EXAMPLES & EXPLANATIONS

Family Law

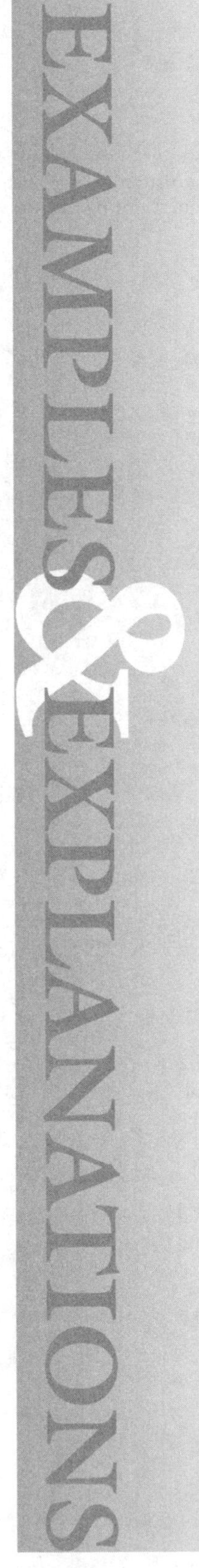

ASPEN PUBLISHERS

Family Law

Second Edition

Robert E. Oliphant
Emeritus Professor of Law
William Mitchell College of Law

Nancy Ver Steegh
Associate Professor of Law
William Mitchell College of Law

AUSTIN BOSTON CHICAGO NEW YORK THE NETHERLANDS

Aspen Publishers
Attn: Permissions Department
76 Ninth Avenue, 7th Floor
New York, NY 10011-5201

To contact Customer Care, e-mail customer.care@aspenpublishers.com, call 1-800-234-1660, fax 1-800-901-9075, or mail correspondence to:

Aspen Publishers
Attn: Order Department
PO Box 990
Frederick, MD 21705

Printed in the United States of America.

1 2 3 4 5 6 7 8 9 0

ISBN 978-0-7355-6289-9

Library of Congress Cataloging-in-Publication Data

Oliphant, Robert E., 1938-
Family law / Robert E. Oliphant, Nancy Ver Steegh. — 2nd ed.
p. cm.
Includes index.
ISBN 978-0-7355-6289-9 (hardcover : alk. paper)
1. Domestic relations — United States — Outlines, syllabi, etc. I. Ver Steegh, Nancy, 1953- II. Title.

KF505.Z9.O43 2007
346.7301′5 — dc22

2006101358

About Wolters Kluwer Law & Business

Wolters Kluwer Law & Business is a leading provider of research information and workflow solutions in key specialty areas. The strengths of the individual brands of Aspen Publishers, CCH, Kluwer Law International and Loislaw are aligned within Wolters Kluwer Law & Business to provide comprehensive, in-depth solutions, and expert-authored content for the legal, professional, and education markets.

CCH was founded in 1913 and has served more than four generations of business professionals and their clients. The CCH products in the Wolters Kluwer Law & Business group are highly regarded electronic and print resources for legal, securities, antitrust and trade regulation, government contracting, banking, pension, payroll, employment and labor, and healthcare reimbursement and compliance professionals.

Aspen Publishers is a leading information provider for attorneys, business professionals and law students. Written by preeminent authorities, Aspen products offer analytical and practical information in a range of specialty practice areas from securities law and intellectual property to mergers and acquisitions and pension/benefits. Aspen's trusted legal education resources provide professors and students with high-quality, up-to-date and effective resources for successful instruction and study in all areas of the law.

Kluwer Law International supplies the global business community with comprehensive English-language international legal information. Legal practitioners, corporate counsel and business executives around the world rely on the Kluwer Law International journals, loose-leafs, books, and electronic products for authoritative information in many areas of international legal practice.

Loislaw is a premier provider of digitized legal content to small law firm practitioners of various specializations. Loislaw provides attorneys with the ability to quickly and efficiently find the necessary legal information they need, when and where they need it, by facilitating access to primary law as well as state-specific law, records, forms, and treatises.

Wolters Kluwer Law & Business, a unit of Wolters Kluwer, is headquartered in New York and Riverwoods, Illinois. Wolters Kluwer is a leading multinational publisher and information services company.

Summary of Contents

Contents

Chapter 16 Determining Paternity 297

Chapter 17 Adoption 317

Preface

We are pleased to provide a substantially updated and revised second edition of *Family Law: Examples & Explanations*. Each of the 24 chapters features recent developments in the law and includes new examples and explanations, many of which are based on fact patterns found in actual cases. Because new developments in family law often reflect underlying societal changes in family structure and demographics, this volume incorporates empirical research and census data that are likely to be of interest to the reader. We also highlight ways that the practice of family law and the role of attorneys have been transformed through the use of processes such as mediation and collaborative law.

This book contains a balanced and in-depth analysis of family law. Because the tapestry of family law is complex, and because we believe that focus is an essential ingredient to learning, we have separated the subject of family law into specific topics that are organized as chapters. Each chapter is subdivided into discrete sections that often include hypothetical examples and illustrative explanations. Wherever possible, we have based our analysis and the examples and explanations on nationally accepted legal principles. However, because family law is so often state specific, the text contains contrasting perspectives from various jurisdictions. To eliminate confusion and to assist with family law research, we have included specific citations to relevant state decisions and legislation associated with the principles under consideration.

We believe that this book provides a clear, well-organized, and efficient learning platform that will assist readers in understanding and appreciating the subject of family law.

Robert E. Oliphant
Nancy Ver Steegh
January 2007

Acknowledgments

We are thankful for the hard work, assistance, and encouragement of the generous people who have helped us write both editions of this book. Foremost among our supporters in the development of the first edition were Aspen editors Lynn Churchill and Eric Holt. Taylor Kearns was likewise instrumental in the preparation of the updated second edition.

William Mitchell College of Law and its administration have been solid supporters of the project since its beginning, and for that we are grateful. Faculty Publication Specialists Linda Thorstad and Cal Bonde were tireless in helping us create the first edition. Ms. Thorstad took the lead in the production of the second edition with substantial proofreading assistance from Ms. Jennifer Miller, and for their commitment to the project, we say, "Thank you for all your efforts."

Several research assistants worked with us on the first edition, including Mr. Arthur Boylan, Mr. Peter Hendricks, Mr. Chris Iijima, Ms. Katherine Kelly, and Ms. Tammy Schemmel. They were tireless in their cite checking and research. We also want to thank William Mitchell Library Director and Associate Dean Ann Bateson and Reference Librarian William Jack for their assistance with the second edition.

Our respective book widow and widower spouses, Susan Oliphant and Jack Ver Steegh, have been patient, tolerant, and supportive as we worked on the manuscripts for both editions. Thank you!

Robert E. Oliphant
Nancy Ver Steegh
January 2007

CHAPTER 1

Marriage — History

1.1. Introduction

A hundred years ago, the body of family law was tiny and judges were granted wide discretion in deciding alimony, child support, and property division issues. Divorces were, of course, rare, as were paternity actions and adoptions. The family was viewed as one unit consisting of the mother, the father, and the children. However, in response to the dramatic changes in American culture over the last hundred years, and in particular since the 1960s, judges and lawyers are now faced with resolving exceedingly complex and often previously undecided family law issues. The body of family law is now large and growing. Often, only experts in the area possess sufficient competence to understand and apply it.

Few dispute the fact that the nature of family life in America has dramatically changed. For example, the definitions of what constitutes a "family" and a "parent" have been altered as divorce has become more common. Civil unions between same-sex couples with children and cohabitation between heterosexual couples add to the challenge of defining the "family."

Data from a variety of sources reflect the changes that have occurred in the culture during the last century. For example, by the early 1990s an estimated 15.5 million children were no longer living with two biological parents and as many as 8 to 10 million children may have been born into families with a gay or lesbian parent. *See Alison D. v. Virginia* M., 569 N.Y.S.2d

586, 589 (Judge Kay dissenting) (N.Y. Ct. App. 1991). A decade later, fewer persons are marrying than ever before; those who do marry are doing so later in life; and more marriages are ended by divorce than by death. The Census Bureau estimates that "25-year-olds marrying for the first time face a 52.5 percent chance overall that their marriage will end in divorce." Moreover, "about 50 percent of first marriages for men under age forty-five may end in divorce, and between 44 and 52 percent [of first marriages for women under age forty-five] may end in divorce." U.S. Census Bureau, U.S. Dep't of Commerce, Number, Timing, And Duration of Marriages and Divorces: 1996, at 18, available at http://www.sipp.census.gov/sipp/p70s/p70-80.pdf.

Data from 1999 indicate that 22 percent of white, non-Hispanic women who gave birth were unmarried. This is up from 9 percent in 1980 and 17 percent in 1990. Forty-two percent of Hispanic women who gave birth were unmarried, which is up from 24 percent in 1980 and 37 percent in 1990. Sixty-nine percent of black women who gave birth were unmarried in 1999, which is up from 56 percent in 1980 and 67 percent in 1990. Stephanie J. Ventura & Christine A. Bachrach, *Nonmarital Childbearing in the United States*, 1940-99, Nat'l. Vital Stat. Rept., Oct. 2000, at 1, 6, available at http://www.cdc.gov/nchs/data/nvsr/nvsr48/nvs48_16.pdf.

The Census Bureau reports that in 2004 unmarried heterosexual couples living with children totaled 43 percent of all American households with children. U.S. Census Bureau, Facts for Features, http://www.census.gov/Press-Release/www/releases/archives/facts_for_features_special_editions/002265.html (July 19, 2004). It has also been reported that 78 percent of single-parent households are headed by women. Terry Lugaila & Julia Overturf, *U.S. Census Bureau, Children and the Households They Live In*: 2000 (2004), available at http://www.census.gov/prod/2004pubs/censr-14.pdf. In 2003, 17.6 percent of children under the age of 18 lived in poverty, even though children made up only 12.5 percent of the total population. U.S. Census Bureau, *Income, Poverty, and Health Insurance Coverage in the United States*: 2003, at 10 (2004), http://www.census.gov/prod/2004pubs/p60-226.pdf. Many of these children lived in families headed by a single woman. Of the 7.6 million families in poverty in 2003, 51 percent (or 3.85 million) were families headed by women without a husband present. *Id. at* 10. Expressed another way, 28 percent of the families headed by single women lived below the poverty line. *Id. at* 13. In addition, 636,000 families headed by single men lived below the poverty line in 2003. *Id.* In the United States the number of custodial fathers has tripled since 1980. U.S. Census Bureau, 1998, http://www.census.gov/population/www/socdemo/hh-fam/cps2004.html).

EARLY HISTORY

1.2. Looking Back Several Centuries: Early Principles and Practices

Family law principles and practices have centuries of custom and tradition behind them, which may explain why change in some areas, such as the effort to allow gays and lesbians to marry, has generated such a strong emotional reaction. Other less controversial laws, such as those associated with consanguinity prohibitions, can be traced to 1400 B.C., when under Mosaic law, a man was barred from marrying his mother, stepmother, sister, half-sister, granddaughter, or granddaughter-in-law. Even today, Mosaic law may occasionally influence the outcome of an issue in a family dispute. *See, e.g., Burns v. Burns*, 538 A.2d 438 (N.J. Super. Ct. 1987) (court ordering spouse to obtain a "get" so party could enter into a Jewish contract of marriage known as a "ketubbah").

The Bible has, no doubt, played a significant role in the development of family law in the United States. The Bible was "nothing short of the underlying fabric upon which American society was founded" and helped form the earliest colonial laws. John W. Welch, *Biblical Law in America: Historical Perspectives and Potentials for Reform*, 2002 B.Y.U. L. Rev. 611, 619 (2002). The theory that, when a couple marry, they become one and that "one" is the husband, most likely derives from the book of Genesis (Genesis 2:24), which states that a husband must leave the home of his parents to be joined to his wife, and "they shall become one flesh." This Biblical view of marriage is repeated by Paul in his Epistle to the Ephesians (Ephesians 5:31).

Other principles and practices of American family law can be found in Roman law, the canon law as developed by the English Ecclesiastical courts, and the early common law.

1.3. Marriage Evolves

Some believe that the concept of marriage began to evolve into a social institution during the period of Roman domination of Europe. *See* John Witte, Jr., *From Sacrament to Contract: Marriage, Religion and Law in the Western Tradition* 3, 20-21 (1997). However, even during this period in history, marriages were viewed as private matters, and there is little evidence indicating that there was significant concern or control by governmental authorities over them. During the fourth and fifth centuries, a systematic theology of marriage began to emerge as the Church of Rome provided a shape for it. *Id.* at 19-21. Under Church doctrine, marriage was characterized as a sacrament and when properly contracted, it opened the flow of divine grace. *Id.* at 27.

In England, marriage regulation eventually fell to the control of the Ecclesiastical or Church courts. The Ecclesiastical law originally followed the Jewish law, as set out in the Old Testament, and viewed marriage as a sacrament. The Church claimed exclusive jurisdiction over what pertained to one's soul, salvation, and sanctification, therefore, it assumed jurisdiction to deal with marriage and separation. The Church's jurisdictional view and its understanding of marriage were solidified by the thirteenth century.

From 1200 to 1500 A.D., the Church was recognized as the one universal sovereign of the West that governed all of Christendom, and the canon law was the one universal law of the West. Despite numerous amendments over the centuries, the thirteenth-century sacramental model of marriage remains reasonably close to the heart of Catholic theology today.

1.4. Reformation, Divorce, and Blackstone

The sixteenth-century Protestant Reformation had a significant impact on how marriage was viewed. The Reformers rejected the Church's view that marriage was a sacrament, even though the concept of the indissoluble marriage had to some extent been mitigated by the law of annulment. Catholic teaching and canon law held that divorce meant only separation from bed and board, a divorce *a mensa et thoro*. The decree of divorce *a mensa et thoro* did not sever the marital tie, and the parties remained husband and wife. The parties could not remarry during the lifetime of their spouse, and the husband was normally required to provide his wife with permanent support. However, the Reformers believed that divorce meant the termination, for cause, of one valid marriage with the right to contract another.

The feud between the Church and Henry VIII may also have influenced how marriage was viewed. In England the canon law had provided the foundation for family law until Henry VIII broke with the Church when it refused to grant him a divorce in 1529. However, after making himself the head of the Church of England, little changed except for the slowly emerging view that marriage may no longer be a union for life.

Divorces were rare, as evidenced by estimates that between 1670 and 1857, only 375 divorces were granted in England. Marriage continued to be viewed by most as a gracious symbol of the divine, a social unit of the earthly kingdom, and a solemn covenant with one's spouse. Patrick McKinley, *Of Marriage and Monks, Community and Dialogue*, 48 Emory L.J. 689, 710 (1999).

Blackstone viewed marriage as the unity of a man and a woman into a single unit. He observed that by marriage "the husband and wife are one person in law: that is, the very being or legal existence is suspended during the marriage, or at least incorporated and consolidated into that of the husband." William Blackstone, *Commentaries on the Laws of England*, 442 (W. Lewis ed., 1897).

Example 1-1

Assume that P and D were married in a sixteenth-century ceremony by the clergy in London, England. Unfortunately, the relationship broke down and each came to hate the other. P sought to divorce D in the Ecclesiastical court. D agreed to the divorce. Would the court grant the couple a divorce?

Explanation

The Ecclesiastical court would not grant a divorce. The Church took the view that there was a solemn covenant between the parties to marry, and no divorce, on any grounds, would be granted. P might attempt to seek an annulment of the marriage or ask for a decree of judicial separation, called divorce *a mensa et thoro* (divorce from bed and board). The decree of divorce *a mensa et thoro* did not sever the marital tie; the parties remained husband and wife. If granted by the Church court, the parties could not remarry during the lifetime of their spouse, and the husband was normally required to provide his wife with permanent support.

1.5. Colonial American Model of Marriage

The English canon and civil laws were imported to this country by the early settlers. The settlers were aware that problems associated with marriage and divorce were governed by canon law in England and were exclusively within the jurisdiction of the Church's Ecclesiastical courts. 2 Pollock & Maitland, *History of English Law* (2d ed.) 366, 392-396. The Ecclesiastical courts were governed by the canon law and it was influential in the development of colonial family law.

During America's colonial period, "the principle objectives of marriage were wealth, social position, and love — usually in that order." John C. Miller, *This New Man, The American* 414 (1974). Most parents considered marriage a matter too serious to be left to the individuals directly concerned. Consequently, it was not uncommon for a young man to seek permission from the parents of a single young woman before he dated her. *Id.* at 413. Legally, the father of the girl had the right to permit or deny consent to marry. Eric Foner & John A. Garraty, *The Reader's Companion to American History* 700 (1991). Unwanted suitors were often discouraged when the father let it be known that he intended to withhold financial assistance if his daughter married a prospective suitor without parental consent.

For the most part, when one married in colonial America, the marriage was intended to last forever, and the law reflected this view by making it difficult for married couples to divorce or separate. Stuart A. Queen, Robert W. Habenstein & Jill S. Quadagno, *The Family in Various Cultures* 214 (1985). For example, to keep marriages secure, husbands were expelled from the Connecticut colony if they were estranged from their wives for more than three years. Jessica Kross et al., *American Eras, The Colonial Era* 278 (1998).

Slaves were not allowed to marry legally in most colonies, and marriages between slaves had to be approved and performed by the slave owner. Foner & Garraty, *supra* at 701. Racial intermarriage in most states was prohibited. For example, in Massachusetts in 1705, a marriage between a white person and a negro or mulatto was prohibited, and a person who violated this law could be fined £50.

1.6. Nineteenth-Century Patriarchic Model of Marriage

During the nineteenth and early twentieth centuries, the patriarchic family model predominated in the United States. The husband was the legal head of the household, responsible for its support and its links to external society, while the wife was the mistress of the home, responsible for the day-to-day management of its internal affairs and the care and education of children.

Early decisions reflected the nineteenth-century view that a husband had a life-long "duty" of support toward his wife. Therefore, should a divorce occur and the wife not be "at fault," an ex-husband was required to provide for her for the rest of her life.

MODERN HISTORY

1.7. Modern Models of Marriage

In the United States it was not until the 1960s that the prevailing views about marriage and divorce came under close, critical scrutiny, resulting in dramatic changes based on newly emerging social values. Many of the changes came about because of an ever more involved United States Supreme Court, and others were the product of state legislation, sometimes based upon model acts but more likely written in response to federal legislative mandates.

Today, there are many arguments surrounding what constitutes a family, the value of marriage, whether gay and lesbians should be allowed to marry, and the proper grounds for a divorce. For example, eminent scholars debate the value of marriage to a society. Professor Lynn Wardle suggests that marriage "is the best, most promising foundation for lasting, growing, individual, and family happiness and security. It also is the very seedbed of democracy. Home is the place where we get our first ideas about ourselves, our attitudes toward other people, and our habits of approaching and solving problems." Lynn E. Wardle, *The Bonds of Matrimony and the Bonds of Constitutional Democracy*, 32 Hofstra L. Rev. 349, 371 (2003).

Professor Martha Albertson Fineman, however, suggests that "for all relevant and appropriate societal purposes, we do not need marriage, per se, at all. To state that we do not need marriage to accomplish many societal objectives is not the same thing as saying that we do not need a family to do so for some. However, family as a social category should not be dependent on having marriage as its core relationship. Nor is family synonymous with marriage." Martha Albertson Fineman, *Why Marriage?*, 9 Va. J. Soc. Pol'y & L. 239, 245 (2001).

Professor Milton C. Gegan questions whether "American Law should more explicitly institutionalize cohabitation by ending the different treatment of marital and non-marital relationships, thereby making available to cohabitors a host of benefits currently available only to those who are married." Milton C. Gegan, Jr., *Calibrated Commitment: The Legal Treatment of Marriage and Cohabitation*, 76 Notre Dame L. Rev. 1435 (2001).

If anything, Family Law continues to evolve and reflect the ever changing American culture. It is a particularly challenging area of study.

CHAPTER 2

Marriage Contracts — Requirements and Restrictions

INTRODUCTION: MARRIAGE CONTRACTS

2.1. How Marriage Contracts Differ from Ordinary Contracts

A marriage contract is viewed in law different from an ordinary civil contract. The distinction was recognized and discussed by the United States Supreme Court over 100 years ago in *Maynard v. Hill*, 125 U.S. 190 (1888). In *Maynard* the Court explained that marriage is an institution of society, founded upon consent and contract of the parties. It stated that marriage contracts differed from ordinary contracts because the rights, duties, and obligations of the parties rested not upon their agreement, but upon the general common or statutory law of the state, which defined and prescribed those rights, duties, and obligations. The Court observed that parties can neither modify nor change a marriage contract without state intervention and that the contract binds them to a lifelong relationship. The Court emphasized that marriage contracts may not be terminated by virtue of a simple agreement made solely between the two parties to it. The state always remains a third party and sets the grounds, if any, for ending the relationship.

EXAMPLES

Example 2-1

Assume that P and D prepare a detailed agreement that they believe will contain the important provisions regarding their contemplated future "marriage." They call a group of friends together, then read the agreement and sign it as a part of their "wedding" ceremony. Although they do not obtain a license to marry, it is clear that they fully intend the relationship to be that of husband and wife and the marriage agreement to act as proof of the formal relationship. When the relationship breaks down a few months later, P brings an action to dissolve the claimed marriage and seeks to utilize the state's divorce statutes. D responds by arguing that there is no marriage for two reasons: First, this state does not recognize common law marriages, which is true. Second, the parties failed to comply with any of the state's statutory marriage requirements such as obtaining a marriage license. P replies that the parties intended to marry, and that the marriage contract was complete when the last party exchanged vows. How will a court most likely rule?

EXPLANATIONS

Explanation

A court will most likely rule that there never was a marriage. For legal recognition of a marriage, the parties must comply with a state's general requirements regarding a marriage application. Here, there is only an agreement between the parties to which the state was never a party. Consequently, the parties were never legally married and cannot benefit from divorce statutes designed by the state to guide and protect the parties when a marital relationship breaks down. Note that, if this state did recognize common law marriages, P would most likely be able to utilize the state's divorce statutes. *See, e.g., Yaghoubinejad v. Haghighi*, 339, 894 A.2d 1173 (N.J. Super. A.D. 2006).

2.2. Capacity — Generally

To marry, one must have the state of mind and the capacity to marry. State of mind consists of voluntarily entering into the relationship with the intent to marry at that time (not a sham). Capacity generally requires that the parties be of opposite gender (male-female), not be married to someone else (bigamy), not be related as defined by local statute, be of the age at which local law permits them to marry, and be capable of understanding the nature of the act.

The Uniform Marriage and Divorce Act (UMDA) section 208(a)(1) states that a marriage is invalid if "a party lacked capacity to consent to the marriage at the time the marriage was solemnized, either because of mental incapacity or infirmity or because of the influence of alcohol, drugs, or other incapacitating substances, or duress, or by fraud involving the essentials of marriage." The issues of capacity and intent are usually litigated in the context of annulment actions.

Example 2-2

Assume that P married D when P was 83 and the marriage took place less than a month before P's death from lung cancer. At the time of the marriage, P was heavily medicated, undergoing chemotherapy, and required the daily assistance of an in-home nurse. P was also hooked up to an oxygen tank during the wedding. Following P's death, P's estate brings an action contesting the marriage, claiming it was void because P did not have the capacity to consent to the marriage. How will a court most likely rule?

Explanation

A court will carefully examine all of the facts surrounding the alleged marriage. Given the facts of this example, it is most likely that a court will find that P lacked the capacity to consent and that the marriage is void. *See In re Estate of Santolino*, 895 A.2d 506 (N.J. Super. 2005).

2.3. Capacity — Guardian's Consent

A guardian may consent to a marriage when the applicant is incompetent or is not of age to consent. *See Knight v. Radomski*, 414 A.2d 1211 (Me. 1980).

2.4. Capacity — Age Restrictions

The state has an interest in preventing unstable marriages among those who lack capacity to act in their own best interests. Consequently, states have set a minimum legal age for marriage that varies from jurisdiction to jurisdiction. For example, in some jurisdictions, a man and a woman 18 or older can marry without parental consent. However, with permission of the underaged person's parents, guardian, or juvenile court, a person 16 or 17 years old may also marry. Some jurisdictions will allow persons to marry with parental permission when the individuals are 15. Although such statutory provisions are rare, a few states have allowed parties younger than 15 or 16 to marry without parental consent when the female is pregnant. In Kansas, the legislature in 2006 eliminated a statute that had allowed persons under 16 to marry when the female was pregnant. The legislation was triggered by a case where a 22-year-old man got a 14-year-old girl pregnant and married her in that state. The Georgia Legislature also abolished a statute in 2006 in that state that had allowed similar underage marriages.

The UMDA, section 205, has influenced how states treat the minimum age of marriage. The UMDA allows a court, upon examination of the parties, to approve certain underage marriages. It declares that after a reasonable effort has been made to notify the parents or guardians of each underage party, the court may order the clerk to issue a marriage license and a marriage certificate form when a party is 16 or 17 and has no parent capable of consenting to marriage.

In most jurisdictions, when there is a court-approved marriage, the judge must first find that the underage party is capable of assuming the responsibilities of marriage and, second, that marriage will serve his or her best interest. Pregnancy alone does not necessarily establish that the best interest of the party will be served.

Statutory age barriers have withstood constitutional challenge. *See, e.g.*, *Moe v. Dinkins*, 533 F. Supp. 623 (S.D.N.Y. 1981), *aff'd*, 669 F.2d 67 (2d Cir.), *cert. denied*, 459 U.S. 827 (1982). When state statutes have been challenged on constitutional grounds, courts have asked whether there is a rational basis for the means selected by the legislature to establish the minimum age to marry and have examined the state interests allegedly advanced by the law. This is the lowest level of scrutiny applied to a statute. For example, in *Moe v. Dinkins* a New York law that required the consent of a parent before a minor between ages 14 to 18 could marry was challenged as violating the fundamental right to marry. The court concluded that the restriction was rational because of the state's concern with unstable marriages and the inability of minors to make mature decisions. The court also observed that the age restriction in the state statute does not bar a marriage between the two applicants forever; rather, it delays their marriage until they are allowed to marry without parental consent. This decision illustrates the two tests the courts apply to restrictions on marriage: while marriage is recognized as a fundamental right, not every state statutory restriction is subjected to strict scrutiny requiring that the state show a compelling interest before it will be upheld. *See, e.g.*, *Zablocki v. Redhail*, 434 U.S. 374 (1978).

EXAMPLES

Example 2-3

Assume that P, age 15, desires to marry X, age 50. P's mother consents to the marriage, but P's father, D, objects. The statute in this jurisdiction permits a minor "between ages 16 to 18 to marry with the consent of one parent and district court authorization." Common law marriages have been abolished.

The trial court held the statute unconstitutional and permitted P, age 15, to marry. D challenged the ruling on appeal. How will a court most likely rule?

EXPLANATIONS

Explanation

It is well settled that states have the right and power to establish reasonable limitations on the right to marry. This power is justified as an exercise of the police power, which confers upon the states the ability to enact laws to protect the safety, health, morals, and general welfare of society. The U.S. Supreme Court has held that parents have a fundamental liberty interest in the care, custody, and management of their children. Even though these rights are fundamental, however, they are not absolute. The state also has an interest in the welfare of children and may limit parental authority. Here, there exists a rational relation between the means chosen by the legislature and legitimate state interests in adopting and enforcing the age restriction. In light of the important state interest in promoting the welfare of children by preventing unstable marriages among those lacking the capacity to act in their own best interests, the restriction would most likely be upheld as constitutional and the alleged marriage would be viewed as void.

2.5. Marriage License

Most jurisdictions impose specific statutory requirements on persons who intend to marry. For example, in all jurisdictions a couple intending to marry must first obtain a marriage license, which usually requires that one of the two persons seeking the license go to the office of a county or district clerk of court.

Once a license is obtained, most states impose a short waiting period between the date the marriage license is sought and the date of the marriage ceremony. The UMDA, section 204, states that a marriage license becomes effective three days after it is issued and expires 180 days later. The waiting period may be waived or modified by a judge in an emergency or under extraordinary circumstances.

Some states take the view that strict compliance with state marriage statutes is mandatory, reasoning that they must guard against recognition of informal relationships. However, in a majority of jurisdictions, only substantial compliance with state marriage statutes is required for a valid marriage. These states reason that they should recognize the parties' reasonable expectations, even though there may be an imperfection in the marriage license or official application.

Although the procedures vary from jurisdiction to jurisdiction, it is common for a clerk to provide a party with a detailed questionnaire to be answered under oath. Once the clerk is satisfied that there is no legal impediment, a fee for administering and sending the required reports to the state is paid. Courts will distinguish between voiding a marriage consummated after the issuance of a marriage license because it was not solemnized and a marriage duly solemnized but deficient for the lack of a marriage license. *Compare Hames v. Hames*, 316 A.2d 379 (Conn. 1972) *with Carabetta v. Carabetta*, 438 A.2d 109 (Conn. 1980). The distinction between outcomes generally rests upon the specific language found in state statutes relating to these subjects.

2.6. Solemnizing a Marriage

Solemnizing a marriage serves several purposes. It provides public notice and a permanent public record of the marriage. It may also satisfy a religious tradition and act to impress on the couple the seriousness of marriage.

The UMDA states that "[a] marriage may be solemnized by a judge of a court of record, by a public official whose powers include solemnization of marriages, or in accordance with any mode of solemnization recognized by any religious denomination, Indian Nation or Tribe, or Native Group." UMDA §206(a).

EXAMPLES

Example 2-4

Assume that P and D have decided to marry while D, the proposed groom, is very ill and confined to the hospital. The hospital chaplain, after checking with authorities, informs the couple that, in order to get married immediately, they are required to get a waiver of the three-day waiting period from a judge so that the license can promptly issue. The parties decide to proceed with a ceremony that very day, despite the absence of a license. They intend to complete the paperwork following the ceremony. The parties are married in an elaborate hospital ceremony; however, D dies one day following the ceremony. A marriage license is never obtained. Following D's death, P seeks an intestate share of D's estate. The relevant statute in this jurisdiction reads: *Previous to any marriage in this state, a license for that purpose shall be obtained from the officer authorized to issue the same, and no marriage hereafter contracted shall be recognized as valid unless the license has been previously obtained, and unless the marriage is solemnized by a person authorized by law to solemnize marriages.* D's estate contends that no marriage existed because a license was not obtained. P argues that the parties were married, as evidenced by the ceremony, and all that is needed is to obtain the license — an act they both intended to carry out. How will a court most likely rule on the validity of the marriage?

EXPLANATIONS

Explanation

A court that strictly relies on the above statutory language will most likely hold that there was not a legal marriage. Had D survived and later obtained and recorded a license, P would have a much stronger argument that a valid marriage should be declared. *See Yun v. Yun*, 908 S.W.2d 787 (Mo. App. W.D. 1995).

EXAMPLES

Example 2-5

Assume P and D obtain a marriage license in state X. State X has a statute declaring that marriages solemnized in another state or country are invalid under X's law when parties residing in X intend to evade X's marriage laws by going to another state or country for solemnization. After obtaining a marriage license in state X, P and D fly to Puerto Rico for a vacation. During the vacation, they have their marriage solemnized by a local pastor. They then return to state X and file their license with the clerk of court. Three years later P files a petition to divorce D in state X. D replies that the couple was never married under the laws of X because the marriage was solemnized outside that jurisdiction. Therefore, the action must be dismissed. Other than the testimony regarding the intent to vacation in Puerto Rico, there is no other evidence regarding an effort to evade X's marriage laws. How will a court most likely rule on the validity of the marriage?

EXPLANATIONS

Explanation

A court will most likely be practical and rule that the marriage is valid. Little will be gained by ruling that the marriage was void after three years. Moreover, there is nothing to suggest that the couple intentionally flew to Puerto Rico to evade the laws of X. *See Barbosa-Johnson v. Johnson*, 851 P.2d 866 (Ariz. Ct. App. 1993).

2.7. Premarital Medical Testing

The UMDA states that "[t]he premarital medical examination requirements serve either to inform the prospective spouse of health hazards that may have an impact on marriage, or to warn public health officials of venereal disease." UMDA §203. The UMDA, however, makes the requirement of a medical examination optional.

The Supreme Court observed nearly 50 years ago that "[t]he blood test procedure has become routine in our everyday life. It is a ritual for those going into the military service as well as those applying for marriage licenses. Many colleges require such tests before permitting entrance and literally millions of us have voluntarily gone through the same . . . routine in becoming blood donors." *Breithaupt v. Abram*, 352 U.S. 432, 436, 448 (1957).

Several states require a marriage license applicant to file a health certificate with the licensing authority. The requirements vary among states, with some asking that applicants certify that they have submitted to a medical examination and do not have a venereal disease, or, if infected, that they are not in the communicable state. Some states also require tests for measles for female applicants. *See, generally*, *People v. Smith*, 23 Cal. Rptr. 5 (Cal. App. 1962); *Hall v. Hall*, 108 S.E.2d 487 (N.C. 1959); *Peterson v. Widule*, 147 N.W. 966 (Wis. 1914) (Upon application for a marriage license the male party to such marriage must, within 15 days prior to the application, be examined by a physician of designated qualifications with reference to the existence or nonexistence of any venereal disease).

The issue of whether a couple may be compelled to undergo compulsory medical testing before they are allowed to marry remains open. Louisiana and Illinois enacted statutes requiring testing for HIV. However, they did not condition issuance of a marriage license on "passing" the test, and the statutes in both states have since been repealed. It is argued that premarital AIDS testing is unconstitutional. A Utah statute that prohibited marriage by a person afflicted with AIDS was ruled invalid because it was in conflict with the Americans with Disabilities Act. *See T.E.P. v. Leavitt*, 840 F. Supp. 110 (D. Utah 1993). In *Matter of Kilpatrick*, 375 S.E.2d 794 (W. Va. 1988), a couple wishing to marry were ordained ministers of the Universal Life Church and challenged the constitutionality of a state statute requiring them to undergo serological tests, claiming that it violated the Free Exercise Clause because it required them to disobey the canon law of their church in order to marry. The state responded that there were three compelling reasons for the test: (1) detection of a communicable disease (syphilis); (2) protection of the health interests of prenuptial couples; and (3) protection of the interests of the future children of the married couple. The court held that the Free Exercise Clauses of the federal and state constitutions were not violated.

EXAMPLES

Example 2-6

Assume that P and D apply for a marriage license in state X. State X requires both to undergo a blood test to determine whether either has a venereal disease. P and D refuse to take the required test and challenge the statutory blood test requirement, arguing that this test violates the Free Exercise

Clause of the First Amendment to the U.S. Constitution. They contend that because the test requires the removal of blood from the body, which is a violation of a canon law of their church, the state is barred from applying the statute to them. How will a court most likely rule?

EXPLANATIONS

Explanation

The court will most likely require that the parties take the test. A majority of jurisdictions have similar statutory provisions requiring tests for venereal disease, tuberculosis, mental incompetence, rubella immunity, or sickle cell anemia. *See* Homer H. Clark, *The Law of Domestic Relations in the United States* §2.11 (2d ed. 1987). These provisions have sustained constitutional attack.

2.8. Premarital Education

The seriousness of marriage makes adequate premarital counseling and education for family living highly desirable. Premarital counseling is viewed as one way to prevent unwise, hasty marriages. Some jurisdictions have proposed reducing marriage license fees for couples who have received premarital education. Where premarital education legislation is in force, it will normally specify that the topics include a discussion of the seriousness of marriage, conflict management skills, and encouragement of counseling should the marriage fall into difficulty. The education is usually provided by a member of the clergy, a person authorized by law to perform marriages, or a marriage and family therapist.

2.9. Form of Marriage — Ministerial Act

Most states do not prescribe a particular form of marriage ceremony except that the parties assent or declare in the presence of a minister or judicial officer solemnizing the marriage, and state in the presence of at least two witnesses, that they take each other to be husband and wife. *See State v. Anderson*, 396 P.2d 558 (Or. 1964). Marriages are commonly performed by a judge of a court of record, a member of the clergy, a clerk of court, or an administrator. Courts are reluctant to invalidate a marriage merely because certain formal requirements were not met, absent specific legislation mandating that the claimed marital relationship is void. This is especially true when the couple have lived together for several years in the belief they were legally married.

Example 2-7

Assume that P and D decide to marry and that P obtains a marriage license, which must be completed and returned to the county clerk's office within 60 days of the wedding ceremony. After obtaining the license, they go through with their marriage ceremony, which is presided over by a minister. The license is signed, but P fails to return it to the local clerk's office for filing. Ten months later, the two break up. D seeks a divorce and P responds that there was never a marriage because the license was never properly filed with the county clerk. How should a court rule on this question?

Explanation

A court will most likely rule that the failure to do a ministerial act, such as returning the marriage license to the county clerk within 60 days of its issuance, cannot render a marriage void and does not by itself defeat the existence of the alleged marriage. *See generally In Re Estate of Mirizzi*, 723 N.Y.S.2d 623 (N.Y. Sur. 2001) (entry of judgment of divorce was mere ministerial act); *Wright v. State*, 81 A.2d 602 (Md. 1951) (certified copy of an official record of a marriage is not the only means of establishing marriage).

COMMON LAW MARRIAGES

2.10. History of Common Law Marriage

"Common law marriage" is a misnomer. Common law marriage probably did not exist in England, the home of the common law. The concept arose in "English Ecclesiastical courts, which administered canon law, rather than in the English common-law courts." John B. Crawley, *Is the Honeymoon over for Common Law Marriage: A Consideration of the Continued Viability of the Common Law Marriage Doctrine*, 29 Cumb. L. Rev. 399, 401 (1998/1999). The House of Lords concluded in *Regina v. Millis*, 8 Eng. Rep. 844 (1843-1844), that common law marriage had never been recognized in England.

The recognition of unsolemnized marriages in English Ecclesiastical courts, the American colonies, and the several states has an equitable basis. In medieval England and the American frontier it was often impossible for couples wanting to marry to find authorized persons to issue marriage licenses and perform ceremonies. *See Crawley, supra* at 403. Common law marriage was viewed as one means of solving these procedural difficulties.

New York was apparently the first state to recognize unsolemnized, or common law, marriages. *See Fenton v. Reed*, 52 N.Y. Sup. (1809) (per curiam). By the end of the nineteenth century, a majority of states recognized unsolemnized, long-term sexual unions as common law marriages. *See* David F. Crabtree, *Development, Recognition of Common-Law Marriages,* 1988 Utah L. Rev. 273, 275 n.12 (listing 34 states, as of 1931, recognizing common law marriages).

The U.S. Supreme Court considered the validity of common law marriage in *Jewell's Lessee v. Jewell,* 42 U.S. 219 (1843). With only eight justices sitting, the Court evenly divided on whether the relationship between the deceased and the surviving companion constituted a valid marriage. Finally, in 1877, the Court recognized a growing acceptance among states of common law marriages and approved the concept. *Meister v. Moore,* 96 U.S. 76 (1877).

The jurisdictions that as of June 2006 recognized common law marriage were Alabama, Colorado, District of Columbia, Idaho, Iowa, Kansas, Montana, Rhode Island, South Carolina, Texas, and Utah. Pennsylvania recently decided not to recognize common law marriages contracted after January 1, 2005.

2.11. Common Law Marriage Defined

Capacity and mutual consent are essential to a common law marriage. A common law marriage is usually defined as a marriage created by the express agreement of the parties without ceremony, and often without a witness. It is an agreement in words — not *in futuro* or *in postea,* but *in praesenti,* uttered with a view and for the purpose of establishing the relationship of husband and wife. No specific form of words is needed, and all that is essential is proof of an agreement to enter into the legal relationship of marriage at the present time.

There are five elements of a common law marriage: (1) an agreement of marriage *in praesenti,* (2) made by parties competent to contract, (3) accompanied and followed by cohabitation as husband and wife, (4) subsequently holding oneself out as being married, and (5) gaining a reputation as being married. All five elements must be proven, although whether the proof must be clear and convincing or merely a preponderance varies among jurisdictions. *See, e.g., Nestor v. Nestor,* 472 N.E.2d 1091 (Ohio 1984) (clear and convincing); *Callen v. Callen,* 620 S.E.2d 59 (S.C. 2005) (preponderance). Although it is usually required that there be a holding out that the parties are married to those with whom they normally come in contact, a common law marriage will not necessarily be defeated if all persons in the community within which the parties reside are not aware of the marital arrangement. Note, however, that decisions have consistently held that merely living together for a period of time does not support the common law marriage relationship. *In re Thomas' Estate,* 367 N.Y.S.2d 182 (N.Y. Sur. 1975).

When the parties are otherwise disabled from testifying regarding the creation of a contract *verba in praesenti*, or when there is a conflict in the evidence regarding the agreement, courts may apply a rebuttable presumption favoring the marriage if sufficient proof is presented of cohabitation and reputation of marriage. *Jeanes v. Jeanes*, 177 S.E.2d 537, 539-40 (1970). This presumption may be overcome by "strong, cogent" evidence that the parties in fact never agreed to marry. *Id. at* 540 of 177 S.E.2d.

In modern America, the impediments to ceremonial marriage that were present in life on the western frontier have long since disappeared. Transportation, communication, and hosts of legal administrators are readily available to help those wanting to marry. Consequently, most states have abolished common law marriage.

2.12. Common Law Age to Marry

Under the common law, infants may marry — males at the age of fourteen and females at twelve — and the consent of parents is not necessary to the validity of the marriage. *Bennett v. Smith*, 1856 WL 6412 (N.Y. Sup. 1856).

EXAMPLES

Example 2-8

Assume that D, age 41, wants to marry P, age 15, in state X. They move in together and, under common law, would be viewed as husband and wife. However, state X has legislation regarding the age to marry that reads in part: "The Uniform Marriage Act of this State sets forth the rules and requirements for ceremonial marriages. The Act reflects the legislative purposes of strengthening and preserving the integrity of marriage and safeguarding meaningful family relationships." The Act provides procedures for the solemnization and registration of marriages. The Act provides that "nothing in this section shall be deemed to repeal or render invalid any otherwise valid common law marriage between one man and one woman." The statutory age of consent for marriage under this Act in State X is 18. The Act also allows persons between 16 and 18 years to marry if they obtain parental consent or, if that is not possible, judicial approval. Can D and P marry in this jurisdiction?

EXPLANATIONS

Explanation

This is an unusual problem and, despite the statutory language, a court will most likely consider the parties married. The age of consent under the common law is 14 for a male and 12 for a female. The statutory language set out above does not clearly modify or abrogate the existing common law. The U.S. Supreme Court held that common law marriages are valid, notwithstanding statutes that require ceremonial marriages to be solemnized by a minister or a magistrate, if no specific provision to the contrary exists. *Meister v. Moore*, 96 U.S. 76, (1877). As the Court explained,

"No doubt, a statute may take away a common law right; but there is always a presumption that the legislature has no such intention, unless it be plainly expressed." *See J.M.H. v. Rouse*, 143 P.3d 1116 (Col. App. 2006); *State v. Ward*, 28 S.E.2d 785 (S.C. 1944); *see also Adams v. Boan*, 559 So. 2d 1084, 1087 (Ala. 1990) (statute requiring person under the age of 18 to acquire consent of parents before marriage not applicable to common law marriage in action for distribution of marital property).

2.13. Common Law Conflicts of Law

Although jurisdictions that recognize common law marriage are declining, its existence is recognized outside the borders of states that do not otherwise recognize such relationships. The reason for this is that, as a general principle, the validity of a marriage is determined by the law of the forum in which it was celebrated, the *lex loci*. Furthermore, a common law marriage entered into in a jurisdiction recognizing these relationships will also be recognized by all other jurisdictions under the Full Faith and Credit Clause. This is true even if there is a strong policy in the new state against common law marriage. *See, e.g., Kelderhaus v. Kelderhaus*, 467 S.E.2d 303 (1996); *Carpenter v. Carpenter*, 617 N.Y.S.2d 903 (1994); *Mott v. Duncan Petroleum Trans.*, 414 N.E.2d 657 (1980); *Netecke v. Louisiana*, 715 So.2d 449 (La. App. 1998). The law of the domicile of the alleged married couple is to be applied to determine whether the marriage is valid. *Colbert v. Colbert*, 169 P.2d 633 (1946).

2.14. Common Law Marriages Decline

It is believed that judicial recognition of common law marriages was a historical necessity, because the social conditions of early pioneer society made access to clergy or public officials difficult. However, as social and economic conditions changed, so did the attitude of the courts: they began to suggest that common law marriage claims were a fruitful source of perjury and fraud, and, while tolerated in some jurisdictions, they were not encouraged. Beginning around the 1930s, there was a progressive change in the judicial view of common law marriages. Courts began to require higher degrees of proof when common law marriages were claimed to exist, and they examined a professed contract with "great scrutiny." Courts also began to place a "heavy burden" on the proponent of a claimed common law marriage to prove its existence. *See Manifredi Estate*, 399 Pa. 285, 292 (Penn. 1960).

It is estimated that "[a]t one time, nearly two-thirds of the states recognized common law marriage; by 2002, only twelve did so, and two of the twelve had adopted strict limitations on its establishment." Marsha Garrison,

Is Consent Necessary? An Evaluation of the Emerging Law of Cohabitant Obligation, 52 UCLA L. Rev. 815, 849 (February 2005).

2.15. Reviving Common Law Marriage

Proponents of reviving the concept of common law marriage claim that it protects the interests of poor and minority women more effectively than any of the theories suggested to address the problems created by its absence. They also claim that most of the original reasons used to support the abolition of common law marriage — fear of fraud, protection of morality and the family, racism, eugenics, and health-related reasons — no longer withstand careful scrutiny. Furthermore, proponents claim that recognition of common law relationships will protect children better than paternity actions. *See* Cynthia Grant Bowman, *Feminist Proposal to Bring Back Common Law Marriage,* 75 Or. L. Rev. 709 (1996); Sonya C. Garza, *Common Law Marriage: A Proposal for the Revival of a Dying Doctrine,* 40 New Eng. L. Rev. 541 (2006).

Example 2-9

Assume that P and D lived together for five years in state X, which recognizes common law marriages. However, they did not hold themselves out as husband and wife. They move to another state, and that state does not recognize common law marriages. When D dies in an industrial accident two years after moving to the new state, P seeks to claim workers' compensation benefits as a "surviving spouse." When P is turned down on the ground that she is not a spouse, she seeks a declaratory judgment that she and D were married under the common law of state X, which would then make her eligible for coverage under the state act. P testifies that she and D had agreed to be husband and wife "but didn't make a big deal about it." A witness testifies for the state that P and D never used the same last name, did not have any joint savings or checking accounts, and did not jointly own any real or personal property. How will a court most likely rule?

Explanation

This is another case where a court will have to examine the facts carefully. Although the parties were apparently competent to make a common law marriage contract, the only evidence is P's testimony that such a contract was made *in praesenti*. However, much of the evidence indicates they were living more like boyfriend-girlfriend than husband and wife. In particular, the complete separation of funds suggests they were not husband and wife. Finally, it is conceded they did not hold themselves out to the community as husband and wife and were not treated and reputed in the community and circle in which they moved as husband and wife. Most likely, a court would not find on these facts that a common law marriage existed.

PUTATIVE SPOUSE DOCTRINE

2.16. Putative Marriage Doctrine — History

Most jurisdictions have adopted either by statute or by common law the "putative marriage doctrine." Under this doctrine, a spouse who believed in good faith that he or she was validly married, and who participated in a ceremonial marriage, is allowed to use a state's divorce provisions even though the marriage is found to be void because of an impediment. Christopher L. Blakesley, *The Putative Marriage Doctrine*, 60 Tul. L. Rev. 1, 6 (1985). The putative marriage doctrine is intended to protect a party who is ignorant of an impediment that makes the marriage either void or voidable. In addition to putative spouse legislation found in many jurisdictions, the doctrine is recognized by the Social Security Act. *See Estate of Leslie*, 207 Cal. Rptr. 561, 567-68 (Cal. 1984).

Putative spousehood terminates upon a party's loss of a good faith belief that he or she is married. A putative marriage is not a marriage; therefore, one normally need not seek an annulment or divorce to terminate a putative relationship. Courts normally grant equitable relief where putative spousehood is recognized.

2.17. Putative Marriage Doctrine — UMDA

The UMDA has been influential in the development of the putative marriage doctrine. The UMDA states that

> [a]ny person who has cohabited with another to whom he is not legally married in the good faith belief that he was married to that person is a putative spouse until knowledge of the fact that he is not legally married terminates his status and prevents acquisition of further rights. A putative spouse acquires the rights conferred upon a legal spouse, including the right to maintenance following termination of his status, whether or not the marriage is prohibited or declared invalid. If there is a legal spouse or other putative spouses, rights acquired by a putative spouse do not supersede the rights of the legal spouse or those acquired by the other putative spouses, but the court shall apportion property, maintenance, and support rights among the claimants as appropriate in the circumstances and in the interests of justice.

UMDA §209, 9A U.L.A. 192 (1998).

EXAMPLES

Example 2-10

Assume that P and D begin living together at a time when D is not divorced from X. P is aware of D's marital status. P and D continue to live together for several years. D dies without ever having obtained a divorce from X. During the time P and D lived together in this jurisdiction, which is one that recognizes common law marriages, P and D held themselves out to the community as husband and wife. They used the same surname, jointly signed notes, opened joint bank accounts, and otherwise held themselves out as husband and wife. P asserts that she and D had a common law marriage and that she should participate in D's estate as his wife. If the court rejects that claim, then should she be viewed as a spouse under the putative spouse doctrine?

EXPLANATIONS

Explanation

Here, D has a preexisting impediment to a common law marriage (D was married to X and never divorced), and P had knowledge of the impediment. P will not have a claim to D's estate as his common law spouse. Only if P did not have knowledge of the impediment and had lived with D in the good faith belief that they were married under the state's common law doctrine, could P claim a share of D's estate. Thus, P's only claim would be as a putative spouse. However, P cannot claim a share of the estate under the putative spouse doctrine because she was aware of the impediment.

2.18. Putative Spouse — Community Property Jurisdictions

In a community property state such as California, as between a putative spouse and the other spouse, or as between the surviving putative spouse and the heirs of his or her decedent other than the decedent's surviving legal spouse, the putative spouse is entitled to share in the property accumulated by the partners during their void or voidable marriage. It is also settled that the share to which the putative spouse is entitled is the same share of the quasi-marital property as the spouse would receive as an actual and legal spouse if there had been a valid marriage; that is, it shall be divided equally between the parties. *Estate of Leslie*, 689 P.2d 133 (Cal. 1984). The proportionate contribution of each of the parties to the property acquired during the void or voidable union is immaterial in this state because it is divided as community property would be divided upon the dissolution of a valid marriage. *See Estate of Hafner*, 229 Cal. Rptr. 676 (Cal. App. 1986) (as between a surviving, innocent wife and the children of bigamous husband, and the surviving, innocent putative spouse, one half of estate awarded to surviving wife and children of decedent for distribution pursuant to probate code and one half awarded to surviving putative spouse as quasi-marital property).

Example 2-11

Assume that P and D married in California. The relationship later broke down, the parties separated, and D informed P that he had begun their divorce. P answered D's dissolution petition and subsequently signed a Marital Termination Agreement. However, during the period of separation, the couple decided to get back together, with D explaining that the divorce was never finalized. In fact, a judgment and decree had been entered divorcing them. They continued to live together for the next two years until D died. D's children from a former marriage challenge any right of P to share in D's estate. P argues that the state statute allows her to take her widow's share. The statute reads as follows: "Whenever a determination is made that a marriage is void or voidable and the Court finds that either party or both parties believed in good faith that the marriage was valid, the Court shall declare such party or parties to have the status of a putative spouse." How will a court most likely treat the challenge?

Explanation

Although the putative spouse principle is usually applied in situations in which a ceremonial marriage becomes void or voidable, most courts would interpret the language of the statute (or the common law if no statute exists) to allow P to recover. Here, P continued to live with a former spouse in good faith ignorance of a divorce and will most likely be deemed to be a putative spouse. *In re Marriage of Monti*, 185 Cal. Rptr. 72 (Cal. 1982); *Manker v. Manker*, 644 N.W.2d 522 (Neb. 2002).

FORMS OF MARRIAGE

2.19. Proxy Marriage

A proxy marriage has been defined as "[A] marriage contracted or celebrated through agents acting on behalf of one or both parties. A proxy marriage differs from the more conventional ceremony only in that one or both of the contracting parties are represented by an agent[,] all the other requirements having been met." *State v. Anderson*, 396 P.2d 558, 561 (Or. 1964). *Black's Law Dictionary*, (8th ed. 2004), p. 995, defines a proxy marriage as "[a] wedding in which someone stands in for an absent bride or groom, as when one party is stationed overseas in the military."

Proxy marriages first became an issue during World War I. This was the first war in which large numbers of American men were sent to fight across great distances. Some servicemen wanted to be able to marry while they were stationed abroad, and because of this, various states revived marriage by proxy, a practice recognized in the old continental law of Europe and in the American colonies through the old English common law.

In *Barrons v. United States* 191 F.2d 92 (9th Cir. 1951), the court considered the validity of a proxy marriage that had taken place in Nevada. At the time of the marriage, the parties were under military orders; one was stationed in California and the other in Africa. Before entering the military, one party had resided in California and the other in Texas. The court found that there was no difference between California and Texas law for the purposes of determining if the marriage in Nevada was valid. The court observed that a "marriage relationship validly created by a proxy ceremony is in no way different from the same relationship created in the more usual manner." It said that a proxy marriage furthered the statutory objectives of the formal solemnization requirements to ensure "publicity and certainty." *Id.* at 95, 96. The "remote possibilities" of fraud and lack of consent were considered "not sufficiently substantial" to render proxy marriages, which in some cases may be the only way in which a desirable legal and social status can be achieved, "at variance with the Nevada marriage laws." *Id.* at 97.

The UMDA, section 206(b), allows recognition of proxy marriages if the proxy acts with written authorization.

EXAMPLES

Example 2-12

Assume that P and D were married at a time when the decedent suffered from an inoperable malignant brain tumor. The county clerk's office had issued decedent and P a marriage license; however, decedent's physical condition prevented him from signing the application in the presence of either the county clerk or one of his deputies. Decedent never appeared before the county clerk. Both an appearance and a signature in the presence of the county clerk are required by this jurisdiction's Marriage and Dissolution law. At the marriage ceremony, decedent did not respond because of his brain tumor, and a third party was used as a proxy to acknowledge the marriage vows. Decedent died four days after the ceremony. The estate challenges the marriage and the use of a proxy to acknowledge the marriage vows. How will a court most likely rule?

EXPLANATIONS

Explanation

This is not a case involving a soldier or a war, and a court would be very concerned about a marriage being solemnized when only one party obtained the marriage license, only one party spoke or acknowledged the vows in any manner at the ceremony, and a representative spoke for the other party with no evidence of a written proxy authorizing said representative. This is not a case analogous to proxy marriage during wartime, and it is not consistent with the requirements of the UMDA. A court will most likely hold that there was never a valid marriage. *See In re Estate of Crockett*, 728 N.E.2d 765 (Ill. App. 5 Dist. 2000).

2.20. Confidential Marriages

In some states there are provisions for "confidential" or "secret" marriages. These statutes were enacted to encourage persons who are living together out of wedlock, much like husband and wife, to formalize the relationship. Where available, the statutes eliminate some of the procedural requirements such as filing a health certificate or obtaining a license. However, they do require ceremony of solemnization. *See, e.g.*, Cal. Fam. Code §§500-536 (2003).

2.21. Tribal Marriages

In some jurisdictions, tribal marriages, contracted in accordance with tribal laws or customs, are recognized. *See, e.g.*, Minn. Stat. §517.18, subd. 4 (2002) (marriages may be solemnized among American Indians according to the form and usage of their religion by an Indian Midé or holy person chosen by the parties to the marriage).

2.22. Covenant Marriage

Since August 1997 couples seeking to marry in Louisiana have had a choice of entering into a "no-fault" marriage contract or a "covenant" marriage contract. Louisiana did not change its existing no-fault divorce law, which continues to be available. Under a covenant marriage, couples pledge to enter matrimony only after serious deliberation, including premarital counseling. They also agree to try to solve potential marriage conflicts through counseling if either spouse requests it prior to beginning a divorce proceeding. Divorce requires either an agreed-upon two-year separation or one with a limited number of grounds such as adultery, abuse, imprisonment for a felony, or abandonment. The law also allows married couples to renew their vows and to recast their marriage under terms of the covenant. The earliest a covenant marriage in Louisiana can be dissolved is one year, and then only under specific circumstances. "No-fault" divorce is not possible when couples enter a marriage covenant. Proponents of covenant marriage believe it will reduce the divorce rate. Covenant marriage laws were enacted in Arizona in 1998 and Arkansas in 2001. It is estimated that in 2004, 36,391 marriage licenses were issued in Louisiana and that 2 percent, or about 728, may have been covenant marriages.

Example 2-13

Assume that P and D marry in Louisiana and sign a covenant marriage contract pursuant to Louisiana law. After six months the couple agree that the marriage is not working, so P files for a "no-fault" divorce and D does not oppose the filing. The local clerk, however, refuses to file the divorce action. P and D seek an order from the court requiring the clerk to file the divorce papers and place the matter on the divorce docket. Will a Louisiana court grant P and D's request?

Explanation

Given the current state of the statutory provisions regarding covenant marriage in Louisiana, the answer is most likely that the court will not allow the filing. The parties would be required to engage in counseling and wait the appropriate amount of time before seeking to dissolve their marital relationship. It is doubtful that a constitutional argument would cause any difference in the outcome. *See generally*, *Sosna v. Iowa*, 419 U.S. 393 (1975).

HISTORIC RESTRICTIONS ON MARRIAGE REMOVED

2.23. Race

In *Loving v. Virginia*, 388 U.S. 1 (1967), the Court reversed the Virginia conviction of an African-American woman who married a white man. It ruled that statutes barring marriage between the races violated the Fourteenth Amendment Equal Protection and Due Process Clause and constituted invidious discrimination. The equal protection ruling was based on restricting the freedom to marry solely because of racial classification. The due process ruling was based on the proposition that the right to marry is a fundamental right, and one could not suppress the right to marry based on racial classification. This case established that the right to marry was a constitutionally protected fundamental right.

Example 2-14

Assume that P, who is white, and D, who is black, attempt to marry. Under a local ordinance, it is illegal for persons of different races to marry. When the clerk of court refuses to issue a license, P and D bring an action challenging the existing ordinance. Most likely, how will a court rule on their challenge?

Explanation

Clearly, the ordinance is unconstitutional. The Court made absolutely clear in *Loving v. Virginia* that a provision that bars marriage between persons of different race or nationality violates the Fourteenth Amendment's equal protection and due process provisions.

2.24. Child Support Obligation

In *Zablocki v. Redhail*, 434 U.S. 374 (1978), the Court held unconstitutional a Wisconsin statute that provided that members of a certain class of Wisconsin residents may not marry, within the state or elsewhere, without first obtaining a court order granting permission to marry. The class was defined by statute to include any "Wisconsin resident having minor issue not in his custody and which he is under obligation to support by any court order or judgment." The Court held that the statute violated the Equal Protection Clause of the Fourteenth Amendment to the U.S. Constitution. The Court found the state interest in providing counseling before marriage and protecting a child's welfare legitimate and substantial. However, on close examination, the statute did not require or provide counseling, and it barred an applicant from marrying without providing funds (child support) to the applicant's children. The Court felt that there were other reasonable avenues open to the state to obtain support for the children. Moreover, the statute failed to consider the possibility that through a new marriage, the applicant might be better able to meet prior support obligations.

The Court has established varying degrees of scrutiny when examining state regulations that infringe on the right to marry. When there is a significant interference with the right to marry, the statute is subjected to rigorous (strict) scrutiny. When the statutory provisions reasonably interfere with the right to marry, they are subject to minimal scrutiny. Strict scrutiny is required only of infringements that "directly and substantially" interfere with the right to marry.

EXAMPLES

Example 2-15

Assume that state X was very concerned about the increasing amount of unpaid child support, the high divorce rate, and the large percentage of children born out of wedlock. To assist the state in collecting support, a statute is enacted providing that, before a person can marry, he or she must complete a section on the marriage application form that asks whether there are any outstanding child support obligations. The applicant must state the total amount owed and suggest how it will be paid. If the section is not completed, a license will not be issued. If it is completed, a license will be issued. P, who owes several thousand dollars in child support, refuses to complete this area of the license application, and a marriage license is denied. P challenges the provision, arguing that the provision discriminates against persons who are poor. How will a court most likely rule?

EXPLANATIONS

Explanation

This provision is quite different from the one discussed in *Zablocki v. Redhail* because there is no actual barrier to the marriage, other than the requirement that an applicant complete the form. A court would most likely apply a rational basis test to the provision and conclude that the state's interest in obtaining information regarding child support obligors outweighs a citizen's interest in refusing to provide the information. This provision would most likely be upheld.

EXAMPLES

Example 2-16

Assume that a state legislature was concerned about the state's high divorce rate and its impact on children. To discourage second marriages, it raised the marriage license fee to $500 for anyone seeking to marry in the state. P, who is indigent, has been divorced and desires to remarry. P claims the statute is unconstitutional. How will a court most likely rule?

EXPLANATIONS

Explanation

Here, P will argue that the statute prevents a person from ever marrying if he or she cannot pay the filing fee. Because of the lifelong barrier, the statute will most likely be subject to strict scrutiny, and the state will have to demonstrate a compelling interest in charging the fee. It is clear that the statute would be struck down. In addition to *Loving* and *Zablocki*, P will cite *Boddie v. Connecticut*, 401 U.S. 371 (1971), in which the Court held that Connecticut could not deny access to divorce courts to those persons who could not afford to pay the required fee. Because of the exclusive role played by the state in the termination of marriages, the Court held that indigents could not be denied an opportunity to be heard "absent a countervailing state interest of overriding significance."

2.25. Prisoners

States have on occasion barred marriage by anyone who seeks to marry while incarcerated for a crime. However, the Court in *Turner v. Safely*, 482 U.S. 78 (1987), while affirming *Butler v. Wilson*, 415 U.S. 953 (1974) (holding that a marriage prohibition when an inmate has received a life sentence is constitutional), declared that a state regulation barring all inmate marriages was not reasonably related to the state interests. In *Turner v. Safely*, the state regulation barred marriages of inmates except when there were compelling reasons such as a pregnancy or a nonmarital child to be born, and then only with the warden's permission, which permission was usually given only in the prospect of illegitimacy. Prison officials unsuccessfully argued that the restriction was related to the state's interest in rehabilitation of the inmate and the prevention of prison security problems.

The Supreme Court in *Turner v. Safely* stated that "several factors are relevant in determining the reasonableness of the regulation at issue," including: (1) "a 'valid, rational connection' between the prison regulation and the legitimate governmental interest put forward to justify it," (2) "whether there are alternative means of exercising the right that remain open to prison inmates," (3) "the impact accommodation of the asserted constitutional right will have on guards and other inmates, and on the allocation of prison resources generally," and (4) "the absence of ready alternatives."

EXAMPLES

Example 2-17

Assume P is convicted of a crime involving the use of prohibited drugs. The trial judge sentences P to a six-month rehabilitative drug program, which requires that P be incarcerated at a minimum security prison. P decides to marry X and seeks to obtain a marriage license without a personal appearance before the clerk of court — a requirement under local law. The prison refuses to transport P to the clerk's office so he can obtain the license with his fiancée. P brings an action against the clerk to require him to travel to the prison. P also contends that it is reasonable and feasible for the clerk or a representative to periodically visit area prisons for the purpose of issuing licenses. In fact, he argues *Turner* requires the clerk to do so. How should a court rule?

EXPLANATIONS

Explanation

This is a close question. The issue not addressed by *Turner* is whether under the totality of all circumstances involved in operating a prison, a prisoner's fundamental right to marry can be enforced irrespective of the cost to the ancillary services, which have no statutory responsibility to ensure that the prisoner and his or her partner get to the marriage license bureau door. A court rejecting the prisoner's request would reason that the court clerk does not have a legal duty to ensure that a prisoner obtains a marriage license. It would say that for a court to direct the clerk to engage in an activity that would entail unknown expenditures of money, manpower, and security concerns and which would divert funds and resources beyond their statutory mandate is inappropriate. *In re Coates*, 849 A.2d 254 (Pa. Super. 2004). This court would likely conclude that *Turner* never intended that its ruling was to be extrapolated to provide that prisoners must be accommodated regardless of cost or security problems in order to comply with the ministerial requirements of obtaining a marriage license.

A court favoring the plaintiff prisoner would most likely view the matter as one where there are low-cost alternatives available. For example, the clerk's office could schedule periodic trips to prisons within the county to conduct examinations and issue marriage licenses two or three times a year. Since the examinations would be performed at predetermined intervals rather than at the prisoners' request, the cost associated with this service would be minimal. Alternatively, the clerk could accept affidavits that were sworn, attested, and notarized at the prison and then mailed to the clerk's office.

MARRIAGE RESTRICTIONS IN PLACE

2.26. Polygamy

Polygamous marriages have not been protected at any time by the laws of the United States. *See Reynolds v. United States*, 98 U.S. 145 (1878); *In re State ex rel. Black*, 238 P.2d 887 (Utah 1955). Because a polygamous relationship is viewed as a type of bigamy, such a relationship is punishable by imprisonment in most jurisdictions. These relationships are viewed as void in all jurisdictions. *See State v. Holm*, 136 P.3d 726 (Utah 2006). Polyandry is likewise prohibited. *See Riepe v. Riepe*, 91 P.3d 312 (Az. App. 2005).

Polygamous marriages are legally recognized in many African, Asian, and Muslim countries. There are four common arguments made in support of polygamy: (1) The Old Testament of the Bible gives religious authority to a man's having more than one wife. (2) Polygamy is justified when the wife is infertile or unwell, permitting a man to have children without divorcing his first wife or leaving her ill provided for is in society's interests. (3) Polygamy prevents immorality such as prostitution, rape, fornication, adultery, and a high divorce rate that destabilizes a society. (4) Polygamy protects widows and orphans and responds to the excess of women over men in a society in time of war or other disasters. Others argue that polygamy offers women a viable solution to successfully balance a career, motherhood, and marriage. Still others argue that the increased incidence of extramarital sex, children born out of wedlock without support from fathers, and the soaring divorce rate suggest polygamy should be reconsidered.

2.27. Bigamy

Bigamy is a statutory crime and is commonly defined as "the act of marrying one person while legally married to another." *Black's Law Dictionary* (8th ed. 2004), p 172. The Utah Supreme Court has held that the term "marry" in the state's bigamy statute makes a married person guilty of bigamy when the person purports to marry another person. Furthermore, the concept of marriage includes both legally recognized marriages and those that are not state-sanctioned. *State v. Holm*, 136 P.3d 726 (Utah 2006) (defendant was legally married to one woman and participated in religious marriage ceremonies with others).

EXAMPLES

Example 2-18

Assume that X marries D1 and D2 outside the United States. Where X and D1 and D2 are married, there is no barrier to having two spouses. Assume X comes to the United States with D1 and D2. Shortly after arriving in the United States, D1 begins divorce proceedings against X. The clerk of court (P) discovers that D1 and D2 are both married to X and refuses to file the papers. What arguments may P and D1 make to the court when D1 challenges P's refusal to allow the filing of the divorce papers? How will a court most likely rule?

Explanation

Most likely P will argue that the action should be dismissed because the relationship in every state in the United States is void, and in most states is a crime punishable by imprisonment. Furthermore, the Full Faith and Credit Clause of the Constitution does not apply to the laws of a foreign government. D1 will argue that because the marriage was valid where it was performed, it is valid everywhere. D1 will also argue that, because she was married first, her marriage is valid while the marriage to D2 is invalid. P will respond that, even though the rule of *lex loci* generally supports D1's position, the rule is tempered by the strong public policy in the forum state that bars bigamous marriages. Moreover, P will contend that the policy of the foreign government is contrary to that of the forum state, and a court should not, under these circumstances, parcel out the sequence of the marriage in order to allow a divorce (noting that, if the divorce is allowed to D1, D2 apparently remains the wife of X). On these facts, the clerk's decision to reject the divorce petition will most likely be upheld. As a possible alternative, D1 may consider using the jurisdiction's putative spouse statute, which permits a person who believed in good faith that he or she was married to another to be treated in an equitable manner. P may counter that the putative spouse doctrine was not intended to apply to polygamous relationships and that D1's ignorance of the forum law is not an excuse for not following it. Although the answer to this somewhat close question turns on the precise language of the forum state's putative spouse statute, a trial court will most likely not recognize D1 as a putative spouse.

2.28. Sham Marriages — Immigration Fraud

Sham marriages are those entered into without the intent to live together as a husband and wife. Sham marriages are sometimes used by foreign aliens in an attempt to gain citizenship in the United States. For example, in *Faustin v. Lewis*, 427 A.2d 1105 (N.J. 1981), the plaintiff seeking a marriage annulment came to this country on a temporary visitor's visa. At that time, the defendant was in the employ of persons engaged in the unlawful business of arranging sham marriages between U.S. citizens and Haitians for a fee of between $500 and $1,200 so that the latter could obtain permanent residence in this country. Defendant, using various names, had married a number of Haitians for this purpose, including the plaintiff. Although it was undisputed that plaintiff and defendant participated in the ceremony solely for the purpose of making plaintiff eligible for lawful permanent residence in the United States, the New Jersey Supreme Court remanded the case to the trial court to allow the plaintiff to seek an annulment.

In response to immigration problems, Congress in 1986 enacted the Marriage Fraud Amendments Act, 8 U.S.C. §1154(h), 1255(e). Section 702 of the Act amends 8 U.S.C. §§1154(h) and 1255(e) to permit an alien who marries during deportation proceedings to establish that the marriage was entered into in good faith, in accordance with law, not for the purpose of procuring the alien's entry as an immigrant, and that no fee or other consideration was given. This amendment applies to marriages entered into before, on, or after the date of enactment. *See* 136 Cong. Rec. H 132334 (Oct. 26, 1990). Prior to this Act, any U.S. citizen claiming that his or her alien spouse was entitled to immediate relative status could seek an adjustment in status for the alien spouse simply by filing a petition with the Attorney General. The Immigration and Naturalization Service (INS) then conducted an inquiry into each petition to determine whether the marriage was bona fide or merely a sham entered into for the purpose of obtaining immigration benefits. If the INS concluded that the marriage was sincere, it granted the alien spouse permanent resident status. No adjustment was granted if the marriage was determined to be a fraud.

2.29. Consanguinity

The historical basis for the consanguinity prohibition is rooted in English Canonical Law, which enforced what is considered to be a Biblical prohibition on incestuous relationships. Another reason advanced for the enactment of incest and consanguinity statutes is a generally accepted theory that genetic inbreeding by close blood relatives tends to increase the chances that offspring of the marriage will inherit certain unfavorable physical characteristics. *See State v. Sharon* H., 429 A.2d 1321 (Del. Super. Ct. 1981).

Consanguinity restrictions bar marriages between persons related by blood within certain degrees of kinship, with the scope of the prohibition varying from state to state. All jurisdictions bar marriages within the immediate family, that is, between a parent and child or brother and sister. These relationships, if they occur, are void. Most states bar marriage between an aunt and nephew or an uncle and his niece. A majority of jurisdictions bar marriage between first cousins, although courts have on occasion waived the application of this prohibition. For example, in an Indiana case, two first cousins had married in Tennessee, where such marriages were legal. Later, after moving to Indiana, where such marriages are illegal, they sought a divorce. The Indiana court found that there was not a strong public policy against such marriages, so the marriage was given comity in Indiana and a divorce granted. *Mason v. Mason*, 725 N.E.2d 706 (Ind. Ct. App. 2002).

Consanguinity statutes that expressly prohibit marriages between brother and sister are applied to bar marriages or sexual relations between blood relatives, including relatives of half-blood. *See State v. Skinner*, 43 A.2d 76 (Conn. 1945); *State v. Lamb*, 227 N.W. 830 (Iowa 1929); *State v. Smith*, 85 S.E. 958 (S.C. 1915).

EXAMPLES

Example 2-19

Assume that D1 and D2 were half-brother and half-sister by blood (born of the same mother, but of different fathers). When she was approximately ten days old, D2 was adopted by family X. D1 became a ward of the state and was raised in or by various state programs. D1 and D2 met, fell in love, and married, knowing that they were half-brother and -sister. The state indicted them under its criminal statutes for entering into a prohibited marriage. They argue that by adoption, a child is given the status of a natural child to his or her adopted parents, and any legal relationship to the child's natural parents is ended. Therefore, the prohibition in the state statute barring the marriage of a half-brother or half-sister was inapplicable due to D2's adoption. How will a court most likely rule on their argument?

EXPLANATIONS

Explanation

A court will most likely reject their argument. In general, a consanguinity statute prohibits marriages between blood relatives in the lineal, or ascending and descending, lines. The policy of maintaining secrecy of adoption records does not bar any and all inquiry into the facts of an adoption. *State v. Sharon H.*, 429 A.2d 1321 (Del. Super. Ct. 1981).

2.30. Affinity

Affinity prohibitions refer to a relationship that exists between two people because of the marriage of one of them to a blood relative of the other. Marriages between persons related through marriage by step relationships are prohibited under most state affinity statutes.

2.31. Adopted Children Marrying Each Other

The prohibition against the marriage of close relatives has long existed; however, the policy argument is not as strong when the parties are related by adoption. Although all states prohibit the marriage of relatives within certain degrees of kinship, most, but not all, prohibit that marriage if the relationship is due to adoption. *See Bagnardi v. Hartnett*, 366 N.Y.S.2d 89, 91 (N.Y. 1975) (marriage between adoptive father and adopted daughter legally permissible); *see also Israel v. Allen*, 577 P.2d 762 (Colo. 1978); *In re Enderle Marriage License*, 1 Pa. D & C Reports 2d 114 (Phila. Cy. 1954). In *Israel v. Allen*, the court held that the Colorado statute prohibiting marriage between a brother and sister related by adoption is unconstitutional. It stated that the statute violated the couple's equal protection rights because it does not satisfy minimum rationality requirements and failed to further a legitimate state interest in family harmony. *But cf. Rhodes v. McAfee*, 457 S.W.2d 522, 524 (Tenn. 1970) (marriage of stepfather to stepdaughter after his divorce of her mother was void ab initio under the laws of Tennessee and Mississippi).

EXAMPLES

Example 2-20

Assume that P and D married. P is D's niece, and when D dies, P seeks her widow's share of D's estate. D's children from a former marriage object. How will a court most likely rule on the objection?

EXPLANATIONS

Explanation

The challenge raised by the children will most likely be sustained and the marriage held as void. The result will turn, of course, on the strength of the public policy reflected by decisions and statutes in the jurisdiction. *See Singh v. Singh*, 569 A.2d 1112 (Conn. 1990) (marriage between persons related to one another as half-uncle and half-niece was void as incestuous).

EXAMPLES

Example 2-21

Assume that P and D are brother and sister related by adoption and are not related by either half or whole blood. When both reach the age of majority, they attempt to marry. However, the clerk of court refuses to issue a license based on a provision in that jurisdiction's law that prohibits "A marriage between an ancestor and a descendant or between a brother and sister, whether the relationship is by the half or the whole blood or by adoption." P and D contend that the statute is unconstitutional. Most likely, how will a court rule?

EXPLANATIONS

Explanation

At least one court considering this issue has found that marriage is a fundamental right and that no compelling state interest is furthered by prohibiting marriage between a brother and sister related only by adoption. Such a provision was held unconstitutional as a denial of equal protection by the Colorado Supreme Court. *Israel v. Allen*, 577 P.2d 762 (Colo. 1978).

SAME-SEX RELATIONSHIPS

2.32. Defense of Marriage Act

When it appeared that Hawaii might become the first state to expressly allow same-sex couples to marry, *Baehr v. Lewin*, 852 P.2d 44 (Haw. 1993), Congress responded by enacting the Defense of Marriage Act, 1 U.S.C. §7 (1996). President Clinton signed into law the Defense of Marriage Act (DOMA) on September 21, 1996. DOMA defines marriage for purposes of federal law as a "legal union between one man and one woman as husband and wife." A "spouse" is defined as referring "only to a person of the opposite sex who is a husband or wife." DOMA requires that these definitions apply "in determining the meaning of any act of Congress, or of any ruling, regulation, or interpretation of the various administrative bureaus and agencies of the United States."

Prior to the 2004 elections, at least 38 states had passed state DOMAs that defined marriage as a union between one man and one woman. DOMA has survived early constitutional challenges in the federal courts. *See In re Kandu*, 315 B.R. 123, 133 (Bankr. W.D. Wash. 2004) (concluding that "DOMA does not violate the principles of comity, or the Fourth, Fifth, or Tenth Amendments to the U.S. Constitution"); *Wilson v. Ake*, 354 F. Supp. 2d 1298 (M.D. Fla. 2005) (finding DOMA "constitutionally valid").

EXAMPLES

Example 2-22

Assume that P and D, a same-sex couple, are married in Massachusetts. They move to Minnesota, where the legislature had adopted a state DOMA. When their relationship breaks down, P seeks to use Minnesota's divorce statutes to obtain alimony and an equitable distribution of the couple's property. D contends P cannot bring a divorce action in this jurisdiction. How will a court most likely rule?

EXPLANATIONS

Explanation

A court will most likely agree with D. Under the state DOMA, Minnesota will not recognize the same-sex marriage even though it is valid in Massachusetts.

2.33. *Lawrence v. Texas*

One of the major obstacles to same-sex marriages has been the decision in *Bowers v. Hardwick*, 478 U.S. 186 (1986). There the Court affirmed a lower court ruling that found a criminal statute punishing sex between consenting adults constitutional. The Court rejected the claim that the right to privacy (*Griswald v. Connecticut*, 381 U.S. 479 (1965)) protected consenting adults from prosecution under the statute. Of interest is the Georgia Supreme Court's subsequent ruling that the statute violated the due process rights of consenting adults under its state constitution. *See Powell v. State*, 510 S.E.2d 18 (Ga. 1988).

Of greater interest and of major importance is *Lawrence v. Texas*, 123 S. Ct. 2472 (2003), in which the Court overruled *Bowers v. Hardwick*. *Lawrence* involved a Texas criminal statute that made it a crime for consenting adults to engage in anal intercourse. Justice Kennedy, writing for the Court, held that the criminal statute violated a liberty interest guaranteed by the Due Process Clause of the Fourteenth Amendment. Justice O'Connor concurred in the opinion, finding that the statute violated the Equal Protection Clause. She would not have overruled *Bowers v. Hardwick*. Justice Scalia dissented and questioned whether homosexual sodomy is now a fundamental right entitled to strict scrutiny.

2.34. Formal Registration of Same-Sex Relationships

Belgium, Denmark, Norway, Iceland, England, and Sweden have adopted provisions that permit formal registration of same-sex relationships. Partners who register under the laws of these countries as domestic partners are treated much as they would be if the marriage laws applied to them.

The European Parliament, which is the legislative body for the European Union, voted in 2003 to recognize same-sex registered partnerships, civil solidarity pacts, and marriages across national borders. Several cities, including San Francisco, Atlanta, Los Angeles, Washington, D.C., Seattle, Madison, and Ann Arbor, Michigan, have ordinances that allow partners to declare that they will be responsible for the other's welfare. It is estimated that more than 300 private employers have benefits packages that extend benefits to the partner of any lesbian or gay employee, if the employee signs an affidavit stating that the couple live together in a committed relationship. *See* Michael T. Morley et al., *Developments in Law and Policy: Emerging Issues in Family Law*, 21 Yale L. & Pol'y Rev. 169 (2003).

France, the Netherlands, and Germany also provide same-sex couples with the benefits of marriage. The Netherlands allows these couples to marry.

2.35. Canada Allows Gays and Lesbians to Marry

In *Halpern v. Attorney General of Canada*, the Court of Appeal for Ontario, *http://www.ontariocourts.on.ca/decisions/2003/june/halpernC39172.htm*, June 11, 2003, a three-member panel of the Ontario Court of Appeal declared unanimously that the definition of marriage as currently set by the federal government — as a union between man and woman — was invalid and must be changed immediately to include same-sex couples. The panel said that marriage does not have a constitutionally fixed meaning. Rather, the term *marriage*, like the term *banking* and the phrase *criminal law*, has the constitutional flexibility necessary to meet changing realities of Canadian society without the need for recourse to constitutional amendment procedures. The court observed that procreation and childrearing are not the only purposes of marriage, or the only reasons why couples choose to marry. Intimacy, companionship, societal recognition, economic benefits, and the blending of two families are other reasons that couples choose to marry. It said that same-sex couples are capable of forming "long, lasting, loving and intimate relationships," *id.* at n.94, and that denying same-sex couples the right to marry perpetuates a contrary view, namely, that same-sex couples are not capable of forming loving and lasting relationships, and thus same-sex relationships are not worthy of the same respect and recognition as opposite-sex relationships. It concluded that the common law requirement that marriage be between persons of the opposite sex does not accord with the needs, capacities, and circumstances of same-sex couples.

American couples, different-sex or same-sex, may go to Canada to marry. Canada, like the United States, has no residency requirement for marriage (though it does have a one-year residency requirement for divorce). Canadian marriage licenses have generally been recognized in the United States, and this recognition will lead to legal challenges in the United States to same-sex couples claiming rights and privileges deriving from their Canadian licenses. Issues the U.S. courts will have to sort out involve adoption rights, inheritance, and insurance benefits, and matters as mundane as sharing health club memberships are likely to arise in courts and state legislatures.

2.36. Common Benefits Relationships — Civil Unions

Although Vermont has provided same-sex couples with rights similar to those enjoyed by married couples under the common benefits provisions of that state's constitution, only Massachusetts has recognized that a same-sex couple may marry. Courts rationalize their "hands-off" position by stating that marriage is a union of man and woman, uniquely involving procreation and rearing of children within a family. *See Skinner v. Oklahoma ex rel. Williamson*, 316 U.S. 535 (1942) (invalidating Oklahoma's Habitual Criminal Sterilization Act on equal protection grounds). In *Skinner*, the Court stated in part, "Marriage and procreation are fundamental to the very existence and survival of the race."

In *Baker v. State*, 744 A.2d 864 (Vt. 1999), the Vermont Supreme Court held that the limitation of state-recognized marriage to opposite-sex couples violated the common benefits clause of the state constitution. It directed the Vermont legislature to fashion a remedy providing same-sex couples with the same benefits and security granted married couples. In response, the Vermont legislature passed a law extending the benefits and protections of marriage to same-sex couples through a system of civil unions. *See* 15 U.S.C. §150 *et seq.*, 18 U.S.C. §5160 *et seq*. However, under the statute, "marriage" remains a union between a man and a woman.

In 2005 Connecticut became the first state to promulgate legislation without a court order that provides same-sex couples with the opportunity to enter into a civil union. Civil Union Law, Conn. Pub. Act 05-10. The law became effective October 1, and it extends to civil union partners "all the same benefits, protections and responsibilities under law . . . as are granted to spouses in a marriage." However, parties to a civil union under Connecticut law are not defined as spouses.

A few other state legislatures have extended limited recognition and benefits to same-sex couples. For example, California's statewide domestic partnership registry extends all nontax rights that are available to married spouses under California law. Derek B. Dorn, *Advising Clients in a State of Uncertainty*, 78-JAN NYSTBJ 40 (January 2006). New Jersey's domestic partnership law "extends certain rights as next of kin but not intestate inheritance or elective share rights. Domestic partners are not treated as spouses for income and estate tax purposes, but the law does exempt transfers to a surviving domestic partner from New Jersey inheritance tax." *Id.* at 42. Domestic partners in Maine and Hawaii are entitled to a variety of benefits, including the intestate inheritance preference and right to elect against a partner's will. *Id.*

2.37. Full Faith and Credit and Civil Unions

In *Burns v. Burns*, 560 S.E.2d 47 (Ga. 2002), in the context of a child visitation dispute, a Georgia court would not recognize a "civil union" entered into in Vermont as an act of marriage. In *Rosengarten v. Downes*, 802 A.2d 170 (Conn. App. 2002), the Connecticut intermediate court affirmed the trial court's judgment dismissing an action to dissolve a same-sex civil union for lack of subject matter jurisdiction. The court relied upon Connecticut General Statutes §45a-727a (4), which provide that "the current public policy of the state of Connecticut is now limited to a marriage between a man and a woman" and the Defense of Marriage Act.

Example 2-23

Assume that P and D, a same-sex couple, form a civil union in Vermont. They move to another state where the legislature had adopted a state DOMA. When their relationship breaks down, P seeks to use that state's divorce statutes to obtain alimony and an equitable distribution of the couple's property. D contends P cannot bring a divorce action in this jurisdiction. How will a court most likely rule?

Explanation

A court will most likely agree with D. Depending upon the wording of the state DOMA, the court may be prohibited from recognizing the civil union.

2.38. Massachusetts Allows Same-Sex Marriage — New Jersey Requires Legislative Action

Although the number of nontraditional families is increasing in the United States, and several jurisdictions have expanded the rights of same-sex couples, only Massachusetts has extended to same-sex couples the right to marry. In jurisdictions where same-sex couples are unable to marry legally, some enter into secular or religious marriage ceremonies.

It is argued that denial of same-sex marriage "has had far reaching implications on same-sex couples and their children. Children of married spouses enjoy unique family stability and economic security due to their parents' legally recognized relationship that children of same-sex couples do not. In addition, in most states, same-sex unmarried couples do not enjoy benefits related to taxation, health insurance, family and medical leave, hospital visitation, workers' compensation and more." Madeline Marzano-Lesnevich, Galit Moskowitz, *In the Interest of Children of Same-Sex Couples*, 19 J. Am. Acad. Matrim. Law 255 (2005). The United States General Accounting Office has identified over 1,000 federal benefits the receipt of which is dependent on marriage. *Id.*

The Massachusetts Supreme Judicial Court, in a 4 to 3 opinion in *Goodridge v. Department of Public Health*, 798 N.E.2d 941 (Mass. 2003), ruled that "barring an individual from the protections, benefits and obligations of civil marriage solely because that person would marry a person of the same sex violated the Massachusetts Constitution." The court held that the state limitation of protections, benefits, and obligations of civil marriage to individuals of opposite sexes lacked rational basis and violated the state constitutional equal protection principles. However, the majority stayed the entry of judgment for 180 days to allow the Massachusetts Legislature to "take such action as it may deem appropriate in light of this opinion." Massachusetts is the third state supreme court to hear such a case.

In *Lewis v. Harris*, 908 A.2d 196 (N.J. 2006), a majority of the New Jersey Supreme Court held that, although a same-sex marriage is not a fundamental right entitled to protection under the liberty guarantee of the New Jersey Constitution, committed same-sex couples are denied equal protection of the law unless they are afforded the same rights and benefits enjoyed by married opposite-sex couples. The court reasoned that the unequal scheme of benefits and privileges afforded same-sex couples was not supported by a legitimate public need, for purposes of equal protection analysis under the New Jersey Constitution. The court directed the New Jersey legislature to, within 180 days, either amend the marriage statutes or enact a statutory structure affording same-sex couples the same rights and benefits enjoyed by married opposite-sex couples. Cf. *Andersen v. King County*, 138 P.3d 963 (Wash. 2006) (neither the Due Process nor Right to Privacy clauses in article I, section 3 and section 7, nor the equal rights amendment of the state of Washington constitution creates a right to marry a person of the same sex); *Hernandez v. Robles*, 7 N.Y.3d 338 (N.Y. 2006) (New York domestic relations law provisions limiting marriage to same-sex couples was supported by rational basis; provisions did not violate due process; and provisions did not violate equal protection).

In 1993 the Hawaii Supreme Court ruled a prohibition preventing same-sex couples from marrying might violate the Hawaii Constitution's ban on sex discrimination and could be upheld only if such a prohibition was justified by a compelling reason. Following remand and a trial court's ruling that same-sex couples could marry, the Hawaii Constitution was amended to permit the state legislature to restrict marriage to men and women only. In 1998, after a state court had ruled that choosing a marital partner is a fundament right, Alaska amended its constitution to require that all marriages be between a man and a woman.

Hawaii has enacted provisions that apply to couples who are "legally prohibited from marrying one another under state law." Haw. Rev. Stat. Ann. §572C-1. It encompasses brothers, sisters, a widowed mother and her unmarried son, and persons of the same gender. It allows individuals to make health care decisions for a partner and a variety of other benefits and rights usually associated with traditionally married couples. It differs from Vermont's approach by including persons with economic, personal, and emotional ties.

2.39. Massachusetts Limits Who May Marry

In *Cote-Whitacre v. Department of Public Health*, 844 N.E.2d 623 (Mass. 2006), the court upheld a statute that prohibited nonresidents from contracting a marriage in Massachusetts if the nonresident intended to continue to reside in another state and that state did not recognize same-sex marriages. The court ruled that couples who resided in states where same-sex marriage had not been expressly prohibited were entitled to proceed to trial, on expedited basis, to present evidence to rebut the Commonwealth's claim that their home states would prohibit same-sex marriages.

TRANSSEXUAL RELATIONSHIPS

2.40. Recognizing Transsexual Marriages

The status of recognition of transsexual marriage is changing, although courts and legislatures have not yet fully resolved the issues involved in such recognition. In M.T. v. J.T., 355 A.2d 204, 211 (N.J. App. Div. 1976), the petitioner underwent a sex change to become a woman and married. When the relationship broke down, she sought support from her husband. He countered that the marriage was void because a man could not marry another man, even one who had had a sex change. He contended that the petitioner was born a male and did not possess the internal organs of a woman. The court rejected the argument, saying that when one has a sex change, for purposes of the state's marriage laws, that person is a woman and entitled to support. Sex reassignment surgery, under that view, merely harmonizes a person's physical characteristics with that identity. It said that the transsexual's gender and genitalia are no longer discordant; they have been harmonized through medical treatment. Plaintiff has become physically and psychologically unified and fully capable of sexual activity consistent with her reconciled sexual attributes of gender and anatomy.

In *Littleton v. Prange*, 9 S.W.3d 223 (Tex. App. San Antonio 1999), the Court of Appeals held that a ceremonial marriage between a man and a transsexual born as a man, but surgically and chemically altered to have the physical characteristics of a woman, was not valid. *See In re Ladrach*, 513 N.E.2d 828 (Ohio Prob. 1987) (post-operative male-to-female transsexual could not obtain marriage license to marry male). The Maryland Court of Appeals in *In re Heilig*, 816 A.2d 68 (Md. 2003), held that it would recognize a transsexual's gender change. However, in *In re Estate of Gardiner*, 42 P.3d 120 (Kan. 2002), the court held that a post-operative male-to-female transsexual is not a woman within the meaning of the statutes recognizing marriage, and a marriage between a post-operative male-to-female transsexual and a man is void as against public policy.

Courts have fewer problems with allowing transsexual name changes. For example, a transsexual male was permitted to change his name from Richard to Susan as part of his sex reassignment therapy. *In re Maloney*, 774 N.E.2d 239 (2002), *In re Bricknell*, 771 N.E.2d 846 (Ohio 2002).

CHAPTER 3

Annulments

3.1. Introduction

Annulment actions today are few and are found most commonly in immigration and Social Security disputes, where a marriage either qualifies or disqualifies an individual from eligibility for certain benefits. In most jurisdictions, statutes treat parties to an annulment in a fashion similar to persons involved in a short-term marriage. Despite the rarity of these actions, most family law students are expected to understand the concepts associated with annulments and to possess the skills necessary to apply basic legal principles to problems associated with them. We have, therefore, included an analysis of the more common principles and issues involved in annulment actions in this chapter.

HISTORY AND DEVELOPMENT

3.2. History

Annulment has its origin in the canon law of the Ecclesiastical Church in England and was recognized for centuries. *See* W. Scott, *Nullity of Marriage in Canon Law and English Law*, 2 U. Toronto L.J. 319 (1937-1938). Annulment jurisdiction was removed from the Ecclesiastical courts and placed in the English civil family court system around 1870.

"VOID" AND "VOIDABLE" DEFINED

3.3. Defining a Void Marriage

Annulment actions involve two types of relationships. The first is a void relationship — one that the law will not recognize under any circumstances. A void marriage is a relationship that is not legally recognized for any purpose. *See Black's Law Dictionary* (8th ed. 2004). For example, a person who is already married may not marry another without obtaining a divorce from the first partner. Absent a divorce, the second relationship is considered void.

A marriage that is void typically is one that offends a strong public policy, including such relations as bigamy, polygamy, and incest. A void marriage normally does not require a judicial declaration or action to establish that it is not valid. However, an action may be filed to provide a person with certainty that the marriage is void and to establish a public record of its invalidity.

3.4. Defining a Voidable Marriage

In contrast to a void relationship, a voidable relationship is one that is recognized as lawful until it is legally voided by a court order. A voidable marriage may occur, for example, when one of the parties lacked the capacity to consent to the marriage contract. Whether a court determines that an action is void or voidable is of practical importance. *See, e.g., Patey v. Peaslee*, 111 A.2d 194 (N.H. 1955) (marriage was voidable, not void; therefore, spouse not barred from intestate share of estate).

3.5. Standing to Pursue an Annulment

Usually, either party or a third party may bring an annulment action to challenge the validity of a marriage. A legal representative of a decedent's estate may normally pursue an annulment action that was commenced prior to death. *See Hall v. Nelson*, 534 N.E.2d 929 (Ohio App. 1987). An underage party has standing to have a marriage annulled. However, a party who is of marriageable age may not attack the validity of his or her marriage to an underage person. The Uniform Marriage and Divorce Act (UMDA) states that "[a] declaration of invalidity . . . may be sought by the underaged party, his parent or guardian." UMDA §208(b).

Example 3-1

Assume that P married D while P was still legally married to X. When D discovered that P was married to X, D sought advice regarding an annulment action. Is a formal annulment necessary?

Explanation

The relationship is void and no legal action is normally necessary on the part of the innocent spouse. However, if a particular statute exists (and they now do in almost all states) or if the party is uneasy about the relationship and wants a public record that no marriage existed, an action to void the relationship may be brought.

RETROACTIVITY OF ANNULMENT RULING

3.6. General Rule

As a general rule, a marriage is void from the time its nullity is declared if one of the parties was incapable of consenting to the marriage for want of understanding. *See Levine v. Dumbra*, 604 N.Y.S.2d 207 (N.Y. 1993).

3.7. Uniform Marriage and Divorce Act

UMDA states that:

> unless the court finds, after a consideration of all relevant circumstances, including the effect of a retroactive decree on third parties, that the interests of justice would be served by making the decree not retroactive, it shall declare the marriage invalid as of the date of the marriage. The provisions of this Act relating to property rights of the spouses, maintenance, support, and custody of children on dissolution of marriage are applicable to non retroactive decrees of invalidity.

UMDA §208(e).

ANNULMENT ACTIONS INVOLVING MENTAL CAPACITY, AGE, DRUGS, OR JEST

3.8. Mental Capacity

A valid marriage requires that both parties possess sufficient mental capacity to understand the nature of the contract and the duties and responsibilities it creates. *Guthery v. Ball*, 228 S.W. 887 (Mo. Ct. 1921).

Example 3-2

Assume that P and D married and that three months after the marriage P (the wife) brought an action to annul the marriage, claiming she did not have sufficient mental capacity to understand the nature of the marriage ceremony. Experts called by P testified that she suffered from a severe and irreversible mental illness long before her marriage and agreed that based on their examinations, she was incapable of understanding the nature, consequences, and effect of marriage. D argued that P had waived the claim by her apparent delay in bringing the action and that the only action that could be brought was one for divorce. How will a court most likely rule?

Explanation

To obtain an annulment on the ground of lack of understanding, it must be shown that the party was incapable of understanding the nature, effect, and consequences of the marriage. Here, there is evidence that the wife suffered from a severe and irreversible mental illness long before her marriage. A court will most likely annul her marriage. *See Levine v. Dumbra*, 604 N.Y.S.2d 207 (N.Y. App. Div. 1993); *Faivre v. Faivre*, 128 A.2d 139 (Pa. Super. Ct. 1956).

3.9. Age

The common law allowed a girl age 12 and a boy age 14 to marry. The marriage would have been valid without the consent of parents or the approval and order of a court. Today, most jurisdictions set the age to legally marry by statute, and the minimum age is around 15 or 16 years with parental or court consent. UMDA requires parental or judicial consent for persons 16 and 17. The Act requires both parental and judicial consent before persons younger than 16 can marry.

If an underage person marries without consent of a parent or the court, the marriage is voidable. An action may be maintained by the infant, by either parent of the infant, or by the guardian of the infant's person. But an annulment action is not allowed at the suit of a party who was of the age of legal consent when it was contracted, or by a party who, for any time after he or she attained that age, freely cohabited with the other party as husband or wife.

Example 3-3

Assume that P, age 23, and D, age 16, marry in a jurisdiction that requires consent of a parent or a court order when a party is under 18. D obtains neither. Three years later, at age 19, D seeks an annulment of the marriage on the ground that it was void when entered. P claims that they are now both adults and that D waived whatever opportunity she might have had to obtain an annulment once she became an adult. How will a court most likely treat the action?

Explanation

The court will most likely deny the request for an annulment. Most courts will take the view that, to obtain an annulment, D should have brought her action before reaching age 18. Here, D failed to do this. In addition, she freely cohabited with P as his wife after reaching the legal age of an adult.

Example 3-4

Assume that P, age 23, and D, age 16, marry in a jurisdiction that requires consent of a parent or a court order when a party is under 18. D obtains neither. A year later, P brings an action to annul the marriage. How will a court most likely rule on P's effort?

Explanation

The court will most likely reject P's effort. The reason is that P is not the party with the age disability; therefore, most courts will not provide P with standing to bring the annulment action. P's only remedy is to seek a divorce.

3.10. Influence of Drugs or Alcohol

An excessive use of intoxicants may render one incapable of contracting a marriage because of the resulting inability to concentrate one's mental faculties or to understand the marital obligations. Absent a showing that the party ratified the marriage by continuing to voluntarily live with the other person following the ceremony, such a marriage may be annulled.

Example 3-5

P and D participated in a marriage ceremony in Nevada on a Sunday, while P was allegedly under the influence of intoxicating liquor and so inebriated that he did not understand the nature of the ceremony or its legal effect. Two days later, when P claimed he was still suffering from the effects of intoxication, D advised P of the marriage. The next day, having fully recovered from his inebriation, P left the hotel room he was sharing with D and had not since cohabited with her. P sought to have the marriage annulled.

At trial, P's testimony was corroborated by a friend who was with him at the time of the marriage. The friend said that P could hardly walk down the aisle and passed out during the wedding dinner following the ceremony. D testified that although she felt that P was drinking "an awful lot, we had talked about getting married and he was able to stand up during the ceremony." The trial court denied the annulment, stating in effect that it did not believe P's testimony. The judge wrote that she was "satisfied that there isn't any minister in the city or anywhere else that is ordained, that will marry a drunken person." P appeals. How will an appellate court most likely rule?

Explanation

It is apparently a matter of common knowledge that some parties submit to a marriage ceremony when one person is under the influence of an intoxicating beverage to the extent that such person is of unsound mind and does not know what is taking place, thus being unable to enter into a contract. *See* cases cited in 28 A.L.R. (1924) 648. One participating in a marriage ceremony while under the influence of intoxicating beverages to such extent as to be of unsound mind and without knowledge of what is happening is entitled to an annulment of the marriage. Here P's testimony was corroborated by a witness. Unless the judge is ready to reject the testimony of both P and his witness, an annulment should be granted. It is also important that shortly after the alleged marriage, P moved out of the hotel room and did not have further relations with D. The trial judge erred in refusing to grant the annulment. *See Dobson v. Dobson*, 193 P.2d 794 (Cal. App. 2d Dist. 1948).

EXAMPLES

Example 3-6

Assume that P and D married, and P claims that he was intoxicated and can recall very little of the marriage ceremony. D concedes that P's recollection of the marriage ceremony is correct. Despite P's intoxication at the time they were wed, P continued to live with D for several months following the marriage and contributed financially to D's support. When P decided that the relationship was not working out, P brought an action to annul the marriage. P produces several witnesses who testify that at the time of the marriage ceremony it was clear that P was *non compos mentis* — that P was very drunk and could not have understood what was occurring. D concedes that the testimony of the witnesses is correct but insists that P does not have a basis for an annulment. How will a court most likely rule?

EXPLANATIONS

Explanation

A court will most likely not grant an annulment. Although P was intoxicated to the degree that he cannot recall what happened at the time of the marriage, P thereafter lived with D and contributed financial support when sober. By this conduct, P effectively condoned the acts done while he was intoxicated as if they had been done when he was absolutely sober.

3.11. Marriage Made in Jest

When two people participate in a mock marriage ceremony as an act of jest, exuberance, hilarity, or dare and harbor no intention to be bound thereby, most courts permit an annulment, reasoning that the public interest would not be served by compelling the persons involved to accept the legal consequences of their imprudent conduct. *Mpiliris v. Hellenic Lines, Ltd.*, 323 F. Supp. 865 (D.C. S.D. Tex. 1969). *See Crouch v. Wartenberg*, 104 S.E. 117 (W. Va. 1920); *Jewett v. Jewett*, 175 A.2d 141 (Pa. Super. Ct. 1961).

ANNULMENT ACTIONS INVOLVING FRAUD

3.12. Misrepresentation

Most states provide that a marriage may be annulled as a result of a fraud that goes to the essence of the marriage because this type of fraud vitiates consent. To justify an annulment finding, the fraud must be of an extreme nature pertaining to one of the essentials of the marriage and must go to present, not future, facts. The test is whether the false representations or concealment defeated the essential purpose of the injured spouse inherent in contracting a marriage. Once a marriage is consummated, courts require a greater quantum of proof of fraud before granting an annulment. When the fraud is discovered by the injured party, an annulment will not be granted unless the couple immediately, voluntarily ceased living together as husband and wife.

The mere fact of lying is not a sufficient basis for a court to grant an annulment. Lies that involve the concealment of incontinence, temper, idleness, extravagance, coldness, or fortune are not recognized as sufficient justification for annulling a marriage. For example, a shoe salesman's false representation that he owned his own shoe store fell short of fraud sufficient to annul a marriage in *Mayer v. Mayer*, 279 P. 783 (Cal. 1929). A future husband's statement that he was a "man of means" when he was really "impecunious" was insufficient to convince a court that fraud was committed. *Marshall v. Marshall*, 300 P. 816 (Cal. 1931). An annulment action was rejected when the husband turned out to be, in the eyes of his wife, a lazy, unshaven disappointment with a drinking problem. An annulment was also rejected when a woman falsely stated prior to marriage that she had been cured of epilepsy. *Lyon v. Lyon* 82 N.E. 850 (Ill. 1907). An annulment was denied when a man claimed that he was chaste even though another woman was pregnant with his child. *Hull v. Hull*, 191 Ill. App. 307 (1915). In each of these examples, the courts found that the claimed fraud did not impair the ability of the parties to live together and perform the obligations and duties of marriage. The courts reasoned that the defrauded party "got possession of the same flesh and bones he bargained for and the law makes no provision for the relief of a blind credulity."

Example 3-7

P and D marry. A month after the marriage, P discovers that D had an affair with his best friend before their marriage. Based on this information, P seeks an annulment of the marriage, arguing that D had concealed her moral character prior to the marriage. How will a court most likely rule?

Explanation

Almost all courts take the view that concealment of defects of character, morality, chastity, habits, and temper generally are not sufficient to obtain an annulment unless there is also evidence of overreaching. Evidence of overreaching includes taking advantage of another because of disparity in age, experience, or knowledge. Here, it is unlikely that a court will grant an annulment.

EXAMPLES

Example 3-8

After a 20-month marriage, P sought to have her marriage to D annulled on the ground that her consent had been fraudulently obtained. D agreed that the marriage should be terminated but requested a divorce. At the trial to determine whether the action should be one of divorce or annulment, P testified she was unaware of D's severe drinking problem until after the marriage and that she was upset to discover this and disappointed in his refusal to seek help. P testified that she knew before the nuptials that D was unemployed but she did not realize he would refuse to work thereafter. P stated that their sex life after marriage was unsatisfactory and that D was dirty and unattractive. In short, he turned from a prince into a frog. D testified to the contrary, but the trial court believed P. Is it likely a court will grant an annulment on the basis that the marriage was fraudulently obtained?

EXPLANATIONS

Explanation

A court will most likely not grant an annulment. The claims by P will be viewed as mere character defects that do not go to the essence of the marriage. In addition, P lived with D and his defects for 20 months. P's remedy is to seek a dissolution of the relationship.

3.13. Pregnancy Claims

There is a fairly even division among authorities as to whether a false representation prior to marriage by the woman that she is pregnant by the man, when actually she is pregnant by another, is sufficient to support a cause of action for annulment of marriage. Some states have held that a false representation of pregnancy that induced the husband to marry is not a ground for annulment. They reason that because premarital sexual intercourse is illegal, the man who engages in it is *in pari delicto*, and may not complain to the courts of any misconduct of the woman growing out of it. They also reason that any single man who engages in sexual intercourse with a single woman has a social obligation to marry her.

However, some jurisdictions, such as Wisconsin, have granted an annulment when a woman lied about her pregnancy before marriage. *See Masters v. Masters*, 108 N.W.2d 674 (Wis. 1961). Wisconsin and New York courts reason that the punishment inflicted by denying an annulment is out of proportion to the offense committed. However, there are aggravated situations where the doctrine of *in pari delicto* has been applied. *See Gondouin v. Gondouin*, 111 P. 756 (Cal. 1910).

3.14. Religious Claims

Religious claims are sometimes the basis for annulment actions. Older decisions suggest that courts were not overly enthusiastic about recognizing such claims. *See Wells v. Talham*, 194 N.W. 36 (Wis. 1923); *Boehs v. Hanger*, 69 N.J. Eq. 10, 59 A. 904 (N.J. 1905). For example, it was held that an annulment would not be granted when a woman falsely represented that she was a good, religious woman when in fact she was a prostitute. *Beckley v. Beckley*, 115 Ill. App. 27 (1904). However, in recent years several jurisdictions have adopted a more liberal view of religion as a basis for annulling a marriage. For example, in *Jordan v. Jordan*, 345 A.2d 168 (N.H. 1975), an annulment was granted on claims that the plaintiff, a Roman Catholic, was unaware of the defendant husband's prior marriage at the time she married him, that she would not have married him had she known, and that she could not live with defendant because of her religious beliefs. Ten years earlier, the same court had denied an annulment under similar circumstances. *Fortin v. Fortin*, 208 A.2d 447 (N.H. 1965).

Today, most courts hold that misrepresentation of strong religious convictions goes to the essence of the marriage contract, particularly if the marriage has not been consummated. The rationale for this view is that religion has a significant impact on family life.

EXAMPLES

Example 3-9

Assume that P and D, who P knew was a deeply religious individual, were married for eight years and one child was born to them when P filed suit for divorce on grounds of extreme and repeated mental cruelty. D was extremely upset because D's religion does not approve of divorce. During discovery, P revealed that she had lied to D before they were married about whether her former husband was alive or dead; she told D her former husband was dead when in fact she had divorced him. D then filed a counter-complaint for an annulment on the ground that D had been induced to marry by P's fraudulent representation that her former husband was dead when in fact he was alive and she was divorced from him. During the hearing, D claimed that his strong religious beliefs would have prevented him from marrying P, a divorced woman, while her former husband was living. D contends that P's false representation was made to induce a marriage and constitutes fraud that goes to the essence of the marriage relationship, thereby providing grounds for annulment. P says that whatever ground D may have had for an annulment is barred by the length of their marriage. How will a court most likely rule on the annulment request?

EXPLANATIONS

Explanation

The parties were married a long time and a statute in a particular state may bar the annulment claim. However, without a statutory barrier, and given the liberal trend in this area, a court might conclude that the representations provide a sufficient basis upon which an annulment may be predicated. To one who is deeply religious, his faith is the foundation on which he builds his life and conducts his everyday affairs. His religious commitment determines his attitudes and behavior toward others. When one partner has discovered that unwittingly he has been duped into a violation of his religious beliefs and that indeed he has been living in a state of calamitous and grievous sin, that discovery may well make continuation of the relationship impossible. In such an instance the fraud eliminates the innocent party's consent to the relationship and goes directly to the essence of the marriage relationship, which is not merely "flesh and bones" but heart and soul and mind as well. *See Wolfe v. Wolfe*, 378 N.E.2d 1181 (Ill. 1978).

ANNULMENT BASED ON COERCION OR DURESS

3.15. Duress

Duress is another ground sometimes used to seek an annulment of a marriage. Duress is legally defined as "a threat of harm made to compel a person to do something against his or her will or judgment." *Black's Law Dictionary* (8th ed. 2004). A marriage that is induced by duress is generally voidable. *Black's Law Dictionary* (8th ed. 2004). The distress must be of such a degree as to prevent the individual from acting as a free agent. Although physical distress is normally the evidence a court looks for in a party seeking an annulment on this ground, some courts will accept evidence of mental stress. To have a marriage annulled on the grounds of coercion or duress, most courts will require clear and convincing evidence of the duress. *Fluharty v. Fluharty*, 193 A. 838 (Del. Super. Ct. 1937).

ANNULMENT BECAUSE OF PHYSICAL INCAPACITY

3.16. Impotence

To justify the grant of an annulment on the ground of impotency, it must be proven that the impotency is natural and incurable. For an annulment, evidence must show that the other spouse was, at the time of marriage, and still is naturally and incurably impotent. *See Manbeck v. Manbeck*, 489 A.2d 748 (Pa. Super. Ct. 1985).

EXAMPLES

Example 3-10

Assume that P sought an annulment of her marriage to D three months after their marriage in a jurisdiction with a statute declaring that an annulment will be granted when there is "[i]ncurable physical impotency, or incapacity for copulation, at the suit of either party; if the party making the application was ignorant of such impotency or incapacity at the time of the marriage." Assume that the evidence at the annulment hearing indicated that D suffered from no physical defect of a sexually incapacitating nature; rather, it appeared that psychogenic causes had made D physically unable to copulate, at least with the woman he had married. D contends that the statute applies only to physical, not psychological, problems. P contends that the statute should be construed to include both physical and psychological causes. How will a court most likely rule?

EXPLANATIONS

Explanation

The court will most likely allow an annulment. The reasoning is that it is not relevant that D's impotence resulted from psychological causes rather than from physical causes. *See Rickards v. Rickards*, 166 A.2d 425 (Del. 1960); *Manbeck v. Manbeck*, 489 A.2d 748 (Pa. Super. 1985) (psychological or emotional disorder from which wife suffered, referred to by physicians as a sexual dysfunction and described as rendering her incapable of participating in normal sexual intercourse, was sufficient evidence on which to base a finding of "impotence" and to warrant an annulment of marriage given sufficient additional evidence to warrant an inference that impotence was incurable). The purpose of the statute is to allow an annulment where there is sufficient evidence to support a finding that the spouse of the party seeking the order is, in fact, impotent.

ANNULMENT AND COHABITATION

3.17. Annulment Barred by Cohabitation

Cohabitation is generally recognized as a defense to a voidable annulment action. If the partners continue to live together while seeking an annulment, courts will often reject the claim. This reflects, of course, a strong public policy favoring marriage.

EXAMPLES

Example 3-11

Assume that P petitions for an annulment in a common law court, claiming that her uncle forced her to marry D. The facts indicate that P and D lived together as husband and wife for two years before P brought her annulment action. D opposes the annulment. How will a court most likely rule?

EXPLANATIONS

Explanation

Here P sought an annulment after two years of living with D on the basis of duress. Most courts would view the fact of cohabitation as an affirmative defense to such a claim, and the action would most likely be dismissed. P may, of course, pursue a divorce action.

SUPPORT AND PROPERTY DISTRIBUTION

3.18. Support

At common law, an annulment resulted in the bastardization of any children born during the marriage. Statutes in all jurisdictions have removed this harsh common law view. UMDA §207(c) provides that children born to a void marriage are legitimate.

3.19. Alimony and Property Division

When an annulment is granted, courts have historically not provided relief similar to that provided when a couple divorce. Consequently, in a traditional annulment situation, the court did not award alimony or divide property as though it were "marital" in nature. However, that view has dramatically changed.

Today legislatures frequently authorize courts to grant alimony in divorce and annulment matters. In a majority of states alimony is awarded by the courts in connection with the termination of void marriages through application of the general divorce statutes of such states. *See Jones v. Jones*, 296 P.2d 1010 (Wash. 1956).

3.20. Reviving a Former Spouse's Support Obligation

When an annulment is granted, it may not revive a former spouse's duty of support that terminated upon the attempted remarriage. *See Gaines v. Jacobsen*, 124 N.E.2d 290 (N.Y. 1954). *Compare In re Marriage of Williams*, 677 P.2d 585 (Mont. 1984) (maintenance obligation neither automatically terminated nor automatically reinstated when remarriage was annulled) *with In re Marriage of Harris*, 560 N.E.2d 1138 (Ill. 1990) (remarriage ceremony terminates maintenance obligation, notwithstanding annulment of remarriage). *See also In re Marriage of Cargill and Rollins*, 843 P.2d 1335 (Colo. 1993) (maintenance obligations of prior marriage could be reinstated following annulment of second marriage, depending on circumstances of individual case; and equities of present case favored resumption of maintenance obligation).

OTHER ISSUES

3.21. Enoch Arden Statute

Enoch Arden statutes take their name from Alfred Lord Tennyson's 1864 poem *Enoch Arden*. Enoch married Annie, who was secretly loved by Phillip Ray, the miller's son. When Enoch did not return from a voyage, Annie and Phillip married, believing Enoch to be dead. Ten years after departing, Enoch returned.

Enoch Arden statutes provide a defense to bigamy when a spouse remarries with the good-faith belief that a former spouse is dead but do not necessarily validate the later marriage. For the later marriage to be upheld, some jurisdictions require an Enoch Arden divorce as a prerequisite to the later marriage. *See, e.g., Randolph v. Randolph*, 212 N.Y.S.2d 468 (N.Y. Sup. Ct. 1961). The effect of the Enoch Arden statute is to create an express statutory exception to the general rule that an annulment of marriage is retroactive.

EXAMPLES

Example 3-12

Decedent (D) was P's first husband. They separated, and P never heard from her first husband again. Six years after the separation, and after her inquiries proved unavailing, P believed that D was dead and P married X. However, D was not dead when P married X; D actually died ten years after the couple separated. P, who was married to X, learned of D's death and his huge estate. P immediately began legal action and secured an annulment of her second marriage. P then asserted a claim that she was D's widow and was entitled to a portion of his estate. The Enoch Arden statute in this jurisdiction reads in part as follows:

> A subsequent marriage contracted by any person during the life of a former husband or wife of such person, with any person other than such former husband or wife, is illegal and void from the beginning, when such former husband or wife is absent, and not known to such person to be living for the space of five successive years immediately preceding such subsequent marriage, or is generally reputed or believed by such person to be dead at the time such subsequent marriage was contracted. In either of which cases the subsequent marriage is valid until its nullity is adjudged by a competent tribunal.

Given the language of the statute, may P make a claim as D's surviving widow that a court will recognize?

EXPLANATIONS

Explanation

P's claim will most likely not be recognized. Courts will take the view that a claimant's status must be determined as of the date of death, and as of that date, P's marriage to X was valid. P's marriage to X could become invalid only as of the date of an annulment decree — necessarily at a time after her status in relation to the estate had been fixed. Most courts will take the view that only if P had secured her annulment while D was still alive could she contend that her marriage to him had become revived so as to give her a widow's status. *See Estate of Lemont*, 86 Cal. Rptr. 810 (Cal. Ct. App. 1970); *Valleau v. Valleau*, 6 Paige (N.Y. 1836).

CHAPTER 4

Who May Divorce? Restrictions and Requirements

4.1. Introduction

This chapter examines the history and development of divorce. It traces the important legal developments in this area of the law from ancient times to the present. Where appropriate, examples are included to explain the application of a legal principle to a practical legal problem.

HISTORY

4.2. Ancient History

Marriage and divorce have existed in some form since ancient times. Under Athenian law, Greek husbands and wives could go their separate ways after the mere filing of notice with a magistrate, with the parties free to marry, divorce, and remarry at will. Around 18 B.C. the act of divorce may have assumed a more formal requirement when the Roman emperor, Caesar Augustus, promulgated the *Lex Julia de Adulteris*, which required that a divorcing couple execute a writing that renounced their marriage—making divorce something more than an informal dissociation.

The pervasive influence of the Roman Catholic Church was being felt in England by the eleventh and twelfth centuries. During this period of history, the Church, through its Ecclesiastical courts and canon law, gained control over marriage and divorce. The Church viewed marriage as a sacrament and indissoluble except by death; not even the Pope could break the bonds of marriage. Church theology was fortified by a conviction that sexual indulgence outside marriage involved mortal sin and created a formidable barrier within marriage to the achievement of spiritual purity. These beliefs were founded, at least in part, on the Gospels. *See, e.g.*, Matthew 19:5-6, 19:3-9; Luke 16:18; Mark 10:11; Ephesians 5:30-31; I Corinthians 7:10-11; and Romans 7:2-4.

LEGAL SEPARATION: DIVORCE *A MENSA ET THORO*

4.3. Generally

Although the Church forbade absolute divorce, when the marriage vows were broken by adultery or acts of cruelty that rendered further cohabitation unsafe, the innocent spouse was permitted, by judicial decree of the ecclesiastical courts, to live apart from the wrongdoer. This relief was afforded by a decree of judicial separation called divorce *a mensa et thoro*, or a divorce from bed and board. The decree of divorce *a mensa et thoro* did not sever the marital tie, and the parties remained husband and wife. *See Schlagel v. Schlagel*, 117 S.E.2d 790, 793 (N.C. 1961). Neither party could remarry during the spouse's lifetime, and the husband was normally required to provide his wife with permanent support. *See Metcalf v. Metcalf*, 51 S.W.2d 675 (Ky. 1932).

4.4. Defined

A *divorce a mensa et thoro* is defined in *Black's Law Dictionary* (8th ed. 2004), p. 515, as "A partial or qualified divorce by which the parties were separated and allowed or ordered to live apart, but remained technically married. This type of divorce, abolished in England in 1857, was the forerunner of modern judicial separation."

4.5. Separate Maintenance: Limited Divorce

Separate maintenance proceedings today are, in part, the residue of the divorce *a mensa et thoro*. Separate maintenance actions are distinguishable from a proceeding for an absolute divorce, and even from a modern proceeding for a limited divorce. Unlike the ancient divorce *a mensa et thoro*, an action for separate maintenance does not expressly or necessarily authorize the wife to live apart from her husband. However, a decree of limited divorce allows the parties to live apart. *See Cregan v. Clark*, 658 S.W.2d 924 (Mo. App. Ct. 1983).

A separate maintenance decree also is intended to provide only for the support of the wife and children, whereas under legal separation or limited divorce, the court may determine child custody and property division, in addition to child support and alimony. *See Anderson v. Anderson*, 382 N.W.2d 620, 621 (Neb. 1986).

"FAULT" EMERGES

4.6. Ecclesiastical Courts and Fault

In the context of divorce, the concept of fault, which has played a significant role in some divorce actions, can be traced to the early Church and the Ecclesiastical courts' exercise of authority over domestic matters. Under the rules established by the Ecclesiastical courts, a person could ask for permission to live apart from a spouse. However, the person seeking the separation had to prove fault on the part of the spouse. To determine fault, the court asked whether the erring spouse had committed one of the sins recognized by the Church. Adultery, physical cruelty, and unnatural sexual practices were recognized as valid reasons for parties to live apart although they were not permanently divorced.

Fault also played a role in determining whether support was to be ordered when a divorce *a mensa et thoro* was granted. For example, if a wife committed adultery during the marriage, she was considered "at fault," and the Ecclesiastical courts were not obligated to require that her husband support her.

ABSOLUTE DIVORCE BECOMES POSSIBLE

4.7. Sixteenth-Century Theory of Absolute Divorce

The theory that one could obtain a permanent divorce apparently emerged during the sixteenth-century Protestant Reformation. The Reformers believed that marriage was not a sacrament in the Roman sense; rather, it was a natural and social institution. Therefore, marriage fell under the natural and civil law, not under Church law.

Another factor that may have influenced the view of divorce during the sixteenth century was the difficulty England's Henry VIII had in securing annulments of marriages to his various wives. When ten years of negotiations with the Pope broke down over a request for the annulment of his marriage to Catherine of Aragon, Henry had Thomas Cranmer, Archbishop of Canterbury, declare the marriage null and void, and he directed Parliament to enact two laws. The first declared Henry the head of the Church in England. The second made the Church of England a separate entity from the Church of Rome.

Despite the break with the Pope, the Protestant Reformation, and the substitution of the Church of England for the Church of Rome, not a great deal changed in England. The Church of England assumed the role of the state church and continued to monopolize the resolution of matrimonial disputes.

EXAMPLES & EXPLANATIONS

Example 4-1

Assume that P and D are English citizens living in the fifteenth century, and P seeks a divorce claiming that D has committed adultery on numerous occasions. D admits his adulterous conduct. P files a request with an Ecclesiastical court to grant an absolute divorce. The request, however, is denied. Was the denial appropriate under the existing law?

Explanation

The Church forbade absolute divorce; therefore, the request would not be granted. However, when the marriage vow was broken by adultery or acts of cruelty that rendered further cohabitation unsafe, the innocent spouse was permitted, by judicial decree, to live apart from the wrongdoer, and Church courts would afford the injured party relief by allowing a decree of divorce *a mensa et thoro*.

PARLIAMENTARY DIVORCE

4.8. Parliamentary Divorce Becomes Available

The theory that Parliament could dissolve marriages had become a fact by the seventeenth century in England. Divorces were sought by English nobility who, unable to obtain a divorce or annulment from the Ecclesiastical courts, turned to Parliament to grant them a divorce. *See Waite v. Waite*, 4 N.Y. 95 (N.Y. 1855). Parliamentary divorces were rare and, as a practical matter, available only to England's "great families" for "special cases." William J. Goode, *World Changes in Divorce Patterns* 136 (1993). It is estimated that the usual expense of obtaining a parliamentary divorce was $3,000 to $4,000.

Waite v. Waite, *supra at* 106. The English legislative divorce concept was transported to America. *See, e.g.*, *Maynard v. Hill*, 125 U.S. 190 (1888).

EARLY AMERICAN VIEW OF DIVORCE

4.9. Colonial Divorce

The American colonies, possibly influenced by the Protestant Revolution in Europe, rejected the establishment of Ecclesiastical courts. Although the colonies differed greatly in their specific approach to divorce, in general they vested power in colonial legislatures or courts of equity to handle divorce matters. However, divorce was not allowed in some of the colonies. *See* Barbara Dafoe Whitehead, *The Divorce Culture* 13 (1997).

4.10. Divorce Following the American Revolution

Following the American Revolution, statutory divorce was introduced in most jurisdictions. During this period, divorce actions were rare and were treated in a manner similar to other civil disputes, that is, as a means of providing compensation to a person who had been wronged. For example, in most jurisdictions, a divorced wife could recover the dowry she brought to the marriage if she could prove to a jury that her husband was guilty of adultery. Furthermore, if she met her burden of proving she was wronged and her dowry did not adequately provide for her, her husband might be required to provide her with a limited means of support from his personal estate. *See Brown's Appeal*, 44 A. 22 (Conn. 1899).

4.11. Jury Trial

During the nineteenth and early twentieth centuries, the issue of whether a divorce should be granted was tried to a jury in most jurisdictions. *See, e.g.*, *Gilpin v. Gilpin*, 21 P. 612 (Colo. 1889). However, today only a few states continue to use a jury in a divorce action. *See, e.g.*, *Waits v. Waits*, 634 S.E.2d 799 (Ga. App. Ct. 2006) (jury's verdict awarded title and possession of the marital residence to Mrs. Waits); *Soldinger v. Soldinger*, 799 N.Y.S.2d 815 (N.Y.A.D. 2005) (testimony in jury trial where plaintiff who claimed abandonment by lockout as a ground for divorce failed to establish a *prima facie* case since, among other things, he admitted that he was not excluded from the marital residence, he retained the keys to the martial residence, and the defendant never changed the locks). In order to obtain a jury trial in a divorce action, the right to trial by jury must arise either by statute or under the state constitution. *See Brennan v. Orban*, 678 A.2d 667, 672 (N.J. 1996). Sometimes, only a specific issue such as custody of a minor child is submitted to a jury trial. *See, e.g., Hausman v. Hausman*, 199 S.W.3d 38, 41 (Tex. App. Ct. 2006).

GROUNDS FOR DIVORCE

4.12. Adultery

One of the oldest and most common grounds for divorce is adultery. Although the crime of adultery could be committed only by a man with a married woman, this view was not extended to civil divorce actions. *See, e.g., Nelson v. Nelson*, 164 A.2d 234, 235 (Conn. Super. Ct. 1960) (husband's adulterous actions provided sufficient ground for divorce, notwithstanding the fact that under criminal statute, adultery relates only to sexual intercourse between a man and a married woman).

EXAMPLES

Example 4-2

Assume that P and D are citizens of a jurisdiction that requires proof of adultery as the ground for divorce. P has discovered that D has been visiting chat rooms on the Internet and has been "carrying on an affair via the Internet with another woman, X." E-mail messages seized from the family computer by P between D and X are described by P as "intimate" and "embarrassing." P testifies that D and X have apparently not met each other in person but have exchanged revealing photos over the Internet. P seeks a divorce and alleges adultery as the basis of the divorce. D moves to dismiss the action. How will a court that has adultery as its only basis for divorce most likely rule?

EXPLANATIONS

Explanation

Most courts will dismiss the action. The reason for the dismissal is that P does not have evidence of any sexual activity between D and X.

4.13. Cruel and Inhuman Treatment

Another basis for divorce found in most states under the common law is "cruel and inhuman treatment." It has also been incorporated into many state statutes. A plaintiff alleging cruel and inhuman treatment, in order to prevail, has to show a course of conduct by the defendant that is harmful to the plaintiff's physical or mental health, which makes continued cohabitation unsafe or improper. The conduct of the defendant has to be serious and not just an indication of incompatibility. *See Hessen v. Hessen*, 308 N.E.2d 891 (N.Y. 1974) (a high degree of proof is required to establish cruel and inhuman treatment).

In some jurisdictions, the cruel and inhuman conduct may be in the form of emotional abuse; however, it must be more than mere "unkindness, rudeness, or incompatibility." *Brooks v. Brooks*, 652 So. 2d 1113, 1124 (Miss. 1995). As a general rule, the charge of cruel and inhuman treatment must be founded on conduct that is continuous and not based on one isolated incident.

Example 4-3

Assume that P and D were married 10 years and had three children. Assume that P brought an action against D for divorce, alleging cruel and inhuman treatment. P's proof consisted of D's alleged public statements disparaging P, which were uttered before professional colleagues and friends. P also alleged a cold and indifferent personal and sexual relationship with D. P claimed that D had caused P to suffer depression; therefore, continued cohabitation with D was not safe. D denied P's allegations and responded that their marital difficulties were attributable to P's problems with drugs, alcohol, and the inability to live a family life with D and the children. As to P's claim of sexual problems, D denied a coldness or indifference. D alleged that their sexual problems stemmed from differing sexual appetites and drives. How will a judge mostly likely rule on P's petition for divorce where the only ground for the divorce is cruel and inhuman treatment?

Explanation

To prevail, P must demonstrate a course of conduct by D that is harmful to P's physical or mental health, which makes continued cohabitation unsafe or improper. The conduct must be serious and not just an indication of incompatibility. The proof of activities that are alleged to constitute cruel and inhuman treatment must be viewed in the scope of the entire marriage. Here, P and D were together some 10 years and had three children before P moved to pursue a divorce. The marriage is of significant length, and the transgressional acts must be viewed in terms of the scope of the marriage, including the fact that it produced three children. The conflicting versions of alleged cruel and inhuman treatment rest entirely on the credibility of the parties. Probably, P's effort to obtain a divorce on this ground will fail. *Spence v. Spence*, 930 So. 2d 415 (Miss. App. 2005) (divorce on ground of habitual cruel and inhuman treatment denied where the only evidence of bad circumstances in the marital home, which was corroborated, was that the spouses had arguments).

4.14. Mental Cruelty

Several jurisdictions established mental cruelty as a ground for divorce under the common law. Mental cruelty has also been incorporated into many state statutes. Although the statutory definitions vary, in general, to prove mental cruelty, the evidence must have demonstrated that the conduct of the offending spouse was unprovoked and constituted a course of abusive and humiliating treatment that actually affected the physical or mental health of the other spouse, making the life of the complaining spouse miserable or endangering his or her life, person, or health. Mental cruelty could be inflicted by the use of words or acts or conduct that constitutes quarreling or fault finding and that affected the health, well-being, or peace of mind of either of the parties. *Cochran v. Cochran*, 432 P.2d 752 (Colo. 1967). Incompatibility of temperament is not viewed as cruelty and a ground for divorce. *Neff v. Neff*, 192 P.2d 344, 345 (Wash. 1948).

4.15. Desertion

Desertion is a ground for divorce found in a majority of American jurisdictions. Matthew Butler, *Grounds for Divorce: A Survey*, 11 J. Contemp. Legal Issues 164, 170, 172 (2000). Desertion occurs when one spouse breaks off marital cohabitation with the intent to remain apart permanently without the consent or against the will of the other spouse. *Barnes v. Barnes*, 16 Va. App. 98, 101, 428 S.E.2d 294, 297 (1993). The cause of action is based upon persistent separation from the spouse against the latter's will for a designated number of years. During the designated period after the initial separation, the erring spouse may return. The offense is not complete until the entire time has expired. A new period of desertion may be commenced when there is a bona fide effort on the part of the deserted spouse to effect a reconciliation. The staying away is a continuous offense.

EXAMPLES

Example 4-4

Assume that P and D were married for five years. However, the relationship broke down and P sued D for divorce, claiming desertion. At the trial, evidence was presented that for the last ten years D believed "more or less" that the marriage was over. During the entire time, D slept "on the couch." D testified that after moving out of the marital home a year before

P filed for divorce, he began "living in a school bus" that he and his son used for hunting. P denied asking or forcing her husband to leave their marital home. Does P have a sufficient basis to support a divorce on the ground of desertion?

EXPLANATIONS

Explanation

Here, a court will most likely rule that P has proven that D deserted her. The reason for the ruling is that the circumstantial evidence supports the conclusion that D broke off marital cohabitation with P with the apparent intent to remain apart permanently. Furthermore, the action by D was without the consent and against the will of P. *See Skeens v. Skeens*, 2000 WL 1459867 (Va. Vt. App. 2000) (unpublished).

4.16. Constructive Desertion

Constructive desertion is a court-created cause of action. The doctrine provides courts with a basis to grant relief on the ground of desertion to a spouse driven from the home by his or her partner.

4.17. Habitual Drunkenness

Habitual drunkenness is a ground for divorce in some states. It has been defined as a fixed habit of frequently getting drunk; it does not necessarily imply continual drunkenness. *Rooney v. Rooney*, 131 S.E.2d 618 (S.C. 1963). One need not be an alcoholic to be guilty of habitual drunkenness, but it is sufficient if the use or abuse of alcohol causes the breakdown of normal marital relations. *Id.* In *McVey v. McVey*, 289 A.2d 549 (N.J. Super. Ct. 1972), the court held that the evidence established the ground of "habitual drunkenness" for a divorce. The husband had progressed from a social drinker to an inebriate who was regularly drunk four or five times a week both at home and in public. The condition existed for a period of 12 or more consecutive months subsequent to the marriage and preceding the filing of a complaint by the wife for divorce. *See Kessel v. Kessel*, 46 S.E.2d 792 (W. Va. 1948) (proof that defendant occasionally became intoxicated from drinking intoxicating liquors does not establish the allegation of habitual drunkenness within the meaning of West Virginia law).

4.18. Indignities

"Indignities" once existed as a ground for divorce in some states. For a spouse to prevail, the evidence had to show a course of behavior toward the spouse that was sufficiently humiliating and degrading as to render the condition of "any woman of ordinary sensibility and delicacy" intolerable and her life burdensome. *Steinke v. Steinke*, 357 A.2d 674 (Pa. Super. Ct. 1975) (husband who for several months was in a program leading up to anticipated sex change and who adopted clothing and physical appearance of a woman entitled wife to divorce on ground of indignities, in absence of showing of mental illness).

TRADITIONAL COMMON LAW DEFENSES TO A DIVORCE ACTION

4.19. Overview — Affirmative Defenses

A group of affirmative defenses to a divorce action arose under the common law. Most of these defenses were related in one way or another to a party's "fault." A majority of jurisdictions have abolished most, if not all, of these defenses.

4.20. Unclean Hands

This defense imposed a burden on the petitioning party to enter court without serious fault. It was sometimes used as a defense in mental cruelty or desertion cases when the petitioner's own acts were questionable. The defense resembles the defense of recrimination.

EXAMPLES

Example 4-5

Assume that P came before a nineteenth-century common law court asking for a divorce from D. D, who was serving a long prison sentence for a felony conviction, was properly served but failed to answer the divorce petition. At the required default hearing where grounds for the divorce had to be proven, the court asked P several questions. The answers revealed that P had been living in a state of adultery during D's absence and had become the mother of an illegitimate child. When these facts were revealed, the court refused to grant P a divorce. Was the court most likely correct in its application of the law?

EXPLANATIONS

Explanation

Most divorce proceedings at common law were regarded as equitable in nature, and various defenses appropriate to courts of equity were available. "Unclean hands, within the meaning of the maxim of equity, is a figurative description of a class of suitors to whom a court of equity as a court of conscience will not even listen, because the conduct of such suitors is itself unconscionable, that is, morally reprehensible." *Pollino v. Pollino*, 121 A.2d 62 (N.J. Super. Ch. 1956). Here, even though there was no opposition to the divorce, a common law court would most likely not allow the divorce action to proceed.

4.21. Recrimination

Recrimination as a defense to a divorce action under the common law meant that if the complaining party was guilty of an offense that would justify a divorce, then a court could not grant the divorce. This defense is a variation on the clean hands defense. For example, if both parties were guilty of adultery, neither could obtain a divorce. However, in some jurisdictions, the guilt of both parties was weighed and must be found equal in order to trigger the recrimination defense. For example, neither drunkenness nor cruelty would normally constitute a sufficient recriminatory defense when weighed against a charge of adultery. *Bast v. Bast*, 82 Ill. 584 (1876). *See also De Burgh v. De Burgh*, 250 P.2d 598 (Cal. 1952) (extensive discussion of history and application of the recrimination defense).

EXAMPLES

Example 4-6

Assume that P sued D in a common law equity court seeking a divorce and alleging as grounds that D had committed adultery. D, while not denying the claim, asserted the defense of recrimination, that is, that P had deserted D. In a jurisdiction that recognizes recrimination but weighs the various guilty acts of the parties, how will a court most likely rule?

EXPLANATIONS

Explanation

A common law court in these circumstances would most likely allow P's claim to proceed. It would take the view that P's desertion cannot exonerate D from the more serious charge of adultery.

4.22. Condonation

Condonation as a defense represented forgiveness, usually conditional, based on a promise not to repeat the offense. The forgiveness could be either actually expressed or implied; in either case, spouses, the forgiver and the forgiven, continued their married life as before. An offense that was condoned could not later be used as grounds for a divorce. *See* Marvin M. Moore, *An Examination of the Condonation Doctrine*, 2 Akron L. Rev. 75 (1969).

Example 4-7

Assume that in this common law jurisdiction P (husband) learned of several adulterous affairs involving D (wife). After a family fight, D left the family home to stay with her mother. P filed an action for divorce, but dismissed it three days later at D's request. D then moved back into their home and they attempted to reconcile as husband and wife and were intimate on several occasions. However, the reconciliation was short-lived, lasting only a few weeks, after which P once again filed a petition alleging D's earlier adultery as the ground for the divorce. D answered and asserted the defense of condonation. D asked the court to dismiss P's divorce action. Will a common law court be likely to recognize the defense of condonation on these facts?

Explanation

Condonation is the forgiveness of an antecedent matrimonial offense on the condition that it shall not be repeated, and that the offender shall thereafter treat the forgiving party with conjugal kindness. Under the common law, the condonation must be free, voluntary, not induced by duress or fraud, and not procured by unconscientious and fraudulent practices. Obviously, it cannot have been obtained by force and violence. Here, P, with knowledge of D's repeated acts of adultery, dismissed his initial divorce action and allowed D to move back in with him, and they were intimate. A common law court will reason that the acts of intercourse by P with D, with knowledge that D had been guilty of adultery, indicate that P has fully condoned the earlier behavior. A common law court would most likely dismiss P's divorce action. *See Tigert v. Tigert*, 595 P.2d 815 (Okla. App. 1979); *Panther v. Panther*, 295 P. 219, 221 (Okla. 1931).

4.23. Collusion

Collusion as a defense under the common law represented an agreement by the two parties to create a false-fact situation upon which a divorce could be granted. For example, collusion occurred when the married partners, having decided that they would divorce, stage a fake adultery scene in an effort to create grounds for divorce. To carry out their scheme, the husband goes to a hotel room, where a paid co-respondent joins him and partially undresses. While the two of them sit on the edge of the hotel bed, the wife, as prearranged, walks in with a detective and photographer. The photographs and testimony of the detective provide the evidence of adultery, and this forms the basis for the divorce action. Because the incident was rigged, the divorce proceeding would be viewed as collusive and as a fraud on the court. A divorce action based on this evidence would be dismissed.

Example 4-8

Assume P sues D for divorce in a jurisdiction that requires proof of misconduct, even if the matter goes by default. In her divorce petition, P alleges that D was an adulterer. D does not answer the petition, and a default hearing is set where P must prove that D committed adultery. At the default hearing, only P appears. She produces a handwritten letter, allegedly by D, in which he confesses to his adulterous behavior. Based on the letter and the testimony of P, who claims she was aware of D's behavior, will a common law court likely grant P a divorce from D?

Explanation

Common law courts would be concerned about the couple colluding to obtain a divorce. The confession of D, the alleged guilty spouse, would be received in evidence. However, because of the potential for collusion, proceedings such as this were subject to close judicial scrutiny. In this hypothetical, a court would be suspicious of the evidence presented by P and it would not be unusual for it to deny a divorce to P on the ground of adultery. *See Grobin v. Grobin*, 55 N.Y.S.2d 32 (N.Y. Sup. 1945) (a divorce will not be granted on spouse's confession of adultery unsupported by any other evidence); *Zoske v. Zoske*, 64 N.Y.S.2d 819 (N.Y. Sup. 1946).

4.24. Connivance

Connivance was a defense under the common law that was sometimes used in divorce litigation where the claim was adultery. This defense was defined as consent by one party to the adulterous act of the other. For example, if the couples swapped spouses for a night at a party, this incident could not later be used as the basis for a divorce. Connivance is sometimes confused with collusion; however, the two are quite different. Collusion occurs when the parties collaborate to impose on the court by fabricating a ground for the divorce. Connivance is consent to an offense that is actually committed.

4.25. Undue Delay

In a few jurisdictions, undue delay in bringing a divorce action was a defense, either because there was a specific statute of limitations or because the courts had held that divorce was within the general omnibus statutes of limitations. In other states, a few courts held that the doctrine of laches was a defense.

4.26. Insanity

Insanity as a defense to a divorce action was recognized by the common law under certain circumstances. *See Shaw v. Shaw*, 269 P. 80 (Wash. 1928). For example, where the ground for a divorce was a claim of cruel and inhuman treatment, the action would fail if it was based on acts attributable to the insanity of the defending party. *Bosveld v. Bosveld*, 7 N.W.2d 782, 785 (Iowa 1943) (insanity is not a ground for divorce and charge of "cruel and inhuman treatment" cannot be based on acts attributable to insanity). The common law view of this defense has been replaced in a majority of jurisdictions by statute.

4.27. Provocation

Provocation was also once a recognized defense to a divorce action in some jurisdictions. The theory was that one could not provoke physical retaliation on the part of his or her spouse and complain of such retaliation unless it was out of all proportion to the provocation. *Trenchard v. Trenchard*, 92 N.E. 243 (Ill. 1910); *De La Hay v. De La Hay*, 21 Ill. 251, 254 (1859); *Gress v. Gress*, 148 N.W.2d 166 (N.D. 1967) (when provocation is asserted as a defense, it is for the trial judge to determine whether sufficient provocation existed and whether the retaliatory action was out of proportion to the provocation).

RELIGION AS A DEFENSE

4.28. Why This Defense Fails

A litigant who challenges a divorce proceeding on religious grounds will fail, as the law clearly does not recognize such a defense. Three United States Supreme Court cases have settled the issue. First, in *Maynard v. Hill*, 125 U.S. 190, 210 (1888), the Court held that marriage was a social relationship governed by the laws of the individual states under their police powers. Second, in *Sherbert v. Verner*, 374 U.S. 398, 403 (1963), the Court reiterated the standard under which First Amendment infringements by state regulation are to be judged, stating that: "any incidental burden on the free exercise of appellant's religion may be justified by a 'compelling state interest in the regulation of a subject within the State's constitutional power to regulate. . . .' " (citing *NAACP v. Button*, 371 U.S. 415, 438 (1963)).

The third case, *Reynolds v. United States*, 98 U.S. 145 (1878), asked whether freedom of religion made a federal law prohibiting polygamy impermissible. It observed that "[m]arriage, while from its very nature a sacred obligation, is, nevertheless, in most civilized nations, a civil contract, and usually regulated by law. Upon it society may be said to be built, and out of its fruits spring social relations and social obligations and duties, with which government is necessarily required to deal." 98 U.S. at 165. The Court also observed that "[l]aws are made for the government of actions, and while they cannot interfere with mere religious belief and opinions, they may with practices. . . . Can a man excuse his practices to the contrary because of his religious belief? To permit this would be to make the professed doctrines of religious belief superior to the law of the land, and in effect to permit every citizen to become a law unto himself. Government could exist only in name under such circumstances." 98 U.S. at 165-167.

In *Williams v. Williams*, 543 P.2d 1401 (Okla. 1975), the appellant complained that her constitutional right to the free exercise of religion was violated when a divorce was granted over her religious objection. The appellate court observed that the trial court only dissolved the civil contract of marriage between the parties and that there was no attempt to dissolve it ecclesiastically. Consequently, there was no infringement of her constitutional right to freedom of religion. *See also Everson v. Board of Educ.*, 330 U.S. 1, 15 (1947); *Sharma v. Sharma*, 667 P.2d 395, 396 (1983); *Martian v. Martian*, 328 N.W.2d 844 (N.D. 1983); *Trickey v. Trickey*, 642 S.W.2d 47 (Tex. Ct. App. 1982).

EXAMPLES

Example 4-9

Assume that P brings an action to divorce D in a no-fault jurisdiction. D challenges the action on the basis of his religious beliefs as a Roman Catholic, in that his faith opposes divorce. D asserts that a divorce decree will violate his rights under the First Amendment to the U.S. Constitution. His sincerity in his position and his devotion to his faith is apparent to the trial judge. Assume that there is sufficient evidence produced by P to justify issuing the divorce decree; however, the court is concerned with the First Amendment argument made by D. How will a court most likely rule?

EXPLANATIONS

Explanation

D will most likely not be successful. The court will view D's religious belief and practice as completely separate from the secular divorce proceeding.

THE MODERN REFORM MOVEMENT

4.29. Common Law Is Replaced by Statutes

The statutory grounds for a divorce in American jurisdictions developed at varying speeds in each state. It is interesting to note, for example, that for many years South Carolina did not have a provision for an absolute divorce, and that until well into the twentieth century, New York granted a divorce only when adultery could be proven. Other jurisdictions created statutes that provided for divorce on a variety of grounds, including desertion and habitual drunkenness. Cruel and inhuman treatment and mental cruelty were added in the twentieth century and became a commonly used basis for a divorce because they covered a number of marital sins.

4.30. Uniform Marriage and Divorce Act — Irretrievable Breakdown of Marriage

In August 1970 the National Conference of Commissioners on Uniform State Laws approved the Uniform Marriage and Divorce Act (UMDA). It was subsequently amended, and in 1974 the American Bar Association's House of Delegates approved the revised Act. *See* Harvey L. Zuckman, *The ABA Family Law Section v. The NCCUSI: Alienation, Separation and Forced Reconciliation over the UMDA*, 24 Cath. U. L. Rev. 61 (1974). Section 305 of the UMDA permitted a divorce when there was an irretrievable breakdown of the marriage and both parties stated under oath or affirmed that this was the case. It also permitted a divorce when one party stated under oath that the marriage was irretrievably broken and the other did not deny it. If one party challenged the allegation, a court was required to make findings that an irretrievable breakdown had occurred or continue the matter for 30 to 60 days with an eye toward recommending that the parties seek counseling.

The phrase *irretrievable breakdown* used as a ground for divorce in the UMDA was somewhat general. The phrase was the end product of intense debate and careful consideration toward accommodating a variety of contradictory interests. *See* Robert J. Levy, *Comments on Legislative History of Uniform Marriage & Divorce Act*, 7 Fam. L.Q. 405 (1973). The UMDA was intended to reduce the acrimony connected with such proceedings as well as the time devoted to such litigation in already overcrowded court calendars.

4.31. Emergence of Modern "No-Fault" Divorce

During the 1970s and 1980s, various states became active participants in a remarkable nationwide family law revolution prompted by changing societal values. For most judges and family lawyers, no-fault divorce was viewed as a dramatic and welcome reform. Under the former system, to obtain a divorce, couples had to prove that one partner was guilty of fault. Often when the parties arrived at court they had already divided their property, lived apart for many years, and had little to dispute. Nevertheless, to prove that grounds for the divorce existed, they were forced to produce witnesses to corroborate their in-court sworn testimony proving that the other party was at fault. This procedure was often followed even when the other party failed to appear at the hearing. The result was that many divorce proceedings were a sham. In other cases in which fault dictated the amount of property to be divided, moral judgments about which party was right or wrong ignored the complexity of the underlying causes of the marital dispute. The process also made the eventual outcome of a divorce action speculative rather than reasonably certain. Too often, husbands and wives were combatants, with each of their lawyers arguing that responsibility for the marriage breakup belonged solely to the other spouse.

No-fault legislation dramatically altered the matrimonial landscape. Under no-fault statutes, divorces were granted when it was clear there were irreconcilable differences. The no-fault statutes eliminated fault and wrong as a substantive ground for dissolution. They also required consideration of the marriage as a whole and made the possibility of reconciliation an important issue. These changes were intended to induce a conciliatory and uncharged atmosphere, which might facilitate resolution of the other issues and perhaps effect a reconciliation.

By the year 2000, virtually every jurisdiction had adopted a provision that permitted a divorce without proof of fault. A typical ground involved a showing that the marriage was irretrievably broken. A statement to the court by either party that this was the case resulted in a divorce. Fault was retained in some jurisdictions as a significant feature in an award of maintenance, but in others it was completely removed from the law.

EXAMPLES

Example 4-10

Assume that P seeks to dissolve the marriage between P and D in a typical no-fault jurisdiction. P and D have been married for 21 years. P is a self-employed trucker, and P's job requires him to do a lot of traveling and to spend long periods away from home. P has asked D to accompany him on the trips, but D has refused. P claims that D has refused to be P's "partner in life." P testifies that there has been an irretrievable breakdown of the marriage and that the marriage is at an end. D responds that the marriage is not irretrievably broken and that all P needs to do is to engage in "some marriage counseling." D testifies that the two should reconcile, even though D is aware that P is involved in a relationship with another woman. The no-fault statute in this jurisdiction reads:

> A dissolution of a marriage shall be granted by a county or district court when the court finds that there has been an irretrievable breakdown of the marriage relationship. A finding of irretrievable breakdown under this subdivision is a determination that there is no reasonable prospect of reconciliation. The finding must be supported by evidence that there is serious marital discord adversely affecting the attitude of one or both of the parties toward the marriage. If after a hearing the court determines that there is a reasonable prospect of reconciliation between the parties, the court should continue the matter for at least 90 days and require the parties to attend marriage counseling.

How will a court most likely rule?

EXPLANATIONS

Explanation

Each marriage relationship is unique; therefore, the court must look at the facts of each individual case to determine whether the marriage is irretrievably broken with no "reasonable prospect of reconciliation." Although it is commendable that D wishes to reconcile and is willing to forgive P for his adulterous affair, most courts will still find that the marriage is irretrievably broken. They will take the position that a healthy marriage can be nurtured only by the love of both husband and wife. The fact that P stated he did not want to be married to D and demonstrated this desire through his romantic relationship with another woman is sufficient evidence to persuade most courts that the marriage is irretrievably broken.

EXAMPLES

Example 4-11

Assume the existence of the same no-fault statute set out above and the facts as stated in the above example. However, assume that there is additional testimony that on various occasions P asked D to accompany him on his trips so that they may attempt to reconcile, although she did not join him on any of those trips. D also asserts that P should have communicated in some way that their marriage was breaking down. How should a court rule?

Explanation

These additional facts will normally not make a difference in the trial court's decision to grant P a divorce. When P filed the divorce petition alleging irretrievable breakdown of their marriage, D should have been on notice that their marriage was in trouble. D was apparently aware of P's extramarital affair, and while D asserts that P had asked her to accompany him on trips in an attempt to reconcile, D did not join him on any of those trips. *See, e.g., Mackey v. Mackey*, 545 A.2d 362 (Pa. Super. Ct. 1988); *Liberto v. Liberto*, 520 A.2d 458, 461 (Pa. Super. Ct. 1987).

Example 4-12

Assume that P files a petition in a jurisdiction that provides alternative grounds for a divorce. In this jurisdiction, a divorce may be obtained on the basis of an irretrievable breakdown or adultery. P alleges that the marriage is irretrievably broken down and that D has committed adultery. At the conclusion of the hearing, the trial court finds that there has been an irretrievable breakdown of the marriage and grants the divorce. P objects to the judge's decision and moves to withdraw the count in P's petition regarding an irretrievable breakdown. P asserts that the court should have made a finding of adultery as the basis for the divorce and argues that during the hearing D admitted carrying on an adulterous relationship during most of the marriage and that D moved out "months ago and is living with another woman." Is the trial judge likely to allow P to withdraw the count?

Explanation

Most courts will conclude that P's position is not supportable. They will conclude that a marriage is irretrievably broken when a husband moves out of the marital property to live with another woman. The policy of most courts will be to make the law for legal dissolution of marriage effective for dealing with the realities of matrimonial experience and to give primary consideration to the welfare of the family rather than the vindication of private rights or the punishment of matrimonial wrongs. To allow P to pursue this remedy would be tantamount to allowing P to invoke the power of the court to vindicate a private right. *See, e.g., Rosenberg v. Rosenberg*, 39 Pa. D. & C.3d 549 1984 WL 2628 (Pa. Com. Pl. 1984).

CHAPTER 5

Child Custody and Parenting Plans

5.1. Introduction

When it functions well, the child custody legal process meets three objectives: It protects the interests of children, it assists parents in restructuring their relationships with the children, and it leads to fair and predictable results for families. Courts and legislatures have historically struggled to achieve these goals against the backdrop of a constantly changing society. Consequently, the law of child custody has evolved significantly over the last century and has changed dramatically in recent years.

As a practical matter, today only a small percentage of child custody disputes are resolved through a trial in the adversarial system. Instead, the vast majority of cases are settled through processes such as mediation and cooperative negotiation. These processes are designed to avoid distributing "blame" between the parties. Rather, the goal is to empower parents to create their own parenting arrangements tailored to meet the needs of the child or children.

THE IMPACT OF DIVORCE

5.2. Effects of Divorce on Children

With nearly 50 percent of marriages ending in divorce, researchers estimate that 40 percent of children have experienced or will experience the divorce of their parents. *See* Stephen J. Bahr, *Social Science Research on Family Dissolution: What It Shows and How It Might Be of Interest to Family Law Reformers*, 4 J.L. & Fam. Stud. 5 (2002).

Much has been written about the effects of divorce on children. There is, for example, general agreement that a child's adjustment to divorce is directly related to the level of conflict between the parents before, during, and after the divorce. A child whose parents exhibit a continuing high degree of conflict experiences more difficulty adjusting than one whose parents have a better relationship. *See* Joan B. Kelly & Robert E. Emery, *Children's Adjustment Following Divorce: Risk and Resilience Perspectives*, 52(4) Fam. Rel. 352 (2003); Joan B. Kelly, *Children's Adjustment in Conflicted Marriage and Divorce: A Decade Review of Research*, 39(8) J. Am. Acad. Child Adolescent Psychiatry 963 (2000). One frequently cited study concludes that children's adjustment to divorce is linked to factors such as the absence of the noncustodial parent, the adjustment of the custodial parent, the conflict between the parents, economic hardship, and stressful life changes. *See* Paul R. Amato, *Children's Adjustment to Divorce: Theories, Hypotheses, and Empirical Support*, 55 J. Marriage & Fam. 23 (1993).

5.3. Impact on Parenting

Although the marital relationship ends, couples with children will continue to deal with each other as parents. Consequently, they must give careful thought to restructuring their parental alliance and renewing their commitment to the children at this critical time.

Divorce or the breakup of a relationship where the parties are not married is a stressful experience for parents as well as children. Parents must typically deal with their own emotional and financial pressures in addition to meeting the heightened needs of their children. The parents' ability to cope with change and minimize ongoing conflict bears directly on the well-being of the restructured family. For example, the quality of the relationship between divorced spouses strongly predicts whether noncustodial fathers will remain involved with the children. *See* P. Lindsay Chase-Lansdale & E. Mavis Hetherington, 10 Life-Span Dev. & Behav. 105 (1990).

Researchers have found that 25 percent of parents ease into a co-parenting relationship, half disengage for a period of time and then become more cooperative, and 25 percent remain at odds indefinitely. *See* Carla B. Garrity & Mitchell A. Baris, *Caught in the Middle* 27 (1994). In fact, some 10 percent of divorcing couples demonstrate "unremitting animosity" as their children grow up. *See* Janet Johnston & Vivienne Roseby, *In the Name of the Child: A Developmental Approach to Understanding and Helping Children of Conflicted and Violent Divorce* 4 (1997). For these couples, "parallel" parenting may be more realistic than co-parenting. Janet R. Johnston, *Building Multidisciplinary Professional Partnerships with the Court on Behalf of High-Conflict Divorcing Families and*

Their Children: Who Needs What Kind of Help? 22 U. Ark. Little Rock L. Rev. 453, 469 (2000).

DEFINING CUSTODIAL RELATIONSHIPS

5.4. Overview

Until recently, when a divorce was granted one parent was awarded custody of the child and the other parent was granted "reasonable" visitation. Visitation would typically occur on weekends and for a few weeks in the summer. However, due to changing sex roles and a heightened awareness of the importance of both parents in child development, a variety of custody arrangements have emerged over the last 40 years. Courts now place less emphasis on predefined labels and put more focus on creating workable day-to-day parenting schedules.

5.5. Legal Custody

Legal custody is a technical term used by courts to describe a parent's authority to make major decisions on behalf of the child. Decisions that the legal custodian might make include those about the child's religion, education, and medical treatment. Legal custody can be awarded to one parent, an arrangement that courts refer to as "sole legal custody," or it can be shared by the parents, referred to as "joint legal custody." The American Law Institute (ALI) refers to legal custody as "decision making responsibility." ALI, Principles of the Law of Family Dissolution: Analysis and Recommendations §2.03(4) (2002).

5.6. Physical Custody

Physical custody is a technical term that describes a parent's right to have the child reside with him or her and the obligation of that parent to provide for the routine daily care and control of the child. Physical custody can be awarded to one parent, which courts refer to as "sole physical custody," or it can be shared, in what courts term a "joint physical custody" arrangement.

5.7. Joint Legal and Physical Custody

When parents share "joint legal custody," which is a technical term used by the court, they agree to work together to make major decisions affecting the child.

For example, they plan to agree on where the child should attend school, whether the child should have a major medical procedure, and what if any religious training the child should receive. Under a typical joint legal custody arrangement neither parent has a superior right to make such decisions. Consequently, a well-drawn joint legal custody agreement will include procedures for resolving conflicts (such as returning to mediation) short of returning to court.

In contrast, when parents share "joint physical custody," also a technical term used by the court, the child maintains a residence in both homes. Joint physical custody does not require precise 50-50 time sharing. In practice, it is sometimes difficult to distinguish a sole physical custody arrangement in which the noncustodial or nonresidential parent has liberal overnight visitation from a joint physical custody arrangement.

Joint custody, as it is commonly practiced, encompasses a wide variety of parenting arrangements. Some couples share legal custody even though one of the parents is the sole physical custodian. Other couples share both legal and physical custody.

Joint legal and physical custody arrangements have become increasingly popular. Researchers estimate that joint legal custody is the final disposition in nearly 80 percent of cases while joint physical custody is the result in 20 percent of cases. *See* Eleanor E. Maccoby & Robert J. Mnookin, *Dividing the Child: Social and Legal Dilemmas of Custody* 108, 113 (1997). Viewed positively, this trend signifies an increasing commitment to cooperative parenting after divorce. *See* Isolina Ricci, *Mom's House, Dad's House: Making Two Homes for Your Child* (1997). However, if underlying parental conflict is not resolved, such arrangements can work to exacerbate the situation. For this reason, joint custody is not favored in cases where the parties have a history of high conflict that may include domestic violence. Janet R. Johnston, *A Child-Centered Approach to High Conflict and Domestic Families: Differential Assessment and Interventions,* 12 J. Fam. Stud. 15 (2006); Janet R. Johnston, *Building Multidisciplinary Professional Partnerships with the Court on Behalf of High-Conflict Divorcing Families and Their Children: Who Needs What Kind of Help?* 22 U. Ark. Little Rock L. Rev. 453 (2000).

The states generally allow joint legal and/or joint physical custody awards that are in the best interests of the child. However, courts and legislatures have adopted a variety of approaches to accomplish this. Some states presume that some form of joint custody is in the best interests of the child if requested by either or both parties. Other states express no such preference, and courts make joint custody decisions based on the merits of each case. A few states disfavor joint custody. In making joint custody awards, courts scrutinize the parents' ability to cooperate and judges evaluate the dispute resolution skills of the parties. *See* Andrew Schepard, *Children, Courts and Custody* (2004).

In the absence of a parenting plan, the ALI presumes that joint decision making (joint legal custody) will be in the best interests of the child if each parent has performed a reasonable share of parenting tasks and there has been no domestic violence or child abuse. ALI, Principles of the Law of Family Dissolution: Analysis and Recommendations §2.09 (2002).

EXAMPLES

Example 5-1

P and D reached an agreement concerning the care of their children after divorce. They agreed to discuss and reach consensus on matters such as the children's religion and schooling. During the school year, they agree that the children are to reside with P Monday through Friday and spend every weekend living with D. During the summer, the children are to reside with D Monday through Friday and live with P every weekend. What technical legal description(s) or term(s) will a court most likely assign to this arrangement?

EXPLANATIONS

Explanation

A court will consider the agreement as constituting joint legal custody because P and D will share the major policy-making decisions regarding the children. P will claim to have sole physical custody because the children will reside with P the majority of the time during the school year and 60 percent of the time on an annual basis. D will argue that this arrangement constitutes joint physical custody because joint physical custody does not necessitate equal time sharing and, over the course of the year, the children will reside with D 40 percent of the time. A court would likely agree with D and consider these parents to have joint legal and physical custody. However, P would be considered to have sole physical custody were it not for the fact that the children will reside substantially with D during the summer.

EXAMPLES

Example 5-2

P and D had one child, who was a preschooler at the time of their divorce. The parties resided 50 miles from each other, and both sought sole physical custody of the child. The court found that neither parent was an ideal custodian, and the evidence showed that their relationship was filled with strife and disagreement. On its own motion and to the surprise of the parents, the court ordered that primary physical custody of the child would alternate between them every year once the child started school. The court viewed this arrangement as a way for the child to have ongoing contact with both parents. P appealed the decision, believing that such an arrangement would not be in the child's best interest because the child would have to change schools every year. What is the likely result on appeal?

EXPLANATIONS

Explanation

In *Headrick v. Headrick*, 916 So. 2d 610 (Ala. Civ. App. 2005), the appellate court frowned on the annually alternating custody arrangement, as most courts do. The court stated: "We conclude, however, that this decision constitutes reversible error because the alternation of residence and primary physical custody guarantees a recurring, yearly disruption in this young child's life for which we find no justification in the record." *Id.* at 614. One of the concerns about joint physical custody generally is that the child may feel as if he or she doesn't have a primary home. Such feelings could be exacerbated by alternating physical custody on a yearly basis. In addition, in this example, the court was not in the position of approving a parenting plan agreed to by the parties. Rather, the court created the alternating arrangement on its own and without the agreement of the parents. Given the fact the parents had a history of conflict, this unorthodox arrangement would likely not benefit the child. *But see Mundy v. Devon*, 2006 WL 902233 (Del. Supr. Apr. 6, 2006) (court approved yearly alternating primary placement). Because of the difficulty of anticipating the needs of the child into the future, P and D would be well advised to attend mediation prior to the time that the child starts school.

5.8. Parenting Plans

As a result of growing concern about the adversarial nature of some child custody proceedings, family law professionals have encouraged courts and legislatures to move away from reliance on custody labels and focus instead on creating detailed agreements built around the needs of the particular family. These parenting plans are frequently developed in mediation and typically cover topics such as parenting time schedules, decision-making protocols, parental cooperation and communication, dispute resolution, and financial support. *See* Schepard, *supra*. Instead of using traditional custody labels, parents may create their own terms or use labels such as "on-duty" and "off-duty" parent or "residential" and "nonresidential" parent.

Consistent with this trend in terminology and perspective, the ALI has replaced the terms *custody* and *visitation* with the concept of "custodial responsibility" in an effort to avoid the win-lose framework present in many custody disputes. ALI, Principles of the Law of Family Dissolution: Analysis and Recommendations §2.03(3), cmt. e (2002). Rather than awarding custody, the ALI encourages parents to allocate parenting responsibility and plan for dispute resolution through the use of detailed parenting plans. §2.05. However, exceptions are made for couples with a history of child maltreatment, domestic violence, substance abuse, or interference with the child's relationship with the other parent. §2.11. Under the ALI proposal, courts should reject parenting plans agreed to by the parents in cases where the agreement was not "knowing or voluntary" or if the plan would be harmful to the child. §2.06.

PRESUMPTIONS

5.9. Overview

Faced with the difficult task of awarding custody, courts and legislatures have historically relied on various preferences and presumptions to lend predictability to decision making and give effect to societal beliefs about the nature of the family.

5.10. Historical Paternal Presumption

Under the English common law fathers had nearly absolute control over their children. At marriage, the wife's legal identity merged with her husband's and she had no right to property or to custody of children born during the marriage. The paternal presumption benefited the child because the mother had no means of supporting the child in the father's absence. The father even had the right to appoint a guardian other than the mother in the event of the father's death. W. Blackstone, *Commentaries on the Laws of England* 446, 453 (9th ed. 1783).

Only if the father engaged in highly immoral conduct might a mother be awarded custody. This paternal presumption began to give way in 1873, when the English Parliament granted women the right to have custody of children who were under the age of 16. Early American decisions adopted the common law view initially, but the paternal preference began to wane by the end of the nineteenth century.

5.11. Historical Maternal Presumption

By the 1920s and 1930s, many American jurisdictions replaced the paternal preference with the "tender years" maternal presumption. Children of "tender years" included preschool children and sometimes children through the age of ten. These young children were seen as best cared for by mothers who would provide for their physical and emotional needs while the father was working away from home. As was stated in *Freeland v. Freeland*, 159 P. 698, 699 (Wash. 1916), the presumption could be overcome by showing that the mother was unfit:

> Mother love is a dominant trait in even the weakest of women, and as a general thing surpasses the paternal affection for the common offspring, and, moreover, a child needs a mother's care even more than a father's. For these reasons courts are loathe to deprive the mother of the custody of her children and will not do so unless it be shown clearly that she is so far an unfit and improper person to be instructed with such custody as to endanger the welfare of the children.

In *Freeland*, the presumption operated in favor of the mother even though she had been "indiscreet in her conduct with men." *See also Krieger v. Krieger*, 81 P.2d 1081 (Idaho 1938) (tender years presumption applied even over preference of eight-year-old child to live with father).

During the late 1960s and early 1970s, societal views shifted and fathers were viewed as being as competent as mothers in raising young children. As a result, courts gradually became more concerned with the best interests of the child than with the sex of the parent. In some jurisdictions, application of the tender years presumption was held to be unconstitutional. *Ex parte Devine*, 398 So. 2d 686 (Ala. 1981).

EXAMPLES

Example 5-3

Assume that P and D were married in 1998 and had one child, who was born in 2002. When P and D decided to divorce, they could not agree on a parenting arrangement, and the matter was set for trial. At the time of the custody hearing the child was 28 months old. The court determined that both P and D were fit parents even though the father (D) showed some immaturity and worked long hours and the mother (P) had some psychological problems. The court granted physical custody to P, taking "personal notice of the natural bond that develops between infants and a mother, especially when the mother breast-feeds the infant" and finding that "by the very nature of the age and gender of the minor child (28-month-old female)," placement with the father "would be a negative aspect in the weighing of the positives and negatives." The father appealed, claiming that the court's reasoning amounted to an application of the historical tender years doctrine. The mother argued that this was a permissible consideration under the best-interests standard. What is the likely result of D's appeal?

EXPLANATIONS

Explanation

If this case had taken place in 1930, the mother of the young child would be the preferred custodian unless she was proven to be unfit. However, today the maternal presumption is no longer in effect and courts do not award custody based on presumptions favoring either sex. Consequently, in *Greer v. Greer*, 624 S.E.2d 423 (N.C. App. 2006), on which this example is based, D prevailed on appeal. In that jurisdiction the "tender years presumption" had been abolished by statute, and the appellate court agreed with D's argument that the trial court improperly applied it in this case.

5.12. Primary Caretaker Presumption

Although most states adopted the sex-neutral "best interests of the child" standard during the 1970s, some states presumed that the interests of a young child are best served by placing him or her with the "primary caretaker." The primary caretaker was defined as the parent who performed the following types of tasks for the child:

- Bathing, grooming, and dressing
- Purchasing, cleaning, and caring for clothes
- Providing medical care, including caring for a sick child and taking him or her to doctor's appointments
- Arranging for social interaction with the child's peers
- Arranging for child care, putting the child to bed, attending to the child during the night, and waking the child in the morning
- Educating
- Disciplining
- Providing religious training
- Teaching elementary skills

The primary caretaker presumption was based on the child's need for a stable and continuous relationship with the primary parent. Preference was given to the parent who was most experienced in caring for the child and who had the strongest history of meeting the child's daily needs. *See Garska v. McCoy*, 278 S.E.2d 357 (W. Va. 1981); *Pikula v. Pikula*, 374 N.W.2d 705 (Minn. 1985).

Opponents of the primary caretaker presumption contended that despite the sex-neutral language, the presumption favored women. Courts sometimes had difficulty identifying a primary parent, and the preference had little application to older children such as teenagers.

States no longer use the primary caretaker preference as a presumption. However, some states currently use it as a factor to be considered among others in determining the best interest of the child.

The ALI has incorporated the primary caretaker tasks into its definition of caretaking functions. *See* ALI, Principles of the Law of Family Dissolution: Analysis and Recommendations (2002). The ALI suggests that, in the absence of an agreed upon parenting plan, post-divorce caretaking should mirror pre-divorce caretaking patterns. §2.03, cmt. g. In other words, caretaking should be allocated in a way that "approximates the proportion of time each parent spent performing caretaking functions" prior to separation. §2.08. If one parent performed the bulk of caretaking functions prior to divorce, the approximation standard would function similarly to the primary caretaker presumption. However, if caretaking tasks were shared more equally during the marriage, that past arrangement would be carried forward after the divorce. *See* Katharine T. Bartlett, *U.S. Custody Law and Trends in the Context of the ALI Principles of the Law of Family Dissolution*, 10 Va. J. Soc. Pol'y & L. 5, 18 (2002).

EXAMPLES

Example 5-4

P (father) sued D (mother) for divorce in 1986. They lived in a state that adopted the primary caretaker presumption. P and D had two children, who were two and five years old. D worked as an airline attendant and was consequently away from home overnight each week from Monday through Friday. She also worked one weekend per month. When she was at home, she helped care for the children by cooking meals, doing laundry, and entertaining them. P worked at home and was responsible for all of the children's care while D was away from home. A year before the divorce, P went into treatment for an alcohol problem, and although he did not drink after his release, D was afraid that P would relapse while caring for the children. Both P and D sought custody of the children. Who would have been likely to prevail if the court applied the primary caretaker presumption to this dispute?

EXPLANATIONS

Explanation

In a jurisdiction that applied the primary caretaker presumption, P would have prevailed as the primary caretaker of the couple's young children. He was the parent who spent more time feeding, disciplining, clothing, bathing, and generally caring for the children. D alleged that she performed these caretaking tasks when she was at home and that she should not be penalized for working long hours to meet the financial needs of the family. However, she would be unsuccessful because the goal of the primary caretaker presumption was to provide stability for the children, who in this case had been primarily cared for by their father, P. D would argue that because of his alcohol problem, P was not a fit parent and, consequently, the primary caretaker doctrine should not have applied. However, treatment for an alcohol problem would not be sufficient to show that D was not a fit parent.

Here no facts are presented showing that D was currently drinking or that his alcohol use was detrimental to the children. Although some states use "primary caretaker" as one factor in determining the best interests of the child, it is no longer used as a custodial presumption. Today, P and D would be encouraged to create a parenting plan that would allow both of them to have strong continuing relationships with the children.

5.13. Natural Parent Presumption

As against third parties, natural parents are entitled to custody of their children unless there is clear evidence of unfitness. "Third parties" include stepparents and grandparents as well as others. *See Webb v. Webb*, 546 So. 2d 1062 (Fla. Ct. App. 1989) (trial court abused discretion in awarding custody to stepparent without clear and convincing evidence that mother was unfit); *Brewer v. Brewer*, 533 S.E.2d 541 (N.C. Ct. App. 2000) (presumed that fit parent will act in best interests of child). *But see Bennett v. Jeffreys*, 356 N.E.2d 277 (N.Y. Ct. App. 1976) (extraordinary circumstances required consideration of best interests of child).

This preference in favor of natural parents remains in effect today. However, courts have struggled with situations in which the parent seeking custody has had little or no contact with the child and the child has lived with a third party for an extended period. *See* Elizabeth Barker Brandt, *De Facto Custodians: A Response to the Needs of Informal Kin Caregivers?* 38 Fam. L.Q. 291 (2004). The ALI has dealt with these situations by broadening the definition of parent to include parents by estoppel and de facto parents. ALI, Principles of the Law of Family Dissolution: Analysis and Recommendations §2.03(b), (c) (2002). A parent by estoppel is a person other than a legal parent who (1) is obligated to pay child support, (2) lived with the child and accepted parental responsibility for at least two years in the good-faith belief that he was the child's father, or (3) lived with the child since birth and acted as a parent pursuant to a parenting or co-parenting agreement. A de facto parent is a person other than a legal parent or parent by estoppel who for at least two years (1) lived with the child and (2) performed the bulk of caretaking functions or as many caretaking functions as the parent with whom the child resided (3) either by agreement or due to the failure or inability of the legal parent to do so.

EXAMPLES

Example 5-5

Assume that P (mother) and D (father) are the parents of one child, C. Because of severe alcohol dependency resulting in her incarceration, P was no longer involved with the child. D worked as a merchant seaman and was at sea for lengthy periods of time. Consequently, C's grandparents cared for C for the majority of a period of four years. The grandparents petitioned the court for custody of C, alleging that C needed stability and that it would be in C's best interest if custody were awarded to the grandparents. D promised to seek other employment and argued that he had acted responsibly in arranging for the child to be cared for in his absence. Without making a finding that D was an unfit parent, the court awarded custody of C to the grandparents, and D appealed. What will D argue and what is the likely outcome?

EXPLANATIONS

Explanation

D will argue that he is entitled to custody of C because he has not been found to be an unfit parent. Under the natural parent presumption, if D is fit, he is entitled to custody even if C might be "better raised" by the grandparents. In *McDermott v. Dougherty*, 869 A.2d 751 (Md. 2005), the court found that the father's employment at sea did not constitute an extraordinary circumstance sufficient to overcome the preference for the natural parent. The court stated:

> In the balancing of court-created or statutorily-created "standards," such as "the best interest of the child" test, with fundamental constitutional rights, in private custody actions involving private third-parties where the parents are fit, absent extraordinary (*i.e.*, exceptional) circumstances, the constitutional right is the ultimate determinative factor; and only if the parents are unfit or extraordinary circumstances exist is the "best interest of the child" test to be considered.

Id. at 808.

MODEL ACTS

5.14. Uniform Marriage and Divorce Act

A majority of the states have adopted statutes providing that custody should be awarded based on the best interests of the child. Section 402 of the Uniform Marriage and Divorce Act states:

> The court shall determine custody in accordance with the best interest of the child. The court shall consider all relevant factors including:
>
> (1) the wishes of the child's parent or parents as to his custody;
>
> (2) the wishes of the child as to his custodian;
>
> (3) the interaction and interrelationship of the child with his parent or parents, his siblings, and any other person who may significantly affect the child's best interest;

> (4) the child's adjustment to his home, school, and community; and
> (5) the mental and physical health of all individuals involved.
>
> The court shall not consider conduct of a proposed custodian that does not affect his relationship to the child.

Some states have included additional factors to be considered in determining the best interests of the child. Examples include factors relating to the child's primary caretaker, the child's cultural background, the effect of domestic abuse on the child, and the propensity of each parent to encourage continuing contact between the child and the other parent.

Although widely used, the best-interest standard has been criticized because of its indeterminate nature. Despite the enumerated factors, judges must exercise substantial discretion in applying the standard, and this can lead to unpredictable and sometimes arbitrary results.

5.15. American Law Institute

The American Law Institute has created an alternative definition of the best interests of the child that makes fairness between the parents clearly secondary to the best interests of the child. *See* ALI, Principles of the Law of Family Dissolution: Analysis and Recommendations (2002). Under §2.02, the child's bests interests are seen as being served by parental planning and agreement, continuity in attachments, contact with both parents, caretaking by skilled and loving adults who place a priority on it, avoidance of conflict and violence, and "expeditious" decision making. The ALI favors the use of agreed parenting plans to achieve these goals. §2.05. However, if agreement is not reached, the ALI suggests allocating custodial responsibility to "approximate" the proportion of caretaking done by each parent prior to the divorce. §2.08. Exceptions may be made to accommodate the wishes of some children, to avoid separating siblings, to avoid harm to the child, and for other reasons listed in §2.08(1). Joint decision-making responsibility is presumed to be in the child's best interest unless a contrary showing is made. §2.09.

STANDARDS FOR DETERMINING THE BEST INTERESTS OF THE CHILD

5.16. Race

The Supreme Court has held that courts cannot use race as the sole or decisive factor in awarding custody. In *Palmore v. Sidoti*, 466 U.S. 429 (1984), the

United States Supreme Court held that the lower court improperly failed to consider the relative qualifications of both parents and erred in depriving the mother of custody of her child because she had entered into an interracial marriage. The ALI prohibits court consideration of race or ethnicity. §2.12(1)(a).

5.17. Religion

If divorcing parents have religious differences, constitutional protections concerning the free exercise of religion may come into play. Consequently, courts cannot favor one religious tradition over another. However, courts can consider the compatibility of a parent's religious behavior with the health and well-being of the child. *See Sagar v. Sagar*, 781 N.E.2d 54 (Mass. App. Ct. 2003). The American Law Institute prohibits consideration of a parent's religious practices other than as necessary to protect the child from harm or to allow the child to continue to practice a religion that is significant to the child. ALI, Principles of the Law of Family Dissolution: Analysis and Recommendations §2.12(1)(c) (2002).

EXAMPLES

Example 5-6

In the case of *Jones v. Jones*, 832 N.E.2d 1057 (Ind. App. 2005), P and D were the divorcing parents of one child. They both practiced Wicca, which is a form of paganism. The court awarded them joint legal custody and awarded D physical custody of their child. The judge directed the parents to "take such steps as are needed to shelter [the child] from involvement and observation of these non-mainstream religious beliefs and rituals." Both parents appealed the decision. What was the outcome?

EXPLANATIONS

Explanation

On appeal, the child's legal custodians (P and D jointly) were found to have the right to determine the child's religious upbringing. The appellate court found that there was no indication that the child would be endangered by Wiccan practice or that the parents disagreed about the choice of religion. Consequently, the appellate court held that the trial court lacked authority to limit the parents' direction with respect to religious practice. (The court did not reach the issue of the parents' constitutional right to control the religious training of the child.)

5.18. Disability

Under §102(5) of UMDA, courts are instructed to consider the mental and physical health of all the parties. This does not give courts license to discriminate against parents with disabilities. Rather, this language has been interpreted to require the courts to make case-by-case determinations concerning the effect of the disability on the child. *See Arneson v. Arneson*, 670 N.W.2d 904 (S.D. 2003); *Schumm v. Schumm*, 510 N.W.2d 13 (Minn. Ct. App. 1993).

5.19. Child's Preference

Most courts will consider "the wishes of the child as to his custodians" as described in §402 of UMDA. However, this broad language is tempered by the court's discretion to determine whether the child has sufficient maturity to express a meaningful preference. Although age is not the sole consideration in making this determination, teenagers are typically consulted. *See* Joan B. Kelly, *Psychological and Legal Interventions for Parents and Children in Custody and Access Disputes: Current Research and Practice*, 10 Va. J. Soc. Pol'y & L. 129 (2002) (discussing ramifications of excluding children from the process); Andrew Schepard, *Children, Courts and Custody* (2004); Randi L. Dulaney, *Children Should Be Seen AND Heard in Florida Custody Determinations*, 25 Nova L. Rev. 815 (2001) (discussing various state statutes regarding child preference). The ALI makes an exception to the "approximation" rule to accommodate the "firm and reasonable preference" of a child of a specific age. ALI, Principles of the Law of Family Dissolution: Analysis and Recommendations §208(1)(b) (2002).

When children are consulted, the court will evaluate the reasons behind the child's expressed preference. For example, in *In re Marriage of Mehlmauer*, 131 Cal. Rptr. 325 (Ct. App. 1976), the court did not defer to the preference of a 14-year-old boy who preferred to live with his father because the father allowed him to wear his hair longer and stay out later. However, in *McMillen v. McMillen*, 602 A.2d 845 (Pa. 1992), the court considered the child's preference where the stepfather frightened and upset the child and the child was left unattended after school.

The child is not asked to express a parental preference in open court. Section 404 of UMDA provides for two alternatives. First, the judge can interview the child in chambers and on the record with the attorneys present. Second, the court can "seek the advice" of a professional who can submit a written report to the court. Either way, care must be taken to avoid undue parental influence or coercion on the child being interviewed. *See Couch v. Couch*, 146 S.W.3d 923 (Ky. 2004) (mother entitled to access in camera interview tape).

Section 310 of UMDA provides that the court may appoint an attorney to act as an advocate for the child. However, this is relatively rare in most jurisdictions. In contrast, courts sometimes appoint a guardian *ad litem* who acts in the child's best interest as opposed to carrying out the child's wishes. Schepard, *supra*; *see also* ALI, Principles of the Law of Family Dissolution: Analysis and Recommendations §2.13 (2002).

5.20. Separating Siblings

Courts avoid separating siblings when making child custody arrangements. Siblings are kept together to maintain stability and promote sibling relationships unless there are compelling reasons to separate them. *See In re Marriage of Heath*, 18 Cal. Rptr. 3d 760 (Cal. App. 2004) (court improperly found detriment to one child based on sibling's disability). The ALI provides for an exception to the "approximation" standard in order to keep siblings together. ALI, Principles of the Law of Family Dissolution: Analysis and Recommendations §2.08(1)(c) (2002).

5.21. Parental Conduct Not Affecting the Child: The Nexus Test

Many states have adopted statutory language contained in §402 of UMDA preventing courts from considering parental conduct that does not affect the parent's relationship to the child. Under the nexus test, evidence concerning parental behavior is relevant to a child custody decision only if the parental behavior affects the parent's relationship with the child; in other words, there must be a nexus between the parental activity and harm to the child. Whether parental conduct affects the child is a question of fact that the trial court must determine on a case-by-case basis. Questions of parental conduct are sometimes raised in cases involving gay and lesbian parents and cases involving cohabiting parents.

5.22. Gay and Lesbian Parents

The nexus test has been used in cases where one parent is gay or lesbian. While some courts have been hesitant to award custody to gay or lesbian parents, other courts have considered what, if any, effect the parent's sexual orientation has upon the child or children. *See Hollon v. Hollon*, 784 So. 2d 943 (S. Ct. Miss. 2001). The nexus test view is consistent with the position taken by the American Psychological Association in passing a resolution stating that sexual orientation should not be the sole consideration in making custody decisions. The ALI specifically prohibits court consideration of the sexual orientation of the parent. ALI, Principles of the Law of Family Dissolution: Analysis and Recommendations §2.12(1)(d) (2002).

5.23. Cohabitation

In the past, a parent's cohabitation with a member of the opposite sex would typically result in loss of custody. *See Jarret v. Jarret*, 449 U.S. 927 (1980). However, under §402 of UMDA, cohabitation is relevant only to the extent that the parent's sexual relationship adversely affects the child or children. Similarly, the ALI prohibits consideration of a parent's extramarital sexual behavior unless it harms the child. ALI, Principles of the Law of Family Dissolution: Analysis and Recommendations §2.12(1)(e) (2002). *See* Margaret F. Brinig, *Feminism and Child Custody Under Chapter Two of the American Law Institute's Principles of the Law of Family Dissolution*, 8 Duke J. Gender L. & Pol'y 301, 312 (2001).

Example 5-7

P (mother) and D (father) are seeking a divorce. They separated in 2004, and they agreed that the couple's three children, ages four, six, and ten, would reside temporarily with D while the divorce was pending. D began cohabiting with C against the wishes of P, who strongly disapproves of cohabitation outside of marriage on moral grounds. P learns that C was twice convicted of shoplifting and that C drinks alcoholic beverages in the presence of the children. Assuming that D is otherwise a fit parent, will P be awarded physical custody based on D's cohabitation?

Explanation

D's cohabitation is relevant to the question of physical custody only if it adversely affects the children. P will argue that the shoplifting convictions and the drinking in front of the children show that C has poor moral character and will be a bad influence on the children. D will argue that P should not be awarded custody based on D's cohabitation with C unless P can prove specific adverse consequences to the children. Because the children were not involved with the shoplifting charges (and may not even be aware of them) and there is no indication that C drinks to excess or has placed the children in danger while drinking, P is not likely to be awarded physical custody of the children based solely on D's cohabitation with C. However, if P can show specific adverse consequences to the children, via expert testimony or otherwise, the cohabitation could become a factor in the outcome of the case. This is an example of a situation where the parties might benefit from creating a mediated parenting plan addressing ground rules for parenting.

5.24. Careers

Despite the gender-neutral language of the "best interests" test, working mothers sometimes fear that their careers could work against them in a custody dispute. This was the case in *Rowe v. Franklin*, 663 N.E.2d 955 (Ohio Ct. App. 1995), in which the court was found to have abused its discretion by focusing on a mother's behavior (including her enrollment in law school) rather than the best interests of the child. *See also Burchard v. Garay*, 724 P.2d 486 (Cal. 1986) (not permissible for court to award custody of child in day care based on economic advantage of father with new stay-at-home wife); *Linda R. v. Richard E.*, 162 A.D.2d 48 (N.Y. 1990) (mother who worked outside the home was not a "remote control" mother). Fathers also sometimes fear that their employment, particularly if they work long hours or travel frequently, may hinder their chances of being awarded sole or joint physical custody of their children. The ALI prohibits consideration of the relative earning capacity of the parents. ALI, Principles of the Law of Family Dissolution: Analysis and Recommendations §2.12(1)(f) (2002).

5.25. Friendly Parent Provision

Most states encourage or require courts to consider the extent to which a proposed custodial parent is likely to encourage ongoing contact between the child and the other parent. These are known as "cooperative" or "friendly" parent provisions, and the idea behind them is to encourage awards of custody to the parent who is most likely to support the child's relationship with the noncustodial parent. Such provisions have come under attack when applied to situations involving domestic violence. Consequently, some states make this factor inapplicable if there is a history of family violence. Peter G. Jaffe et al., *Child Custody and Domestic Violence: A Call for Safety and Accountability* 68 (2003). *See also* ALI, Principles of the Law of Family Dissolution: Analysis and Recommendations §2.11(1)(d) (2002).

EXAMPLES

Example 5-8

Assume that P and D live in a jurisdiction that has adopted UMDA (see Section 5.14 *supra*) and that the legislature has amended the Act to include the following additional factor: "(6) the disposition of each parent to encourage and permit frequent contact with the other parent by the child." Both P and D seek sole legal and physical custody of their child when P files for divorce. They are unable to agree on custodial arrangements and they have a history of conflict. The court awards P sole physical custody but, over P's objection, orders joint legal custody, stating that without such an order P would not "foster the relationship" between D and the child. Will P prevail on appeal?

EXPLANATIONS

Explanation

P is not likely to prevail on appeal because judges consider the proclivity of a proposed custodian to foster the child's relationship with the other parent when they award legal and physical custody. *Kay v. Ludwig*, 686 N.W.2d 619 (Neb. Ct. App. 2004). More typically, friendly parent provisions are raised in connection with physical custody rather than legal custody awards. P and D may benefit from mediation addressing their decision-making process; otherwise, shared legal custody could result in an increased (rather than decreased) level of conflict.

5.26. Domestic Violence

In the past, as the states moved away from fault divorce and adopted provisions preventing courts from considering parental conduct that did not affect the child, some courts failed to view spouse abuse as relevant to child custody decisions. Jaffe et al., *supra*. Today, nearly every state requires courts to consider the presence of domestic violence when awarding custody. Some have created rebuttable presumptions against awarding custody to a parent with a history of domestic violence. These states have relied on recent studies documenting harm to children who witness or overhear domestic violence. *See* Nancy K.D. Lemon, *Statutes Creating Rebuttable Presumptions Against Custody to Batterers: How Effective Are They?* 28 Wm. Mitchell L. Rev. 601 (2001).

EXAMPLES

Example 5-9

Assume that P and D live in a jurisdiction that has adopted UMDA (see Section 5.14 *supra*) and that the legislature has amended the Act to add the following additional factors: "(6) the effect on the child of domestic abuse that has taken place between the parents; and (7) the disposition of each parent to encourage and permit frequent contact with the other parent by the child." D has been violent with P on several occasions. When P files for divorce, P and D each seek custody of the two children. D has never physically harmed the children, but P claims that the children have witnessed the violence and that D should not have custody of the children. How is a court likely to analyze the situation with respect to child custody?

Explanation

Under UMDA, the court is required to consider a number of factors in determining the best interests of the children. The court will exercise its discretion in determining which factors are most important in a given case. P will argue that the children are directly affected by the domestic violence because they have witnessed and thus been harmed by the abuse. D will argue that D has never physically harmed the children and that if awarded custody, P will not be disposed to allowing D to have continuing contact with the children (P will not be a "friendly" parent). Assuming that P has evidence of the abuse, a court is likely to award custody to P and carefully structure visitation or parenting time for D. If P lived in a jurisdiction that had adopted a rebuttable presumption against custody awards to abusers, P would be awarded custody if P could prove abuse of sufficient frequency and severity to trigger the presumption.

5.27. American Law Institute View of Domestic Violence and Custody

The ALI requires special written findings before a parent who has engaged in domestic violence is allowed to have custodial responsibility or decision-making responsibility for a child. The burden is placed on the parent who has committed domestic violence to show that such contact will not endanger family members. ALI, Principles of the Law of Family Dissolution: Analysis and Recommendations §2.11(3) (2002).

COURT SERVICES: INVESTIGATION AND EDUCATION

5.28. Reports of Professionals

Courts frequently place substantial weight on the investigative reports of professionals such as social workers and child psychologists. These reports may be ordered by the court and admitted into evidence. However, under §405 of UMDA, any party can require the professional and the people the professional has interviewed to testify. The investigation is usually performed by a court agency, a state social services department, or a private agency under contract to the court.

Either or both parties may hire qualified professionals to provide expert testimony on their behalf should the case go to trial. This process can be time-consuming and expensive.

Under various state statutes and depending on the resources available, a guardian *ad litem* may be appointed to represent the interests of the child. The guardian *ad litem* investigates the situation, reports to the court, and advocates for the child's best interests. Although the guardian *ad litem* may be an attorney, this role differs from traditional attorney-client representation because the guardian *ad litem* formulates his or her own opinion concerning the best interests of the child rather than acting as an advocate of the child's expressed preference. (See Section 5.19 *supra*.)

5.29. Use of Neutral Experts and Facilitators

Parents are encouraged to create parenting plans because parents are most familiar with the needs of their children and they are in the best position to create workable long-term arrangements. This less adversarial approach has resulted in a decreased need for custody evaluations and expert witnesses. However, parents may benefit from consulting with neutral experts who perform an educational rather than an evaluative function. For example, parents in mediation may meet with a neutral child psychologist to better understand the developmental needs of their children with respect to divorce. In this role, the child psychologist does not "take sides" but provides helpful information to the parents so that they can make more child-centered decisions. Parents also benefit from working with a process facilitator such as a mediator (see Chapter 25).

5.30. Parent Education

In an effort to reduce conflict and help parents develop strategies to work cooperatively, some jurisdictions offer, and in some cases require, that parents attend sessions addressing the impact of divorce on children, co-parenting after divorce, and conflict resolution. The purpose of such classes is to ease the children's adjustment to divorce, prevent long-term emotional difficulties, and avoid relitigation of custody and visitation issues.

Some jurisdictions mandate attendance at these educational sessions, and parents who fail to comply risk being held in contempt of court and other sanctions. Other states have implemented adult education programs but leave the issue of compulsory attendance to the discretion of the court. A few states make attendance entirely optional. *See* Solveig Erickson & Nancy Ver Steegh, *Mandatory Divorce Education Classes: What Do the Parents Say?* 28 W. Mitchell L. Rev. 889, 895 (2001).

Some preliminary research indicates that attending parent education classes early in the divorce process is more valuable than attending them later on. Although early attendance has been linked to reduced rates of relitigation of custody, support, and visitation issues, few states require attendance within 45 days of service of the divorce complaint.

Do parental divorce programs work? So far, research indicates that parents are learning valuable parenting and communication skills and that children are being exposed to less parental conflict as a result of parent education programs. *See* Jack Arbuthnot & Donal Gordon, *Does Mandatory Divorce Education for Parents Work?* 34 Fam. & Conciliation Cts. Rev. 60, 79 (1996). Parents also report that they appreciate the classes. Consequently, it is likely that such programs will be significantly expanded throughout the nation.

Despite these positive reviews, victims of domestic violence should not attend general parent education courses because of safety issues and because messages about co-parenting and enhanced communication can be dangerous for them. Instead, when domestic violence has occurred, specialized programs stressing safety planning and separate parenting should be provided. Geri S. W. Fuhrmann et al., *Parent Education's Second Generation: Integrating Violence Sensitivity*, 37 Fam. & Conciliation Cts. Rev. 24 (1999).

EXAMPLES

Example 5-10

P has filed for divorce from D. They have three young children. They live in a jurisdiction where the court has the discretion to order them to attend a parent education program. The judge assigned to their case orders them both to attend such a program. D does not want the divorce and refuses to attend the parenting sessions. What is likely to happen?

EXPLANATIONS

Explanation

By failing to attend the parent education program, D is in violation of a court order and is likely to be held in contempt of court. D may be allowed to "purge" civil contempt by attending the program. Otherwise, D may be jailed for a period of time. In either event, P will be allowed to proceed with the divorce.

5.31. Differentiated Case Management

Recognizing that families have different needs, some courts customize the handling of dissolution cases using triage procedures and multidisciplinary screening teams. Once identified, high-conflict and violent families can be referred to appropriate services. Even in jurisdictions where differentiated case management has been implemented, screening for domestic violence and high conflict is best accomplished when all family law professionals, including attorneys, actively participate.

5.32. Parenting Coordinators

Because high-conflict cases require additional oversight, some courts have begun to use parenting coordinators. Parenting coordinators typically help families resolve day-to-day matters such as scheduling, transportation, and child care. In some cases they facilitate communication between the parents; in other cases, they exercise limited decision-making authority. *See* Association of Family and Conciliation Courts Task Force on Parenting Coordination, *Parenting Coordination: Implementation Issues*, 41 Fam. Ct. Rev. 533 (2003).

EXAMPLES

Example 5-11

During the divorce process a mental health expert recommended that P and D work with a parenting coordinator. They consequently agreed to the entry of a court order appointing a parenting coordinator to assist with communications, resolve minor issues, monitor problems, and make recommendations about parenting time. The appointment was made pursuant to a state statute placing strict guidelines on the role. Despite having initially agreed, P later challenged the use of a parenting coordinator. She alleged that the parenting coordinator micro-managed the family and usurped her right to make decisions for her child. What is the likely result?

EXPLANATIONS

Explanation

In *Barnes v. Barnes*, 107 P.3d 560 (Okla. 2005), the court upheld the appointment of a parenting coordinator, noting that the role was a clearly limited one. The court held that the Oklahoma Parenting Coordinator Act did not violate equal protection and that P's substantive due process rights were not violated by the appointment.

CHAPTER 6

Modifying Custody — Relocating to Another Jurisdiction

6.1. Introduction

This chapter examines a variety of legal problems associated with two reasonably discrete types of custody modification actions. The first type of action involves the typical request for a change of custody from one parent to the other, after an initial order has been made and primary or sole custody awarded to one parent, and relocation is not an issue. The second type of action involves an analysis of issues associated with a custodial parent's request to relocate to another state or to a foreign country with the minor child or children after an initial order awarded primary or sole custody to the parent requesting the move.

JURISDICTION

6.2. Subject Matter Theory

Once a custody order is entered, states uniformly agree that they have subject matter jurisdiction to modify the order during the minority of the child or children. This principle rests upon the well-accepted theory that the state always sits as a third party to divorce proceedings and carries the responsibility of ensuring that the best interest of a child is protected during minority. *See Troxel v. Granville*, 530 U.S. 57, 68-69 (2000) (so long as a parent adequately cares for his or her children (i.e., is fit), there will normally be no reason for the state to inject itself into the private realm of the family to further question the ability of that parent to make the best decisions concerning the rearing of that parent's children). The state always has a role as *parens patrie* as well as an interest in protecting a child where allegations of abuse, neglect, or abandonment have been made. *Roth v. Weston*, 789 A.2d 431 (Conn. 2002).

6.3. *Res Judicata*; Presumption; Change in Circumstances Required

After a court enters a final judgment in a dissolution action that provides for the custody of a child, the judgment is *res judicata* of the facts and circumstances at the time the judgment became final. Once the judgment is entered, a presumption arises that favors its reasonableness. The presumption serves the practical purpose of providing stability and continuity to the original action because subsequent modification actions attacking the original judgment are considered highly disruptive to children. *George v. Helliar*, 814 P.2d 238 (Wash. App. 1991). The presumption is rebuttable, and a court usually places a heavy burden on the moving party to prove the circumstances necessary for modification. *Groves v. Groves*, 567 P.2d 459, 463 (Mont. 1977). The presumption may, of course, be overcome if the court is persuaded that a change in circumstances since the original judgment justifies such action. *See, e.g., Wade v. Hirschman*, 903 So. 2d 928 (Fla. 2005).

UNIFORM MARRIAGE AND DIVORCE ACT (UMDA): MODIFICATION ABSENT A RELOCATION REQUEST

6.4. Stability Is the Goal

The Uniform Marriage and Divorce Act (UMDA), §409(b), has influenced custody modification legislation in many jurisdictions. The UMDA reflects a desire to provide a minor child with stability once a custody ruling is issued, which is why §409(b) states that more than a change in circumstances must be shown if custody is to be modified. For example, when sole physical custody is awarded to one parent under this section of the UMDA, custody may be modified only upon a showing of changed circumstances, which are defined alternatively as follows: (1) the present custodial parent agrees to the custody change; or (2) the child has been integrated in the petitioner's family with the consent of the custodial parent; or (3) the child's present environment seriously endangers his physical, mental, moral, or emotional health, and the harm likely to be caused by a change of environment is outweighed by its advantages. UMDA §409(b); 9A U.L.A. 628 (1987 & Supp. 1996).

6.5. Time Limitations on Modification Actions

The UMDA recommends that states adopt time barriers that a noncustodial parent must overcome in order to successfully bring a modification action once an initial judgment has been entered. The purpose of these time barriers is to provide a minor child with as much stability as possible. For example, absent a showing of consent, integration, or endangerment, §409(a) of the UMDA bars a custody modification action for two years following an initial decision. *See Frieze v. Frieze*, 692 N.W.2d 912 (N.D. 2005); *In re Marriage of Marsh*, 799 N.E.2d 1037 (Ill. App. 2003). Many states have adopted some form of the UMDA limitations.

Example 6-1

Assume that P and D divorce, and the trial judge awards sole physical and legal custody of X, age 13, to D, his mother. Six months after the judgment is entered (and no appeal was taken), P brings an action asking that the judgment be modified so that P is awarded sole legal and physical custody of X. In the moving papers, P asserts that X has told P that D is drinking heavily and has a boyfriend who was once convicted of drunk driving. In an affidavit submitted to the court in response to P's moving papers, D denies that she is drinking heavily, saying that X has made up the story. She says that X is angry after being grounded for a month for bad behavior. D concedes that her boyfriend was convicted of drunk driving five years ago; however, there are affidavits from him and his AA counselor stating that he has been "dry for two years."

Assume that this jurisdiction has adopted the above provisions of the UMDA and in addition requires a prima facie showing of endangerment before a modification hearing will be granted. The trial judge has two questions: Is the above action time-barred? If it is not, has the party moving for modification made out a prima facie showing of endangerment? How will most courts answer these two questions?

Explanation

The answer to the "time-barred" question is easy. Section 409 of the UMDA bars a change-of-custody hearing for two years following an initial custody decision. Here, the original custody order was entered only six months ago. Therefore, the action is time-barred unless the moving party can establish a prima facie case of endangerment. More formally stated, the moving party must show that that the child's present environment seriously endangers his or her physical, mental, or emotional health, and the harm likely to be caused by a change of environment is outweighed by its presumed advantages.

Most likely, courts will find that the noncustodial parent's evidence in support of his allegations falls short of establishing a prima facie case that justifies reopening the original order. The noncustodial parent would have a better chance of a favorable decision had he produced evidence from experts and disinterested non-expert third parties to support his claims. The custodial parent countered the drinking allegations with her responsive affidavit and the affidavits of her boyfriend and the AA counselor. Furthermore, the claimed evidence of drinking doesn't appear to be something new; therefore, a judge could reasonably assume that if such evidence existed, it should have been produced at the original custody hearing held only six months earlier.

SELECTED STATE STANDARDS FOR CUSTODY MODIFICATION NOT INVOLVING RELOCATION

6.6. Overview of Procedures and Standards

The procedures and standards employed by courts considering a modification request vary among jurisdictions. As illustrated below, states use somewhat different procedures and standards when approaching the issue.

6.7. California: "Significant Change"

In California, once a trial court has entered a final or permanent custody order indicating that a particular custodial arrangement is in the best interest of the child, the paramount need for continuity and stability in custody arrangements — and the harm that may result from disruption of established patterns of care and emotional bonds with the primary caretaker — weigh heavily in favor of maintaining that custody arrangement. In recognition of this policy concern, California has articulated a variation on the best-interest standard, known as the "changed circumstance" rule, that a trial court must apply when a parent seeks modification of a final judicial custody determination. Under the rule, custody modification is appropriate only if the parent seeking modification demonstrates a significant change of circumstances indicating that a different custody arrangement would be in the child's best interest. It is thought that this rule serves to protect the weighty interest in stable custody arrangements, and that it fosters judicial economy. *In re Marriage of Seagondollar*, 43 Cal. Rptr. 3d 575 (Cal. App. Ct. 2006).

6.8. Florida: No Proof of Detriment Needed

In *Wade v. Hirschman*, 903 So. 2d 928 (Fla. 2005), the Florida Supreme Court resolved a conflict among the district courts of appeal regarding the law applicable to custody modification proceedings. In deciding *Wade*, the Florida Supreme Court held that in a modification of child custody proceeding, "satisfaction of the substantial change test is necessary in order to overcome the *res judicata* effect of the final judgment." *Id.* at 934. The substantial change test requires that the moving party prove "both that the circumstances have substantially, materially changed since the original custody determination and that the child's best interests justify changing custody." *Id.* at 931 n. 2 (quoting *Cooper v. Gress*, 854 So. 2d 262, 265 (Fla. App. Ct. 2003)). In addition, "the substantial change must be one that was not reasonably contemplated at the time of the original judgment." *Id.* (quoting *Cooper*, 854 So. 2d *at* 265). The court stated that proof of detriment "is not an element of the substantial change test necessary to modify a child custody award." *See Kendall v. Kendall*, 832 So. 2d 878, 879-80 (Fla. App. 2002); *Glover v. Glover*, 820 So. 2d 324, 324 (Fla. App. 2001); *Young v. Young*, 732 So. 2d 1133, 1134 (Fla. App. 1999).

6.9. New York: Totality of Circumstances

In New York the legal standards for determining custody and visitation modifications are basically the same, although the extent and magnitude of the proposed modification have some bearing on the court's ultimate determination. *See Matter of Engwer v. Engwer*, 762 N.Y.S.2d 689 (N.Y. 2003). The standard requires that the petitioner "demonstrate a change in circumstances warranting modification of the visitation or custody order to advance the best interest[s] of the children." *Matter of Reese v. Jones*, 671 N.Y.S.2d 170 (N.Y. 1998); *Matter of La Bier v. La Bier*, 738 N.Y.S.2d 132 (N.Y. 2002). A change-of-custody standard requires a clear demonstration of a significant change of circumstances, which, based on the totality of circumstances, warrants a modification of custody in the best interests of the children before moving them. *Renzulli v. McElrath*, 712 N.Y.S.2d 267 (N.Y. Sup. 2000).

6.10. Ohio: Change Can't Be Inconsequential

Modification of parental rights in Ohio can occur only if (1) there was a change in circumstances since the parties filed their parenting plan with the court; (2) a modification was deemed to be in the best interests of the parties' children; and (3) the harm likely to be caused by a change of environment is outweighed by the advantages of the change of environment to the children. *Rohrbaugh v. Rohrbaugh*, 136 Ohio App. 3d 599 (2000). Furthermore, the "change of circumstances" required to modify parental rights "must be a change of substance, not slight or inconsequential change." *Davis v. Flickinger*, 77 Ohio St. 3d 415, 418 (Ohio 1997).

6.11. Pennsylvania: Substantial Change Not Required

In Pennsylvania, the paramount concern in child custody proceedings is the best interest of the child. *Jordan v. Jackson*, 876 A.2d 443 (Pa. Super. 2005); *Clapper v. Harvey*, 716 A.2d 1271 (Pa. Super. 1998). It is settled law in Pennsylvania that a custody order is subject to modification without proof of a substantial change in circumstances when it is shown that change is in the best interests of the child. *Moore v. Moore*, 634 A.2d 163, 169 (Pa. 1993). Whenever a court is called upon to address the best interests of a child, traditional burdens or presumptions such as substantial change in circumstances, the fitness of one parent over another, or the tender years doctrine must all give way to the paramount concern: the best interests of the child. *Id.* In determining best interests of the child, a court must consider all factors that legitimately affect the child's physical, intellectual, moral, and spiritual well-being. *Swope v. Swope*, 689 A.2d 264 (Pa. 1997).

6.12. Texas: Heightened Burden

A party making a child custody modification request is apparently entitled to a jury trial in Texas. To support modification of an order regarding custody in Texas, a trial court must find that the modification would be in the best interest of the child and that the circumstances of the child have materially and substantially changed since the date of the original order. Tex. Fam. Code Ann. §156.101(1) (West Supp. 2005). The party seeking modification has the burden to establish these elements by a preponderance of the evidence. *Agraz v. Carnley*, 143 S.W.3d 547, 552 (Tex. App. 2004); *In re* T.D.C., 91 S.W.3d 865, 871 (Tex. App. 2002); *Considine v. Considine*, 726 S.W.2d 253, 255 (Tex. App. 1987). The best interest of the child is always the primary consideration of the court in determining custody. Tex. Fam. Code Ann. §153.002 (West 2002).

In a modification action, a threshold inquiry is whether the moving party has met the imposed burden of showing a material and substantial change; otherwise the trial court must deny the motion to modify. *Bates v. Tesar*, 81 S.W.3d 411, 427 (Tex. App. 2002). To prove that a material change in circumstances has occurred, the petitioner must demonstrate what material changes have occurred in the conditions existing at the time of the entry of the prior order as compared with the circumstances existing at the time of the hearing on the motion to modify.

The Texas legislature has established a system that attempts to create stability in the custody of children. *Burkhart v. Burkhart*, 960 S.W.2d 321, 323 (1997). A person seeking to change the designation of the person who has the exclusive right to determine the child's primary residence within a year after such a designation was ordered faces a heightened burden. *Id.* In such a circumstance, the petitioner must file an affidavit that supports a the existence of one of three conditions, including a finding that "the child's present environment may endanger the child's physical health or significantly impair the child's emotional development." *See* Tex. Fam. Code Ann. §156.102(b)(1) (West Supp. 2005). If the court determines, based on the affidavit, that the facts stated are adequate to support such an allegation, the court shall set a time and place for the hearing. *Id.* §156.102(c). Otherwise, the trial court "shall deny the relief sought and refuse to schedule a hearing for modification." *Id.*

EXAMPLES

Example 6-2

Assume that this jurisdiction does not have a time barrier for bringing modification actions similar to that found in UMDA. Also assume that P and D were divorced and that D was awarded sole physical custody of child X. According to the findings made by the judge at the custody proceeding, she was concerned about X's mother's (P's) abuse of drugs and alcohol. A year after the original custody decision, P sought to modify custody so that she would have sole physical custody of X. At the initial custody proceeding the Department of Social Services (DSS) had been involved because of concerns over P's fitness to care for X, age ten. The concerns were prompted in large part by the mother's history of drug abuse. At the modification proceeding, P called a social worker, who testified that P was having "great success in overcoming her alcohol and drug dependence" and that X "would be better nurtured by P." D's lawyer argued that there had not been a change in circumstances, and even if there were, the change would not justify modifying custody. D testified that X was enrolled in school and was doing a good job (X's report cards supported D). Custodial parent D testified that X had made friends in the neighborhood, that X attended church with D on a regular basis, and that X was on a Little League baseball team. D testified that X appeared to enjoy the home setting. How will a court likely rule?

EXPLANATIONS

Explanation

Most courts that use a two-pronged test would find that P has satisfied the first prong: There has been a substantial change in circumstances since the trial (i.e., she has her drug problem under control). However, there is no evidence of consent, integration, or endangerment. There is likewise scant evidence to support the conclusion that X's best interests would be served by changing custody from D to P. Because stability and continuity are so important to a judge considering a modification request, and D has produced evidence demonstrating X's relationship to the neighborhood and school, most courts will conclude that P's evidence has failed to overcome the presumption favoring the custodial parent. *See Ardizoni v. Raymond*, 667 N.E.2d 885 (Mass. App. Ct. 1996). Even without the presumption, it is doubtful that a court would change custody on the above facts.

TYPICAL MODIFICATION CLAIMS

6.13. Unwarranted Denial of Visitation

Although successful custody modification actions based solely on denial of visitation are rare, a majority of jurisdictions have by statute declared that unwarranted denial of or interference with duly established visitation constitutes contempt of court and may be sufficient cause for reversal of a custody ruling. *See, e.g.*, Iowa Code §598.23(2)(b) (2006); New Hampshire Code Rev. Stat. Ann. 458:17, V(a)(2) (2004) (modification allowed if court finds repeated, intentional, and unwarranted interference by a custodial parent with the visitation or custodial rights of the noncustodial parent). However, unwarranted denial of or interference with visitation is not dispositive but is usually viewed as only one of several factors to be considered in contemplating a custody modification action. *See, e.g., In re Marriage of Ciganovich*, 61 Cal. App. 3d 289 (1976); *Slinkard v. Slinkard*, 589 S.W.2d 635 (Mo. App. 1979); *Lopez v. Lopez*, 639 P.2d 1186 (N.M. 1981); *Lemcke v. Lemcke*, 623 N.W.2d 916 (Minn. App. 2001); cf. *Entwistle v. Entwistle*, 402 N.Y.S.2d 213 (1978) (custodial parent's interference with the other parent's visitation rights is so inconsistent with the child's best interests as to per se raise a strong probability that custodial parent is unfit).

6.14. Failure to Pay Child Support

A noncustodial parent is often required by a court order or by an agreement between the parties to make child support payments. When the noncustodial parent fails to make such payments, the custodial parent will sometimes resort to a self-help method of enforcement. The self-help consists of withholding court-ordered visitation privileges from the noncustodial parent until that parent pays the support.

Courts are unwilling to support a custodial parent in the withholding effort. Also, as a general rule, courts will not terminate visitation solely for reasons unrelated to the welfare of the child, and a failure to pay support is usually not included within the scope of this principle. *See Stewart v. Soda*, 226 A.D.2d 1102 (N.Y. 1996). Note, however, that some "older" decisions have prevented visitation where an agreement between the parties conditioned visitation upon payment of child support. *See* 65 A.L.R. 1155 (1988).

Example 6-3

Assume when P and D divorce that P is awarded sole physical and legal custody of X and that D is ordered to pay P $1,000 per month in child support. When D fails to make three consecutive child support payments, P refuses to allow D to visit with their minor child. D reacts to P's withholding of visitation by bringing a motion to enforce the court-ordered visitation or, alternatively, to modify the custody decree and give D sole legal and physical custody of the child. P responds by asking the court to hold D in contempt because of his failure to pay child support and to deny D visitation on the ground that he has either forfeited or abandoned the child by failing to pay support. The court issues a contempt citation against D for failure to pay support as ordered. P then argues that the contempt order bars D from making a custody request of any kind; he does not have "clean hands." How will a court rule on the motions by the parties?

Explanation

First, it is unlikely that a court will accept the abandonment argument because of the short period of time between the initial court order and P's action to deny visitation; moreover, D is seeking visitation with X. Second, most courts will not apply the clean hands doctrine, reasoning that a child's best interests are at stake. Third, courts will apply the general rule that proof of unwarranted denial of or interference with established visitation rights may be sufficient cause for reversal of custody. However, as noted above, courts view a denial or interference with visitation as not necessarily controlling in a custody modification proceeding, though it must be considered along with the other factors. Finally, the court will most likely keep custody with the custodial parent and order visitation with the noncustodial parent to be resumed. It will also likely continue to utilize its civil contempt power to force D to pay the ordered support.

6.15. Integration into Noncustodial Parent's Home

Most jurisdictions recognize that custody may be modified when the child has been integrated into the noncustodial parent's family with the consent of the custodial parent. *See* §409, 9A U.L.A. 62829 (1987). Consent has been defined as "a voluntary acquiescence to surrender of legal custody." *In re Marriage of Timmons*, 617 P.2d 1032 (Wash. 1980). Most courts view integration as more than expanded visitation. It includes the performance of normal parental duties such as washing clothes, providing meals, attending to medical needs, assisting with homework, and guiding the children physically, mentally, morally, socially, and emotionally. *See, e.g.*, *In re Marriage of Wechselberger*, 450 N.E.2d 1385 (Ill. App. Ct. 1983). The time spent by the children with the proposed custodial parent must be of sufficient duration that they have become settled into the home of that parent as though it were their primary home. *See In re Marriage of Paradis*, 689 P.2d 1263 (Mont. 1984). Consideration may also be given to which residence the children consider to be their true home. *In re Custody of Thompson*, 647 P.2d 1049 (Wash. App. 1982). *See generally* Annot., 35 A.L.R. 4th 61 (1985).

Example 6-4

Assume that upon dissolution of P and D's marriage sole physical custody of their three children was awarded to D (mother), and P (father) was ordered to pay child support. Six years after the original judgment was entered, P filed a motion asking that the judgment be modified so that he is awarded sole physical custody of the three children. The testimony at the modification hearing showed that when the dissolution decree was entered, P was granted visitation consisting of alternating weekends and Wednesday afternoons. However, shortly after the divorce became final, P remarried and requested additional visitation with the children. Because the children enjoyed the time they spent with P, D agreed to more visitation, although the original visitation judgment was not amended. At the time P filed the modification action, the evidence showed that the three children were spending about an equal percentage of time with P and with D.

In opposition to the motion, D presented evidence that since the divorce she had continued to exercise daily control over the lives of the children, even when they stayed with P. She testified that she made the major decisions on their behalf and maintained other parenting duties, such as assisting with homework; attending parent-teacher conferences; transporting them to athletic activities and lessons; assisting in their expenses; and providing love, support, and encouragement. P testified that he was working a great deal and found it difficult to attend many of the events and conferences involving his children, although his wife was able to make many of them. D testified that it was never her intent for the expansion of visitation to constitute a change in her capacity as sole legal custodian for the children, that she had begun to reduce the amount of time the children spent with D, and that she believed D was bringing the motion in an attempt to reduce his child support obligation. P responded that "the fact is, the children had been integrated" into his home with D's permission. How will a court most likely rule on P's claim that the children have been integrated into his home?

EXPLANATIONS

Explanation

A court will, of course, conduct a factual inquiry and will most likely conclude that there has been a substantial change in circumstances. It appears, however, that there was neither consent nor complete integration of the minor children into P's household. Moreover, D continued to make the major decisions and exercise control of the children, although she agreed to the change in the amount of time to be spent with the noncustodial parent. The evidence produced by P will be viewed by most courts as falling short of the kind of knowing integration that statutes and case law require to support a modification request. *See, e.g., In re Marriage of Pontius*, 761 P.2d 247 (Colo. App. 1988).

6.16. Endangerment

One of the more common grounds for seeking modification of custody is a claim that the present environment endangers a child's physical or emotional health or impairs a child's emotional development. For example, in *Molitor v. Molitor*, 718 N.W.2d 13 (N.D. 2006), the noncustodial father claimed endangerment following an incident in which the custodial parent had discovered her oldest child and her new husband's two children "huffing" gasoline in the basement of her house. An argument ensued between her and the three children, during which time the mother of her new husband's children phoned, overheard the argument, and contacted the police. In rejecting the noncustodial father's claim, the court concluded that the incident was the result of the behavior of the child's sibling and step-siblings in the mother's home, and that the child was not in danger. *See Sharp v. Bilbro*, 614 N.W.2d 260, 263 (Minn. App. 2000), *review denied* (Minn. Sept. 26, 2000) ("endangerment" implies a significant degree of danger or likely harm to the child's physical or emotional state); *In re K.L.R.*, 162 S.W.3d 291 (Tex. App. 2005) (endangerment found where former wife was about to move child to house of unknown quality and environment, her physical condition was deteriorating, she had been arrested on two felony charges and subsequently spent time in jail, and noncustodial father feared she might flee jurisdiction with child).

6.17. Stipulations: Agreements Between the Parties

When there is an agreement between the parties regarding a child custody arrangement, several jurisdictions presume that the agreement is in the best interests of the child. *See, e.g., In re Marriage of Jennings*, 50 P.3d 506 (Kan. App. 2002). This presumption must be overcome when a modification motion is brought. Custody agreements are, of course, always subject to the overarching power of the court to determine the best interests of the child.

Some jurisdictions have indicated that agreements in parenting plans can alter the statutory review standard should either parent seek future modification of a decree. *See, e.g., Eschbach v. Eschbach*, 451 N.Y.S.2d 658 (N.Y. 1982). Where the parties have entered an agreement as to which parent should have custody, priority—not as an absolute but as a weighty factor—should, in the absence of extraordinary circumstances, be accorded to that agreement. *Id.* Priority is accorded to the first determination of custody in the belief that the stability produced by this policy is in the child's best interests. *Id.*

Other jurisdictions treat a permanent custody order obtained by stipulation as little different from a permanent custody order obtained via litigation. *See, e.g., In re Marriage of Burgess*, 913 P.2d 473 (Cal. 1966). These jurisdictions apply the changed circumstance rule regardless of whether the initial determination of custody resulted from the parents' agreement, from a default judgment, or from litigation.

EXAMPLES

Example 6-5

Assume that a judgment of divorce was entered incorporating the terms of a stipulated agreement between the husband and wife. The judgment stated that P "shall not remove the children outside the town of X until the youngest child shall have reached the age of eighteen (18) years." P was awarded sole legal and physical custody of the children.

Six months after the judgment was entered, P asked that she be allowed to move the children from the town of X to a large metropolitan city 200 miles away from where P and D were living. P argued that as the custodial parent, she is allowed to make major decisions regarding the family, including moving to another location. In addition, she argued that she intended to marry Y, who was employed in a "good job" in the city. D opposed P's motion, arguing that P's right to move the children had been clearly addressed in the divorce action and that the court should honor the agreement. On these facts, should the court enforce the stipulation restricting movement that was contained in the judgment?

EXPLANATIONS

Explanation

Although various jurisdictions will approach the issue from somewhat different perspectives, the trial judge's ruling regarding the stipulation will most likely be upheld. The court will reason that P knowingly entered into an agreement that contained express and unmistakable relocation restrictions. Although P may be subject to financial and other advantages by moving to the big city, the court will most likely be unwilling to allow the change because of the stipulation made by the parties only a few months earlier. *See Zindulka v. Zindulka*, 726 N.Y.S.2d 173 (N.Y. App. Div. 3 Dept. 2001).

CHILD'S PREFERENCE

6.18. Maturity

Whether a child's preferences and feelings regarding custody and visitation will be given weight by the trial judge in the ultimate determination necessarily depends on all the facts, including the child's age and ability to intelligently form and express those preferences and feelings. *Azia v. DiLascia*, 780 A.2d 992 (Conn. App. Ct. 2001). Although the express wishes of the child are not controlling at a modification proceeding, they are entitled to great weight, particularly where the child's age and maturity would make his or her input particularly meaningful. *McMillian v. Rizzo*, 817 N.Y.S.2d 679 (N.Y.A.D. 2006). Also, when a child states a preference, a court will evaluate the opinion in light of a child's general susceptibility to influence, parental and otherwise. *See Clara L. v. Paul M.*, 673 N.Y.S.2d 657 (N.Y. App. Ct. 1998). The child's wishes must be founded on good conditions. *Myers v. DiDomenico*, 657 A.2d 956, 958 (Pa. 1995).

The predominant importance of the choice of an older child is recognized in most jurisdictions. *See, e.g., State ex rel. Feeley v. Williams*, 222 N.W. 927,

928 (Minn. 1929) (preference of 12½-year-old child given great weight in maintaining her custody with aunt and uncle); *David M. v. Margaret M.*, 385 S.E.2d 912, 920 (W. Va. 1989) (preference of child 14 years old or older is determinative); *Marcus v. Marcus*, 248 N.E.2d 800, 805 (Ill. App. 1969) (error to award custody of 14-year-old to mother against his stated preference to remain with grandmother); *Patrick v. Patrick*, 212 So. 2d 145, 147 (La. Ct. App. 1968) (award of custody of 17- and 18-year-old children to father reversed when children expressed preference to remain with mother; from practical viewpoint, it would be "vain and useless act" to order children who are approaching age of majority to live with parent with whom they do not wish to live). While some courts have placed particular emphasis on a teenager's preference, terming it "an overwhelming consideration," all courts agree that a teenager's preference will not necessarily be controlling, regardless of the strength of the conviction.

EXAMPLES

Example 6-6

Assume that P and D divorced and that P was awarded sole physical custody of the two minor children of the marriage. Five years after the divorce, D began to suspect that P was having an affair. D hired private detectives to investigate P's behavior. After receiving various reports from the private detectives, D brought a motion to modify custody of the two minor children, then ages 16 and 17. D argued that the children were being raised in an immoral atmosphere by P and that he should have sole legal and physical custody of them. The evidence to substantiate the claim of the alleged adulterous acts was circumstantial and consisted of the testimony of the detectives, who had observed P enter a hotel on five occasions with a male and leave the hotel several hours later. The children both appeared as witnesses and expressed their strong desire to remain with P. Despite the testimony, the trial judge ordered that custody be changed to D. P appealed and raised a number of issues, one of which was that the trial judge had failed to give sufficient weight to the children's testimony. How will an appellate court most likely treat the issue of the children's preference?

EXPLANATIONS

Explanation

On these facts, an appellate court might not even reach the issue of the children's preference because of a failure to show the kind of changed circumstances that most courts would recognize as significant. However, if the appellate court should consider their preferences, it is difficult to believe that, given the ages of the children, anyone can practically contradict their choice, even if their opinions are shown to be misguided (and there is no such showing). Because of the apparent maturity of the children, after weighing their opinions, the appellate court will most likely reverse the lower court ruling. P will retain custody.

RELOCATING (REMOVING) A CHILD TO ANOTHER STATE: SOLE PHYSICAL CUSTODY

6.19. Trends

The current trend in relocation decisions is to examine the facts of each case rather than apply an automatic presumption favoring one of the parents. This trend is being fueled by an ongoing dialogue among social scientists regarding the psychological impact relocation has on children. Some social science studies suggest that the psychological welfare of a child depends more on the well-being of the family unit with whom the child primarily resides than on maintaining frequent and regular contact with the other parent. *See, e.g.*, Janet M. Bowermaster, *Sympathizing with Solomon: Choosing Between Parents in a Mobile Society*, 31 U. Louisville J. Fam. L. 791, 884 (1992) (custodial parents should be allowed to relocate with their child in good faith to pursue "their best opportunities"); Judith S. Wallerstein & Tony J. Tanke, *To Move or Not to Move: Psychological and Legal Considerations in the Relocation of Children Following Divorce*, 30 Fam. L.Q. 305, 311, 318 (1996) (social science research on custody does not support the presumption that frequent and continuing access to both parents is in the child's best interests; therefore, a parent with primary physical custody generally should be able to relocate with the child).

However, other social science research suggests that children are better off if they have frequent contact and good relationships with both parents. *See, e.g.*, Marion Gindes, Ph.D., *The Psychological Effects of Relocation for Children of Divorce*, 10 J. Am. Acad. Matrimonial Law. 119, 132 (1998). Some contend that any move, even a relatively short one, is a stressful event for a child and can have a negative impact on the child's well-being. *See, e.g.*, Joan B. Kelly & Michael E. Lamb, *Using Child Development Research to Make Appropriate Custody and Access Decisions for Young Children*, 38 Fam. & Conciliation Cts. Rev. 297, 309 (2000) (regardless of who is the primary caretaker, a child benefits from extensive contact with both parents); David Wood et al., *Impact of Family Relocation on Children's Growth, Development, School Function, and Behavior*, 270 JAMA 1334, 1337 (1993) ("[a] family move disrupts the routines, relationships, and attachments that define the child's world"). This difference of opinion explains, at least in part, the disparate approaches among the various jurisdictions to relocation issues.

6.20. Relocation Law Is Nationally Diverse

Across the country, the law applicable to interstate relocation of a child by a parent is diverse. For example, when a relocation request is made in New York, all relevant facts are considered, but the predominant emphasis is placed on what outcome is most likely to serve the best interests of the child. *See Fisher v. Fisher,* 137 P.3d 355 (Hawaii 2006). In California, the custodial parent has a presumptive right to relocate with the minor child, subject to the power of the court to restrain a change that would prejudice the rights or welfare of the child. *Id.*

In some jurisdictions, the custodial parent seeking permission to relocate bears the initial burden of demonstrating, by a preponderance of the evidence, that the relocation is for a legitimate purpose and that the proposed relocation is reasonable in light of that purpose. Once the custodial parent has established a prima facie case, the burden shifts to the noncustodial parent to prove, by a preponderance of the evidence, that the relocation would not be in the best interests of the child. *See, e.g., Ireland v. Ireland,* 717 A.2d 676 (Conn. 1998) (limited to post-judgment relocation matters); *Ford v. Ford,* 789 A.2d 1104 (Conn. 2002).

EXAMPLES

Example 6-7

Assume that when P and D's marriage dissolved, the court awarded joint legal custody of their minor son to the parties but placed primary physical custody with P. Assume that this jurisdiction applies the modification views expressed in *Ireland v. Ireland,* discussed above. The order allowed D to visit his son every other weekend. At the time of the dissolution, P and D resided in Connecticut. Three years after the divorce, P remarried. P's new husband is a computer consultant, and his major consulting contract ended when the company he was working with crashed because of financial problems. He undertook a search for another job and secured a position in California. P informed D of her plan to join her husband in California with their son and moved to modify the existing decree so that she could relocate there with the child. Is the court likely to grant P's request to relocate?

EXPLANATIONS

Explanation

In this jurisdiction it appears that P bears the initial burden of showing by a preponderance of the evidence that the relocation is for a legitimate purpose and that the proposed relocation is reasonable in light of that purpose. Given the fact that P's new husband lost his job and found a new one in California, a court would most likely rule that P has carried her burden. Once the custodial parent (P) has established a prima facie case, the burden shifts to the noncustodial parent to prove, by a preponderance of the evidence, that the relocation would not be in the best interests of the child. In an *Ireland* jurisdiction, there is a tendency to recognize the "new family" consisting of the custodial parent and child, and the noncustodial parent will have a great deal of difficulty preventing the relocation. The relocation will most likely be allowed.

6.21. Right to Travel

Courts cannot agree on the interplay of a parent's right to travel and a parent's right to the care and control of his or her child in the context of a best-interest analysis. *See In re Marriage of Graham & Swim*, 121 P.3d 279 (Colo. App. 2005), *overruled by In re Marriage of Ciesluk*, 113 P.3d 135 (Colo. 2005); *LaChapelle v. Mitten*, 607 N.W.2d 151 (Minn. Ct. App. 2000); *Watt v. Watt*, 971 P.2d 608 (Wyo. 1999); *Jaramillo v. Jaramillo*, 823 P.2d 299 (N.M. 1991).

Although courts considering this question have acknowledged that the right to travel is implicated when a child's majority-time parent seeks to remove the child from the state, they disagree on how to balance the right to travel with the rights of the minority-time parent in a best-interest-of-the-child analysis. Three distinct approaches have emerged, which are illustrated by decisions from Wyoming, Minnesota, and New Mexico. *In re Marriage of Ciesluk*, 113 P.3d 135 (Colo. 2005). Wyoming elevates the relocating parent's right to travel over the other, competing interests. *See Watt*, 971 P.2d *at* 615-616. Minnesota disregards the need to balance the parents' competing constitutional rights in favor of elevating the child's welfare to a compelling state interest. *See LaChapelle*, 607 N.W.2d *at* 163-164. New Mexico treats all the competing interests equally, holding that both parents' constitutional interests, as well as the best interests of the child, are best protected if the parents share equally in the burden of showing how the child's best interests will be impacted by the proposed relocation. *See Jaramillo*, 823 P.2d at 307-309.

Some courts have held that removal cases do not implicate a parent's right to travel because removal statutes do not outright prohibit a parent's traveling, but prohibit only a parent's traveling with a child. *See, e.g., Lenz v. Lenz*, 40 S.W.3d 111, 118 n.3 (Tex. App. 2000), *rev'd on other grounds, Lenz v. Lenz*, 79 S.W.3d 10 (Tex. 2002). Colorado has apparently agreed with New Mexico that "a legal rule that operates to chill the exercise of the right, absent a sufficient state interest to do so, is as impermissible as one that bans exercise of the right altogether." *Jaramillo*, 823 P.2d at 306.

MODEL RELOCATION DRAFTING EFFORTS

6.22. American Law Institute (ALI)

The American Law Institute (ALI) Principles reflect "the policy choice that a parent, like any other citizen, should be able to choose his or her place of residence, and that the job of rearing children after divorce should not be made too financially or emotionally burdensome to the parent who has the majority share of custodial responsibility." ALI, Principles of the Law of Family Dissolution, ch. 2, §2.17, cmt. d (2002).

Where physical custody is shared, the best-interest calculus pertaining to removal is appreciably different compared with those situations that involve sole physical custody. ALI, Principles of the Law of Family Dissolution: Analysis and Recommendations, §2.17(1), (4)(c) (2002). Where physical custody is shared, a judge's willingness to elevate one parent's interest in relocating freely with the children is often diminished. Edwin J. Terry et al., *Relocation: Moving Forward, or Moving Backward?* 15 J. Am. Acad. Matrimonial Law. 167, 212-213 (1998).

6.23. American Academy of Matrimonial Lawyers (AAML)

The American Academy of Matrimonial Lawyers (AAML) Model Act has 22 sections and covers notice, procedures for objection, and remedies. It "is meant to serve as a template for those jurisdictions desiring a statutory solution to the relocation quandary." *Perspectives on the Relocation of Children*, 15 J. Am. Acad. Matrimonial Law. 1, 2 (1998).

Among its recommendations, the Model Act identifies seven nonexclusive factors that courts should consider in determining relocation issues: (1) the nature, quality, and extent of involvement, and the duration of the child's relationship with the person proposing to relocate and with the non-relocating person, siblings, and other significant persons in the child's life; (2) the age, developmental stage, and needs of the child, and the likely impact the relocation will have on the child's physical, educational, and emotional development, taking into consideration any special needs of the child; (3) the feasibility of preserving the relationship between the non-relocating person and the child through suitable [visitation] arrangements, considering the logistics and financial circumstances of the parties; (4) the child's preference, taking into consideration the age and maturity of the child; (5) whether there is an established pattern of conduct of the person seeking relocation, either to promote or to thwart the relationship between the child and the non-relocating person; (6) whether the relocation of the child will enhance the general quality of life for both the custodial party seeking the relocation and the child, including but not limited to financial or emotional benefit or educational opportunity; (7) the reasons of each person for seeking or opposing the relocation; and (8) any other factor affecting the best interests of the child. 15 J. Am. Acad. Matrimonial Law. §405 (1998).

SELECTED STATE RELOCATION STANDARDS

6.24. California: Custodial Parent Has Initial Burden

In *In re Marriage of Burgess*, 913 P.2d 473, 480-481 (Cal. 1996), the California Supreme Court modified its approach of requiring a custodial parent to prove that relocation was "necessary" before permitting the move. The court concluded that the necessity of relocating "has little, if any, substantive bearing on the suitability of a parent to retain the role of a custodial parent." *Id.* The court noted that given the fact that both parents may need to secure or retain employment or pursue educational or career opportunities, "it is unrealistic to assume that divorced parents will permanently remain in the same location after dissolution or to exert pressure on them to do so." *Id.* at 480-481.

The court in *In re Marriage of Burgess* held that in making an initial custody decision, if one or both of the parents was planning to move away, "the trial court must take into account the presumptive right of a custodial parent to change the residence of the minor children, so long as the removal would not be prejudicial to their rights or welfare. In considering all the circumstances affecting the 'best interest' of minor children, it may consider any effects of such relocation on their rights or welfare." *Burgess* 913 P.2d at 473. *See Ragghanti v. Reyes*, 20 Cal. Rptr. 3d 522 (Cal. App. 2004). The likely impact of the proposed move on the noncustodial parent's relationship with the children is a relevant factor in determining whether the move would cause detriment to the children. *In re Marriage of Lamusga*, 88 P.3d 81 (Cal. 2004). However, when one parent has sole custody, that parent is not justified in moving simply because he or she has chosen, for any sound good-faith reason, to reside in a different location.

California courts have also observed that a custody decision allowing one parent to move the children out of California necessarily interferes with the other parent's ability to have frequent and continuing contact with them. Such a decision is one of the most serious that a family law court is required to make, and should not be made in haste. *In re Marriage of McGinnis*, 9 Cal. Rptr.

2d 182 (Cal. 1992), *disapproved on other grounds in In re Marriage of Burgess*, 913 P.2d 473 (Cal 1996). The best interests of the children require that competing claims be considered in a calm, dispassionate manner and only after the parties have had an opportunity to be meaningfully heard.

6.25. Connecticut: Legitimate Purpose

The custodial parent seeking permission to relocate outside Connecticut with the child or children has the initial burden of demonstrating, by a preponderance of the evidence, that (1) the relocation is for a legitimate purpose and (2) the proposed relocation is reasonable in light of that purpose. Once the custodial parent makes such a prima facie showing, the burden shifts to the noncustodial parent to prove, by a preponderance of the evidence, that the relocation would not be in the best interests of the child. *Ireland v. Ireland*, 246 Conn. 413, 717 A.2d 676 (1998).

6.26. Florida: Detailed Standards Promulgated in 2006

Florida's legislature promulgated a lengthy, detailed relocation statute that became law in 2006. Fla. Stat. §61.13001 (2006). Among the many new provisions is one defining what constitutes a change of residence. Under the statute, a change of residence address means the relocation of a child to a principal residence more than 50 miles away from his or her principal place of residence at the time of the entry of the last order establishing or modifying the designation of the primary residential parent or the custody of the minor child, unless the move places the principal residence of the minor child less than 50 miles from the nonresidential parent. There are detailed procedures regarding relocation notice, agreements, sanctions, and substantive principles to apply. The statute declares that no presumption shall arise in favor of or against a request to relocate with the child when a primary residential parent seeks to move the child and the move will materially affect the current schedule of contact, access, and time sharing with the non-relocating parent or other person.

The parent or other person wishing to relocate has the burden of proof if an objection is filed and must then initiate a proceeding seeking court permission for relocation. The initial burden is on the parent or person wishing to relocate to prove, by a preponderance of the evidence, that relocation is in the best interest of the child. If that burden of proof is met, the burden shifts to the non-relocating parent or other person to show by a preponderance of the evidence that the proposed relocation is not in the best interest of the child. The statute contains 11 factors a court must consider when making a relocation decision.

6.27. New Jersey

In *Baures v. Lewis*, 770 A.2d 214 (N.J. 2001), the court held that under the New Jersey removal statute, a custodial parent may move with the children as long as the move does not interfere with the best interests of the children or the visitation rights of the noncustodial parent. *Baures*, 770 A.2d at 227. Guided by two previous state Supreme Court cases, *Holder v. Polanski*, 544 A.2d 852 (N.J. 1988), and *Cooper v. Cooper*, 491 A.2d 606 (N.J. 1984), the court clarified the legal standards for removal. The court had previously required that the custodial parent seeking relocation to another state prove a "real advantage" to that parent from the move, but in *Holder* it rejected that requirement as failing to allow custodial parents the same freedom enjoyed by noncustodial parents to seek a better life. *Holder*, 544 A.2d at 856; *see Baures*, 770 A.2d at 227.

The court then established a new two-part test requiring a good-faith reason for the move and proof that the child will not suffer from it. *Holder*, 544 A.2d at 856; *see Baures*, 770 A.2d at 230. In *Baures*, the court listed many factors relevant to proving the two parts, including the reasons for and against the move; comparison of education, health, and leisure opportunities; whether special needs or talents of the children can be accommodated; the effect on extended family relationships; the effect on visitation and communication with the noncustodial parent to maintain a full and continuous relationship with the child; and whether the noncustodial parent has the ability to relocate. *Baures* 770 A.2d at 229-230.

6.28. New York: Full, Detailed Inquiry

In *Tropea v. Tropea*, 87 N.Y.2d 727 (N.Y. 1996), the New York Court of Appeals defined the manner in which relocation cases are to be decided in that state. It rejected various formulas and presumptions that had been suggested by lower appellate courts in the past. It held that each relocation request must be considered on its own merits with due consideration of all the relevant facts and circumstances and with predominant emphasis being placed on what outcome is most likely to serve the best interest of the child. It held that the respective rights of the custodial and noncustodial parents, while still recognized as significant factors, were subservient to the rights and needs of the child. In summarizing its holding, the court noted that "in all cases, the courts should be free to consider and give appropriate weight to all of the factors that may be relevant to the determination. In the end, it is for the court to determine, based on all of the proof, whether it has been established by a preponderance of the evidence that a proposed relocation would serve the child's best interests."

6.29. Pennsylvania: Initial Burden on Custodial Parent

In Pennsylvania, if either party desires to relocate after a custody order has been made, a trial court, on its own motion or upon the motion of either party, may review the existing custody order. *Gruber v. Gruber*, 583 A.2d 434, 440 (1990). When a custodial parent seeks to relocate at a geographical distance, and the noncustodial parent challenges the move, the custodial parent has the initial burden of showing that the move is likely to significantly improve the quality of life for that parent and the children. In addition, each parent has the burden of establishing the integrity of his or her motives in either desiring the move or seeking to prevent it.

A best-interest analysis must incorporate three factors originally outlined in *Gruber v. Gruber*, 583 A.2d 434 (Pa. Super. 1990): (1) The court must assess the potential advantages of the proposed move and the likelihood that the move would substantially improve the quality of life for the custodial parent and the children and is not a momentary whim on the part of the custodial parent. (2) Next, the court must establish the integrity of the motives of both the custodial and the noncustodial parent in either seeking the move or seeking to prevent it. (3) Finally, the court must consider the availability of realistic, substitute visitation arrangements that will adequately foster an ongoing relationship between the child and the noncustodial parent. *Billhime v. Billhime*, 869 A.2d 1031, 1037 (Pa. Super. 2005).

The custodial parent must convince the court that the move is not sought for whimsical or vindictive reasons. Likewise, the noncustodial parent must show that resistance to the move stems from concern for the children and his or her relationship with them. The court must then consider the feasibility of creating substitute visitation arrangements to ensure a continuing, meaningful relationship between the children and the noncustodial parent.

6.30. Texas: Right to Jury Trial

In Texas, a party may demand a jury trial on the issue of primary residence. *Lenz v. Lenz*, 79 S.W.3d 10 (Tex. 2002); *see* Tex. Fam. Code §105.002(c)(1)(D). As a consequence, the analytical framework is different for a reviewing judge, even though much of the evidence will be of the same kind that a judge in another jurisdiction where a jury trial on custody is not permitted might take into account. When reviewing the jury verdict, the court conducts a legal-sufficiency review to determine whether the evidence supports the jury's verdict in favor of removing a residency restriction. Texas courts view the evidence relevant to the best-interest factors in a light that tends to support the jury's verdict. See *Bradford v. Vento*, 48 S.W.3d 749, 754 (Tex. 2001).

6.31. The "New Family" Theory

Several states have accepted and applied the theory that divorce results in the creation of a new family unit, including the custodial parent with sole legal and physical custody of the child. Jurisdictions applying this theory have concluded that what is beneficial to the new family unit as a whole also benefits its individual members. *See, e.g.*, *Rebsamen v. Rebsamen*, 107 S.W.3d 871 (Ark. 2003); *Rosenthal v. Maney*, 745 N.E.2d 350 (Mass. App. Ct. 2001); *Anderson v. Anderson*, 56 S.W.3d 5 (Tenn. Ct. App. 1999); *D'Onofrio v. D'Onofrio*, 365 A.2d 27, 29-30 (N.J. Super. Ct. Ch. Div.), *aff'd*, 365 A.2d 716 (1976) (children belong to a different family unit after a divorce); Joan G. Wexler, *Rethinking the Modification of Child Custody Decrees*, 94 Yale L.J. 757, 808 (1985). The new family unit is entitled to a measure of constitutional protection against unwarranted governmental intrusion, which is similar to that accorded to an intact, two-parent family. *In re Marriage of Mentry*, 190 Cal. Rptr. 843, 848-849 (1983).

Unless a court modifies its custody order, a custodial parent is permitted to make the significant, life-influencing decisions affecting his or her child as long as the parent remains fit to have custody, although the noncustodial parent's interests retain great importance. *Ascuitto v. Farricielli*, 711 A.2d 708 (Conn. 1998) (recognizing importance of familial relationship between noncustodial parent and child in context of parent-child immunity). The child's interests can become so intricately interwoven with the well-being of the new family unit that the determination of the child's best interest requires that the interests of the custodial parent be taken into account. *See, e.g.*, *Mize v. Mize*, 621 So. 2d 417, 419 (Fla. 1993) (it follows that what is good for custodial parent's well-being is good for child's well-being).

EXAMPLES

Example 6-8

Assume that this dispute takes place in a jurisdiction that applies the "new family" theory discussed above. P and D dissolve their relationship. D (mother) is awarded sole legal and physical custody of their two children. Three months after the judgment is entered, D brings a motion to leave the forum state with the children, ages four and seven, and move to another state that is 1,000 miles away. D produces evidence that she has been accepted into law school in the distant state. Since the divorce, the noncustodial father, P, has exercised his visitation rights with the children on Saturday and Sunday of every other week and has seen them every Wednesday evening for two or three hours. It is obvious that P and D are still extremely angry with each other over the divorce. P argues that D is getting revenge by seeking to leave the state with the children because P just married his secretary. D produces evidence that makes it clear she applied and was accepted at the law school 1,000 miles away. She has also produced a plan that outlines how the children will be cared for while she is in law school. D agrees that P may have extended visits with the children in the summer. Most likely, how will a court rule on D's request to relocate?

Explanation

Obviously, one must carefully analyze the problem because of the varying standards states use to resolve this issue. However, a jurisdiction that applies the "new family" theory will most likely allow D to relocate to another state. The "new family" theory is, in reality, a presumption favoring the custodial parent. The party opposing relocation must offer reasonably strong evidence to establish that the relocation is not in the best interest of the child or that the relocation is intended to interfere with visitation. There is little evidence to support such a claim. Furthermore, it is doubtful that many courts would grant P a hearing on the relocation question absent evidence showing endangerment in the papers opposing the move.

JOINT PHYSICAL OR "SHARED" CUSTODY AND RELOCATION REQUESTS

6.32. Overview

When the parties following a divorce have joint physical custody of a child, many courts will view the situation as one in which there is no noncustodial parent. Therefore, when a joint-custody parent opposes relocation, that parent is normally not saddled with any burden to come forward. Conversely, the joint-custody parent desiring to remove the child must first petition the court to modify the residential parent status. The burden of showing that the move is in the best interests of the child remains with the parent seeking the modification. *See, e.g., Mason v. Coleman*, 850 N.E.2d 513 (Mass. 2006); *In re Marriage of Burgess*, 913 P.2d 473, 483 n.12 (Cal. 1996) (when parents have shared joint physical custody, relocation of one of them justifies modification of custody under a best-interest test); *Ayers v. Ayers*, 508 N.W.2d 515, 519 (Minn. 1993) (in shared custody cases, relocation amounts to a modification of the custody award, and thus must be justified by the relocating parent); *cf. Jaramillo v. Jaramillo*, 823 P.2d 299, 309 (N.M. 1991) (when parties share custody equally, neither has the burden of proof in removal matter). The burden normally does not shift to the parent resisting the move to prove that the change would adversely affect the child. *See Stringer v. Vincent*, 411 N.W.2d 474 (Mich. App. 1987); Edwin J. Terry et al., *Relocation: Moving Forward, or Moving Backward?* 15 J. Am. Acad. Matrimonial Law., 167, 212-213 (1998).

Generally, when parents have equal physical custody and one parent decides to move, it is no longer a question of having "permission to move"; the question becomes who should, under the circumstances, receive primary custody of the child. If neither parent has been exercising a significant majority of custodial responsibility for the child, the court will reallocate custodial responsibility based on the best interests of the child, taking into account all relevant factors, including the effects of the relocation on the child.

Example 6-9

Assume that P and D have joint legal and physical custody of child C, with each parent having physical custody for one-half of the week. C is eight years old. Assume that three months after the divorce was final, P filed a motion asking to be granted primary physical custody of C and for permission to relocate to West Virginia with the child. In the motion to relocate, P maintained that as a result of her mother's recent death, she desired to return to her childhood home in West Virginia, to be close to her siblings. P explained that she had inherited a substantial sum of money from her mother, as well as part ownership of her mother's house. Her siblings have agreed to permit her to live in the house, rent free, while she finishes college and earns a teaching license. P explained that her mother's death not only resulted in closer contact with her siblings, but also renewed the importance of this contact. P also explained that she had exhausted her career opportunities as a secretary in the city where she currently lived. She stated that teaching would offer her a career, rather than a "job," and because her hours would mirror the minor child's school schedule, C would no longer need outside day care.

D (father) opposed her motion, arguing that a move to West Virginia offered no actual advantage to the child and would disturb the current, functioning joint custody arrangement. D, in response, asks for sole physical custody of the child. Assume the court has held an evidentiary hearing to address P's motion to relocate. How will the court most likely rule?

Explanation

The court will not, of course, bar P from leaving the state. However, it may well consider giving sole physical custody to D if P moves to West Virginia. It may reason that the best interests of the child are to keep him in as stable an environment as possible — a familiar neighborhood and school system. This is a close issue but one P will most likely lose.

RELOCATING TO A FOREIGN COUNTRY

6.33. Hague Convention

The law governing child custody disputes between the United States and foreign countries is found in the Hague Convention on the Civil Aspects of International Child Abduction, entered into force December 1, 1983, (for the United States July 1, 1988) and the International Child Abduction Remedies Act (ICARA), 42 U.S.C. §11601 *et seq*., which is the statute that implements the Hague Convention and states that its provisions "are in addition to and not in lieu of the provisions of the Convention." 42 U.S.C. §11601(b)(2)(A).

The Hague Convention establishes legal rights and procedures for the prompt return of children who have been "wrongfully removed to or retained in" a nation that is a party to the Convention. Hague Convention, art. 1; 42 U.S.C. §11601(a). The nations that have adopted the Hague Convention have as their purpose "to protect children internationally from the harmful effects of their wrongful removal or retention and to establish procedures to ensure their prompt return to the State of their habitual residence, as well as to secure protection for rights of access." Hague Convention, preamble. The Hague Convention is intended "to preserve the status quo" with respect to child custody and to deter feuding parents from "crossing international boundaries in search of a more sympathetic [custody] court." *Miller v. Miller*, 240 F.3d 392, 398 (4th Cir. 2001). The scope of a court's inquiry under the Hague Convention is limited to the merits of the claim for wrongful removal or retention. *See* 42 U.S.C. §11601(b)(4); Hague Convention, art. 16. Consequently, a court is not to examine the merits of any underlying custody case when determining which country should hear the matter. *See Miller*, 240 F.3d at 398; Hague Convention, art. 19.

ICARA established procedures for implementing the Hague Convention in the United States, and it defined and allocated the burdens of proof for various claims and defenses under it. *See* 42 U.S.C. §11601 *et seq*. ICARA requires that a petitioner under the Hague Convention establish, by a preponderance of the evidence, that the child whose return is sought has been "wrongfully removed or retained within the meaning of the Convention." 42 U.S.C. §11603(e)(1)(A).

When a citizen from a foreign country brings an action in the United States claiming that the matter should not be heard here, the individual petitioner must prove by a preponderance of the evidence (1) that the child was habitually resident in the foreign county at the time the child was retained by the other parent in the United States, (2) that the retention was in breach of the petitioner's custody rights under the laws of the foreign nation, and (3) that the petitioner had been exercising those custody rights at the time of retention. *See Miller*, 240 F.3d at 398; Hague Convention, art. 3.

The party opposing the return of a child may prevail if he or she establishes certain defenses designated by ICARA and available under the Convention. For example, the opposing party might prevail if it is established by clear and convincing evidence (1) that there is a grave risk that returning the child to the foreign country would expose the child to physical or psychological harm or otherwise place him or her in an intolerable situation (Hague Convention, art. 13b), or (2) that the return of the child would not be permitted by the fundamental principles of the United States "relating to the protection of human rights and fundamental freedoms" (Hague Convention, art. 20). The opponent might also prevail if it is established by a preponderance of the evidence that the petitioner "was not actually exercising the custody rights at the time of . . . retention" (Hague Convention, art. 13a) or if it is shown that "the child objects to being returned and has attained an age and degree of maturity at which it is appropriate to take account of [the child's] views." Hague Convention, art. 13, §2.

The distinction between a Hague Convention petition brought pursuant to ICARA and a petition to determine the legal custody of a minor is that a Hague Convention petition affects custody, but it is not a custody determination. *See* Hague Convention, art. 19. The Hague Convention states that courts "shall not decide on the merits of rights of custody until it has been determined that the child is not to be returned under this Convention." Hague Convention, art. 16. The intention and effect of the Hague Convention, then, is to "lend priority to the custody determination hailing from the child's state of habitual residence." *Miller*, 240 F.3d at 399. As a result, a state court of competent jurisdiction may proceed to determine legal custody only when that court or a federal district court first finds that the petitioner cannot prove wrongful removal or retention or when the respondent establishes one of the available affirmative defenses.

Courts disagree on various provision of the Hague Convention, including the definition of "habitual residence." *See, e.g., Humphrey v. Humphrey*, 434 F.3d 243 (4th Cir. 2006) (father required to establish habitual residence by a preponderance of evidence); *Gitter v. Gitter*, 396 F.3d 124 (2d Cir. 2005) (courts must focus on parental intent when deciding habitual residence). Note that cases brought pursuant to ICARA and the Hague Convention are tried to a judge, as neither ICARA nor the Hague Convention provides for trial by jury and the available remedy — return of the child — is equitable in nature. *See Silverman v. Silverman*, 338 F.3d 886 (8th Cir. 2003).

Forty-four countries (including the United States) have joined the Hague Convention on the Civil Aspects of International Child Abduction.

Removing a child from the United States, or retaining a child who has been in the United States outside the United States with intent to obstruct the lawful exercise of parental rights, is a federal felony punishable by up to three years in prison. 18 U.S.C. §1204.

Interstate Custody Struggles: The Uniform Child Custody Jurisdiction Act and the Parental Kidnapping Prevention Act—History, Restrictions, and Requirements

7.1. Introduction

This chapter focuses on the history and development of the Uniform Child Custody Jurisdiction Enforcement Act (UCCJEA) and highlights several of its important features. The act becomes important whenever a dispute erupts over custody of a minor child and the child's parents claim that different states have jurisdiction to decide the issue. All states have adopted some form of the UCCJEA. The chapter also analyzes important features of the Parental Kidnapping Prevention Act (PKPA). The PKPA is a federal statute that preceded the UCCJEA and was intended by the federal government to establish uniformity among the states when dealing with interstate child custody disputes. Both the UCCJEA and PKPA must be considered when a child is involved in an interstate custody dispute.

HISTORY

7.2. Overview

The question of which state has jurisdiction to decide custody of a minor child when the parties involved in the conflict are citizens or residents of different states has been difficult for courts to resolve. Despite repeated efforts, the states have not been able to achieve uniform agreement as to which of two conflicting jurisdictions is better suited to decide the jurisdictional question related to the custody of a minor child. In an effort to remedy the situation, model acts have been proposed with the hope that states would uniformly adopt the language in them and that this would result in a standardized approach to the jurisdiction issue.

The first model act was the Uniform Child Custody Jurisdiction Act (UCCJA), which was promulgated in 1968. In 1980 Congress stepped in and enacted the Parental Kidnapping Prevention Act (PKPA) out of frustration with the inability of states to agree on a uniform approach to conflicting jurisdictional claims. Finally, in 1997, another model act, the Uniform Child Custody Jurisdiction Enforcement Act (UCCJEA), was promulgated in an effort to reconcile the PKPA with the older UCCJA. Today, most jurisdictions have enacted some version of the UCCJEA. However, despite these efforts, areas of unsettled jurisdictional conflict remain among some of the states when parents become locked in an interstate custody struggle.

7.3. Traditional View of Custody Jurisdiction — "Domicile"

The traditional view of custody jurisdiction in the United States was that only a court of the state where a child was domiciled could issue a custody decree. *See* Restatement, Conflict of Laws §§1, 17 (1934). The domicile rule was based on the theory that only the child's domicile state possessed a sufficient relationship with the child to give that state a legitimate interest in determining custody. However, the domicile rule was criticized as rigid and as not focusing on the real issue: the best interests of the child. *See* George W. Strumburg, *The Status of Children in Conflicts of Laws*, 8 U. Chi. L. Rev. 42 (1940); Russell M. Coombs, *Interstate Child Custody: Jurisdiction, Recognition, and Enforcement*, 66 Minn. L. Rev. 711 (1982). In theory, strict application of the domicile rule could leave a state without authority to act in the best interest of a child who was before the forum and in grave need of protection.

7.4. Modification Theory Spawns Unrest

In a decision that generated jurisdictional unrest, the United States Supreme Court held that because a custody decision is modifiable in the state where it was originally entered, the Full Faith and Credit Clause did not prevent modification by other states. *New York ex rel. Halvey v. Halvey*, 330 U.S. 610 (1947). In response to this decision, some state courts began to exercise their custody modification power liberally, which may have encouraged forum shopping among warring parents.

7.5. Personal Jurisdiction and Status

The Court injected another level of unrest into the interstate custody debate in 1953. In *May v. Anderson*, 345 U.S. 528 (1953), a plurality held that in a child custody case, personal service upon a nonresident defendant outside the state whose court had awarded the custody decree was insufficient to confer *in personam* jurisdiction, also holding that a sister state was not bound to accord full faith and credit to that decree. In *May v. Anderson*, the father had obtained an ex parte Wisconsin divorce that granted him custody of his minor children. He then attempted to enforce the decree in Ohio, where the mother now resided. She refused to return the children to Wisconsin while she was exercising visitation with them in Ohio. The Court held that Ohio did not have to recognize the custody order because the order was entered by a Wisconsin court that did not have personal jurisdiction over the mother. The ruling is significant because the parties had agreed in the divorce action that the children were domiciled in Wisconsin.

The decision in *May v. Anderson* has been the subject of considerable academic dialogue. *See, e.g.*, Bridgette M. Bodenheimer & Janet Neeley-Kvarme, *Jurisdiction over Child Custody and Adoption after Shaffer and Kulko*, 12 U.C. Davis L. Rev. 229 (1979); Bridgette M. Bodenheimer, *The Uniform Child Custody Jurisdiction Act: A Legislative Remedy for Children Caught in the Conflict of Laws*, 22 Vand. L. Rev. 1207, 1232-1233 (1969).

Some argue that the better view of jurisdiction in interstate custody disputes is found in Justice Jackson's dissent. Justice Jackson believed that custody should be viewed not with the idea of adjudicating rights in the children, as if they were chattels, but rather with the idea of making the best disposition possible for the welfare of the children. He said that to speak of a court's "cutting off" a mother's right to custody of her children, as if it raised problems similar to those involved in "cutting off" her rights in a plot of ground, is to obliterate these obvious distinctions. Justice Jackson observed that personal jurisdiction of all parties to be affected by a proceeding is indeed highly desirable, to make certain that the parties have had valid notice and opportunity to be heard. "But the assumption that it overrides all other considerations and in its absence a state is constitutionally impotent to resolve questions of custody flies in the face of our own cases." *Id.* at 541.

Justice Frankfurter, who concurred, felt that although Ohio was not required to give full faith and credit to the Wisconsin order, the Due Process

Clause did not prohibit Ohio from recognizing it "as a matter of local law" or comity. *Id.* at 535-536. The Restatement (Second) of Conflict of Laws seems to agree with the Frankfurter interpretation of the law. "Under this view, a state may, as a matter of local law, recognize the custody disposition made by another state, regardless of lack of personal jurisdiction." Bodenheimer & Neeley-Kvarme, *supra* at 251.

The *May* decision has also been explained as a case involving a lack of personal jurisdiction because Wisconsin did not have language in its long-arm statute authorizing extraterritorial service of process over the mother, who was served with process in Ohio. Most states have now adopted long-arm statutes with specific language that makes them applicable to cases growing out of domestic difficulties. These statutes are given their intended effect. *See Mitchim v. Mitchim*, 518 S.W.2d 362 (Tex. 1975).

Several state courts considering interstate custody disputes in which personal jurisdiction over one of the parties is absent have rejected the plurality view of personal jurisdiction found in *May v. Anderson*. Instead, they have seized upon a "status" theory, which allows a court to make a custody decision if the state where the proceeding is being held has the most significant connections with the child and the child's family at the time of the hearing. *See Burton v. Bishop*, 269 S.E.2d 417 (Ga. 1980); *Yearta v. Scroggins*, 268 S.E.2d 151, 153 (Ga. 1980); *McAtee v. McAtee*, 323 S.E.2d 611, 616-617 (W. Va. 1984); *Hart v. Hart*, 695 P.2d 1285 (Kan. 1985); *Genoe v. Genoe*, 500 A.2d 3, 8 (N.J. Super. Ct. App. Div. 1985); *In re Marriage of O'Connor*, 690 P.2d 1095, 1097 (Or. Ct. App. 1984); *In re Marriage of Hudson*, 434 N.E.2d 107, 117-118 (Ind. Ct. App. 1982); *McArthur v. Superior Court*, 1 Cal. Rptr. 2d 296 (Cal. App. 6 Dist. 1991).

EXAMPLES

Example 7-1

Assume that P and D were married and living in Iowa. After five years of marriage, the relationship broke down, and D left Iowa and established his domicile in California. The children remained with P in Iowa. A year later, P brings a divorce action in Iowa. D ignores the matter and makes no appearance in Iowa in response to a summons and dissolution petition served on him in California. P has asked in her legal papers for sole physical and legal custody of the children. In its default judgment, the Iowa court awards sole physical and legal custody of the parties' children to P, observing that the children are domiciled in that state with P. A few months later, after the children visit with D in California, D refuses to return them to P in Iowa. D then brings an action in California asking that he be granted sole legal and physical custody of the children. P argues that only Iowa may resolve this issue. How might the outcome of the California action differ, depending on which of the theories previously discussed the court may choose to apply?

Explanation

First, if the court applies the traditional domicile rule, it will rule that it lacks jurisdiction to litigate the issue because the children are domiciled in Iowa. Second, even if California has a long-arm statute covering domestic matters, it will most likely find that the mother does not have sufficient contacts with California to satisfy constitutional requirements. (Review the jurisdiction chapter if you have trouble with this point.) Third, should the court strictly follow the plurality view in *May v. Anderson*, it will most likely refuse to enforce the Iowa ruling on the theory that Iowa lost personal jurisdiction over D before the divorce action was initiated, when D became a citizen of California. It will reason that without personal jurisdiction over both parties, the Iowa court was without power to enter an enforceable judgment regarding custody outside its borders. Fourth, the court might apply the "status" theory and consider the custody request because D and the children are within California and before the court. Under this theory, a state may alter a child's custody status without having jurisdiction over both parties if at the time of the hearing it has the most significant connections with the child and the child's family. This theory suggests that "status" (custody) implies more than the state's concern with the relationship of the parties. It encompasses the right and obligation of the state in its *parens patriae* role to consider the welfare of the child subject to its jurisdiction and to make a determination that is in the best interests of the child. *In re Marriage of Leonard*, 175 Cal. Rptr. 903 (Ct. App. 1981). A fifth approach is that espoused by Justice Frankfurter. Application of this theory would result in California, as a matter of local law, recognizing the Iowa custody disposition, regardless of a lack of personal jurisdiction over D.

UNIFORM CHILD CUSTODY JURISDICTION ACT (UCCJA)

7.6. Overview

Because of the inability of states to cooperate in interstate custody matters, an initial effort to create a uniform system to resolve these disputes was launched in 1968, when the National Conference of Commissioners on Uniform State Laws created a model act that it labeled the UCCJA. 9 U.L.A. (Part 1A) 261 (1998). The model act had several purposes: First, it sought to avoid jurisdictional competition and conflict among courts of different states in matters of child custody and to promote cooperation among the courts in matters of child custody. Second, by promoting cooperation among the courts of different states, the Act sought to achieve a custody decree rendered in the state best suited to determine the best interests of the child. Third, the Act was aimed at deterring abductions and other unilateral removals of children undertaken by parents to obtain favorable custody awards.

The UCCJA was subsequently adopted by all 50 states; however, the versions promulgated by legislatures were not identical. Because of the dissimilarities, tension among the states developed over the goal of achieving stability of custody decrees and providing a system with sufficient flexibility to accommodate the best interests of the child. The Oregon Supreme Court critically characterized the UCCJA as "a schizophrenic attempt to bring about an orderly system of decision and at the same time to protect the best interests of the children who may be immediately before the court." *In re Marriage of Settle*, 556 P.2d 962, 968 (Or. 1976), *overruled*, *Matter of Custody of Russ*, 620 P.2d 353 (Or. 1981). It became clear after a number of years that the initial effort to achieve uniformity had fallen far short of the mark.

FEDERAL PARENTAL KIDNAPPING PREVENTION ACT (PKPA)

7.7. Overview

Although the UCCJA was promulgated to provide guidance and uniformity among the states in child custody disputes, state legislatures were not uniform in their statutory adoptions. The result was that noncustodial parents sometimes exploited the situation by forcibly taking children from the state issuing the custody decree to another state with less stringent jurisdictional requirements, or by refusing to return the children to the custodial parent following visitation. The noncustodial parent would then turn to the courts of his or her state and seek to obtain a favorable custody ruling.

In an effort to discourage interstate forum shopping and to allocate powers and duties between courts of different states, in 1980 Congress enacted the PKPA, 28 U.S.C. §1738A (1988). *See* Russell M. Coombs, *Progress Under the PKPA*, 6 J. Am. Acad. Matrim. Law. 59 (1990). Despite its title, the Act is not limited to cases involving parental kidnapping but applies broadly to civil interstate custody disputes. *See* Anne B. Goldstein, *Tragedy of the Interstate Child, A Critical Reexamination of the Uniform Child Custody Jurisdiction Act and the Parental Kidnapping Prevention Act*, 25 U.C. Davis L. Rev. 845 (Summer 1992). Unlike the UCCJA, the PKPA prioritizes the bases of jurisdiction. It gives priority to the "home state" of the child. It also provides that once a state has exercised jurisdiction, the initial decree-granting state retains exclusive continuing jurisdiction if it remains the residence of the children or any contestant.

7.8. PKPA Application and Limitations

The effect of sections 1738A(d) and 1738A(f) of the PKPA is to limit custody jurisdiction to the first state to properly enter a custody order, as long as two sets of requirements are met. 28 U.S.C. §1738A(d)(f) (1998). First, the Act establishes a federal standard for continuing exclusive custody jurisdiction in the state that initially possessed jurisdiction over the parties at the time the custody order was entered (according to criteria in the Act).

Second, the Act incorporates a state law inquiry. To retain exclusive responsibility for modifying its prior order, the first state must still have custody jurisdiction as a matter of its own custody law. However, even if the federal and state criteria for continuing jurisdiction are met, the first state can, if it decides to do so, relinquish jurisdiction in favor of a court better situated to assess the child's needs.

In addition to sorting out the civil jurisdictional issues between states, the Act contains criminal provisions. For example, persons who "snatch" children may be criminally prosecuted under the Act. *See* 28 U.S.C. §1738A (1988). In child snatching cases, the Act also provides for a federal warrant and permits the intervention of the Federal Bureau of Investigation.

The Supreme Court in *Thompson v. Thompson*, 484 U.S. 174 (1988), declared that under the provisions of the PKPA, once a state properly exercises jurisdiction, other states must give full faith and credit to the determination and no other state may exercise concurrent jurisdiction, even if it would be entitled to under its own laws. The Court stated that the chief aim of Congress in enacting the Law was to extend the Full Faith and Credit Clause to custody determinations.

EXAMPLES

Example 7-2

Assume that P and D are divorced in state X at a time when state X has personal jurisdiction over both parties. P is awarded sole physical and legal custody of child C. Following the divorce, D moves to state Y, and P and C remain in state X. Assume that a year after the divorce, D becomes very concerned about the care and treatment afforded child C. During one of the periods that child C is visiting D in state Y, D brings an action in a state Y family court seeking to modify the custody decree in state X. P asks the court to dismiss the action in state Y on the grounds that only state X has jurisdiction in this matter. Most likely, how will a court rule?

Explanation

A court will most likely rule in favor of P. Here, state X has retained jurisdiction under its own laws. State X possessed initial custody jurisdiction when it entered its first order, and it has remained the residence of C and P. A custody modification action must be brought in state X, unless state X declines to exercise jurisdiction, which in this hypothetical is unlikely. *See Matthews v. Riley*, 649 A.2d 231 (Vt. 1994).

7.9. Continuing Jurisdiction — Application

It is useful to examine more closely the concept of "continuing jurisdiction" under the PKPA. Under the Act, the court asked to modify an existing custody order determines whether the rendering court has continuing jurisdiction under the law of the rendering state. *See Cann v. Howard*, 850 S.W.2d 57, 60 (Ky. Ct. App. 1993); *Pierce v. Pierce*, 197 Mont. 16, 640 P.2d 899, 903 (Mont. 1982).

In determining continuing jurisdiction under section 1738A(d), the Act does not mandate a home state preference. Once a court acquires jurisdiction under the PKPA, whether it retains jurisdiction is wholly a matter of state law and the residence of one contestant. 28 U.S.C. §1738A(d); *see* §1738A(c)(2)(E) (determinations made by courts with continuing jurisdiction are consistent with PKPA and are entitled to interstate recognition and enforcement). The Act "does not affect the discretion of a state to limit its own continuing jurisdiction. The statute only curtails the freedom of another state to modify the decree for the period of time the rendering state's jurisdiction continues under its own law." Russell M. Coombs, *Interstate Child Custody: Jurisdiction, Recognition, and Enforcement*, 66 Minn. L. Rev. 711, 852 (1982). The possibility of continuing jurisdiction beyond the home state discourages parties from relocating to reestablish a home state only for the purpose of modifying an unfavorable custody arrangement. In providing for continuing jurisdiction, the PKPA fosters a stable home environment and family relationships for a child, promotes "negotiated settlement of custody disputes, and facilitates visitation between a child and the other noncustodial parent." Matthews, *supra* at 239.

7.10. Private Right of Action

Prior to 1988, several courts of appeal had concluded that the PKPA gave warring parents in different states an implied cause of action in federal court, where their custody contest could be resolved. *See, e.g., Meade v. Meade*, 812 F.2d 1473 (4th Cir. 1987). In *Thompson v. Thompson*, 484 U.S. 174 (1988), the Court addressed the question of whether the lower courts were properly interpreting the language of the PKPA so as to provide this private right of action. The Court held that the Act did not create an implied private right of relief in federal court to determine which of two conflicting state custody decrees is valid. It reasoned that the statutory language of the PKPA and its legislative history both indicated that Congress had not intended to create a new cause of action and did not intend federal courts to "play an enforcement role" in custody disputes. *Id.* at 184.

UNIFORM CHILD CUSTODY JURISDICTION AND ENFORCEMENT ACT (UCCJEA) IS PROMULGATED

7.11. Overview

In 1997, 17 years after Congress enacted the PKPA, another effort to solidify a uniform approach among the states regarding interstate custody disputes was launched: the National Conference of Commissioners on Uniform State Laws promulgated the Uniform Child Custody Jurisdiction Enforcement Act (UCCJEA), 9 U.L.A. (Part 1A) 649 (1997). The goal was to reconcile differences between the UCCJA found in all states and the PKPA. Since the release by the commissioners of the model UCCJEA, some version of it has been adopted in all jurisdictions.

The general objectives of the UCCJEA remain the same as those found in the UCCJA, including the goal to address problems associated with the growing number of custody disputes between geographically separated parents. *See Phillips v. Beaber*, 995 S.W.2d 655, 659 & n.2 (Tex. 1999). Like its predecessor, the UCCJEA is concerned with the refusal of some courts to give finality to custody decrees issued by other states, and it seeks to discourage the use of the interstate system for continuing controversies over child custody. It also is intended to deter the abduction of children.

Unlike the UCCJA, the UCCJEA prioritizes among the four bases of jurisdiction and follows the PKPA by giving priority to the child's home state. It also restricts the use of emergency jurisdiction to the issuance of temporary orders. A court may exercise emergency jurisdiction to protect a child, the child's siblings, or the child's parents. *See* Joan Zorza, *The UCCJEA: What Is It and How Does It Affect Battered Women in Child-Custody Disputes*, 27 Fordham Urb. L.J. 909, 917 (2000). The UCCJEA follows the PKPA in that a modification action can be brought only in the state that made the initial custody determination so long as a child or parent involved in the original custody ruling remains in that state.

7.12. Scope

There are four areas where the UCCJEA may play an important role in the outcome of an interstate custody dispute: (1) in initial child custody determinations; (2) when continuing jurisdiction exists because the court originally possessed personal jurisdiction over the parties to the action; (3) when a modification motion is brought to change an existing custody determination; and (4) in situations where an emergency exists and a court must act to protect the child.

In general, the UCCJEA applies to the following: custody, modification of custody, visitation disputes that arise in divorce and separation proceedings, domestic violence matters, and paternity disputes. It may also apply to neglect, dependency, guardianship, termination of parental rights, and grandparental visitation. It does not apply to adoption proceedings. *See* UCCJEA prefatory note, §4, 9 U.L.A. (Part 1A) 649 (1997).

7.13. Subject Matter Jurisdiction — Waiver

Adjudication under the UCCJEA requires that a court possess subject matter jurisdiction. Subject matter jurisdiction cannot be conferred by waiver, consent, or estoppel. *See In re Marriage of Arnold and Cully*, 222 Cal. App. 3d 499, 504 (1990). Therefore, the jurisdictional requirements of the UCCJEA must be satisfied whenever a court makes a custody determination.

7.14. Exclusive Continuing Jurisdiction

Continuing jurisdiction was not specifically addressed in the UCCJA. Its absence caused considerable confusion, particularly because the PKPA, in section 1738(d), required other states to give full faith and credit to custody determinations made by the original decree state, pursuant to the decree state's continuing jurisdiction, so long as that state has jurisdiction under its own law and remains the residence of the child or any contestant.

However, section 2 of the UCCJEA provides the rules of continuing jurisdiction and establishes a jurisdictional hierarchy to provide guidance to courts deciding child custody and visitation cases. At the top of the hierarchy is the court that possesses exclusive continuing jurisdiction. This is the most preferred jurisdictional basis and is applied if it is available, unless the court that has the preferred jurisdictional basis declines to exercise jurisdiction.

Once a court makes an initial custody determination consistent with the UCCJEA, that court is viewed as retaining exclusive continuing jurisdiction over the matter unless neither the child nor at least one parent or person acting as a parent has a significant connection with the state originally issuing the order and substantial evidence in that state is no longer available concerning the child. In general, the state issuing the original decree continues to have jurisdiction to decide a custody dispute regardless of the length of the absence of the child and the other parent from the jurisdiction.

If a court has entered a valid custody order and one of the parties or the child continues to live in the state, that court has the exclusive right to decide if the order should be modified. The court with exclusive continuing jurisdiction has a right of first refusal. Courts of other states may not modify an order (assuming a parent or child continues to live in the state that issued an order) unless the court that issued the order gives permission for another state to decide the issue.

Example 7-3

Assume P and D divorce in state X, and P is awarded sole legal and physical custody of P and D's minor child. P leaves state X with the child and resides in California for one year. P brings an action in California to modify D's visitation with the minor child. D has never visited California. D argues that under the UCCJEA, the action can only be brought in state X, where D continues to reside. P argues that because she and the child are before the court, it can alter the status of the original custody order. How will a judge most likely rule?

Explanation

A trial judge most likely will agree that the matter cannot be heard in California. A court other than the issuing court may modify a custody determination only if the issuing court determines that it no longer has exclusive continuing jurisdiction. Here, one of the parties continues to live in state X, the state that issued the original custody order. State X does not appear to have lost jurisdiction or to have given it up. The ruling is also consistent with PKPA.

7.15. Home State Jurisdiction

One of the measures used by the UCCJEA to resolve jurisdictional disputes when considering an initial custody request is to determine whether the forum is the home state of the child. Home state is defined as the state where the child lived with a parent or a person acting as a parent for at least six consecutive months immediately before commencement of the proceeding. If the child is less than six months old, the home state is the state in which the child lived from birth. The definition of "home state" in the UCCJEA is identical to the definition found in the PKPA. UCCJEA §102(7), 9 U.L.A. (Part 1A) 133 (1997); 28 U.S.C. §1738A(b)(4) (1994).

A court has jurisdiction to make an initial child custody determination if the state is the home state of the child on the date the proceeding is commenced. It also has such jurisdiction if the child no longer lives there, but the state was the home state of the child within six months before the proceeding commenced, and a parent or person acting as a parent continues to live in the state. A temporary absence from the forum state does not change the application of "home state" as found in the UCCJEA. In situations in which a parent has improperly removed a child from the home state, the home state may retain jurisdiction beyond six months.

7.16. No "Home State"

If there is no home state, or the home state court declines to exercise jurisdiction, a court of another state may assume jurisdiction if it qualifies as one with "significant connections" to the action. UCCJEA §201(a)(2), 9 U.L.A. (Part 1A) 144 (1997).

7.17. Emergency Jurisdiction

A state court may assume temporary jurisdiction over a custody dispute if the child is present in the state and it is necessary to protect the child because he or she is subjected to or threatened with mistreatment or abuse. A trial court enjoys broad discretion in issuing orders for immediate protection of a child. UCCJEA §204 cmt., 9 U.L.A. (Part 1A) 677 (1997) (states' duties to recognize, enforce, and not modify custody determinations of other states do not take precedence over the need to protect child). *See Garza v. Harney*, 726 S.W.2d 198, 202 (Tex. Ct. App. 1987). States have a *parens patriae* duty to children within their borders, and the possibility that allegations of immediate harm might be true is generally sufficient for a court to assume temporary emergency jurisdiction in the best interests of the child under the UCCJEA. *In re Nada R.*, 108 Cal. Rptr. 2d 493, 500 (Ct. App. 2001); *Hache v. Riley*, 451 A.2d 971, 975 (N.J. Super. Ct. Ch. Div. 1982).

Any order issued under emergency circumstances must be temporary in nature. It must specify a period that the court considers adequate to obtain an order from the state with jurisdiction. The temporary order remains in effect only until proper steps are taken in the original forum state to adequately protect the children or until the specified period expires.

Once a court assumes temporary emergency jurisdiction, it has a duty to communicate with the other state that has asserted custody jurisdiction and should retain a record of those communications. This mandatory duty of cooperation between the courts of different states is a hallmark of the UCCJEA, and the cooperation is intended to lead to an informed decision on custody. One of the reasons for consulting with the other state's court is to determine the duration of the temporary order. *In re C.T.*, 121 Cal. Rptr. 2d 897, 906 (Ct. App. 2002); *see also* Patricia M. Hoff, *The ABC's of the UCCJEA: Interstate Child-Custody Practice Under the New Act*, 32 Fam. L.Q. 267, 284 (1998).

Temporary emergency jurisdiction is reserved for extraordinary circumstances, and the trial court's assumption of temporary emergency jurisdiction does not include jurisdiction to modify the original court's child custody determination. UCCJEA §204 cmt., 9 U.L.A. (Part 1A) 677 (1997); *see Abderholden v. Morizot*, 856 S.W.2d 829, 834 (Tex. Ct. App. 1993) (holding that exercise of emergency jurisdiction does not confer authority to make permanent custody disposition or modify custody decree of court with jurisdiction). A court's exercise of emergency jurisdiction is temporary in nature and may not be used as a vehicle to attain modification jurisdiction for an ongoing, indefinite period of time.

EXAMPLES

Example 7-4

Assume that in a paternity action, the Texas trial judge awarded P (the father) custody of the minor child C who was born to D and P. C resided with P at P's parents' home in Texas. D made an unannounced visit to P's home and abducted C. P tried to locate D and the minor child C, who had moved to North Carolina, but he was unsuccessful.

Several months after D abducted C, a North Carolina County Department of Social Services (DSS) filed a petition alleging C to be a neglected and dependent juvenile. The petition asserted that she was not receiving proper care, supervision, or discipline from her parent, guardian, custodian, or caretaker; that she had been abandoned; and that she lived in an environment injurious to her welfare. Although the North Carolina trial judge knew of the Texas order giving P custody, she made no effort to contact the Texas court. At an adjudication hearing, the court found C to be a neglected and dependent juvenile and placed her in DSS custody. P, who eventually learned of the proceeding, filed an appeal and argued that the trial court should have granted full faith and credit to the Texas order and awarded him custody of C. How will an appellate court most likely rule, and of what relevance are the UCCJEA's emergency provisions to the resolution of this issue?

Explanation

The trial court's decision will most likely be reversed. The order finding C to be a neglected and dependent juvenile and placing her in custody of the county department of social services violated the emergency jurisdiction provisions of UCCJEA. The reasoning is that the order does not appear to be temporary, and although the North Carolina judge knew about the prior Texas custody decree, there was no effort to immediately contact the Texas court to determine that court's willingness to assume jurisdiction.

Example 7-5

Assume that P and D divorced in Illinois, and a court there awarded sole legal and physical custody of child C to D. Both parents were before the court when it issued the order. P subsequently moved to Pennsylvania. Also assume that about ten years following the entry of the divorce judgment, C called P claiming that her new stepparent was abusing and mistreating her. P immediately sought an emergency order under the UCCJEA in Pennsylvania. P argued that Pennsylvania has jurisdiction to issue an emergency order regardless of whether the child is present in the state. How will a court most likely rule?

Explanation

A Pennsylvania court will most likely reject P's request. Section 204 of the UCCJEA codifies and clarifies several aspects of what has become common practice in emergency jurisdiction cases under the UCCJEA and PKPA. First, a court may take jurisdiction to protect a child even though it can claim neither home state nor significant connection jurisdiction. Second, the duties of states to recognize, enforce, and not modify a custody determination of another state do not take precedence over the need to enter a temporary emergency order to protect the child. However, this section of the UCCJEA must be read in context with the federal PKPA. The PKPA states a custody determination can be made by a state if it has jurisdiction under state law and the child is physically present in such state and if (1) the child has been abandoned or (2) it is necessary in an emergency to protect the child because he has been subjected to or threatened with mistreatment or abuse. 28 U.S.C. §1738A(c)(2)(C) (1994). This language is more explicit than the UCCJEA in defining that presence, as well as an additional emergency situation, is required. When the federal PKPA precludes exercise of UCCJEA jurisdiction, state courts "must give preemptive effect to the federal enactment." *See McLain v. McLain*, 569 N.W.2d 219, 224

(Minn. Ct. App. 1997). Because Pennsylvania meets none of the requirements for exercise of jurisdiction under either the UCCJEA or the PKPA, it is preempted from assuming jurisdiction. The action must be brought in Illinois.

7.18. International Application of UCCJEA and Related Laws

International abduction of children by parents is a serious problem, and the UCCJEA has attempted, at least in part, to deal with it. Under the UCCJEA, another country is treated as if it were a state of the United States for purposes of applying Articles 1 and 2 of the Act. The Act provides that custody determinations of other countries will be enforced if the facts of the case indicate that jurisdiction was in substantial compliance with the requirements of the act. However, at least one jurisdiction has said that certain provisions of the UCCJEA do not apply to international custody disputes. *See, e.g., Temlock v. Temlock*, 898 A.2d 209 (Conn. 2006) (although Connecticut adopted the provisions set forth in §§105(b) and (c) of the Model Act that address foreign judgments, it chose not to treat foreign countries as states for purposes of other provisions, including its *forum non conveniens* provision, by excluding §105(a) of the Model Act).

Congress addressed international child abduction in 1993 when it promulgated the International Parental Kidnapping Act (IPKA), 18 U.S.C. §1204 (2006). The Act imposes criminal penalties on parents who illegally abduct children. For example, the Act makes it a federal felony for a parent to wrongfully remove or retain a child outside the United States. Defenses to the criminal action include the following: (1) The defendant was granted custody or visitation pursuant to the UCCJEA. (2) The defendant is fleeing from domestic violence. (3) The defendant was unable to return a child to the custodial parent because of circumstances beyond his or her control and the defendant made reasonable attempts to notify the other parent.

Another area of law relevant to international child abduction is the Hague Convention on the Civil Aspects of International Abduction. The United States began implementing the Convention in 1980 when Congress promulgated the International Child Abduction Remedies Act (ICARA), 42 U.S.C. §§11601-11610 (2006). The Hague Convention is intended to secure the return of children who are wrongfully removed from or retained in a signatory state and to return them to the country of their habitual residence, which must be another contracting nation, where the merits of the custody dispute can be decided.

7. Interstate Custody Struggles

Courts have disagreed on various provisions of the Hague Convention, including the definition of "habitual residence." *See, e.g.*, *Humphrey v. Humphrey*, 434 F.3d 243 (4th Cir. 2006) (father required to establish habitual residence by a preponderance); *Gitter v. Gitter*, 396 F.3d 124 (2d Cir. 2005) (courts must focus on parents' intent when deciding habitual residence).

CHAPTER 8

Visitation and Parenting Time

8.1. Introduction

When a divorce takes place, children's relationships with caring adults are restructured. Some of these relationships, such as those between parents and children, are legally protected and enforced. Other relationships, including those with grandparents and stepparents, may only be legally recognized under certain circumstances and conditions.

In all but the most extreme cases, continuing and regular contact with both parents will speed the child's adjustment to his or her new family situation. If parents share joint physical custody and create a parenting plan, they are likely to spend considerable effort scheduling time for the child to spend with each parent. Alternatively, if one parent has sole physical custody, the noncustodial parent has traditionally been considered the "visiting" parent and is awarded "visitation rights" or "parenting time."

As sex roles have become less rigid, society has increasingly recognized the contribution of both parents in child rearing. As a result, family law professionals have questioned the designation of one parent as a "noncustodial visitor" after divorce. Consequently, some jurisdictions no longer use the term *visitation* and instead have replaced it with the term *parenting time*. This shift in terminology recognizes that from the child's point of view, even though living arrangements change with divorce, both former spouses remain parents throughout the child's life. The term *parenting time* is broad enough to encompass cases of joint physical custody (parents share roughly equal amounts of parenting time) as well as cases of sole physical custody (one parent exercises more parenting time). This approach is also consistent with the approach taken in mediation, during which parents are encouraged to focus on the needs of the children instead of becoming fixated on winning a custody label.

Many children benefit from continuing relationships with adults other than their natural parents. Interested people such as grandparents and step-parents have increasingly turned to the courts to assure that their relationships with children will continue. Legislatures and courts struggle with this area, recognizing some relationships but not others.

MODEL ACTS

8.2. Uniform Marriage and Divorce Act: Reasonable Visitation

Section 407(a) of the Uniform Marriage and Divorce Act (UMDA) provides that a "parent not granted custody of the child is entitled to reasonable visitation rights unless the court finds, after a hearing, that visitation would endanger seriously the child's physical, mental, moral, or emotional health."

In practice, the "reasonable visitation" standard requires parents to make visitation arrangements on their own after the divorce. Although some parents are able to reach amicable agreements, many find this to be a source of serious and ongoing conflict. These couples frequently seek post-decree assistance from the court in defining "reasonable" and "unreasonable." Consequently, courts and legislatures often require specific and detailed visitation orders in divorce decrees. In addition to scheduling hours for visitation, final orders should address issues such as transportation, holidays, and vacations.

In a situation in which one parent is granted sole physical custody of the children, the visiting parent is typically awarded visitation every other weekend, one evening during the week, alternating holidays, and several weeks during the summer.

EXAMPLES

Example 8-1

Assume that P and D divorced and agreed that D would have physical custody of the children because P traveled extensively for work — she was out of the country for six to eight weeks at a time and then returned home for two to four weeks. P was granted "reasonable" visitation with the two children. One child, X, was 16 years old, and another child, Y, was 3 years old. The couple experienced continued difficulty working out a visitation arrangement. P claimed that she was entitled to have the children stay with her during the two to four weeks that she was in the United States. D argued that such an arrangement would amount to joint physical custody and would undermine his award of sole physical custody. He also argued that long blocks of visitation would be disruptive to the children. If the couple chose not to mediate, what would a judge be likely to decide?

EXPLANATIONS

Explanation

The court is being called upon to interpret and enforce the divorce decree entitling P to reasonable visitation. Because of P's unusual work schedule, she is not able to visit with the children every other weekend or have midweek face-to-face contact. The court will look at the best interests of the children in determining what visitation is reasonable under the circumstances However, this situation is complicated by the fact that one child is 3 and one child is 16. The 3-year-old likely needs more frequent physical contact with P, whereas the 16-year-old can supplement face-to-face time with e-mail and phone conversations. Consequently, what is reasonable for one child may not be reasonable for the other. The court might order that both children spend every weekend with P when she is in town and that the 3-year-old spend an additional overnight during the week with P.

8.3. American Law Institute

The American Law Institute (ALI) replaces the traditional use of *custody* and *visitation* with the term *custodial responsibility*. ALI, Principles of the Law of Family Dissolution: Analysis and Recommendations §2.03(3) (2002). Comment (e) to §2.03 explains,

> While any beneficial effects of this shift in terminology on people's perceptions of parenthood cannot be measured, it is assumed that the unified concept of custodial responsibility has some potential to strengthen the usual expectation that both parents have responsibility regardless of the proportion of time each spends with the child, and that neither parent is a mere "visitor."

Section 2.11 limits allocation of responsibility to parents who have abused, neglected, or abandoned a child; inflicted domestic violence; abused drugs and alcohol; and interfered with the other parent's access without cause. Limitations imposed can include reduction or limitation of custodial responsibility; supervision of custodial time; exchange of a child through an intermediary; restraints on communication and proximity; abstinence from prior drug and alcohol use; denial of overnight custodial responsibility;

restrictions on persons present; requiring posting of bond; and completion of a treatment program.

STANDARDS FOR DENYING OR LIMITING VISITATION

8.4. Court Denial of Parenting Time or Visitation

Because parents have a constitutional right to have contact with their children, courts will only deny visitation in the most extreme and egregious cases. The burden is on the parent contesting the visitation to show that the child would be seriously endangered by contact with the other parent. *See Sterbling v. Sterbling*, 519 N.E.2d 673 (Ohio Ct. App. 1987). For example, in *Nelson v. Jones*, 781 P.2d 964 (Alaska 1989), even supervised visitation was denied to a father guilty of sexual abuse. Similarly, an incarcerated parent may be denied visitation under some circumstances. In *Harmon v. Harmon*, 943 P.2d 599 (Okla. 1997), the court delineated factors to be considered in deciding whether a father in a correctional facility had visitation rights. These factors included the age of the child, the distance to be traveled, the physical and emotional effect on the child, whether the parent had exhibited genuine interest in the child, past history of contact, and the nature of the crime committed.

8.5. Restrictions on Parenting Time or Visitation

Courts rarely deny a parent the right to see a child. However, with the proper showing, courts will place restrictions on the exercise of visitation. For example, a parent might only be able to have contact with a child in a supervised setting (either formally supervised by professional staff at a visitation center or supervised more informally by friends or family), or a parent may be denied overnight contact.

In order to place restrictions on a parent's right to visit, the court must find that "visitation would endanger seriously the child's physical, mental, moral, or emotional health." *See* UMDA §407. Proof beyond mere allegations is required.

Research shows that when supervised visitation at visitation centers has been ordered, it has usually been in the cases of children who previously were severely traumatized. These children have typically been abused or neglected, have witnessed domestic violence, have lived with a mentally ill parent, or have been abducted. *See* Janet R. Johnston & Robert B. Straus, *Traumatized Children in Supervised Visitation: What Do They Need?*, 37 Fam. & Conciliation Cts. Rev. 135 (1999).

8.6. Child Abuse and Domestic Violence

When a parent has committed child abuse or is guilty of domestic violence, the other parent may be understandably frustrated by the court's insistence on allowing even limited visitation. In such circumstances, if visitation is going to occur, the parent and child are best protected if the court requires that the visitation be formally supervised. *See Mallouf v. Saliba*, 766 N.E.2d 552 (Mass. App. Ct. 2002); *Hollingsworth v. Semerad*, 799 So. 2d 658 (La. Ct. App. 2001). *But see Sevland v. Sevland*, 646 N.W.2d 689 (N.D. 2002) (allowing unsupervised visitation in a case involving domestic violence).

8.7. Alcohol and Substance Abuse

Supervised visitation may be required if the visiting parent's alcohol or drug use makes visitation unsafe for the child. *See Allen v. Allen*, 787 So. 2d 215 (Fla. Dist. Ct. App. 2001) (requiring supervision because of the mother's alcohol use); *see also Fine v. Fine*, 626 N.W.2d 526 (Neb. 2001) (requiring supervised visitation because of the parent's mental illness, history of domestic violence, and substance abuse); *White v. Nason*, 874 A.2d 891 (Me. 2005) (contempt action against father for violation of prohibition on substance use while children were in his care).

EXAMPLES

Example 8-2

Assume that P (mother) and D (father) are getting divorced. They have one child, X. D has been arrested several times for alcohol- and drug-related offenses, but he does not believe that he has a substance abuse problem. D argues that he neither drinks nor uses drugs in the presence of the child and that he should be entitled to spend unrestricted time with X. P asserts that D's drinking and drug use are out of control and that X would be in danger spending time alone with D. The trial court orders D to abstain entirely from alcohol and drug use at all times, whether he is with X or not. Will this restriction be upheld on appeal?

Explanation

Most likely, a court would order that visitation with X take place in a supervised setting so that D could be prevented from seeing the child if D is under the influence. By complying with the order for supervised visitation and consistently appearing for visitation in a sober state, D could establish his trustworthiness and at some point petition the court to be allowed to spend unsupervised time with X. However, this example is based on *Cohen v. Cohen*, 875 A.2d 814 (Md. App. 2005), where the court went a step further and ordered the father to stop drinking and using drugs even outside of the presence of the child. Although this is much more unusual than ordering supervised visitation, the appellate court upheld the lower court order requiring the father to abstain entirely from alcohol use.

8.8. Child Abduction

If there is credible evidence that a parent with court-ordered visitation will abduct or has abducted the child, visitation is likely to be supervised to prevent abduction from occurring. For example, in *Chandler v. Chandler*, 409 S.E.2d 203 (Ga. 1991), the court ordered supervised visitation after one parent took the child out of state without notice. However, in *Abouzahr v. Abouzahr-Matera*, 824 A.2d 268 (N.J. Super. Ct. 2003), a parent was allowed to exercise visitation in Lebanon so long as the parent gave four weeks' advance notice.

8.9. Cohabitation

If the visiting parent cohabits with a person of the opposite sex, the other parent may petition to limit overnight visits with the child. However, such a restriction is not likely to be granted unless the cohabitation has a serious adverse impact on the children. *See Higgins v. Higgins*, 981 P.2d 134 (Ariz. Ct. App. 1999); *Harrington v. Harrington*, 648 So. 2d 543 (Miss. 1994). *But see Muller v. Muller*, 711 N.W.2d 329 (Mich. 2006) (upholding order that "neither party shall have an unrelated member of the opposite sex overnight while having parenting time with the minor children").

8.10. Parent Who Is Gay or Lesbian

Although courts take opposing views on the issue, the emerging view is that a parent who is gay or lesbian is entitled to overnight visitation unless the parent opposing it can show specific endangerment to the child's physical or emotional health. *See Downey v. Muffley*, 767 N.E.2d 1014 (Ind. Ct. App. 2002); *In re Marriage of Dorworth*, 33 P.3d 1260 (Colo. Ct. App. 2001); *Boswell v. Boswell*, 701 A.2d 1153 (Md. App. 1997); and *Johnson v. Schlotman*, 502 N.W.2d 831 (N.D. 1993).

8.11. HIV-Positive Parent

Courts have refused to restrict overnight visits with HIV-positive parents. *See North v. North*, 648 A.2d 1025 (Md. App. 1994).

8.12. Religious Differences

A parent without legal custody can be restricted from imposing his or her religious views on a child during visitation, and the visiting parent may be required to bring a child to religious services chosen by the legal custodian. *See Lange v. Lange*, 502 N.W.2d 143 (Wis. Ct. App. 1993) and *Zummo v. Zummo*, 574 A.2d 1130 (Pa. Super. Ct. 1990). However, within limits, a visiting parent may take the child to religious services of his or her own choosing during visitation. *See Wood v. DeHahn*, 571 N.W.2d 186 (Wis. Ct. App. 1997); *In re Marriage of McSoud*, 131 P.3d 1208 (Colo. Ct. App. 2006). In order to restrict this activity, the objecting parent may need to show that the child would be physically or emotionally harmed by it. *Zummo v. Zummo*, 574 A.2d 1130 (Pa. Super. Ct. 1990).

EXAMPLES

Example 8-3

P (mother) was awarded legal and physical custody of X, and D (father) was awarded visitation with X. As the sole legal custodian, P decided to raise X as a Jehovah's Witness, over D's objection. As a part of her faith tradition, P objected to D's giving gifts to X and to D's encouraging X to participate in various holiday activities. Because of ongoing conflict about the child's religious affiliation, the court entered an order prohibiting D from interfering with X's religious training — D could not visit X on Christmas Eve or Christmas Day or allow X to participate in holiday activities, including gift-giving and trick-or-treating. D objected to the court order as an improper restriction on his visitation. Will such an order be upheld on appeal?

EXPLANATIONS

Explanation

As the sole legal custodian, P has the right to determine X's religious upbringing, even over the strong objection of D. In *A.G.R. ex rel. Conflenti v. Huff*, 815 N.E.2d 120 (Ind. Ct. App. 2004), the court upheld a similar order because the custodial parent's right to determine religious training could only be limited by a showing that the child's physical health or emotional development would be "significantly impaired." In this example, D did not allege any harm to the child resulting from the religious practice. The appellate court found that the trial court's order did not unreasonably interfere with the visiting parent's right to parenting time because the father received the same amount of time with the child that he otherwise would.

EXPANDING THE DEFINITION OF PARENT

8.13. Stepparent Visitation

After a divorce, some stepparents have sought visitation with their stepchildren. Visitation is sometimes granted if the stepparent has acted *in loco parentis* with the stepchild prior to the divorce. *See Simmons v. Simmons*, 486 N.W.2d 788 (Minn. Ct. App. 1992); *Weinand v. Weinand*, 616 N.W.2d 1 (Neb. 2000); *In re Marriage of Riggs and Hem*, 129 P.3d 601 (Kan. Ct. App. 2006); *Visitation Rights of Persons Other than Natural Parents or Grandparents*, 1 A.L.R.4th 1270 (1980). However under the common law, stepparents have no protected right to ongoing contact with stepchildren at divorce or upon the death of the biological parent-spouse. *See Seyboth v. Seyboth*, 554 S.E.2d 378 (N.C. Ct. App. 2001) (visitation by stepparent was denied because there was no showing that the natural parent was unfit).

EXAMPLES

Example 8-4

Assume that after a father and mother divorce, the father has physical custody of their child, X. The father remarries, and X's new stepmother, S, functions as a parent to him. Approximately two years after the father's remarriage, he is killed in a car accident. Although X's biological mother assumes physical custody of X, the stepmother petitions for visitation with X. A state statute allows a person standing *in loco parentis* to a child to petition for visitation if it is in the child's best interest, and one of the legal parents is deceased. The statute defines *in loco parentis* as "a person who has been treated as a parent by the child and who has formed a meaningful parental relationship with the child for a substantial period of time." The biological mother opposes the visitation on the basis that X already has a biological and legal mother. The court agrees and denies the visitation on the grounds that the stepmother could not establish *in loco parentis* status unless she "stood in the place of either Father or Mother" before the father's death. What is the likely outcome on appeal?

EXPLANATIONS

Explanation

In *Riepe v. Riepe*, 91 P.3d. 312 (Ariz. Ct. App. 2004), the appellate court held that the statute did not require the stepmother to show that her relationship with the child was the same as or superior to the child's relationship with the biological parents in order to be awarded visitation. The case was remanded so that the stepmother could establish that she was treated as a parent by the child and that she had a meaningful relationship with the child for a substantial period of time as required under the statute. On remand in such a case, it is likely that the biological mother would argue that a two-year relationship did not amount to a substantial period of time and that the relationship was not a meaningful one. Note that if the parties lived in a state without an *in loco parentis* statute, the stepmother would likely not be awarded visitation because under the common law, stepparents do not generally have an enforceable right to ongoing contact with a stepchild. *See Dodge v. Dodge*, 505 S.E.2d 344 (S.C. Ct. App. 1998) (where mother died, stepfather had no derivative right to visitation).

8.14. Visitation by Nonbiological Gay or Lesbian Co-parent

Historically, courts have not granted visitation to lesbian or gay nonbiological co-parents (who have not formally adopted the child) after the relationship between the adult partners ends. For example, in *Nancy S. v. Michele G.*, 279 Cal. Rptr. 212 (Cal. Ct. App. 1991), the court refused to recognize the nonbiological mother as a parent under the Uniform Parentage Act or as a de facto parent. *See also Alison D. v. Virginia M.*, 572 N.E.2d 27 (N.Y. 1991) and Robin Cheryl Miller, *Child Custody and Visitation Rights Arising from Same-Sex Relationship*, 80 A.L.R.5th 1 (2000).

However, more recently, some courts have ordered visitation in an exercise of the court's equitable power or based on the specific language of a "third-party" visitation statute. *See In re Custody of H.S.H.-K.*, 533 N.W.2d 419 (Wis. 1995); *E.N.O. v. L.M.M.*, 711 N.E.2d 886 (Mass. 1999); *V.C. v. M.J.B.*, 748 A.2d 539 (N.J. 2000); and *Laspina-Williams v. Laspina-Williams*, 742 A.2d 840 (Conn. Super. Ct. 1999) (same-sex partner had standing under visitation statute). *See also* Melanie B. Jacobs, *Micah Has One Mommy and One Legal Stranger: Adjudicating Maternity for Nonbiological Lesbian Coparents*, 50 Buff. L. Rev. 341 (2002).

EXAMPLES

Example 8-5

Assume that P (legal mother) and D (same-sex partner) lived in a committed relationship for more than ten years. Because same-sex couples were not allowed to adopt children, the child was adopted by P individually. Both P and D were extensively involved in parenting the child, and they shared all major parenting decisions, including those related to education, religion, and medical care. After P and D part ways, D seeks visitation with the child under a statute allowing such a proceeding by a person "who has had physical care of a child for a period of six months or more." If P opposes D's request, what is the likely outcome?

EXPLANATIONS

Explanation

D will argue that she has physically cared for the child for more than six months as required by the statute, and she will likely succeed with this argument. In the similar case of *In re E.L.M.C.*, 100 P.3d 546 (Colo. Ct. App. 2004), an adoptive legal mother, P, unsuccessfully argued that her former partner was required to establish a legal relationship to the child, that the visitation request must be incident to a dissolution proceeding, and that the legally recognized parent must have relinquished care of the child. Of course, D would have great difficulty obtaining parenting time over P's objection if D lived in a state that had not adopted a statute recognizing psychological parenthood.

8.15. Parents by Estoppel and De Facto Parents

Under the ALIs Principles of the Law of Family Dissolution: Analysis and Recommendations §2.18, individuals other than legal parents can be allocated parental responsibility either as a parent by estoppel (§2.03(b)) or as a de facto parent (§2.03(c)). A parent by estoppel is a person other than a legal parent who (1) is obligated to pay child support; (2) lived with the child and accepted parental responsibility for at least two years in the good-faith belief that he was the child's father; or (3) lived with the child since birth and acted as a parent pursuant to a parenting or co-parenting agreement. A de facto parent is a person other than a legal parent or parent by estoppel who for at least two years (1) lived with the child and (2) performed the majority of caretaking functions or as many caretaking functions as the parent with whom the child resided (3) either by agreement or because of the failure or inability of the legal parent to do so. Although a parent by estoppel has more rights than a de facto parent, both statuses require the adult in question to have significantly functioned as the child's parent and are consequently theoretically consistent with acting *in loco parentis*. However, the ALI analysis appears to be broad enough to encompass petitions for parenting time by stepparents, lesbian and gay parents, and some grandparents.

ENFORCING VISITATION (PARENTING TIME)

8.16. Overview

If parenting time arrangements are not carefully structured or if the divorced parents have not resolved underlying emotional issues, visitation can be an ongoing source of serious conflict. In such situations, the parties can mediate their differences or return to court to seek enforcement of visitation provisions. Some parents who engage in ongoing post-decree litigation benefit from marriage-termination counseling.

8.17. Contempt and Modification of Custody

If the parties cannot reach an amicable resolution through agreement, the parent being denied visitation may bring a contempt action to enforce a visitation order. *See Ellis v. Ellis*, 840 So. 2d 806 (Miss. Ct. App. 2003). In extreme cases, the parent denying visitation could lose custody. *See Egle v. Egle*, 715 F.2d 999 (5th Cir. 1983).

8.18. Compensatory Visitation

If a parent has wrongfully been denied visitation, that parent may be entitled to "makeup" or compensatory visitation. *See* Mich. Comp. Laws Ann. §552.642 (2003) and Minn. Stat. §518.175 subd. (6)(b) (2002).

EXAMPLES

Example 8-6

P was awarded sole physical custody of the parties' two children, and D was awarded visitation every other weekend, alternate Monday evenings, and on some holidays. Six months after the divorce, based on a motion to modify and an action for contempt, the court ordered that P could not schedule any activities for the children during D's visitation periods unless D agreed ahead of time in writing. Eighteen months later, after some consultation with D, P enrolled the children in a religious education class that took place on one of D's visitation evenings. D brought a contempt action against P and sought additional visitation time. The trial court found P in contempt and awarded

D an additional ten hours per month of visitation time. If P appeals, what is the likely outcome?

Explanation

In an analogous case, *In re Kosek*, 871 A.2d 1 (N.H. 2005), the appellate court upheld the lower court's finding of civil contempt and the award of additional visitation time. The appellate court reasoned that the increase in visitation was an appropriate sanction for civil contempt and that the new visitation schedule was not contrary to the best interests of the child.

8.19. Withholding Child Support

In most states, a parent cannot deny parenting time because the visiting parent has not paid child support. Similarly, a child support obligor must continue to pay child support even if parenting time is denied. *See Carter v. Carter*, 479 S.E.2d 681 (W. Va. 1996); *Seidel v. Seidel*, 10 S.W.3d 365 (Tex. Ct. App. 1999).

8.20. Wishes of the Child

Absent specific restrictions on parenting time, parents are expected to encourage and support a child's relationship with the other parent. Consequently, a parent cannot deny the other parent visitation based on a child's desire not to visit. *Schutz v. Schutz*, 581 So. 2d 1290 (Fla. 1991). Nevertheless, parenting time is more difficult to enforce if teenagers are opposed to it. For example, in *Worley v. Whiddon*, 403 S.E.2d 799 (Ga. 1991), a 14-year-old's wishes were considered but were not dispositive.

Example 8-7

Assume that when P (mother) and D (father) divorce, they have a 16-year-old son, X. Father and son have a difficult relationship despite the fact that both have attended counseling. Because of their history and X's age, the judge orders that D's continuing contact with X be "contingent upon the contact being mutually requested." D appeals the order. What is the likely outcome?

EXPLANATIONS

Explanation

D will argue that the conditional order could have the effect of denying his right to parenting time and that parenting time cannot be restricted without a finding that visitation would endanger the child. P might argue that a 16-year-old should not and cannot be forced to spend time with a parent if the teenager is strongly opposed to doing so. In the final analysis, although a court may consider the child's wishes with respect to the scheduling of parenting time, courts do not generally allow children to choose whether or not to spend time with a nonresidential parent. *In re Marriage of Kimbrell*, 119 P.3d 684 (Kan. Ct. App. 2005).

EXAMPLES

Example 8-8

Assume that P (mother) and D (father) were divorced and that P was granted physical custody of their two children. A high level of conflict between P and D continued after the divorce, and they returned to court several times on post-decree motions. One summer, one of the children (age 11) wanted to participate in sports and a band program that conflicted with D's parenting time. Through her own attorney (hired by P), the 11-year-old filed a motion to modify parenting time in the parents' divorce. What is the likely result?

EXPLANATIONS

Explanation

Under similar facts in *In re Marriage of Osborn*, 2006 WL 1506152 (June 2, 2006), a father argued that no change in circumstances was shown and that consequently, modification of the visitation order was improper. He also argued that the child lacked standing to bring the modification action. The appellate court ultimately agreed with the father and held that the child lacked standing to file the motion to modify.

MODIFYING VISITATION (PARENTING TIME)

8.21. Uniform Marriage and Divorce Act Provisions

Like custody and child support, parenting time orders can be modified. Section 407 of the UMDA allows for modification in the best interests of the child, "but the court shall not restrict a parent's visitation rights unless it finds that the visitation would endanger seriously the child's physical, mental, moral, or emotional health." Typical restrictions are those discussed in earlier sections.

GRANDPARENT VISITATION

8.22. History

At common law, grandparents generally had no legally enforceable right to visit their grandchildren. However, as both the number of living grandparents and the divorce rate increased, more formal recognition was given to the grandparent-grandchild bond in hope of adding stability to the lives of children experiencing divorce. *See* Maegen E. Peek, *Grandparent Visitation Statutes: Do Legislatures Know the Way to Carry the Sleigh Through the Wide and Drifting Law?*, 53 Fla. L. Rev. 321 (2001). Thanks in large part to the efforts of organized grandparent groups, by 1994 every state had adopted a grandparent visitation statute. These statutes vary widely in scope—some apply only if the parents divorce, die, or have their parental rights terminated, and other statutes apply regardless of the status of the child's immediate family unit.

8.23. *Troxel v. Granville*

State statutes providing for grandparent visitation have been subject to reexamination since the United States Supreme Court decided *Troxel v. Granville*, 530 U.S. 57 (2000). In *Troxel*, the Court struck down a Washington statute allowing "any person" to petition for visitation rights "at any time" that "visitation may serve the best interests of the child." The Court held that the statute as applied was an unconstitutional infringement on a fit parent's fundamental right to make decisions about the care and custody of minor children. The Court determined that some deference or "special weight" must be given to parental decisions because it is presumed that fit parents will act in their children's best interests. The court's decision rested in part on the breadth of the Washington statute, but the court stopped short of holding that specific types of statutes would violate due process.

The somewhat ambiguous nature of the decision spawned additional litigation as state courts considered the constitutionality of their visitation statutes in light of *Troxel*. Examining courts focused on the extent to which statutes deferred to the decisions of fit parents and the presence of statutory factors in addition to the "best interests of the child." Some state statutes have been found constitutional, whereas others have been held unconstitutional facially or as applied. For a discussion of the cases decided subsequent to *Troxel*, *see* Kristine L. Roberts, *State Supreme Court Applications of* Troxel v. Granville *and the Courts' Reluctance to Declare Grandparent Visitation Statutes Unconstitutional*, 41 Fam. Ct. Rev. 14 (2003). *See also* George L. Blum, *Grandparents' Visitation Rights Where Child's Parents Are Living*, 71 A.L.R.5th 99 (1999).

Example 8-9

Assume that mother, M, and father, F, are married, and they live together with their two children. They reside in a jurisdiction with a statute allowing grandparents reasonable visitation of grandchildren if such visitation would be in the child's best interest and if a substantial relationship has been established between the child and the grandparent. The grandparents had ongoing contact with the grandchildren from their birth until recently, including regular phone contact, holiday visits, and overnight visits. However, since the grandmother mistakenly alleged that one of the children had been sexually abused, M and F have refused to let the grandparents see the child. The grandparents sue for visitation with both children over the objection of M and F. M and F argue that they are fit parents in a continuing nuclear family and that it is their prerogative to deny visitation to the grandparents. The grandparents argue that the statute makes no distinction between intact families and those experiencing divorce or other disruption. What is the likely outcome?

Explanation

Because the mother and father are fit parents in a "continuing nuclear family," they argue that their decision not to allow visitation should be given absolute deference by the court. However, the grandparents argue that the statute makes no distinction between intact families and other families. In a recent case, *Davis v. Heath*, 128 P.3d 434 (Kan. Ct. App. 2006), a court faced with this situation awarded visitation to the grandparents, holding that the language of the statute did not distinguish between intact and other families, that the parents' decision to terminate visitation was unreasonable, that the evidence showed that the grandmother and grandchild had a substantial relationship, and that visitation was in the child's best interest. *But see Santi v. Santi*, 633 N.W.2d 312 (Iowa 2001) (statute permitting visitation without circumstance such as divorce, death of parent, or adoption declared unconstitutional).

CHAPTER 9

Child Support

9.1. Introduction

This chapter examines many of the child support issues that arise in paternity disputes and divorce actions. Issues related to modification of an existing child support award are considered in Chapter 10.

HISTORY

9.2. Elizabethan Poor Laws

Evidence of one of the first efforts to create a formal obligation to provide child support is found in the Elizabethan Poor Laws that were passed at the beginning of the seventeenth century. Passage of the Poor Laws resulted from economic conditions that created a large class of landless, often destitute laborers with children. "The Poor Relief Act of 43 Eliz. Ch. 2 required the father and the mother, among other relatives, of every poor, old, blind, lame, and impotent person, or other poor person unable to work, to relieve and maintain such person at their own charges, if they were of sufficient ability to do so." M.C. Dransfield, Annotation, *Parent's Obligation to Support Adult Child*, 1 A.L.R.2d 910, 935 (1948). These laws transformed the moral duties of family members toward each other and of the community toward its members into legal obligations. They also provided the first public welfare program, funded through taxation, to assist needy members of the community whenever family support was unavailable.

9.3. Common Law

In America, the common law imposed the duty of supporting minor children on their parents. However, as a general rule, there was no obligation placed on a parent to support an adult child. M.C. Dransfield, *Parent's Obligation to Support Adult Child*, 1 A.L.R.2d 910, 914 (1948). The states eventually removed any doubt regarding parental responsibility for the support of their children by enacting laws making it a criminal offense for a parent to desert or willfully neglect to provide support for a minor child.

Some common law courts felt that "nature" provided an adequate parental incentive to support children born to a marriage should a divorce occur. For example, in *Plaster v. Plaster*, 47 Ill. 290 (1868), the court observed that:

> [N]ature has implanted in all men a love for their offspring that is seldom so weak as to require the promptings of law, to compel them to discharge the duty of shielding and protecting them from injury, suffering and want, to the extent of their ability. Hence the courts are seldom called upon to enforce the duty of parents. The law of nature, the usages of society, as well as the laws of all civilized countries, impose the duty upon the parent of the support, nurture and education of children.

Id. at 291.

Unfortunately, the hoped-for natural inclination of a parent to provide support for a child has not been realized. Today, with thousands of divorces, involving large numbers of children, occurring on an annual basis, extensive state and federal legislation drives a variety of programs intended to ensure that minor children receive financial support from their parents and, as a last resort, from the state.

9.4. European View

Contemporary American law reflects the view that the cost of raising children is a private matter, with the parents having that responsibility. In contrast, some European countries play a more active role by subsidizing day care for children and providing state-supported health care for them.

The legal landscape in America, however, has dramatically changed in the last 40 years because of the federal government's involvement. Before the federal government acted, states had primary responsibility to award and enforce child support.

ROLE OF FEDERAL GOVERNMENT

9.5. Child Support and Establishment of Paternity Act of 1974

The federal government began collecting national data regarding child support awards and payments because of concern over rising rates of single parenting and welfare dependence. Since this fledgling effort, a multitude of federal programs to deal with child support have been enacted.

One of the first federal efforts was the Child Support and Establishment of Paternity Act of 1974, 42 U.S.C. §§651-655. The law was aimed at recipients of public assistance and required that they cooperate in establishing and enforcing support orders and cooperate in locating potential obligors. The act had three primary objectives. The first was to reduce public expenditures on welfare by obtaining child support from noncustodial parents on an ongoing basis. The second objective was to help families obtain support so that they could move off of public assistance. The third objective was to stimulate state action to establish paternity for children born outside marriage and obtain child support for them.

Under this early federal legislation, basic responsibility for administering the support program was left to individual states and local governments. However, the federal government dictated the major features of the programs by linking funding to specific state legislative activity, providing technical assistance, and giving direct assistance to help states locate absent parents.

9.6. State Guidelines Mandated

In 1984 Congress mandated that every state seeking federal funding to support its welfare program establish advisory child-support guidelines. Child Support Enforcement Amendments of 1984, Pub. L. No. 98-378, 98 Stat. 1305. States that rejected creating statewide guidelines risked losing a large percentage of federal funding for their Aid to Families with Dependent Children (AFDC) program. *See* 42 U.S.C. §§651, 667(a)-(b) (1984). The guidelines were intended to reduce widely differing amounts of child support from being ordered from courtroom to courtroom and to provide judges with a reasonably objective basis for determining support. The legislation also required that states enact statutes providing for expedited processes for obtaining and enforcing support orders.

Congress strengthened the guidelines in 1988 with the passage of the Family Support Act, which required that the state guidelines be applicable in all cases and operate as rebuttable presumptions of the correct support amount to be awarded in a divorce or paternity action. The Act also mandated that any deviation from the presumptive amount be supported by a decision maker's specific findings, in writing or on the record. 42 U.S.C. §667(b)(2). *See also* Helen Donigan, *Calculating and Documenting Child Support Awards Under Washington Law*, 26 Gonz. L. Rev. 13 (1990-1991).

9.7. Child Support Recovery Act of 1992

The Child Support Recovery Act of 1992 made it a federal crime for an obligor to willfully fail to pay child support to a child in another state. *See* 18 U.S.C. §228.

9.8. Omnibus Budget Reconciliation Act of 1993

The Omnibus Budget Reconciliation Act of 1993 mandated that states adopt in-hospital programs to facilitate voluntary acknowledgment of paternity in cases of children born out of wedlock. 42 U.S.C. §666. It also required that states create a rebuttable or conclusive presumption of paternity when genetic testing indicated a man was the father of a child born out of wedlock. It modified the Employee Retirement Income Security Act (ERISA) to require that employers make group health care coverage available to the noncustodial children of their employees. This resulted in the implementation at the state level of Qualified Medical Child Support Orders (QMCSO), which ordered an employer and insurance carrier to include the child in the employer's insurance program.

9.9. Full Faith and Credit Act of 1994

In a further effort to address interstate child support issues, Congress enacted the Full Faith and Credit for Child Support Orders Act (FFCCSOA) in 1994. This Act was intended to establish national standards to facilitate the payment of child support, discourage interstate conflict over inconsistent orders, and avoid jurisdictional competition. FFCCSOA, codified at 28 U.S.C. §1738B, requires that state courts afford full faith and credit to child support orders issued in other states and refrain from modifying or issuing contrary orders except in limited circumstances. Under section 1738B(e), a child support order may be modified by a sister state only if the rendering state has lost continuing, exclusive jurisdiction over the child support order, which in turn occurs only if (1) neither the child nor any of the parties continue to reside in the state, or (2) each of the parties has consented to the assumption of jurisdiction by another state. 28 U.S.C. §1738B(e)(2) (2003). Under the Supremacy Clause of the United States Constitution, FFCCSOA is binding on all states and supersedes any inconsistent provisions of state law, including any inconsistent provisions of uniform state laws such as URESA.

9.10. The Welfare Reform Act of 1996

The Welfare Reform Act of 1996 mandated that states adopt a version of the Uniform Interstate Family Support Act by January 1, 1998, and required that they develop expedited procedures that move away from complaint-driven approaches to collection of support and toward more efficient and faster administrative provisions. It also encouraged states to use liens, seizures of funds, license suspension, and administrative subpoenas to collect outstanding child support.

9.11. Personal Responsibility and Work Opportunity Reconciliation Act of 1996

The Personal Responsibility and Work Opportunity Reconciliation Act of 1996 (PRWORA) required each state desiring to receive block grants to develop a state directory of new hires that met federal requirements by either October 1, 1997, or October 1, 1998, depending upon whether a state had a new hire reporting law in effect before August 22, 1996. 42 U.S.C. §§601 *et seq*. The law required the Department of Health and Human Services to develop a national directory of new hires by October 1, 1997.

States were also required to adopt laws that allowed for the automatic placement of liens on an obligor's property when the obligor was in arrears.

CHILD SUPPORT DEFINED

9.12. Generally

Child support is traditionally defined as a payment by one parent (often the noncustodial or nonresidential parent) to the other parent for the support of their common child. As a general rule, the law takes the view that it is in the best interests of a child that both parents be obligated to pay support; therefore, the fact that a custodial parent is able to support a child without financial assistance from the noncustodial parent does not necessarily shield the noncustodial parent from making support payments. An order for child support transfers the income from one parent to the other so that the combined incomes of both parents are available for the child's support.

A child support order is typically part of a divorce decree or paternity judgment and is usually payable on a monthly basis. Many states require that child support be paid by wage assignment (automatic deductions from the paycheck) whenever available because this procedure reduces the need for subsequent enforcement actions.

WHAT IS INCOME FOR SUPPORT?

9.13. Generally

All jurisdictions have adopted provisions to generally guide judges in determining what resources should be considered income for the purpose of calculating child support. The phrase "income from any source," as used in most child support guidelines, is broadly construed and normally includes all financial payments, whatever the source. The determination of income for child support purposes under the guidelines is not necessarily controlled by definitions of gross income used for federal or state income tax purposes. The following is a nonexclusive list of some of the resources courts in most jurisdictions will consider as income and available when calculating child support:

1. Wage and salary income and other compensation for personal services (including commissions, overtime pay, tips, and bonuses)
2. Interest, dividends, and royalty income
3. Self-employment income
4. Net rental income (defined as rent after deducting operating expenses and mortgage payments, but not including noncash items such as depreciation)
5. All other income actually being received, including severance pay, retirement benefits, pensions, trust income, annuities, capital gains, social security benefits, unemployment benefits, disability and workers' compensation benefits, interest income from notes regardless of the source, gifts and prizes, spousal maintenance, and alimony

Examples of resources that some courts do not include in their calculation include (1) return of principal or capital, (2) accounts receivable, or (3) benefits paid in accordance with aid for families with dependent children. The duty to pay child support extends not only to an obligor's ability to pay from earnings, but also to his ability to pay from any and all sources that may be available.

The following sections illustrate some of the issues courts face when determining whether a particular resource is income for the purpose of calculating child support.

Example 9-1

Assume that P and D are divorcing and the court is calculating child support for their child. P will have sole physical custody of the child, and D will pay child support to P. D claims that D earns $15,000 per year and receives $46,000 in gifts and loans from his parents. D argues that the gifts and loans should not be viewed as "net income" under the statute and thus be available income for child support purposes. P alleges that the loans and gifts are "net income" and should not be excluded. What is the likely result?

Explanation

One of the key determinations in calculating child support is the determination of net income. The payer is likely to claim various deductions in order to lower child support liability. The payee will seek to have questionable income included for purposes of calculating child support. In a case with similar facts, *In re Marriage of Rogers*, 280 Ill. Dec. 726 (2003), the court held that the value of the gifts and loans could not be deducted from net income and that both were available for child support purposes. Given that D has more income from gifts and loans than from earnings, holding otherwise in this case would have substantially deprived the child of support.

9.14. Obligation of a Parent Who Is a College Student

In *In re* L.R.P., 98 S.W.3d 312 (Tex. Ct. App. 2003), a college student with a net monthly resource of $2,000 was required to pay 20 percent of that amount, or $400, as child support. He argued that the court erred in calculating his net monthly resources because it included funds he received from his father, and his father had no legal obligation to provide him with money. In rejecting his claim, the court said that the Texas child support statute defines resources to embrace in part "all other income actually being received," including "gifts and prizes." *Id.* at 314 (quoting Tex. Fam. Code Ann. §154.062(b)(5)). The student's father did not give him occasional gifts of money; rather, he provided a fixed amount of money each month to pay for his living expenses. The court analogized the monthly amount the college student's father sent to him to spousal maintenance, finding that it is the kind of ongoing support that falls within the purview of the statute.

9.15. Student Loan Payments

The Nebraska Supreme Court allowed a college student to deduct $178.09 for the monthly student loan payment he was required to make in determining modification of his child support obligation. The court stated that the student

> incurred his student loan in order to obtain the education necessary to gain employment as a teacher. By setting the initial child support at $50 per month, the trial court made it possible for [the student] to obtain his present income. Most courts recognize that fostering further education of young parents in such a fashion benefits the child throughout the child's life. It seems undesirable to undermine that policy by ignoring the fact that such students must later repay the student loans they incurred in the process.

Elsasser v. Fox, 584 N.W.2d 832, 835 (Neb. Ct. App. 1998).

9.16. Deducting Monthly Amounts Paid to Bankruptcy Court

In *Erica J. v. Dewitt*, 659 N.W.2d 315 (Neb. 2003), the court held that a payment to a bankruptcy plan of $100 per month in and of itself is not sufficient to rebut the presumption that the Nebraska Child Support Guidelines should be applied or to require a deviation from the guidelines to avoid an unjust result. The Montana Supreme Court held that a deduction for bankruptcy payments was in error because it was not provided for under the state's guidelines. *See In re Marriage of Nikolaisen*, 847 P.2d 287 (Mont. 1993).

9.17. Vested Stock Options

In *MacKinley v. Messerschmidt*, 814 A.2d 680 (Pa. Super. Ct. 2002), the court held that once vested, stock options constituted available income that had to be imputed to the parent holding them, for purposes of calculating the parent's child support obligation, regardless of whether the parent chose to exercise the options. When determining income available for child support, the court must consider all forms of income. *Blaisure v. Blaisure*, 577 A.2d 640, 642 (Pa. Super. Ct. 1990) (court must consider every aspect of parent's financial ability, including stocks). A stock option, typically a "form of compensation," is defined as "an option to buy or sell a specific quantity of stock at a designated price for a specified period regardless of shifts in market value during the period." *Black's Law Dictionary* 1431 (8th ed. 2004).

An option is "vested" when all conditions attached to it have been satisfied, and it may be exercised by the employee.

9.18. Employer's Contribution to Pension Plan

In *Portugal v. Portugal*, 798 A.2d 246, 253 (Pa. Super. Ct. 2002), the court held that an employer's contributions to a pension plan constitute income for purposes of support "if the employee could access his employer's contributions (regardless of penalties) at the time of the support calculation." The court reasoned that children should not be made to wait for support and that parents should not be permitted to defer income to which they are entitled until they choose to avail themselves of it. *But see Bruemmer v. Bruemmer*, 616 S.E.2d 740 (Va. Ct. App. 2005) (mandatory deductions excluded from income for child support purposes).

9.19. Stepparent Income

Most child support statutes do not permit a state agency or court to substitute a stepparent for a parent when determining the basic child support obligation. Furthermore, a court normally cannot consider the income of a stepparent in calculating the presumptively correct child support amount for a child. *See, e.g., Gal v. Gal*, 937 S.W.2d 391, 394 (Mo. Ct. App. 1997).

9.20. Lump-Sum Payments and Commissions

Regular commissions and lump-sum payments may be used to set the amount of child support. Lump-sum payments may also be withheld from an obligor to pay past-due support or to pay future support if there is a history of willful nonpayment. *See In re Marriage of Heiner*, 136 Cal. App. 4th 1514 (Cal. App. 2006) (evaluating whether lump-sum personal injury award is income for the purpose of child support).

9.21. Seasonal Employment

Seasonally employed obligors are generally required to make equal monthly payments throughout the year. Because the expenses of raising a child are not seasonal, judges generally require equal monthly payments despite the seasonal nature of the income.

9.22. Overtime

The law in most jurisdictions does not impose an obligation on obligors to work overtime. However, if an obligor has a history of working overtime, the courts may conclude that overtime is a normal, regular source of income and consider it when setting support. Similarly, if the overtime is a condition of employment, it is normally considered an income. *See Markey v. Carney*, 705 N.W.2d 13 (Iowa 2005).

9.23. Military Retirement Pay and Allowances

A military member's entire pay and allowances may be considered in the determination of child support amounts. *See Alexander v. Armstrong*, 609 A.2d 183 (Pa. Super. Ct. 1992) (father's military allowances were included in his income for purposes of child support); *Hautala v. Hautala*, 417 N.W.2d 879 (S.D. 1988) (military allowances are a species of remuneration subject to child support payments); *Merkel v. Merkel*, 554 N.E.2d 1346 (Ohio Ct. App. 1988); *Jackson v. Jackson*, 403 N.W.2d 248 (Minn. Ct. App. 1987); *Peterson v. Peterson*, 652 P.2d 1195 (N.M. 1982).

Collection of child support through direct payment by the Defense Finance and Accounting Service is determined by individual military service rules, which differ among the branches of service. Involuntary attachment of child support payments is provided for under federal law, but requires a court order.

ESTABLISHING CHILD SUPPORT

9.24. Overview

States have adopted various models of child support guidelines in response to the federal threat to withhold funds from states without them. *See* 42 U.S.C. §§651-667 (1982 & 1984 Supp. II) and 45 C.F.R. §302.56 (1989). The guidelines differ from state to state, and the more common models are briefly described in the following sections.

9.25. Income Shares Model

The income shares model has been adopted by a majority of jurisdictions and operates on the theory that a child involved in a divorce or paternity determination should receive the same proportion of parental income as if the family had continued to live together. *See, e.g.*, *Voishan v. Palmer*, 609 A.2d 319 (Md. 1992).

The income shares model, in its simplest form, requires at least three steps to calculate a child support award. First, using a statutory formula, the net incomes of both parents are calculated, combined, and then pro rated. For example, assume that the particular statutory formula resulted in a determination that parent A had a net income for child support purposes of $1,000, and the same formula resulted in a determination that parent B had a net child support income of $3,000. The parents would then be viewed as contributing 25 percent and 75 percent, respectively, to the support of a single child.

The second step is to apply the combined income to a guideline chart that suggests the amount of support that should be paid. For example, a state-mandated chart might suggest that with one child, when the combined net income is $4,000, the appropriate total amount of support is $1,000. Parent A would be required to pay 25 percent ($250), and parent B would pay 75 percent ($750). Thus, the parents are viewed as sharing equally in achieving the living standard for the child.

The final step in the application of this model normally allows a court to consider extraordinary medical expenses incurred by the child and a custodial parent's work-related child care expenses.

Example 9-2

Assume that P and D are divorcing in a state using the income shares method of child support calculation. They have one child. Assume that, for the purpose of calculating child support, P has a net income of $2,000 and that D has a net income of $4,000. Imagine that the amount of child support to be paid at a net income level of $6,000 is $2,000. How much child support will P and D pay?

Explanation

P has one-third of P and D's combined income, and D has two-thirds of their combined income. Consequently, P will pay one-third of $2,000 ($666.67) per month, and D will pay two-thirds of $2,000 ($1,333.33) per month. Rather than exchanging checks every month, D will probably just pay the difference ($666.66) to P each month.

9.26. Percentage of Income Model

The percentage of income model is sometimes viewed as the easiest of the various models to apply because of the limited need for calculations. When one parent is awarded sole physical and legal custody of a child, the model looks only at the noncustodial obligor's net income, although when joint physical custody (or shared custody) is ordered, this model considers both parents' incomes.

States adopting this model provide an obligor with a simple formula to use when calculating net income figures. To begin the calculation, one takes an obligor's gross income and deducts those items allowed by the statute. The list of deductions is short and usually includes only items such as taxes, medical insurance, social security, and reasonable pension payments. An obligor is not allowed to deduct living expenses when making the calculation. For example, assume that A is awarded sole legal and physical custody of child C. B, the noncustodial parent, has a gross income of $5,000 per month. To arrive at a net income figure for child support, B is allowed to deduct state and federal taxes, social security payments, health care payments, and reasonable pension payments from the $5,000. Assume that the allowed deductions reduce B's income to $4,000. In an attempt to reduce the child support obligation, B attempts to introduce evidence of monthly car payments, apartment rent, food, gas, and so on. If permitted, these may reduce B's monthly net income to less than $500. In states that use the percentage of income model, the latter expenses will be ignored — the only expenses to use when calculating support are the former. Therefore, the court will use $4,000 as the obligor's net income when calculating child support.

Once net income is calculated, that figure is applied to a guideline formula, which is increased by the number of children to receive support. For example, assume that application of the formula to an obligor's gross income resulted in a net monthly income child support figure of $4,000. Also assume that there was one child born of the marriage. Using a typical guideline chart (see Example 9-3), one would find the column headed by "1" (the number of children) and follow it down to $4,000 net income. Where the column and the $4,000 intersect, one finds 25 percent. This means that in this jurisdiction, monthly child support is 25 percent of $4,000, or $1,000. Courts will usually consider increasing the support amount when there are extraordinary medical expenses and work-related child care expenses.

EXAMPLES

Example 9-3

Assume that P and D divorce in a percentage of income jurisdiction, and they have two children. P is awarded sole legal and physical custody of the children, and D is ordered to pay child support in accordance with the following guidelines. After taking the deductions allowed by the statute, D's net income is $900 per month. Using the following table, calculate how much monthly child support D most likely will have to pay.

Net Monthly Income of Obligor	Number of Children 1	2	3	4	5	6	7 or more
	Percentage of Income						
$551-600	16%	19%	22%	25%	28%	30%	32%
$601-650	17%	21%	24%	27%	29%	32%	34%
$651-700	18%	22%	25%	28%	31%	34%	36%
$701-750	19%	23%	27%	30%	33%	36%	38%
$751-800	20%	24%	28%	31%	35%	38%	40%
$801-850	21%	25%	29%	33%	36%	40%	42%
$851-900	22%	27%	31%	34%	38%	41%	44%
$901-950	23%	28%	32%	36%	40%	43%	46%
$951-1,000	24%	29%	34%	38%	41%	45%	48%
$1,001-5,000	25%	30%	35%	39%	43%	47%	50%

EXPLANATIONS

Explanation

D will most likely be required to pay $243 per month. D's net income is between $851 and $900 per month, and D is supporting two children. D will pay 27 percent of D's net income in child support ($900 × .27 = $243).

EXAMPLES

Example 9-4

Assume that P and D live in a jurisdiction that calculates child support using the percentage of income method. Using the earlier chart, assume that P has sole legal and physical custody of the two children from P's marriage to D. D's net income after allowable statutory deductions is $3,000 per month, and P's net income after deductions is $4,000 per month. How much child support will each pay?

EXPLANATIONS

Explanation

D will pay \$900 per month to P (\$3,000 × .30 = \$900). However, even though P has the higher income, P will not pay any child support to D. P is the physical custodian of the two children, and P will be providing food, clothing, shelter, and such directly to the children. P's contribution was taken into consideration when the percentage of income chart was developed.

9.27. Melson Model

A few states use a third model, the Melson formula, which is a variation of the income shares model. Among its features is an attempt to ensure that each parent can be self-supporting before arriving at a child support determination. The theory is that a parent who is not self-supporting is an unlikely child support candidate. *See Dalton v. Clanton*, 559 A.2d 1197 (Del. 1989); *Turner v. Turner*, 586 A.2d 1182 (Del. 1991).

DEVIATING FROM GUIDELINES

9.28. Limited Discretion

Courts are given limited discretion to deviate from the guidelines, although as a practical matter, few judges stray very far from them. In most jurisdictions, the guidelines are strictly applied. For example, in *Zabloski v. Hall*, 418 N.W.2d 187 (Minn. Ct. App. 1988), a well-known rock singer, Daryl Hall, was required to pay only \$1,000 a month in child support for a child born out of wedlock, despite the fact that at the time of the support dispute, he had a net yearly income of approximately \$1.4 million. *But see In re Keon C.*, 800 N.E.2d 1257 (Ill. Ct. App. 2003) (court allowed upward deviation to an amount that exceeded the monthly expenses of the custodial parent's household).

When courts deviate from the presumed guidelines, most states require specific findings explaining and supporting the deviation. *See In re Marriage of Thanhouser*, 108 P.3d 667 (Ore. Ct. App. 2005) (case remanded to determine presumed award and for findings supporting deviation).

9.29. Special Circumstances

Special circumstances may require payment of a greater amount of child support than the amount set out by the statutory guidelines. Special circumstances, such as extraordinary medical expenses, special educational needs, unusual travel expenses incurred for child visitation, uninsured catastrophic losses, and the cost of basic living expenses for children from another relationship, can affect the amount of child support that is to be paid under the guidelines. *But see Scott v. Scott*, 879 A.2d 540 (Conn. App. 2005) (private boarding school was not "therapy," and parent was not required to pay additional cost).

Example 9-5

Assume that P and D divorce in a percentage of income state and that P is awarded sole legal and physical custody of the two children of the marriage. P does not work outside the home, and D's gross monthly income is $4,500. After the statutory deductions are made, child support is set at $1,350 per month ($4,500 × .30 = $1,350), leaving D with $3,150 net. D submits his monthly expenses and lists the following: $1,500 house payment, $500 car payment, $200 utilities, $300 attorney fees, $400 permanent maintenance, $500 on credit cards, $200 miscellaneous (total $3,600). D argues for a downward deviation in child support because he cannot make the payments. How will a court most likely rule?

Explanation

The court will most likely not grant a downward deviation. It is assumed that the plight of D and other similarly situated obligors was thoroughly explored by the legislature when the guidelines were enacted. The guidelines function as a presumption that can be overcome only in extraordinary circumstances.

9.30. Imputation of Income

The amount of child support paid is related to the income of the parent or parents supporting the child. However, if a parent is unemployed or underemployed, courts will sometimes impute income to the parent and base the child support order on the imputed income. For example, income equivalent to the minimum wage may be imputed to a voluntarily unemployed obligor. Similarly, if a parent is voluntarily underemployed, the court may base the child support order on the net income that the obligor previously earned. *See Christofferson v. Giese*, 691 N.W.2d 195 (N.D. 2005) (imputation must be based on actual income over prior 12 months rather than an extrapolation).

9.31. Joint Physical Custody

When parents share joint physical custody or the nonresidential parent has extended parenting time, some states provide a child support offset, whereas others view such an arrangement as warranting a deviation from the child support guidelines. *See Cheverie v. Cheverie*, 898 So. 2d 1028 (Fla. Dist. Ct. App. 2005) (downward deviation from child support guidelines where parent has more than 40 percent of the overnights); *Glassner v. Glassner*, 828 N.W.2d 642 (Ohio Ct. App. 2005) (fact that parents with great income disparity shared equal time with children doesn't justify deviation of child support to zero).

EXAMPLES

Example 9-6

Assume that P and D divorce in a percentage of income state that uses the table shown in Example 9-3. They are awarded joint legal and joint physical custody of their only child. P's net monthly income after the statutorily allowed deductions is $4,000, and D's net monthly income after the statutorily allowed deductions is $1,000. Assuming that the child spends approximately equal time with each parent, how will child support be awarded using the above guidelines?

EXPLANATIONS

Explanation

Each parent will pay the amount established by the guidelines for the period of time that he or she does *not* reside with the children. Another way to think of it is that D will pay $1,000 per month for half of the year for a total of $6,000 (when the child is with P), and P will pay $240 per month for half of the year (when the child is with D) for a total of $1,440. ($4,000 × .25 × 6 = $6,000; $1,000 × .24 × 6 = $1,440.) P and D may regularize payments by having D pay P $380 per month for the entire year.

ADDITIONAL SUPPORT

9.32. Medical Support

In 1988 the federal government mandated that the states enact provisions for "child[ren]'s health care needs, through health insurance coverage or other means." *See* 45 C.F.R. §302.56(c)(3).

State courts have found it within the trial court's discretion to require payment of uninsured medical expenses in addition to the child support award. *See generally Lulay v. Lulay*, 583 N.E.2d 171, 172 (Ind. Ct. App. 1991) (finding the commentary to the Child Support Guidelines allows for apportionment of uninsured medical expenses because the guidelines do not mandate any specific treatment of these expenses); *Holdsworth v. Holdsworth*, 621 So. 2d 71, 78 and n.1 (La. Ct. App. 1993) (holding medical and dental expenses not covered by insurance were properly apportioned half to each party in addition to the child support award as determined under the guidelines); *Jamison v. Jamison*, 845 S.W.2d 133, 136-137 (Mo. Ct. App. 1993) (holding it was within the court's discretion to order the obligor to pay half of the uninsured medical expenses, in addition to the child support award determined under the guidelines); *Lawrence v. Tise*, 419 S.E.2d 176, 183 (N.C. App. 1992) (holding ordinary medical expenses not covered by insurance are to be apportioned between the parties at the discretion of the trial court, in addition to the child support award as determined by the guidelines). *But see Hazuga v. Hazuga*, 648 N.E.2d 391, 395 n.1 (Ind. Ct. App. 1995) (noting that the guidelines had been amended and therefore declined to follow *Lulay v. Lulay*); *Family Services ex rel. J.L.M. by C.A.M. v. Buttram*, 924 S.W.2d 870, 871 (Mo. Ct. App. 1996) (ordering father to pay for medical insurance as well as 50 percent of all uncovered medical expenses was a deviation under the guidelines).

9.33. Child Care Costs

In addition to child support, costs associated with child care may be awarded to the parent with sole physical custody. The expense may be apportioned between the parents pursuant to a legislative formula. However, the parent who actually pays the child care expense receives payment from the other parent.

There appears to be an increasing amount of litigation over child care expenses. *See, e.g., Mace v. Mace*, 610 N.W.2d 436 (Neb. Ct. App. 2000) (ex-wife entitled to modification of dissolution decree in order to require former husband to pay proportionate share of her work-related day care expenses); *Hoplamazian v. Hoplamazian*, 740 So. 2d 1100 (Ala. Civ. App. 1999) (court improperly added mother's work-related child care costs to father's basic child support obligation when mother was not seeking employment); *Cupstid v. Cupstid*, 724 So. 2d 238 (La. Ct. App. 1998) (ex-wife proved change in circumstances justifying increase in former husband's child support obligation when she returned to work and began incurring child care expenses); *Rosen v. Lantis*, 938 P.2d 729 (N.M. Ct. App. 1997) (court had authority under guidelines to adjust child support obligation in post-dissolution proceeding based on mother's testimony that she was incurring child care costs because of her employment); *Gal v. Gal*, 937 S.W.2d 391 (Mo. Ct. App. 1997) (day care costs incurred while mother attending nursing school full-time could be included as an extraordinary expense in calculating father's child support obligation); *Sigg v. Sigg*, 905 P.2d 908 (Utah. Ct. App. 1995) (court's decision requiring ex-wife to be solely responsible for one-third of day care costs, then splitting the remaining costs between ex-wife and ex-husband, was not based on fact and was an abuse of discretion).

OTHER SUPPORT CONSIDERATIONS

9.34. Duration of Child Support

The duration of child support depends on state law. All states require both parents to be financially responsible for their child during the child's minority, generally through the child's high school years. A few states have extended the time for financial responsibility beyond the minority of the child. *See Childers v. Childers*, 575 P.2d 201 (Wash. 1976) (court could require parent to support a "defective" child beyond the age of majority—court also has discretion, under proper circumstances and after consideration of all relevant factors, to extend support for the education of normal children past the age of majority).

In many jurisdictions, a support order ends either when the child turns 18 or when the child completes secondary school, but not later than when the child reaches age 20. Couples are free, of course, to negotiate a court order that provides for support to continue beyond the statutory cut-off dates. *See, e.g., Solomon v. Findley*, 808 P.2d 294 (Ariz. 1991) (parties' contract for post-majority support is enforceable in breach of contract action, unlike divorce statutes that end support when child reaches majority age). Support can continue indefinitely for a child incapable of self-support because of a physical or mental condition. *See Haxton v. Haxton*, 705 P.2d 721 (Or. 1985). Parents should be aware that privately negotiated agreements can be altered by the court if the judge determines the agreement is not in the best interests of the child.

Courts in many states have approved parental funding of a college education. For example, under an Iowa statute, parents can be ordered to provide financial support for children attending college. Iowa Code §§598.21(5A), 598.1(8); *In re Marriage of Moore,* 702 N.W.2d 517 (Iowa Ct. App. 2005); *In re Marriage of Mullen-Funderburk and Funderburk,* 696 N.W.2d 607 (Iowa 2005). *See also* Ind. Code §31-16-6-2 (educational support order). In states without statutes authorizing contribution, settlement agreements relating to college expenses may be enforced as contractual obligations. *Nicoletti v. Nicoletti,* 901 So. 2d 290 (Fla. Dist. Ct. App. 2005); *Medearis v. Baumgardner,* 2006 WL 770464 (Tenn. App. 2006); *Spalding v. Spalding,* 907 So. 2d 1270 (Fla. Dist. Ct. App. 2005). *See* ALI, Principles of the Law of Family Dissolution: Analysis and Recommendations §3.12 (2002) (discusses provision of postsecondary education under "Providing for a Child's Life Opportunities").

Child support can be terminated in the event of the death of the child, if the child goes on active duty in the armed forces, or if the child becomes emancipated or self-supporting.

9.35. Monitoring Support

Courts do not generally allow the obligor (person making the support payments) to monitor how the support is used by the obligee. Should the obligee fail to meet the child's needs, the remedy could involve a charge of child abuse or neglect. In extreme cases, abuse or neglect would be a basis for a change in custody.

9.36. Bankruptcy

Not all debts can be discharged in bankruptcy. Those that cannot be discharged are set forth in the Bankruptcy Code, 11 U.S.C. §523 (1994). Among the nondischargeable debts is a debt for child support. *Id.* §§523(a)(5). *Rosen v. Lantis,* 938 P.2d 729 (N.M. 1997). Any back payments owed for child support cannot be included as a debt and cannot be discharged in a bankruptcy proceeding. *See Mattingly v. Mattingly,* 164 S.W.3d 518 (Ky. Ct. App. 2005) (obligation to pay college expenses was in the nature of child support and not dischargeable). *But see In re Hartnett,* 330 B.R. 823 (Bkrtcy. S.D. Fla. 2005) (child support debt was dischargeable where paternity testing showed debtor was not the father of the children).

9.37. Employer Limitation on Withholding Income

The amount an employer may withhold from an employee's income is limited by the Federal Consumer Credit Protection Act (CCPA), 15 U.S.C.A. §1673 (1997). CCPA limitations are as follows: 50 percent of disposable income if an employee is living with a second family; 55 percent of disposable income if an employee is living with a second family and there are arrearages 12 or more weeks overdue; 60 percent of disposable income if an employee is not living with a second family; and 65 percent of disposable income if an employee is not living with a second family and there are arrearages 12 or more weeks overdue. The CCPA limitations do not apply to independent contractors. An employer may not discharge, refuse to hire, or otherwise discipline an employee because a support withholding order exists against the employee.

9.38. Federal Income Tax Treatment

For federal income tax purposes, child support payments are not income to the obligee. The parent who makes the payments cannot deduct the amount as an expense on his or her federal tax return.

9.39. Obligee Withholds Visitation

As a general rule, if an obligor fails to make child support payments, the obligee cannot interfere with visitation between the obligor and the minor child. *See Engrassia v. Di Lullo*, 454 N.Y.S.2d 103 (App. Div. 1982) (failure of noncustodial parent to make child support payments, without other evidence, was insufficient basis upon which to deny visitation). The child support obligation and the right to child visitation are viewed by most courts as separate issues. The reason for the distinction is that visitation is ordered because it is in the best interest of the child to promote love and affection with both parents, custodial and noncustodial. When the parties cannot effectuate visitation, the appropriate remedy is to seek the assistance of the court. *Pierpont v. Bond*, 744 So. 2d 843 (Miss. Ct. App. 1999). Although the coercive effect of withholding child support may, when appropriate, be used to encourage the allowance of visitation, its use is only available upon approval of the court. Child support is payment based on the financial needs of the child and the ability of both parents to provide for these needs and is not viewed as directly related to the psychological needs of a minor child. *See Lindsay, v. Lindsay*, WL 197111 (Tenn. Ct. App. 2006) (father could not be ordered to pay an additional $50 in child support every time he missed visitation).

EXAMPLES

Example 9-7

Assume that P and D divorce and that P is awarded sole legal and physical custody of their child, C. D is awarded parenting time with C every other weekend and for four weeks during the summer. D is ordered to pay child support in the amount of $200 per month. D believes that P is using the child support money to go out drinking and to attend concerts with friends rather than for the benefit of C. Consequently, D asks P for proof that the money is being spent on C, and when P refuses to provide an accounting, D stops paying child support. P tells D that P can barely make ends meet financially and that C has been unable to participate in some school activities because P cannot finance them without the child support payments from D. In exasperation, P refuses to allow D to visit with C until D resumes child support payments. D brings an action to enforce visitation, and P brings an action for enforcement of the child support order. How will a court most likely rule?

EXPLANATIONS

Explanation

Sadly, both P and D could be held in contempt of court. In most states, the physical custodian is not required to provide an accounting concerning child support expenditures, and D wrongfully violated the support order by unilaterally stopping payment. The right to visitation is not conditioned on payment of support, so P could not prevent D from visiting with C even though D's child support payments were in arrears. As described here, this is a situation where the parties might benefit from going to mediation to resolve the ongoing conflict between them.

9.40. Stepparent Liability

The common law did not impose a legal duty on a stepparent to provide support for a minor stepchild. *See Ulrich v. Cornell*, 484 N.W.2d 545, 548 (Wis. 1992). It also took the view that one's standing *in loco parentis* is voluntary and temporary and may be abrogated at will by either person standing *in loco parentis* or by a child. Without a statute and absent an adoption or unusual circumstances, a stepparent is not responsible for providing support for a spouse's children.

Courts are cautious about imposing an ongoing support obligation on a stepparent who voluntarily supports a child, because stepparents could be generally discouraged from providing such support for fear of becoming permanently obligated to do so. However, a few states have adopted provisions requiring a stepparent to support stepchildren as long as the stepparent is married to the children's natural parent. *See, e.g.*, Wash. Rev. Code §26.16.205, which reads as follows:

> The expenses of the family and the education of the children, including stepchildren, are chargeable upon the property of both husband and wife, or either of them, and they may be sued jointly or separately. When a petition for dissolution of marriage or a petition for legal separation is filed, the court may, upon motion of the stepparent, terminate the obligation to support the stepchildren. The obligation to support stepchildren shall cease upon the entry of a decree of dissolution, decree of legal separation, or death.

See also Washington Statewide Org. of Stepparents v. Smith, 536 P.2d 1202 (Wash. 1975) (statute does not unconstitutionally impair marriage contracts or violate the Equal Protection Clause because cohabitants are not held to the same standard).

Under North Dakota law, a stepparent may be liable for necessaries for a spouse's dependent children: if they are "received into the stepparent's family. . . . [T]he stepparent is liable, to the extent of his or her ability, to support them during the marriage and so long thereafter as they remain in the stepparent's family." N.D. Stat. §14-09-09 (West 2005).

When stepparents divorce, most jurisdictions take the view that the support obligation, if any, ends. *See Bagwell v. Bagwell*, 698 So. 2d 746 (La. Ct. App. 1997) (no obligation after divorce). *But see Johnson v Johnson*, 617 N.W.2d 97 (N.D. 2000) (stepparent liable on equitable adoption theory).

EXAMPLES

Example 9-8

Assume that P and D married in the state of Washington and that P brought two children from a former marriage into the relationship. Although the children regularly visited with their biological father, X, and received child support from him, D treated the children as though they were his biological children. During the last year of the marriage, X fell ill and died. About eight months later, P and D's marriage dissolved. P argues that under the Washington statute (Wash. Rev. Code §26.16.205 *supra*), D must continue to pay child support. How will the court most likely rule?

EXPLANATIONS

Explanation

The court will most likely reject P's claim. Although the statute mandates that D provide support to the children during D's marriage to P, there is no requirement that the support continue after the marriage. There is also no evidence presented that would equitably estop D from asserting that he is not the children's father. Therefore, he is not liable for their support.

CHAPTER 10

Child Support Modification and Enforcement

10.1. Introduction

Agreements and court orders regarding child support may be modified as circumstances change. For example, if parents alter their custodial arrangements, the issue of child support will be revisited. Similarly, if the obligor loses his or her job, or if the obligor has a substantial increase in income, the amount of child support is likely to be readjusted. In the unfortunate event that an obligor doesn't pay child support as ordered, the order may be enforced through a variety of legal measures.

STANDARDS FOR MODIFYING EXISTING AWARD

10.2. Substantial Change in Circumstances

Most jurisdictions have statutory provisions that permit an order for child support to be changed or modified. Although the language used by state legislatures varies, in general, modification may occur when a "substantial change in circumstances" has taken place since the issuance of the support order, a change that makes enforcement of the existing award unfair. The parent seeking the change has the burden of proof.

A substantial change in circumstances can take many forms. The change may concern an alteration in a parent's financial situation — such as loss of a job, receipt of a large inheritance, or winning a lottery. The change in circumstance could be the result of a new situation for the child — such as large unanticipated medical expenses, the need for special education, or other unexpected requirements. A typical statute may read as follows:

> Support orders may be modified if there is: (1) a substantial increase or decrease in either parent's earnings, or (2) a substantial increase or decrease in the needs of a parent or child, or (3) a change in a child's or parent's cost of living, or (4) a change in custody, and any of these changes makes the terms of the original order unreasonable or unfair.

EXAMPLES

Example 10-1

Assume that in a paternity action, D was adjudicated the father of three children. At the time that the original child support order was entered, D was not employed, and the court imputed federal minimum-wage income to him and entered a child support order for $250 per month. D was later convicted of a federal crime and sent to prison. D moves for a reduction in child support, asserting that he lacks financial resources because of imprisonment. Will the support order be modified?

EXPLANATIONS

Explanation

D will argue that his incarceration is a substantial change in circumstances sufficient to reduce his child support obligation. One difficulty D has in making this argument is that D's *income* (or lack thereof) did not change when he went to prison. However, D will argue that his *ability* to earn income changed substantially. In the similar case of *A.M.S. ex rel. Farthing v. Stoppleworth*, 694 N.W.2d 8 (N.D. 2005), the court held that the statutory support guideline amount could not be rebutted through a showing of incarceration because the obligor had brought the situation upon himself. The court found that imprisonment was not a circumstance beyond the control of the obligor and was consequently not the type of change that warranted modification of the child support order.

10.3. Statutory Presumption — Substantial Change

Some jurisdictions have created rebuttable statutory presumptions for use in modification cases. Such presumptions typically provide that modification is warranted if the parent seeking the change establishes that the child support order would be increased or decreased by more than 20 percent. For example, in *MacLafferty v. MacLafferty*, 829 N.W.2d 938 (Ind. 2005), the obligor sought to modify a child support order because of an increase in the physical custodian's income. The relevant statute provided that modification could only be made upon a showing that (1) the current order was unreasonable because of substantial changed circumstances or (2) the support order had been in effect for more than one year and the modified guidelines payment would result in an increase or decrease of more than 20 percent. The modification was denied because the changed circumstance only resulted in a 14 percent difference in the child support order.

Example 10-2

Assume that P and D are the unmarried parents of a child, X. When child support was determined, P had a weekly income of $450, and D, an NBA player, had a weekly income of $121,327. Under the child support guidelines, D was ordered to pay $760 per week in child support. Three years later, P brings an action to modify child support because D's annual income has increased from $6,309,004 to $9,061,875. The relevant statute provides that modification requires a showing that (1) the current order is unreasonable because of substantial changed circumstances or (2) the support order has been in effect for more than one year, and the modified guidelines payment would result in an increase or decrease of more than 20 percent. D argues (correctly) that under the child support guidelines, his increased income would only result in a 1 percent increase ($7.15 per week). P argues that X is entitled to live at the standard of living X would have had if X resided with D and that a deviation from the guidelines is warranted. What is the likely result?

Explanation

This example is similar to the case of *Davis v. Knafel*, 837 N.E.2d 585 (Ind. App. 2005), in which the court denied the modification request. P failed to show that D's increased income would result in more than a 20 percent change in the guidelines support order. P also failed to establish substantial changed circumstances *occurring since the entry of the original support order* that would render the support order unreasonable. For example, the court was not persuaded that D's purchase of a $1,700,000 residence was a change in lifestyle, stating that P "fails to show how this is a change in lifestyle for a man who already owned two homes in two different states and who earns several million dollars per year." *Id* at 589.

10.4. Standard Cost of Living Adjustment

Most child support orders provide for a biennial adjustment in the amount to be paid based on a change in the cost of living. An order may direct that a trial court use a cost-of-living index published by the Department of Labor or provide for use of a local index that more accurately reflects the economy in a particular area of the country. *See, e.g., Fronk v. Wilson*, 819 P.2d 1275 (Mont. 1991) (American Chamber of Commerce Researchers' Association Cost of Living Index obtained from the State of Montana's Census and Economic Information Center was admissible).

The cost-of-living requirement may be waived if the court makes an express finding that the obligor's income or occupation does not provide for a cost-of-living increase. A cost-of-living provision providing for a biennial adjustment reflects an obligor's increase in income and the children's needs, which also are rising with inflation.

10.5. Standard for Making Award Retroactive

The court has broad discretion to set the effective date of a support modification. *Borcherding v. Borcherding*, 566 N.W.2d 90, 93 (Minn. Ct. App. 1997). Typically, a modification of support or maintenance may be made retroactive from the date of service of the motion for modification on the responding party. *See, e.g.*, Minn. Stat. §518.64, subd. 2(d) (Supp. 1999).

Example 10-3

Assume that P and D divorce and that D is ordered to pay $300 per month to P in child support. Five years later, P seeks to increase the child support award by $300 per month. The litigation and appeal concerning the increase last two years, from 2004 until 2006, as D unsuccessfully challenges the modification. When P wins on appeal, P believes that D owes P a lump-sum payment of $3,600 (the support increase over the two-year period). D argues that this is a windfall to P and that the increase should begin from the date of the appellate court's decision. How will a court most likely treat this dispute?

Explanation

A court will most likely reject D's argument. P has been required to support the parties' child for nearly two years without receiving all the assistance P was entitled to from D. For this reason, the back support now owed to P will not be considered a windfall, and the court will not abuse its discretion in making the modification retroactive to the time when D was served with the motion papers.

10.6. Standard When Obligor Changes Jobs

Generally, when a party voluntarily assumes a lower-paying job, courts will not automatically modify the support obligation. Furthermore, a party ordinarily will not be relieved of a child support obligation by voluntarily quitting work or by being fired for misconduct.

When seeking a reduction in child support payments because of a change in employment, the moving party must usually establish that the voluntary change in employment, which resulted in a reduction of income, was not made for the purpose of avoiding child support payments. The moving party must also show that a reduction is warranted based on efforts to mitigate any income loss. In effect, the moving party must present evidence as to why she or he voluntarily left the prior employment and also as to why the acceptance of a lower-paying job was necessary. Otherwise, for calculation of child support, the moving party will be considered to have an income equal to his or her earning capacity. *See Chen v. Warner*, 695 N.W.2d 758 (Wis. 2005) (mother's decision to forego employment outside the home was "reasonable under the circumstances").

Courts have applied one of three tests to determine whether to modify a child support order when a parent voluntarily terminates employment. Each of the tests evidences its own strengths and weaknesses, and each reflects the public policy of its adopting jurisdiction. The first of these tests, the good-faith test, considers the actual earnings of a party rather than his or her earning capacity, so long as he or she acted in good faith and not primarily for the purpose of avoiding a support obligation when terminating employment. *In re Marriage of Horn*, 650 N.E.2d 1103, 1106 (Ill. App. Ct. 1995); *Giesner v. Giesner*, 319 N.W.2d 718, 720 (Minn. 1982); *Schuler v. Schuler*, 416 N.E.2d 197, 203 (Mass. 1981); *Fogel v. Fogel*, 168 N.W.2d 275, 277 (Neb. 1969); *Thomas v. Thomas*, 203 So. 2d 118, 123 (Ala. 1967); *Lambert v. Lambert*, 403 P.2d 664, 668 (Wash. 1965); *Nelson v. Nelson*, 357 P.2d 536, 538 (Or. 1960). The good-faith test is criticized because it assumes that a divorced or separated party will continue to make decisions in the best overall interest of the family unit, when often, in fact, the party will not. The test is also criticized as focusing on the parent's motivation for leaving employment rather than on the parent's responsibility to his or her children and the effect of the parent's decision on the best interests of the children.

The second approach is the strict rule test, which disregards any income reduction produced by voluntary conduct and looks at the earning capacity of a party in fashioning a support obligation. Child support remains based solely on earning capacity. The strict rule test is viewed by some as too inflexible because it considers only one factor, the parent's earning capacity.

The third approach, which is referred to as the intermediate test, balances various factors to determine whether to use actual income or earning capacity in making a support determination. The intermediate balancing test considers a number of factors and places the obligation to pay child support first and other financial obligations second. The court asks whether the parent's current educational level and physical capacity provide him or her with the ability to find suitable work in the marketplace. If so, the decision to leave employment is less reasonable. If the parent leaves employment to seek additional training, and if the additional training is likely to increase the parent's earning potential, the decision is more likely to be found reasonable. A court will also consider the length of the parent's proposed educational program because it matters whether the children are young enough to benefit from the parent's increased future income.

Example 10-4

Assume that the marriage between P and D dissolved and that D was ordered to pay $1,200 per month for child support. When the support was ordered, D was employed by the Air Force, earning an annual salary of $48,000, plus benefits. D also holds a master's degree in business administration. D terminated his employment with the Air Force and entered law school. He earns a monthly reserve pay from the Air Force of $308 and his ex-wife, a full-time student/caretaker, earns about $1,000 per month. D alleged a substantial and continuing change in circumstances in that his income was reduced because he terminated his position with the Air Force and entered law school. In his petition, appellant requested a reduction in child support payments from $1,200 to $200 per month. P contended that D could move to a nearby state where night law school is offered and be employed during the day. D's children at the time were ages four and six.

Explanation

This is a close question and depends at least in part on the standard the court uses in reviewing the facts. A court could allow the order to be reduced to the guidelines amount based on D's lower income. It is reasonable to believe that a law degree would enable D to embark on a career that could well result in enhanced economic fortunes, and the increased income would inure to the benefit of his children, given their present ages. The suggestion that D attend night school in another state may be viewed as unreasonable because it would require relocation away from his children. The fact that D chose to stay in state near the children not only is reasonable, but also shows D's desire to remain active in his children's upbringing, an important consideration to D and his children. *See Little v. Little*, 969 P.2d 188 (Ariz. Ct. App. 1998). However, in this example, P would have a difficult time supporting two children on a total income of $1,200 per month, and the first obligation of the court is to assure that the children are cared for financially.

Consequently, a court is unlikely to approve a reduction in child support based on a voluntary action of the obligor that leaves the children in need.

DURATION OF CHILD SUPPORT

10.7. Obligor's Death

Under the common law, a father's death terminated his obligation of support for his minor children. However, by statute, states have altered that perspective. *See, e.g.*, Ariz. Rev. Stat. §25-327(c). A court also has the power to require a parent to obtain or maintain insurance on the parent's life for the benefit of the parent's children. *Pittman v. Pittman*, 419 So. 2d 1376 (Ala. 1982); *Wolk v. Wolk*, 464 A.2d 780 (Conn. 1983); *Allen v. Allen*, 477 N.E.2d 104 (Ind. Ct. App. 1985); *Krueger v. Krueger*, 278 N.W.2d 514 (Mich. Ct. App. 1979); *Stein v. Sandow*, 468 N.Y.S.2d 910 (N.Y. App. Div. 2d Dept. 1983). It is recognized that a child is no less dependent on a parent after the parent's death than before and that the burden of support may fall in total or in part on society if the surviving parent is unable to fully carry the burden.

The Uniform Marriage and Divorce Act (UMDA) repudiates the common law rule that an obligor's support obligation ends upon death by providing that a parent's child support obligation is terminated "by emancipation of the child but not by the death of a parent obligated to support the child. When a parent obligated to pay support dies, the amount of support may be modified, revoked, or commuted to a lump sum payment to the extent just and appropriate in the circumstances." UMDA §316(c).

The UMDA also states that the parties or the court may provide for the contingency of the premature death of the parent in the original decree. But even if no such provision is incorporated into the original decree, the act permits courts to modify the support provisions at a later time, even after the death of the parent. In providing for the death of the parent, the act requires courts to use the criteria considered in the court's original order and in modifying a child support order. The intent of these provisions is to encourage divorcing parents to provide support for their children during their entire minority. UMDA Commissioners' Note to §316(c). In the absence of the parents voluntarily making such provisions for their children, however, these provisions give the court the discretion and authority to *sua sponte* secure the children's support after the parent's death.

10.8. Emancipation of Child

A child support obligation may end when the minor child is emancipated. Emancipation of a child occurs when the fundamental dependent relationship between parent and child is concluded, the parent relinquishes the right to custody and is relieved of the burden of support, and the child is no longer entitled to support. Emancipation may occur by reason of the child's marriage, by court order, or by the child attaining a certain age. Although in most states there is a presumption of emancipation at age 18, that presumption is rebuttable. *Filippone v. Lee*, 700 A.2d 384 (N.J. Super. Ct. App. Div. 1997). The emancipation issue is fact-specific, and the essential inquiry is whether the child has moved "beyond the sphere of influence and responsibility exercised by a parent and obtains an independent status of his or her own" *Bishop v. Bishop*, 671 A.2d 644 (N.J. Super. Ct. 1995). *See In re Marriage of Heddy*, 535 S.W.2d 276, 279 (Mo. Ct. App. 1976). Consent of the custodial parent, either express or implied, is a prerequisite to emancipation. *Vinson v. Vinson*, 628 S.W.2d 376 (Mo. Ct. App. 1982). The mere fact that a child is employed and retains her earnings does not by itself establish that parental control has been relinquished or that the obligation to support has been terminated. *Id.* at 377.

A state may recognize constructive emancipation under the common law. *See, e.g., In re Marriage of George*, 988 P.2d 251 (Kan. Ct. App. 1999). In *Harris v. Rattini*, 855 S.W.2d 410, 412 (Mo. Ct. App. 1993), the Missouri Court of Appeals for the Eastern District held that a child who drops out of school before his or her eighteenth birthday, takes a part-time job, and has no mental or physical incapacity is emancipated, and child support is no longer required. By way of contrast, in *Detwiler v. Detwiler*, 57 A.2d 426 (Pa. Super. Ct. 1948), the Superior Court of Pennsylvania found that a 17-year-old who dropped out of school and earned his own income, but lived at home, was not emancipated. The court found that the parents had not relinquished control over the child. In *In re Marriage of Clay*, 670 P.2d 31 (Colo. Ct. App. 1983), the Colorado Court of Appeals held that a 16-year-old daughter who was dependent on her mother for financial support, who had not established a residence away from both her parents, who was not married to the father of her child, and who did not receive support from her child's father was not emancipated and was entitled to support.

Although a child is generally emancipated upon reaching majority, courts in some jurisdictions have authority to order that an obligor pay support beyond the age of majority when a child is in college. *See, e.g., Main v. Main*, 684 P.2d 1381 (Wash. Ct. App. 1984). See Chapter 9.

An otherwise unemancipated teenager who is dependent on parental support is not disqualified from receiving it because she has become pregnant and she elected to give birth to a child as an unmarried mother. Her own motherhood in these circumstances does not render her emancipated. *See, e.g., Filippone v. Lee supra; In re Marriage of Clay*, 670 P.2d 31, 32 (Colo. Ct. App. 1983); *Doerrfeld v. Konz*, 524 So. 2d 1115, 1116-1117 (Fla. Dist. Ct. App. 1988); *Hicks v. Fulton County Dept. of Family and Children Services*, 270 S.E.2d 254, 255 (Ga. Ct. App. 1980); *French v. French*, 599 S.W.2d 40, 41 (Mo. Ct.

App. 1980); *Wulff v. Wulff*, 500 N.W.2d 845, 851 (Neb. 1993); *Thompson v. Thompson*, 405 N.Y.S.2d 974, 975 (Fam. Ct. 1978), *aff'd*, 419 N.Y.S.2d 239 (App. Div. 1979); *Griffin v. Griffin*, 558 A.2d 75, 80 (Pa. Super. Ct. 1989), *app. denied*, 571 A.2d 383 (Pa. 1989).

Residing apart from a minor's parents does not by itself result in the minor's emancipation. *Quinn v. Johnson*, 572, 577, 589 A.2d 1077 (N.J. Super. Ct. 1991). A troubled minor's removal from his parents' home to a public or private institutional alternative or even to the home of friends or relatives does not relieve the parents of their support obligation during minority, provided the child is not entirely self-supporting. *See In re Marriage of Donahoe*, 448 N.E.2d 1030, 1033 (Ill. App. Ct. 1983); *Quillen v. Quillen*, 659 N.E.2d 566, 576 (Ind. Ct. App. 1995), *vacated in part, adopted in part*, 671 N.E.2d 98 (Ind. 1996); *In re Marriage of Bordner*, 715 P.2d 436, 439 (Mont. 1986); *Hildebrand v. Hildebrand*, 477 N.W.2d. 1, 5 (Neb. 1991); *In re Owens*, 645 N.E.2d 130, 132 (Ohio Ct. App. 1994); *Trosky v. Mann*, 581 A.2d 177, 178 (Pa. Super. Ct. 1990); *In re Marriage of George*, 988 P.2d 251 (Kan. Ct. App. 1999).

Military service normally acts to emancipate a minor. However, in *Baker v. Baker*, 537 P.2d 171 (Kan. 1975), the father argued that when his son went into the Navy, he became emancipated, and that relieved the father of any further obligation of support. The court held that entry into the Navy was not grounds for automatically terminating child support but could be considered as a factor for reducing or terminating the support payments.

Example 10-5

Assume that P and D are divorced. They have one child, X, and D pays child support to P for the support of X. When X is 16, she marries Y, with the permission of P. However, X continues to live with P, and P continues to support her. Seven months later, X's marriage is annulled on the ground of fraudulent inducement on the part of Y. D stopped paying child support when X married Y, believing her to be emancipated. However, after the annulment, P again seeks child support from D, arguing that X was returned to her unemancipated status and consequently is entitled to support. How will a court likely rule?

Explanation

In *State ex rel. Dept. of Economic Sec. v. Demetz*, 130 P.3d 986 (Ariz. Ct. App. 2006), the court considered a similar situation. D argued that X's marriage was voidable, not void, and that the marriage was consequently valid when it occurred, thus emancipating X. The court disagreed, holding that once the annulment became final, the marriage was "deemed invalid from its inception." The court found that D's obligation to support X was revived when X's marriage was annulled.

ENFORCEMENT EFFORTS

10.9. Contempt of Court

Although family courts have many tools with which to enforce orders, one of the most powerful is the ability to hold an obligor in civil or criminal contempt. The purpose of civil contempt is to obtain compliance with the court order. In a civil contempt action, the person being held in contempt is said to hold the keys to the jailhouse door in his or her pocket — jail is conditioned on nonpayment, and the obligor is released when payment is made. *See Branum v. State*, 829 N.E.2d 622 (Ind. Ct. App. 2005) (in civil contempt case, court was required to ascertain that the obligor had ability to pay and to advise that the obligor could obtain release from incarceration through compliance). The purpose of criminal contempt is to punish, and the obligor typically completes a determinate sentence. Despite the bright line between the two types of contempt, in practice, courts sometimes fail to distinguish between them.

When criminal contempt is sought, the defendant-obligor is entitled to additional constitutional protections. In *Hicks v. Feiock*, 485 U.S. 624 (1988), the obligor failed to make child support payments, and the issue was whether the Due Process Clause of the Fourteenth Amendment prohibited the state court from placing the burden on the obligor, rather than the state, to establish the obligor's inability to make payments. The Court held that shifting the burden to the defendant in a criminal case violated due process. However, if the proceeding had been civil in nature, the obligor would not have enjoyed this constitutional protection.

Courts are split over the question of whether appointment of counsel is constitutionally required for an indigent civil contempt defendant. *See Rodriquez v. Eight Judicial Dist. Court ex rel.*, 102 P.3d 41 (Nev. 2004) (Sixth Amendment right to counsel not applicable in civil contempt). *But see Pasqua v. Council*, 892 A.2d 663 (N.J. 2006) (civil contempt obligors entitled to counsel under Due Process Clause and State Constitution).

Most states provide explicit statutory authority for courts to use contempt proceedings to enforce maintenance and child support obligations. In contrast, property settlements are categorized as ordinary debts and are not subject to enforcement through contempt. In most jurisdictions, property settlements are instead enforced through execution on the judgment.

10.10. Criminal Nonsupport

All states have statutes that punish an obligor who willfully fails to pay child support. For example, Wisconsin law declares that:

> [a]ny person who intentionally fails for 120 or more consecutive days to provide spousal, grandchild or child support which the person knows or

> reasonably should know the person is legally obligated to provide is guilty of a Class I felony. A prosecutor may charge a person with multiple counts for a violation under this subsection if each count covers a period of at least 120 consecutive days and there is no overlap between periods.

Wis. Stat. §948.22(2).

Such provisions have withstood constitutional attacks alleging that the obligor is being imprisoned for nonpayment of a debt. In rejecting this argument, courts reason that unlike a debt arising from a contract, a child support obligation is based on a court order. *O'Connor v. O'Connor*, 180 N.W.2d 735, 738 (Wis. 1970). *See Lyons v. State*, 835 S.W.2d 715, 718 (Tex. Ct. App. 1992).

EXAMPLES

Example 10-6

Assume that the state of X charged D with criminal nonsupport. D and his ex-wife were divorced, there were three children born of the marriage, and D was ordered to pay child support in the amount of $150 per month. In a very brief jury trial, the ex-wife testified that from the date of the decree until the date of trial (two years), she had received no child support payments from D. D did not testify and was convicted of criminal nonsupport and sentenced to five years in prison. In this jurisdiction, the criminal nonsupport statute provides that "any person who intentionally fails, refuses, or neglects to provide proper support which he or she knows or reasonably should know he or she is legally obligated to provide to a spouse, minor child, minor stepchild, or other dependent commits criminal nonsupport."

In her instructions to the jury, the trial judge stated. "Regarding criminal non-support, the elements of the State's case are: (1) The alleged crime occurred on or about a certain date. The alleged crime occurred in this County, and this state. (2) The defendant then and there failed to provide proper support for his minor children when he knew or reasonably should have known he was legally obligated to provide support pursuant to the Order of the Court." D argues that the conviction should be reversed because the words "intentionally fails, refuses, or neglects" were not included in the court's instruction. The State argues that D did not properly object to the court's instruction. The trial transcript shows that D's counsel objected to the court's instruction in the following manner: "[T]he defendant does object concerning the elements." How will a court most likely treat D's argument?

EXPLANATIONS

Explanation

The conviction most likely will be reversed. Although the objection could have been more specific, it was sufficient to inform the court of the claimed defect. Intent is an essential element of the crime of criminal nonsupport. In this hypothetical case, the court did not instruct the jury on all of the essential elements of the crime charged. An instruction omitting an essential element is prejudicially erroneous. *State v. Noll*, 507 N.W.2d 44 (Neb. Ct. App. 1993). *See also State v. Nuzman*, 95 P.3d 252 (Ore. Ct. App. 2004) (state had burden to show that nonpayment was without lawful excuse).

10.11. Interception of Tax Refunds

In 1981 the federal income tax refund offset program was enacted into law. Pub. L. No. 97-35, §2331, 95 Stat. 860-863 (1981). Initially, this program was restricted to public assistance cases and enforced delinquent child support obligations by intercepting part or all of the obligor's federal income tax refund. The program was expanded in 1984 to allow for its use in nonassistance cases.

The Debt Collection Improvement Act (DCIA) of 1996, Pub. L. No. 104-134, was enacted into law on April 26, 1996. The primary purpose of the DCIA is to increase the collection of nontax debt owed to the federal government. The DCIA contains important provisions for use in the collection of past-due child support obligations.

The DCIA was further strengthened by Executive Order 13019— Supporting Families: Collecting Delinquent Child Support Obligations, dated September 26, 1998. This order allows the Secretary of Treasury, in consultation with the Secretary of Health and Human Services, to develop and implement procedures necessary to collect child support debts by administrative offsets. *See* 31 C.F.R. 285.1 and 285.3.

10.12. Garnishment

The Child Support and Establishment of Paternity Act of 1974, 42 U.S.C. §659, made it possible for a federal employer to withhold child support and pay an obligor directly from the withheld funds.

10.13. Credit Bureau Reporting

In many jurisdictions, a report to a credit bureau may be triggered if a noncustodial parent owes $1,000 or more in past-due child support.

10.14. Driver's License Suspension

In a number of jurisdictions, when a noncustodial parent is behind in paying child support by a certain number of weeks or months, the obligor's license may be suspended. Before the suspension becomes effective, the obligor is entitled to due-process protections, including written notice and a reasonable period in which to rectify the arrearage.

10.15. Recreational License Suspension

Some jurisdictions suspend the hunting and fishing licenses of obligors who are behind in support payments for a certain period, usually six months.

10.16. Publication of a "Most Wanted" List of "Deadbeat Obligors"

When obligors generate substantial sums in arrears, some jurisdictions publish their names in a local newspaper or place their names and sometimes their photos on a government website.

10.17. Occupational License Suspension

Some states have provisions that permit license suspension for obligors working in occupations that require a license from the state, county, or municipal board or agency. Persons subject to suspension may include realtors, barbers, doctors, and lawyers. For example, Georgia's Code of Professional Responsibility for lawyers incorporates state law and provides that when a court makes a finding that a member of the bar has willfully failed to timely pay a child support obligation, and such refusal continues for 30 days after the determination becomes final, the bar member "shall be deemed not to be in good standing and shall remain in such status until such time as the noncompliance is corrected." *See Matter of Carlson*, 489 S.E.2d 834 (Ga. 1997).

10.18. Passport Denial

Section 370 of the Personal Responsibility and Work Opportunity Reconciliation Act (PRWORA) of 1996 (Pub. L. No. 104-193, 110 Stat. 2105) amended the Social Security Act by adding subsection 452(k). This subsection became effective October 1, 1997, and provides for the denial, revocation, and restriction of U.S. passports. A passport application may be denied when the noncustodial parent is $5,000 or more past due in a child support obligation. PRWORA §§312, 653(a).

10.19. Seizing Awards

Reemployment insurance, workers' compensation payments, and lottery winnings may be seized.

10.20. Seizing Assets Held

A child support office may also take assets held in financial institutions or in retirement funds.

10.21. Obtaining a Wage Assignment

An obligee may seek to obtain an order that directs an employer to deduct the child support payment from the earnings of an employee-obligor parent and then make this payment directly to the obligee parent. Violation of a wage assignment order could result in the employer becoming responsible for such payment to the obligee parent. Assignment orders can be obtained through a relatively simple court procedure. Once obtained, the wage assignment order must be served on the employer of the obligor parent before it becomes effective.

Additional measures found in some states include the following: (1) *Freezing bank accounts* until support is paid. A bank is relieved from liability for damages, should it have acted inappropriately. Both the various state departments of revenue and the federal Internal Revenue Service can also seize funds from these accounts. (2) *Using traditional creditor's legal remedies* such as execution and garnishment against any other property the obligor may own. Some states will place liens on real estate owned by an obligor who is in arrears in child support payments.

FEDERAL COLLECTION EFFORTS

10.22. Federal Crime

The Child Support Recovery Act (CSRA) of 1992, 18 U.S.C. §228(a), made it a federal crime to willfully fail to pay a past-due support obligation, where the child was located in a state separate from that of the obligor. Past-due support is defined as either an amount determined by a state court that remains unpaid for longer than one year or one that exceeds $5,000. An obligor who violates the federal statute can be fined and imprisoned for not more than six months for the first offense or two years maximum and can be ordered to make restitution for subsequent offenses. Support must have been unpaid for at least a year and exceed $5,000. *But see U.S. v. Pillor*, 387 F. Supp.2d 1053 (N.D. Cal 2005) and *U. S. v. Morrow*, 368 F. Supp. 863 (C.D. Ill. 2005), holding that mandatory CSRA rebuttable presumption that the obligor has the ability to pay violates due process by shifting burden regarding willfulness.

In 1998 CSRA became the Deadbeat Parents Punishment Act (DPPA), and two new federal felony categories were created that carry a maximum of two years in prison plus fines and restitution at the discretion of the court. Crossing state lines with the intent to evade child support payments is now a felony for parents owing $5,000 or more or for parents whose payments have remained unpaid for more than a year. Out-of-state parents owing $10,000 or more or who fail to pay for two years will also be subject to felony charges.

10.23. Uniform Interstate Family Support Act (UIFSA)

The enforcement of a child support order, even when the parents and children are residents of the same state, is difficult. However, when the parents live in different states, enforcement is much more difficult.

Before the 1950s, a parent who wanted to ensure support against the other parent who lived in another state had to travel to the support debtor's state to take legal action. However, since that time, a uniform act has existed in one form or another allowing states that subscribe to it to enforce each other's support orders. In 1950 the National Conference of Commissioners on Uniform State Laws prepared a model act that was eventually adopted in some form in all jurisdictions, URESA, which is short for Uniform Reciprocal Enforcement of Support Act.

In 1968, URESA was amended, and the new act was called RURESA, short for Revised Uniform Reciprocal Enforcement of Support Act. By 1992, all of the states had enacted RURESA or URESA. Even American Samoa, Puerto Rico, Guam, and the Virgin Islands had adopted a version of either URESA or RURESA.

The purpose of URESA, and later, RURESA, was to provide for the enforcement of support obligations in another state without requiring commencement of legal proceedings there. However, the uniform acts gave state legislators great latitude to amend the uniform act, while adopting other parts of it. In addition, it became evident that the process was slow, with petitions taking from four to eight months with a considerable amount of paperwork and administration.

With state efforts falling short, the federal government sponsored the revision of the uniform interstate support legislation, which resulted in the Uniform Interstate Family Support Act, or UIFSA. In 1996, Congress enacted a law requiring all 50 states to adopt UIFSA by January 1, 1998. UIFSA was intended to replace URESA and RURESA provisions in the states.

When a party seeks to modify a support order issued by another state, UIFSA applies. *See* Kurtis A. Kemper, *Construction and Application of Uniform Interstate Family Support Act,* 90 A.L.R.5th 1 (2001). Consequently, a party seeking to modify a support order from another state must establish jurisdiction pursuant to the act.

There are nine articles to UIFSA:

Article 1 contains general provisions, including definitions.
Article 2 contains the provisions concerning jurisdiction.
Article 3 contains the provisions relating to the duties of the state in a UIFSA action.
Article 4 contains the provisions relating to the establishment of an order.
Article 5 contains the provisions relating to direct enforcement of an order of another state without the need for registration.
Article 6 concerns the enforcement and modification of support orders after registration.
Article 7 concerns paternity actions.
Article 8 concerns interstate rendition.
Article 9 contains miscellaneous provisions.

The jurisdictional rules are set out in Part A of Article 2 of UIFSA, sections 201 and 202. Section 201 establishes UIFSA's bases for jurisdiction over a nonresident — that is, its long-arm jurisdiction — by providing that a state may exercise jurisdiction over an individual if:

1. the individual has been properly served in the state;
2. the individual submits to the jurisdiction of the court by entering a general appearance or by filing a responsive document;
3. the individual resided with the child for whom support is being sought within the state;
4. the individual provided prenatal expenses or child support while residing within the state;
5. the child resides within the forum state because of some activities of the individual;
6. the individual engaged in sexual intercourse in the state;

7. the individual asserted parentage in the state's registry or in another appropriate agency; or
8. there is any other basis consistent with the constitutions of this State and the United States for the exercise of personal jurisdiction.

One scholar has stated that the first basis is a codification of *Burnham v. Superior Court*, 495 U.S. 604 (1990), which affirmed the constitutionality of asserting personal jurisdiction based on personal service within a state (the tag rule). *See* John J. Sampson & Paul M. Kurtz, *UIFSA: An Interstate Support Act for the 21st Century*, 27 Fam. L.Q. 85, 114 (Spring 1993).

Jurisdiction under UIFSA rests on the concept of continuing, exclusive jurisdiction to establish and modify the levels of child support due a particular child. "Thus, once a court enters a support decree with jurisdiction, it is the only body entitled to modify it so long as it retains continuing, exclusive jurisdiction under the Act. Another state, while required by the Uniform Interstate Family Support Act to enforce the existing decree, has no power under that Act to modify the original decree or enter a support order at a different level," as long as one of the parties remains in the issuing state. *Id.* at 88. *See* Tina M. Fielding, *UIFSA: The New URESA*, 20 U. Dayton L. Rev. 425, 461 (1994).

UIFSA requires that states recognize the continuing, exclusive jurisdiction of a tribunal of another state that issued a child support order. The trial court may modify the child support order (1) upon both parties' consent to the court assuming jurisdiction, section 205(a)(2), or (2) if after registration of the order, the trial court determines that the child, the individual obligee, and the obligor do not reside in the issuing state.

Under UIFSA, an issuing state loses continuing, exclusive jurisdiction to modify child support provisions of a divorce decree once both parents and all their children move away from that state. UIFSA permits only one tribunal at a time to have jurisdiction to modify a child support order. If the parties and their child no longer reside in the state that issued the original child support order, and one party seeks to modify an existing child support order, they must bring the action in the state where the nonmoving party resides, except for modification by agreement.

EXAMPLES

Example 10-7

Assume that P and D dissolve their marriage in Iowa and that a trial judge with jurisdiction over both parties issues a child support order in 2004. P is the custodial parent or obligee, and D is the obligor. P and the minor child move to Texas in 2005. D moves to New York in 2006. P seeks legal advice as to which state she should bring a modification of support action in under UIFSA. What advice will you give P?

EXPLANATIONS

Explanation

Under UIFSA, Iowa lost jurisdiction to modify its own order when D moved to New York, unless P and D consented in writing to Iowa retaining modification jurisdiction. Iowa retains jurisdiction to enforce any amount of arrears owed because of the Iowa order. However, P should be advised to bring her modification action in Texas.

EXAMPLES

Example 10-8

Assume that P and D dissolve their marriage in Iowa and that a trial judge with jurisdiction over both parties issues a child support order in 2004. P is the custodial parent or obligee, and D is the obligor. P and the minor child move to Texas in 2005. D remains in Iowa. P seeks legal advice as to which state she should bring a modification of support action in under UIFSA. What advice will you give P?

EXPLANATIONS

Explanation

Iowa retains modification jurisdiction as long as D is a resident, and Iowa has enforcement jurisdiction because it never lost it.

EXAMPLES

Example 10-9

Assume that P and D dissolve their marriage in Iowa and that a trial judge with jurisdiction over both parties issues a child support order in 2004. P is the custodial parent or obligee, and D is the obligor. P and the minor child remain in Iowa when D moves to New York in 2005. P seeks legal advice as to which state she should bring a modification of support action in under UIFSA. What advice will you give P?

EXPLANATIONS

Explanation

If D is the person who moved, but P and the child remained in Iowa, Iowa retains enforcement jurisdiction and modification jurisdiction because P and the child remained in that jurisdiction. Because D was originally a resident of Iowa at the time of the initial order, or consented to "personal jurisdiction," Iowa retains the ability to modify this order, provided that at least one parent remains in that state.

10.24. Other Jurisdictional Issues

The traditional jurisdictional issues regarding collection of child support are treated in Chapter 27, which covers jurisdiction. Please see that chapter for a discussion of the issues involving this topic. In this chapter, we have included a brief discussion of UIFSA, which is a provision with specific jurisdictional provisions applicable to child support modification actions.

CHAPTER 11

Alimony and Necessaries

11.1. Introduction

Alimony is the obligation of one party to provide the other with support in the form of income. It is also commonly labeled *maintenance* or *spousal support*. However, for simplicity's sake, we have chosen to use the word *alimony* in this book. This chapter focuses on when and how alimony is awarded, either through negotiated settlement or court order.

Although the two concepts are sometimes confused, alimony differs from property division in a variety of ways. First, alimony obligations cannot be discharged in bankruptcy whereas some property obligations may be the object of discharge. Second, alimony is considered taxable income to the recipient and is deductible by the payer. Property settlements have no similar tax treatment. Third, alimony awards may be modified in the future, but property settlements are viewed as final. Fourth, alimony awards traditionally terminate upon the remarriage of the recipient, in contrast to property awards, which are not affected by remarriage. Finally, failure to pay alimony can be enforced by contempt proceedings, and enforcement of property awards generally occurs through traditional debtor-creditor remedies.

The current law with respect to alimony has deep historical roots stretching back for centuries. Three historical "customs" have particularly shaped modern doctrine, and the chapter begins with an explanation of these. The first is the custom of providing gifts to a husband to protect the wife upon marriage. The second is the Unity Doctrine, and the third is the need for finding fault before a legal support obligation would be considered.

HISTORY

11.2. Ancient Customs

The Anglo-Saxon custom of transferring a wife's property to her husband upon marriage probably began around A.D. 800. When a couple married, the bride's parents and relatives gave a husband all her property (her dowry) in return for his promise of care and protection. This early custom was apparently absorbed into the canon law and later found its way in part into English and American common law.

11.3. Ecclesiastical Courts

Another significant factor in the development of modern alimony is the Unity Doctrine, which arose from the early theological teachings of the Church that when a couple married, they became one person. As noted earlier, once a couple married, the wife's person was merged into the husband. The concept took many forms, and its effects were numerous. For example, because one could not sue one's self, neither married partner could sue the other, and a husband was responsible for defending his wife against any third-party actions involving her interests. It was not until the late 1800s, when Married Women's Acts were passed in most jurisdictions, that the law began to change.

11.4. Divorce from Bed and Board

A third factor affecting how alimony was viewed is fault, which is linked to the early Church's teaching that marriage is indissoluble and divorce is a mortal sin. Although the Church banned absolute divorce, it created alternatives when faced with the practical problem of married couples who wanted to live apart. One option was to annul the marriage, a *divorce a vinculo*, thus avoiding a divorce and permitting remarriage. Another canonical option was a divorce from bed and board (*a mensa et thoro*). Under this early separation scheme, a couple could separate and live apart from each other without obtaining an absolute divorce. However, a separation was granted only if a wife could provide a good reason for living apart from her husband. The policy of the law, as administered by the Ecclesiastical courts, looked toward a reconciliation of the parties and preservation of the marriage relation; therefore, the allowance was for the reasonable support of the wife only. The courts sometimes sought to do justice by increasing the allowance in cases where the property originally came from the wife;

however, the alimony still remained based on the wife's reasonable support during the separation.

11.5. Fault Adopted by Secular Systems

Ecclesiastical fault was incorporated into the judicial thinking of most early secular family law. Divorce was a remedy available only to an innocent party who had been "wronged" by a guilty party. It was believed appropriate to punish a wife whose behavior constituted grounds for divorce by either denying alimony altogether or awarding a much smaller sum than she might otherwise receive. The law reasoned that by her wrongful misconduct, she had forfeited any claim to her husband's financial protection.

Conversely, a husband whose marital fault was serious may have had to pay additional alimony either as compensation to the wife for the wrongs done to her or as a means of punishing the husband who was at fault. Alimony awards reflected the judiciary's perceptions of public morality, and the sanctions were considered appropriate when a citizen breached the community's acceptable moral standards.

11.6. Common Law

At common law, a woman entering a common law marriage faced severe legal disabilities. The husband and wife were considered one person, and that one person was the husband. Once married, all a wife's personal property came under the husband's control. During marriage, the wife had no legal rights to her husband's real property.

Under early English common law, a husband was under a duty to maintain his wife in accordance with his means; however, there was no corresponding duty placed on a wife. A husband was to provide a suitable home and necessaries such as food and clothing.

A wife was normally not entitled to alimony in a separate home, absent good reason to live apart from her husband. A husband did not have a duty to maintain his wife if she deserted the marriage, although the duty was revived if she returned. If she committed adultery, which the husband did not condone or which had not been contrived, his duty of support normally ceased.

If a wife was living apart from her husband because of his desertion or misconduct, she was entitled to support, as long as she was free from misconduct herself. If a husband failed to provide for her, she could pledge his credit for necessaries that were suitable given their lifestyle prior to the separation. *See* Brenda M. Hoggett, David S. Peal, *The Family Law and Society, Cases and Materials* 81 (Butterworths 1983).

During the nineteenth century, the common law in the United States in jurisdictions that permitted a divorce recognized the unfairness of leaving a wife in near poverty following a divorce or legal separation. Courts began to require that an ex-husband provide support—sometimes by returning all or a portion of the wife's dowry and at other times by requiring that he provide her with a portion of his personal property. The common law reasoned that the award was supported by public policy, which declared that it was the duty of the husband to support his wife for life.

The common law limited a husband's support obligation and imposed no reciprocal support duty on the wife. However, a husband's duty of support did not necessarily require that he make periodic alimony payments or provide funds from his income. Divorces were, of course, rare and effectively discouraged by most religious institutions.

11.7. Alimony for Husbands

The lingering impact of the historical view that should there be a divorce, a wife owed no reciprocal duty to support a husband continued in this country until the Supreme Court decided *Orr v. Orr*, 440 U.S. 268 (1979). The Court invalidated an Alabama statute that imposed alimony obligations on husbands, but not on wives. The Court observed that because the statute provided that different treatment be accorded persons on the basis of sex, it established a classification subject to strict scrutiny under the Equal Protection Clause of the Fourteenth Amendment. To withstand such scrutiny, gender classifications must serve important governmental objectives and must be substantially related to achievement of those objectives. *Califano v. Webster*, 430 U.S. 313, 316-317 (1977).

Alabama argued that its interests included providing help for needy spouses and claimed that the statute used sex as a proxy for need. It also argued that the statute was intended to compensate women for past discrimination during marriage, which had left them unprepared to fend for themselves in the working world following divorce. These arguments did not persuade the Court. Though conceding that they were legitimate governmental objectives, the Court ruled that the statute was not "substantially" related to the achievement of those objectives. *Orr*, 440 U.S. at 286. It observed that even if sex were a reliable proxy for need, and even if the institution of marriage did discriminate against women, the state did not adequately justify the salient features of the statutory scheme.

The Court also observed that under the statute, individualized hearings at which the parties' relative financial circumstances are considered were already occurring, and therefore, no reason existed to use sex as a proxy for need. It reasoned that needy males could be helped along with needy females with little, if any, additional burden on the state.

THE NECESSARIES DOCTRINE

11.8. Husband's Common Law Duty

At common law, it was the duty of the husband to provide for a wife's necessaries. In return, a wife was obliged to provide domestic services that pertained to the comfort, care, and well-being of her family and consortium to her husband. *See Ritchie v. White*, 35 S.E.2d 414, 416-417 (N.C. 1945).

When a woman married, the common law took the view that she forfeited her legal existence and became the property of her husband, and her services and earnings belonged to him. Because the wife could not contract for food, clothing, or medical needs, her husband was obligated to provide her with such "necessaries," and if the husband failed to do so, the doctrine of necessaries made him legally liable for essential goods or services provided to her by third parties. Most courts viewed the husband's duty as arising from the fact of the marriage, not from any express undertaking on his part. The duty also rested on a recognition of the traditional status of the husband as the financial provider of the family's needs.

In the mid-nineteenth century, the enactment of Married Woman's Acts in most states partially removed the disabilities of married women, which at common law had prevented them from retaining their earnings and owning property.

11.9. Gender-Neutral Application

Most jurisdictions that have considered the issue of necessaries in the last three decades have held that the doctrine should be applied in a gender-neutral fashion. *See, e.g., Nicholson v. Hugh Chatham Memorial Hosp.*, 266 S.E.2d 818, 823 (N.C. 1980); *Jersey Shore Med. Ctr.-Fitkin Hosp. v. Baum's Estate*, 417 A.2d 1003, 1009 (N.J. 1980). In contrast, some states have eliminated it altogether. *See, e.g., Condore v. Prince George's County*, 425 A.2d 1011, 1019 (Md. 1981).

All agree that the old notion that it is the man's primary responsibility to provide a home and its essentials is no longer justified. A female is also no longer destined solely for the home and the rearing of the family, and the male only for the marketplace and the world of ideas. *Orr, supra; Stanton v. Stanton*, 421 U.S. 7, 14-15 (1975). The traditional formulation of the necessaries doctrine, predicated on anachronistic assumptions about marital relations and female dependence, cannot withstand scrutiny under the compelling interest standard. *See Cheshire Med. Ctr. v. Holbrook*, 663 A.2d 1344 (N.H. 1995).

EXAMPLES

Example 11-1

Assume the years are 1830 and 2006 and that a husband and wife live in a jurisdiction that recognizes the necessaries doctrine. Assume that the husband is admitted to the hospital and that the wife signs a form authorizing medical treatment for him. However, the wife refuses to sign a form that guarantees payment for the medical treatment. Assume that the husband recovers and that the hospital seeks payment of the expenses from the wife. The wife replies that the doctrine of necessaries is limited to a husband providing for a wife. Furthermore, she claims that medical expenses are not encompassed within the doctrine. How would a court most likely rule in 1830? In 2006?

EXPLANATIONS

Explanation

Until recently, the wife's argument would have been sustained. Under the common law, the wife was usually dependent on her husband for financial support. However, a majority of jurisdictions have either abolished the doctrine or replaced it with one that makes both spouses equally liable for necessaries. Furthermore, medical expenses are viewed in most jurisdictions that retain the necessaries doctrine as encompassed within it. When both parties are viewed as liable for necessaries, in the absence of an agreement by a spouse to undertake a debt, the creditors may be required to seek initial redress from the spouse incurring the debt, and only if those assets are insufficient may the creditors then reach the other spouse's assets. In this example, therefore, the creditors would most likely be required to initially pursue their claim with the husband. If the husband failed to satisfy the debt, the wife would be liable.

UNIFORM ACTS

11.10. The Uniform Marriage and Divorce Act

During the 1970s, many states adopted all or a portion of the Uniform Marriage and Divorce Act (UMDA). The UMDA was originally ratified by the National Conference of Commissioners on Uniform State Laws in 1970, and after three additional drafts, the American Bar Association endorsed it in 1974. The UMDA was remarkable because it departed from awarding maintenance based on fault when a marriage relationship ended. For example, the commentary to section 308 of the Act reads in part, "Assuming that an award of maintenance is appropriate under subsection 308(a), the standards for setting the amount of the award are set forth in subsection 308(b). Here, as in Section 307, the court is expressly admonished not to consider the misconduct of a spouse during the marriage."

The UMDA also contained a provision regarding homemakers that has been adopted by statute in a majority of jurisdictions. The provision recognized the value of the contributions of a full-time homemaker to the marital partnership and upon divorce entitled the homemaker to share equitably with the wage-earning spouse in the marital property.

11.11. Standard for Determining Amount and Duration Under UMDA

The statutes in the various states provide criteria for judges to apply when determining whether a party is eligible for alimony, the amount to be awarded, and its duration. Considerable discretion is left with the judge in making the award. The UMDA contained a provision that has been adopted in whole or in part in many states:

> The maintenance order shall be in amounts and for periods of time the court deems just, without regard to marital misconduct, and after considering all relevant factors including: (1) the financial resources of the party seeking maintenance, including marital property apportioned to him, his ability to meet his needs independently, and the extent to which a provision for support of a child living with the party includes a sum for that party as custodian; (2) the time necessary to acquire sufficient education or training to enable the party seeking maintenance to find appropriate employment; (3) the standard of living established during the marriage; (4) the duration of the marriage; (5) the age and the physical and emotional condition of the spouse seeking maintenance; and (6) the ability of the spouse from whom maintenance is sought to meet his needs while meeting those of the spouse seeking maintenance.

11.12. American Law Institute Standards

The American Law Institute (ALI) has proposed a "loss compensation" theory to use when alimony is to be considered. ALI, Principles of the Law of Family Dissolution: Analysis and Recommendations §5.05 (2002). Under this theory, one spouse makes compensatory spousal payments to the other spouse for certain losses that have been experienced by the second spouse. The ALI suggests that compensable losses include the loss of a standard of living and a loss incurred because the one spouse was primarily responsible for child care during the marriage. Under the ALI proposal, a spouse would be entitled at dissolution to compensation for the earning-capacity loss arising from his or her disproportionate share, during marriage, of the care of the marital children, or of the children of either spouse.

For example, assume that H and W were married for 20 years and that during that time their relationship was "traditional" in the sense that H worked at developing a business while W remained at home caring for their three children. If W proves that she provided a disproportionate share of the parental child care, the ALI proposal would create an inference that child care responsibilities adversely affected her earning capacity.

The ALI proposal states that a presumption of entitlement to compensation is rebutted by evidence that the claimant did not provide a disproportionate share of the parental child care; however, "the inference that child-care responsibilities adversely affected the claimant's earning capacity is not rebuttable. The reasons are partly pragmatic, and arise from the difficulty of establishing what an individual's earning capacity would have been had the individual made different life choices years earlier." *Id.*

A spouse would also be entitled at dissolution to compensation for earning-capacity losses arising from the care provided during marriage to a sick, elderly, or disabled third party, in fulfillment of a moral obligation of the other spouse or of both spouses jointly. An award is allowed only to a claimant whose earning capacity at divorce is substantially less than that of the other spouse. ALI, Principles of the Law of Family Dissolution: Analysis and Recommendations §5.11(1). For example, assume that H and W were married for 25 years before their marriage broke down. Also assume that H's mother M lived with H and W during the last five years of the marriage. In the twenty-first year of H and W's marriage, M was diagnosed with cancer but continued to live with H and W. W left her part-time employment to care for M at home. After a three-year struggle with cancer, M died. A year later, H and W filed to dissolve their marriage. The ALI would view the care for M as H's moral obligation and, during their marriage, the shared moral obligation of both H and W.

STATE GROUNDS AND STANDARDS FOR DETERMINING NEED FOR ALIMONY

11.13. Fault

As a result of extensive reform movements in the 1960s, all jurisdictions adopted some form of no-fault divorce by 2002. Although no-fault was the sole ground for a divorce in 17 jurisdictions by 2002, in 31 others, it was one of several grounds for divorce — and many traditional grounds remained. *See* Linda D. Elrod & Robert G. Spector, *A Review of the Year in Family Law: State Courts React to Troxel*, 35 Fam. L.Q. 577, 620 (2002). No-fault divorce is designed to reduce acrimony between the parties by abolishing the requirement of proving that one spouse was at fault for the dissolution of the marriage.

Although no-fault divorce grounds are recognized in almost all states, a majority of jurisdictions may consider marital fault when awarding alimony. Some states treat fault as one factor among several when considering whether to award alimony. *See Patterson v. Patterson*, 917 So. 2d 111 (Miss. App. 2005). Some preclude an award of alimony to a spouse who has been at fault. *See Washington v. Washington*, 846 So. 2d 895 (La. App. 2003); *Congdon v. Congdon*, 578 S.E.2d 833 (Va. 2003) (whether denial of alimony would result in manifest injustice is based on the parties' economic circumstances and their fault). *But see Mani v. Mani*, 869 A.2d 904 (N.J. 2005) (fault only relevant if it has affected the parties' economic life or where it "so violates societal norms that continuing the economic bonds between the parties would confound notions of simple justice").

A court in a jurisdiction that permits considerations of fault when awarding alimony is faced with the question of what type of conduct constitutes "fault." Although the standard varies, generally, to constitute legal fault, misconduct must be of a serious nature and must be an independent contributory or proximate cause of the separation. Such acts are often viewed as synonymous with the fault grounds that previously entitled a spouse to a separation or divorce and may include adultery, conviction of a felony, habitual intemperance or excesses, cruel treatment or outrages, public defamation, abandonment, an attempt on the other's life, status as a fugitive, and intentional nonsupport. Mutual incompatibility and general unhappiness with the marital relationship are generally not viewed as lawful causes for leaving the family home. Lawful cause sufficient to justify a spouse's departure from the marital domicile is equivalent to grounds for alimony.

Example 11-2

Assume P and D are divorcing after 18 years of marriage. D has been violent with P throughout the marriage, and D has been convicted of a domestic violence-related felony. Because of D's alcoholism and other personality problems, D is not self-supporting and would qualify for an alimony award under the alimony statute. However, the state where P and D reside also has a statute creating a rebuttable presumption against an award of spousal support to an abusive spouse. P claims that D is precluded from receiving alimony, but D argues that D will be destitute without it. What is the likely result?

Explanation

This example is based on the somewhat similar case of *In re Marriage of Cauley*, 41 Cal. Rptr. 3d 902 (Cal. App. 2006), where the court considered the effect of such a rebuttable presumption statute and held that D was precluded from receiving alimony under it.

11.14. Two-Step Process to Determine Eligibility

A two-step process is usually used to determine whether alimony should be awarded. The first step involves an assessment of the ability of the parties to provide alimony and their need for such support. Once this threshold is met, the second step is to calculate an amount of alimony to be awarded, if any, and its duration.

Step 1 — Financial ability. Typically, a court must find that a party seeking alimony lacks sufficient property to provide for his or her reasonable needs and is unable to be self-supporting through appropriate employment. Appropriate employment usually means employment that is suited to the individual and employment that reflects the expectations and intentions established during the marriage. *See, e.g., In re Marriage of Olar*, 747 P.2d 676, 681-682 (Colo. 1987). The "reasonable needs and unable to support" criteria tend to be interpreted somewhat broadly. *Id.* at 681.

Step 2 — Amount and duration of alimony. Once it is determined that some alimony should be awarded, the next step is to establish the amount and duration. Most jurisdictions have created statutes that contain factors a court is to consider when setting the amount and length of an award. The following is a typical list:

- A spouse's capacities and abilities
- Business opportunities
- Education
- Relative physical conditions
- Relative financial conditions and obligations
- Disparity of ages
- Sizes of separate estates
- Nature of the property
- Disparity in earning capacities or incomes
- Duration of marriage

As noted earlier, courts may consider marital fault in addition to whether one of the parties to the marriage has wasted community assets. The fact that there are ten "non-fault" factors, as well as the fact that the list is nonexclusive, provides a court with broad discretion in making its ultimate determination.

Most courts view the duration of the marriage as particularly important because it is often the major factor creating the disparity in the parties' earning capacities. This is especially true in cases involving a homemaker spouse. Regardless of the spouses' respective roles, duration provides a benchmark for determining reasonable needs — the longer the marriage, the more precisely reasonable needs can be measured by the standard of living established during the marriage.

In addition to the length of the marriage, another critical factor is the role the recipient spouse played during the marriage and the income that spouse is likely to achieve in relation to the standard of living set during the marriage. The latter factor, in turn, is closely related to the recipient spouse's age, health, child care duties, and access to income-producing assets. Depending on the facts of a particular case, it may be appropriate for a court to award permanent maintenance in short-term marriages — those less than 15 years. *See Greene v. Greene*, 895 So. 2d 503 (Fl. Ct. App. 2005) (15-year marriage is a "grey area").

FORMS AND DURATION OF ALIMONY

11.15. Rehabilitative Alimony

Rehabilitative alimony is commonly viewed as a short-term award, which is ordered to enable the former spouse to complete the preparation necessary for economic self-sufficiency. It usually ceases when the dependent spouse is in a position of self-support.

Rehabilitative alimony may be an appropriate consideration if, for example, a spouse gave up or postponed her own education to support the household during the marriage and requires a lump sum or a short-term award to achieve economic self-sufficiency. Its purpose is to enhance and improve the earning capacity of the economically dependent spouse. Its focus is on the ability of a dependent spouse to engage in gainful employment, combined with the length of the marriage, the age of the parties, and the spouse's ability to regain a place in the workforce.

11.16. Reimbursement Alimony

Reimbursement alimony is sometimes characterized as "not truly support but an equitable creation designed to eliminate injustice." Frank Louis,

Limited Duration Alimony, 11 N.J. Fam. Law. 133, 137 (1991). It is intended to compensate a spouse who has made financial sacrifices, resulting in that spouse's reduced standard of living, in order to enable the other spouse to forgo gainful employment while securing an advanced degree or professional license to enhance the parties' future standard of living. Reimbursement alimony is usually limited to monetary contributions made with the mutual and shared expectation that both parties to the marriage would derive increased income and material benefits. Some have questioned whether reimbursement alimony is truly alimony, given that it is based primarily on past contributions rather than future needs.

11.17. Limited Durational Alimony

The focus of limited durational alimony is distinctly different from rehabilitative or reimbursement alimony. Limited durational alimony is not intended to facilitate the earning capacity of a dependent spouse or to make a sacrificing spouse whole. Instead, it is appropriate when an economic need for alimony is established, but the marriage was of short duration, and permanent alimony is therefore not appropriate. *See Gordon v. Rozenwald*, 880 A.2d 1157 (N.J. Super. A.D. 2005) (limited duration alimony appropriate for marriage of short duration). Those circumstances stand in sharp contrast to marriages of long duration in which economic need is also demonstrated. With respect to shorter marriages, limited durational alimony provides an equitable and proper remedy. However, in cases involving longer marriages, permanent alimony is appropriate, and an award of limited durational alimony is clearly circumscribed, by equitable considerations and often by statute.

An award of limited durational alimony should reflect the underlying policy considerations that distinguish it from rehabilitative and reimbursement alimony. Limited durational alimony is conceptually more closely related to permanent alimony than to rehabilitative or reimbursement alimony. The latter two types of alimony represent forms of limited spousal support for specified purposes; once the purpose is achieved, entitlement to that form of alimony ceases. Permanent and limited durational alimony, by contrast, reflect the important policy of recognizing that marriage is an adaptive economic and social partnership, and an award of either validates that principle.

11.18. Incapacity Alimony

This is alimony that is granted when a court finds a spouse to be physically or mentally incapacitated to the extent that the ability of the incapacitated spouse to support himself or herself is materially affected. *See Ferro v. Ferro*, 796 N.Y.2d 165 (N.Y.A.D. 2005) (disability must prevent spouse from earning a living).

11.19. Caregiver Alimony

This is alimony that is granted when a court finds that a spouse must forgo employment to care for a child with a physical or mental incapacity.

11.20. Permanent Alimony

There are two commonly expressed rationales for making an award of permanent alimony. The first is to compensate the recipient spouse for benefits conferred on the other spouse by being responsible for homemaking and child rearing. The primary benefit conferred on the other spouse is increased earning capacity because, while enjoying family life, he or she was free to devote all productive time to income activity outside the home. The second rationale is to compensate for the lost opportunity costs associated with homemaking. Earning capacity may be reduced either by not being employed outside the home or by holding employment subject to the needs of the family. Courts recognize this lost opportunity cost when they refer to the fact that a claimant for alimony remained in the home in the traditional role of full-time homemaker during the marriage. *See In re Marriage of Olson*, 705 N.W.2d 312 (Iowa 2005) (long-term homemaker with health problems entitled to "traditional alimony" for life or as long as incapable of self-support).

A transfer of earning power occurs during a traditional marriage in which the homemaker spouse's efforts have increased the other's earning capacity at the expense of the homemaker. Alimony is an award formulated to compensate for that transfer by sufficiently meeting reasonable needs for support not otherwise met by property division and personal income. *See* Joan M. Krauskopf, *Rehabilitative Alimony: Uses and Abuses of Limited Duration Alimony*, 21 Fam. L.Q. 573 (1988). *Klein v. Klein*, 555 A.20 382, 387 (Vt. 1988).

Although courts often state that permanent maintenance is appropriate in long-term marriages, as discussed previously in Section 11.14, there is no precise point at which marriages are defined as long-term. In general, awards of permanent maintenance may be made in marriages of 15 years or more. *See* Joan M. Krauskopf, *supra*, at 586, 579-580 (1988) (citing trend upholding permanent maintenance awards in cases involving marriages of 15 to 20 years).

Example 11-3

Assume that P and D were married for 30 years before their marriage ended in divorce. P is 50, and D is 48, and both are in good health. During the marriage, P managed the household and was the primary caretaker for the three children. The youngest of the three children was emancipated the previous year. Testimony at trial indicates that P is a high school graduate with limited employment prospects. An expert testified that P could earn from $18,000 to $24,000 annually. D has worked outside the home for the last 25 years as an assembly line worker in a car factory. D has gross annual income of approximately $58,000. P's lawyer has asked the trial judge to award P permanent alimony. D's lawyer argues that D should pay nothing or that the court should award rehabilitative or durational alimony. What will P's lawyer argue, and how will a court most likely decide the alimony issue?

Explanation

P's lawyer may concede that rehabilitative and limited durational maintenance awards are intended to assist the recipient spouse in becoming self-supporting but will contend they are not appropriate in this case. P's lawyer may argue that this is a long-term marriage and that alimony serves to compensate a homemaker for contributions to family well-being not otherwise recognized in the property distribution.

P's lawyer may also argue that the compensatory aspect of alimony reflects the reality that when one spouse stays home and raises the children, not only does that spouse lose future earning capacity by not being employed, but that spouse also increases the future earning capacity of the working spouse. In addition, the working spouse, while enjoying family life, is free to devote productive time to career enhancement. When determining the extent of the compensatory component of an alimony award, a court should give particular consideration to the role of the recipient spouse during the marriage and to the length of the marriage. It is likely that permanent maintenance will be awarded to P.

Example 11-4

Assume that P and D live in a jurisdiction with a statute that allows an award of alimony, either rehabilitative or permanent, to a spouse where the court finds that (1) the spouse lacks sufficient income and/or property to provide for his or her reasonable needs and (2) the spouse is unable to support himself or herself through appropriate employment at the standard of living established during the marriage. The alimony must be in the amount and for the duration the court deems just, based on the consideration of seven nonexclusive factors. Part of the purpose of the statute is to provide spousal support in relation to the standard of living established during the marriage. Another purpose is to recompense a homemaker for contributions made during the marriage.

Also assume that P and D had been married for ten years when their marriage ended. At the time of the divorce, there were no children. P is 55 years old, had back problems for which she received disability benefits, and has not worked outside the home for many years. During the marriage, P helped D obtain a college degree by mail, particularly by typing papers. At the time of the separation, P had an independent income of $670 per month, the bulk of which came from the disability payment. Despite receipt of disability benefits, P is capable of working and earning an income of approximately $800 per month. Her monthly living expenses are about $1,000 per month, including mortgage payments on her home. D's gross income from his work is $45,000 per year and is expected to increase in the future. D's monthly living expenses at the time of the divorce hearing were about $1,800 per month. What are the likely prospects of P being awarded permanent alimony?

EXPLANATIONS

Explanation

In addition to the length of the marriage, the critical factors in determining the duration of an alimony award are the role the recipient spouse played during the marriage and the income that spouse is likely to achieve in relation to the standard of living set in the marriage. The latter factor, in turn, is closely related to the recipient spouse's age, health, child care duties, and access to income-producing assets. Although P is capable of employment, she is 55 years of age and has not worked outside the home for many years. Furthermore, she has a back problem for which she receives the disability payments. In addition, P was the homemaker, and she supported D's efforts to obtain a degree, which has allowed him to obtain the earning capacity he now enjoys. A permanent alimony award is probably necessary to keep P in the standard of living established during the marriage.

OTHER ISSUES REGARDING ALIMONY

11.21. Percentage Formulas

In general, courts have not favored the use of formulas for determining alimony awards. *See, e.g., Kunkle v. Kunkle*, 554 N.E.2d 83, 89-90 (Ohio 1990) (citing cases in other jurisdictions). Particularly disfavored are awards requiring one spouse to pay a percentage of gross or net income to the other spouse. *See, e.g.*, *McClung v. McClung*, 465 So. 2d 637, 638 (Fla. Dist. Ct. App. 1985) (reversing award requiring husband to pay 50 percent of combined net incomes of parties); *Bourassa v. Bourassa*, 481 N.W.2d 113, 115 (Minn. App. 1992) (disallowing award requiring husband to pay 40 percent of his gross monthly income to wife); *Kunkle*, 554 N.E.2d at 88-90 (overturning award requiring husband to pay wife one-third of his gross earned income). When percentage awards are allowed, the cases often involve unusual circumstances. *See, e.g.*, *Hefty v. Hefty*, 493 N.W.2d 33, 36 (Wis. 1992) (considering fluctuation of husband's bonus income, court properly awarded wife fixed monthly sum plus 20 percent of any bonus pay).

11.22. Life Insurance

Some courts have held that requiring the obligor to provide security, such as life insurance, to the recipient against the risk of the obligor's death violates the rule that the obligation to pay alimony normally ends with the obligor's death. *See, e.g.*, *Eagan v. Eagan*, 392 So. 2d 988 (Fla. Dist. Ct. App. 1981); *Perkins v. Perkins*, 310 So. 2d 438 (Fla. Dist. Ct. App. 1975); *Putnam v. Putnam*, 154 So. 2d 717 (Fla. Dist. Ct. App. 1963). *But cf. Stith v. Stith*, 384 So. 2d 317 (Fla. Dist. Ct. App. 1980) (policies of life insurance may be awarded as lump-sum alimony).

11.23. Tax Treatment of Alimony

A payment to a spouse under a divorce or separation instrument is alimony if the spouses do not file a joint return and the payment meets both of two requirements. First, the payment must be based on the marital or family relationship; second, it must not be child support. In addition, the spouses must be separated and living apart for a payment under a separation agreement or court order to qualify as alimony. In general, alimony is considered taxable income to the recipient and is deductible by the payer.

CHAPTER 12

Modifying Alimony

12.1. Introduction

This chapter examines the principles used by courts when considering whether to modify an existing alimony award. An award may generally be modified, even if it has been denominated as "permanent" in the decree, based on a substantial change in financial status or circumstances. Linda D. Elrod & Robert G. Spector, *A Review of the Year in Family Law: Redefining Families, Reforming Custody Jurisdiction, and Refining Support Issues*, 34 Fam. L.Q. 607, 618 (2001). However, because courts and legislatures are not uniform in their approach, the particular law of each jurisdiction must be examined to determine when modification is appropriate.

When an alimony award is made, and a substantial change in circumstances later occurs in the life of either the obligor or the obligee, a court may be confronted with the question of whether to increase, decrease, or eliminate an alimony award or leave it untouched. What constitutes a change in circumstances is a factual inquiry that is said to rest within the trial court's discretion. In general, a trial court's modification decision will not be overturned on appeal absent an abuse of that discretion.

UNIFORM MARRIAGE AND DIVORCE ACT (UMDA)

12.2. UMDA's Unconscionability Standard

The Uniform Marriage and Divorce Act (UMDA) suggests that an existing spousal-support award can be modified only if a change in circumstances has occurred that is so substantial and continuing as to make the terms of the original agreement unconscionable. UMDA §316(b) (1974). This standard has not gained widespread acceptance among the states, which appear to have adopted a less restrictive view.

12.3. States Impose Standards Lower Than UMDA

State legislatures have established modification standards that are not necessarily uniform. For example, Colorado was greatly influenced by the UMDA and originally adopted a standard declaring that an award may be modified "only upon a showing of changed circumstances so substantial and continuing as to make the terms unconscionable." However, in 1986 it amended the statute by replacing "unconscionable" with "unfair." Colo. Rev. Stat. §14-10-122 (1986 Supp.). This made modifying an existing award less burdensome.

PRELIMINARY PROCEDURAL CONSIDERATIONS

12.4. Existing Order or Reservation of Jurisdiction

Courts can generally modify an alimony award only if there is an order currently in effect or if the court reserved subject matter jurisdiction over the issue at the time of the divorce. *See Midzak v. Midzak*, 697 N.W.2d 733 (S.D. 2005) (court expressly reserved jurisdiction). If a court did not award alimony in the original proceeding and failed to reserve jurisdiction, most jurisdictions hold that alimony cannot be awarded at a later date. Similarly, once an alimony order has expired, most courts hold that it cannot be reinstated or modified.

EXAMPLES

Example 12-1

Assume that P and D were divorced in 1997 and that D was ordered to pay alimony until November 30, 2002. D made the final alimony payment on October 15, 2002, approximately six weeks early. On October 30, 2002, P moved to modify the judgment, seeking a permanent alimony order. D moved for summary judgment on the grounds that the court no longer had jurisdiction over the issue of alimony because the order had been fully paid. P argued that D's voluntary early payment did not alter the due date and that the alimony order remained in effect because the final payment had not yet accrued. What is the likely result?

EXPLANATIONS

Explanation

This example is based on the situation in *In re Marriage of Harkins*, 115 P.3d 981 (Ore. App. 2005). In that case, the court agreed with D and held that the court no longer had authority to modify the alimony award because payment had been made in full. Although some courts may take different view, a wise practitioner will advise his or her client to petition for modification well in advance of the termination of the alimony order.

12.5. Burden of Proof and Standard for Change

The party seeking modification normally bears the burden of proving that a change in circumstances has occurred — that is, that there have been changes in the needs of the recipient and in the financial abilities of the obligor. *In re Marriage of Logston*, 469 N.E.2d 167, 176 (Ill. 1984); *Rice v. Rice*, 528 N.E.2d 14, 15 (Ill. App. Ct. 1988). For example, a former spouse's otherwise unsupported assertion that inflation had affected her ability to support herself was not sufficient to warrant modification of an existing alimony award. *Hillier v. Iglesias*, 901 So. 2d 947 (Fla. App. 2005). However, a showing of inability to obtain health insurance was a substantial change in circumstances for purposes of modification. *Metz v. Metz*, 618 S.E.2d 477 (W. Va. 2005).

States differ concerning how substantial the change in circumstances must be in order to warrant modification. *See Tsai v. Tien*, 832 N.E.2d 809 (Ohio App. 2005) (change need not be substantial or drastic but must be more than a nominal change); *Metz v. Metz*, 618 S.E.2d 477 (W.Va. 2005) (substantial change in circumstances); *Withers v. Withers*, 390 So. 2d 453 (Fla. Dist. Ct. App. 1980), *cert. denied*, 399 So. 2d 1147 (Fla. 1981) (substantial change not contemplated at time of judgment); *Zan v. Zan*, 820 N.E.2d 1284

(Ind. App. 2005) (change so substantial and continuing that original terms are unreasonable); *Beard v. Beard*, 751 N.Y.S.2d 304 (App. Div. 2002) (current order creates an "extreme hardship").

12.6. "Bad Bargain" Not a Reason for Modification

Before a court may exercise its discretion to modify an alimony award, a change in circumstances existing at the time of the original decree must have occurred. As a general rule, the court is not to reflect on whether the decree was "equitable" when entered, but only on whether the economic circumstances of the parties have changed since the award such that the original award is now either insufficient or excessive. Most agree that it is not the role of trial courts to relieve a party of his or her bad bargain.

IMPACT OF AGREEMENTS ON SUBSEQUENT MOTIONS FOR MODIFICATION

12.7. Stipulations — Nonmodification Clauses

Courts struggle with the question of whether an alimony award limiting the duration of alimony payments that is the result of an agreement between the parties may be subsequently modified. Most courts distinguish a court-imposed alimony award from an alimony agreement reached by the parties through negotiation and may make modification more difficult if the duration was negotiated.

In several jurisdictions, courts faced with a modification request will apparently only consider whether an originally agreed-upon alimony award involved fraud, duress, or other imperfections of consent or manifest inequities. *See Parrillo v. Parrillo*, 336 S.E.2d 23 (Va. 1985). In the absence of evidence of these claims, the agreements are generally enforced. This view rests on a freedom of contract theory, which, it is thought, will produce mutually acceptable accords, to which parties will voluntarily adhere. It also reflects a belief that the actual purpose behind any particular provision of a settlement agreement made by the parties may remain forever hidden from the trial judge. Courts reason that they may not have possessed authority to impose the kind of alimony award that the parties forged in a settlement agreement; therefore, they cannot subsequently modify the obligation without the consent of the parties.

Courts will also treat stipulations that are incorporated into a judgment differently from stipulations that the court merely refers to and approves. In the latter situation, the arrangement is a contractual determination, not a judicial one; therefore, it is no more subject to change by the court than the terms of any other private agreement. *Marriage of Rintelman v. Rintelman*, 348 N.W.2d 498 (Wis. 1984); *Miner v. Miner*, 103 N.W.2d 4 (Wis. 1960). However, in the former situation, when the court adopts the parties' stipulation and incorporates it into the court's judgment, the award is generally viewed as subject to modification.

OBLIGOR'S CHANGE IN CIRCUMSTANCES

12.8. Obligor's Unanticipated Increased Income

An unanticipated large increase in the obligor's income may constitute a substantial, material change in circumstances. However, if the increase does not make the original alimony award unfair, and the original award maintains the original standard of living, most jurisdictions will not grant an increase in maintenance.

When assessing increases in the recipient's need for alimony, the trial court will usually consider both increases in the actual expenses of the recipient and changes in the recipient's nonsupport income. The trial court will balance the relative economic circumstances of both parties at the time of the request for modification against any increase in the recipient's earnings. The fact that the recipient's income has increased does not necessarily indicate that the recipient's long-term economic circumstances have been improved to such an extent that alimony is no longer required or should be reduced. A court, of course, should not speculate about the equities of the original award, but should confine its evaluation to increases in the recipient's needs since the divorce.

EXAMPLES

Example 12-2

Assume that P and D divorced after a 20-year marriage. At the time of the divorce, they were both unemployed; however, D was receiving $3,000 each month from a trust. The court ordered that D pay P $500 per month in permanent alimony. A year after the divorce, D obtained a position that paid $5,000 a month. P remained unemployed and moved to increase alimony to $1,000 a month. How will a court most likely treat the motion?

EXPLANATIONS

Explanation

P will argue that D's financial worth has increased substantially and that D can afford to pay additional alimony. P will explain that P cannot make ends meet on $500 per month and that P should be entitled to a standard of living more commensurate with that of the marriage. D will argue that P's needs haven't increased since the original alimony order was entered and that one of the purposes of divorce is to end the parties' financial interdependency. However, if P can clearly establish need, the court most likely will grant the request. *See Irwin v. Irwin*, 539 So. 2d 1177 (Fla. App. 1990).

12.9. Obligor's Retirement

When the retirement of an obligor is voluntary or foreseeable at the time of the divorce, several jurisdictions have denied a modification of alimony request. *See Wheeler v. Wheeler*, 548 N.W.2d 27 (N.D. 1996); *Leslie v. Leslie*, 827 S.W.2d 180, 183 (Mo. 1992); *Ellis v. Ellis*, 262 N.W.2d 265, 268 (Iowa 1978); *Deegan v. Deegan*, 603 A.2d 542 (N.J. Ct. App. 1992) (retirement should have been considered when parties originally divorced). Although most courts take the view that traditional standards regulating modification of support agreements should be applied to motivate parties to provide for such contingencies in their dissolution agreement, strict application of these standards in the retirement context can create unreasonable hardships. *Cf. Sifers v. Sifers*, 544 S.W.2d 269, 269-270 (Mo. Ct. App. 1976) (denying modification when obligor "voluntarily" retired, even though he was 62, had a malignant kidney removed, and was unable to find employment in the industry in which he had worked all his life). Courts have also said that at some point, parties must recognize that just as a married couple may expect a reduction in income because of retirement, a divorced spouse cannot expect to receive the same high level of support after the supporting spouse retires. *See In re Marriage of Reynolds*, 74 Cal. Rptr. 2d 636, 640 (Ct. App. 1998).

Courts caution that although bona fide retirement after a lifetime spent in the labor force is somewhat of an entitlement, an obligor cannot merely utter the word "retirement" and expect an automatic finding of a substantial and material change in circumstances. Rather, a court should examine the totality of the circumstances surrounding the retirement to ensure that it is objectively reasonable. In *Ebach v. Ebach*, 700 N.W.2d 684 (N.D. 2005), the court considered the following nonexclusive list of factors in determining the totality of the circumstances:

> A court may consider, for instance, the age gap between the parties; whether at the time of the initial [spousal support] award any attention was given by the parties to the possibility of future retirement; whether the particular retirement

> was mandatory or voluntary; whether the particular retirement occurred earlier than might have been anticipated at the time [spousal support] was awarded; and the financial impact of that retirement upon the respective financial positions of the parties. It should also assess the motivation which led to the decision to retire, i.e., was it reasonable under all the circumstances or motivated primarily by a desire to reduce the [spousal support] of a former spouse. A court may also wish to consider the degree of control retained by the parties over the disbursement of their retirement income, e.g., the ability to defer receipt of some or all. It may also wish to consider whether either spouse has transferred assets to others, thus reducing the amount available to meet their financial needs and obligations.

Id. at 689.

The burden of establishing that the retirement is objectively reasonable is on the party seeking modification of the award. *Seal v. Seal*, 802 S.W.2d 617, 620 (Tenn. Ct. App. 1990).

Example 12-3

Assume that P and D had been married for 25 years before they divorce. The court ordered that D pay P $1,500 a month permanent alimony. Following the divorce, P lived on the alimony payment plus a few hundred dollars she took from her IRA each month. The IRA had a value of about $50,000. At the time of the divorce, D was earning about $5,000 a month. When he reached age 60, D voluntarily retired because he was offered a retirement package that would guarantee him $2,000 per month for life. He was also suspicious that he would be laid off or fired, and he felt that coping with the boss was getting increasingly difficult. D now moves to reduce his alimony obligation. How will a court most likely treat D's motion?

Explanation

D may have a difficult time obtaining a reduction, even though D acted in good faith. P will argue that she has relied on the alimony and that early retirement should have been addressed at the time of divorce. A court may reduce the obligation if D has only the $2,000 to live on. Otherwise, the award may well stand. *See Deegan v. Deegan*, 603 A.2d 542 (N.J. App. 1992).

12.10. Obligor's Change of Occupation

Generally, when a party voluntarily assumes a lower-paying job, there will be no recomputation of the alimony payment. Courts have consistently ruled that obligors act in bad faith when they voluntarily leave steady employment without alternate plans for income or for positions that are less likely to provide sufficient income. *See Curtis v. Curtis*, 442 N.W.2d 173, 177-178 (Minn. Ct. App. 1989) (holding obligor acted in bad faith when he voluntarily left his employment of ten years without alternate employment plans); *Warwick v. Warwick*, 438 N.W.2d 673, 678 (Minn. Ct. App. 1989) (holding obligor acted in bad faith by resigning from his job, unjustifiably limiting his income); *Juelfs v. Juelfs*, 359 N.W.2d 667, 670 (Minn. Ct. App. 1984) (holding obligor in bad faith for voluntarily quitting long-time employment in favor of running business that had little chance of producing similar income).

A party ordinarily will not be relieved of an alimony obligation by voluntarily quitting work or by being fired for misconduct. When seeking a reduction in alimony payments because of a change in employment, the obligor must establish first that the voluntary change in employment, which resulted in a reduction of income, was not made for the purpose of avoiding alimony payments and, second, that a reduction in alimony is warranted based on the party's efforts to mitigate any income loss. In effect, the moving party must present evidence as to why he voluntarily left the prior employment and also as to why the acceptance of a lower-paying job was necessary. Otherwise, for calculation of a maintenance obligation, the moving party will be considered to have an income equal to his earning capacity.

Some courts may grant a temporary reduction or suspension in alimony when the obligor has suffered a reduction in income without deliberately seeking to avoid paying alimony and is acting in good faith to return his income to its previous level. However, a reduction in alimony will be denied when the moving party has not made a good-faith effort to obtain employment commensurate with his qualifications and experience. *See, e.g., Yepes v. Fichera*, 230 A.D.2d 803 (N.Y. App. Div. 1996).

An award of alimony may be based on the obligor's ability to work as distinguished from actual income. In some states, such as California, the court considers the spouse's ability to work, willingness to work, and opportunity to work. When ability and opportunity are present, and willingness is absent, the court has the discretion to apply the earnings capacity standard. Cf. *Pencovic v. Pencovic*, 287 P.2d 501 (Cal. 1955) (the earning capacity standard is properly used when the paying parent willfully refuses to seek or accept gainful employment).

A court is likely to reject the view that a finding of good faith prevents use of the earning-capacity standard. Although deliberate avoidance of family responsibilities is a significant factor in the decision to consider earning capacity, a trial court's consideration of earning capacity is not limited to cases in which a deliberate attempt to avoid support responsibilities is found. *See In re Marriage of Ilas*, 16 Cal. Rptr. 2d 345 (Cal. App. Dept. Super. Ct. 4 Dist. 1993).

Example 12-4

Assume that P and D divorced and that D was ordered to pay alimony to P based on D's employment as a computer hardware specialist earning $111,000 per year. D lost his job because of a reduction in work force, and one month later, he took a position as a massage therapist earning $300 per week (approximately $15,000 per year). D petitioned to reduce the alimony payment, arguing that the order should be based on his present lower income given that his change of position was involuntary. P argues that the alimony payment should be calculated based on the prevailing wage for computer service technicians because D elected to pursue a less lucrative career. What is the likely result?

Explanation

In the similar case of *Storey v. Storey*, 862 A.2d 551 (N.J. Super. 2004), the court imputed to D annual earnings of $60,000, the prevailing wage for a computer service technician. Although D's departure from his job was involuntary, the court held that because he had selected a less lucrative career, D had the burden of establishing that the resulting benefit to him substantially outweighed the disadvantages to P. The court found that D's decision was not reasonable under the circumstances.

Example 12-5

P and D's 15-year marriage was dissolved, and the court ordered D to pay $250 per month in alimony for 60 months. At the time of the dissolution, D was employed as a line technician earning about $24 per hour. He resigned from this position after about 18 years with the company. His resignation was precipitated by his failing a random drug test. A few months later, D also quit a second job because of a mutual disagreement with his employer. At D's request, the district court reduced his alimony obligation to $125 per month because he was now earning about half of what he had been earning at the time of the divorce. P appealed. How would an appellate court most likely treat the reduced alimony?

Explanation

As a general rule, a petition for modification will be denied if the change in financial condition is because of fault or voluntary wastage or dissipation of one's talents and assets. It is undisputed that in this case, there has been a change in D's financial condition and that he is now earning approximately half as much as he once earned. However, the issue is whether the change was because of D's fault or voluntary wastage or dissipation of his talents and assets. Most courts would rule that the reduction in income was D's own fault and would not permit a modification on these facts. The appellate court would most likely reverse the trial court.

OBLIGEE'S CHANGE IN CIRCUMSTANCES

12.11. Obligee Takes a Job Outside the Home

Courts are sometimes asked to modify an alimony award when the obligee takes a job following a divorce. At least two factors are important in deciding the issue. First, was it foreseeable at the time of the divorce that the obligee would seek employment? Second, does the new job provide funds that will allow the obligee to live at the standard of living enjoyed during the marriage? If the answer to the former question is yes, most courts will not modify an existing award. If the answer to the second question is yes, courts are more willing to reduce or eliminate an award.

In *Block v. Block*, 717 N.Y.S.2d 24 (App. Div. 2000), the court rejected a modification request when the ex-wife procured employment before the expiration of durational alimony. The alimony award was scheduled to expire when the parties' youngest child entered kindergarten. The court observed that although the original order awarding alimony stated that it would be "difficult" for the wife to return to work before the parties' youngest child entered kindergarten, "that possibility was not ruled out, and it certainly was not an unforeseeable event that could not have been taken into account in setting the original award." *Id.* at 87. *See Matter of Hermans v. Hermans*, 547 N.E.2d 87 (N.Y. 1989) (particularized showing of facts concerning the personal and financial circumstances of the parties both at the time of the original divorce settlement and at the present time is required, and changes in the prevailing social and legal climate that may have occurred since the parties were divorced do not satisfy this standard); *Wheeler v. Wheeler*, 230 A.D.2d 844 (N.Y. App. Div. 1996) (court erred in terminating maintenance when obligee's earning potential increased as a result of her receiving a nursing degree when there was a substantial increase in the obligor's income between the time of the parties' divorce and the modification hearing).

TERMINATING ALIMONY

12.12. Remarriage

In most jurisdictions, alimony is automatically terminated upon remarriage, unless the parties' agreement or the divorce decree expressly provides that the flow of alimony is to remain unimpeded by the recipient spouse's remarriage. *See Gibb v. Sepe*, 690 N.W.2d 230 (N.D. 2004) (express agreement that alimony would continue after remarriage enforced). The theory is that remarriage is legally connected with need, and the link is broken because the new spouse has formed a legal relationship with another and has assumed a joint legal duty of support. *See, e.g., Voyles v. Voyles*, 644 P.2d 847 (Alaska 1982); *Burr v. Burr*, 353 N.W.2d 644 (Minn. Ct. App. 1984), *Van Bloom v. Van Bloom*, 246 N.W.2d 588 (Neb. 1976).

Some states, however, do not require automatic termination of an alimony award on remarriage of the recipient spouse. Instead, they hold that remarriage establishes a prima facie case for termination or reduction of the alimony payments. *See, e.g., Oman v Oman*, 702 N.W.2d 11 (S.D. 2005); *Keller v. O'Brien*, 652 N.E.2d 589, 593 (Mass. 1995); *Marquardt v. Marquardt*, 396 N.W.2d 753, 754 (S.D. 1986). In these jurisdictions, the receiving spouse may continue to receive maintenance, but only in an extraordinary circumstance. *See, e.g., In re Marriage of Gillilland*, 487 N.W.2d 363, 366 (Iowa Ct. App. 1992) (extraordinary circumstance found when standard of living provided by new spouse with annual income of $30,000 would not meet standard of living during previous marriage to husband who earned $220,000 annually); *Bauer v. Bauer*, 356 N.W.2d 897, 898-899 (N.D. 1984) (extraordinary circumstance found when payer spouse and recipient spouse had large disparity in education and payer spouse's unfulfilled agreement to pay for recipient spouse's education was incorporated in original decree).

12.13. Recipient Cohabits

The majority rule regarding the effect of post-divorce cohabitation on spousal support is that the right to receive spousal support becomes subject to modification or termination only if the recipient spouse's need for the support decreases as a result of the cohabitation. *See Gayet v. Gayet*, 456 A.2d 102, 104 (N.J. 1983); Annotation, *Divorced Woman's Subsequent Sexual Relations or Misconduct as Warranting, Alone or with Other Circumstances, Modification of Alimony Decree*, 98 A.L.R.3d 453 (1980 & Supp. 1996). When there is a showing of financial dependence by the alimony recipient upon the third-party cohabitant, a court will likely reduce spousal support. *See Gayet*, 456 A.2d at 104; *Woodard v. Woodard*, 696 N.W.2d 221 (Wis. App. 2005) (obligee benefited from cohabitant's income); *Miller v. Miller*, 892 A.2d 175 (Vt. 2005) (cohabitation must improve financial circumstances enough to substantially reduce need for maintenance). Similarly, if alimony payments are used to benefit the cohabitant, most courts will reduce or eliminate them. *See, e.g., In re Marriage of Tower*, 780 P.2d 863, 866-867 (Wash. Ct. App. 1989). As stated by the New Jersey Supreme Court, "modification [of spousal support] for changed circumstances resulting from cohabitation [is warranted] only if one cohabitant supports or subsidizes the other under circumstances sufficient to entitle the supporting spouse to relief." *Gayet*, 456 A.2d at 104.

Of course, the amount of spousal support that is reduced, if any, depends on a factual examination of the financial effects of the cohabitation on the recipient spouse. *See Ricketts, supra*, at 154. Shared living arrangements, unaccompanied by evidence of a decrease in the actual financial needs of the recipient spouse, are generally insufficient to call for alimony modification. *See In re Marriage of Bross*, 845 P.2d 728, 731-732 (Mont. 1993); *Mitchell v. Mitchell*, 418 A.2d 1140, 1143 (Me. 1980) (cohabitant's benefit from a recipient spouse's expenditures on heating fuel, which would have a similar cost absent the shared living arrangements, does not show a decreased need for alimony). When a restriction regarding cohabitation is a part of a marital termination agreement, courts have tended to enforce the provision. *See Bell v. Bell*, 468 N.E.2d 849 (Mass. 1984).

Some jurisdictions, by statute or judicial decision, require elimination of spousal support upon a showing of post-divorce cohabitation. *See* S.C. Code 1976 §20-3-150 (West 2005); *Gayet*, 456 A.2d at 103-104; *Lucas v. Lucas*, 592 S.E.2d 646 (interpreting statute providing for possible termination of spousal support where a de facto marriage exists). Others have concluded that the mere fact of cohabitation is just a factor for the court to consider in the changed-circumstances assessment. *See Alibrando v. Alibrando*, 375 A.2d 9, 13-14 (D.C. 1977).

EXAMPLES

Example 12-6

Assume that P and D divorce after a traditional 20-year marriage. P is required to pay D $1,000 per month permanent alimony. Six months after the divorce is final, D moves in with X. P brings a motion to eliminate the alimony award, arguing that it is unfair to require him to pay alimony when his ex-wife and another man are living together much like husband and wife. P argues that cohabiting is so similar to remarriage that it terminates spousal support. D responds that X is not supporting her and has no legal obligation to do so. P also notes that there is not a provision in the final divorce decree that eliminates alimony should she move in with another person following divorce. How will the court most likely rule?

Explanation

The trend is to reject the argument that cohabitation alone can be the basis for terminating alimony. In determining the effect of post-divorce cohabitation on a recipient spouse's alimony entitlement, financial, rather than moral, aspects of the cohabitation should be the primary consideration.

In ruling on P's request, the trial court may consider what effect, if any, D's cohabitation with another person has had on D's financial circumstances. If X makes financial or other tangible contributions toward the living expenses of D, D's ability to support herself may be increased, her needs may be reduced, and the alimony award may in some cases be reduced accordingly; conversely, when the expenses of D are increased because of D's voluntary support of persons whom D is under no duty to support, a court may disregard those expenses to extent they are claimed by recipient as evidence of increased "need." Here, a court would have to conduct an evidentiary hearing to make these determinations. Only then could it make a sound decision. *See Gilman v. Gilman*, 956 P.2d 761 (Nev. 1998).

12.14. Death

Obviously, the recipient's death ends the need for support. However, when a lump-sum alimony award has been ordered, it is viewed by some courts as vested in the obligee, and a spouse's estate may receive the payment. *See, e.g., Maxcy v. Estate of Maxcy*, 485 So. 2d 1077, 1078 (Miss. 1986). When the obligor dies, the maintenance obligation generally terminates, unless stated otherwise in the court order. *See Findley v. Findley*, 629 S.E.2d 222 (Ga. 2006) (death of obligor terminates obligation to pay alimony); *Haville v. Haville*, 825 N.E.2d 375 (Ind. 2005) (order may continue spousal maintenance beyond the death of the obligor).

12.15. Annulment

States may by statute view an annulment of the alimony recipient's remarriage like a divorce and prohibit reinstatement of the terminated alimony obligation of the previous spouse. *See, e.g., Hodges v. Hodges*, 578 P.2d 1001, 1005 (Ariz. Ct. App. 1978); Ferdinand S. Tinio, *Annulment of Later Marriage as Reviving Prior Husband's Obligations Under Alimony Decree of Separation Agreement*, 45 A.L.R.3d 1033 (1972).

12.16. Retroactivity

Most jurisdictions take the view that orders modifying alimony agreements can be made retroactive only to the date of filing a modification motion. However, the rule is not applied when the filing was delayed because of a misrepresentation by another party, so long as the motion is filed in a timely fashion upon discovery. *See, e.g.*, *Albert v. Albert*, 707 A.2d 234 (Pa. Super. Ct. 1998); *In re Marriage of Elenewski*, 828 N.E.2d 895 (Ill. App. 2005).

CHAPTER 13

Dividing the Marital Estate upon Divorce

13.1. Introduction

When couples divorce and are unable to amicably agree on how their property is to be divided, and they reject mediation or some form of arbitration, the only recourse is to litigate the matter before a judge in family court. This chapter surveys the law and illustrates the application of the more common legal principles used by courts to resolve property disputes.

When valuing and distributing property, a court is said to have three tasks. First, it must gather and then classify all the assets involved in the action to determine those that are subject to distribution as martial property and those that are nonmarital property and will remain the separate property of each party. The property having been classified, the next step is to place a reasonable value on the assets that are subject to distribution and those that are the separate property of each spouse. Finally, the court must reach a decision on what is an equitable distribution of the martial assets.

SEPARATE PROPERTY SYSTEM THEORY

13.2. Overview

During the past century, states have used three general theories when considering the question of how to divide marital assets upon divorce. *See* Stephen J. Brake, *Equitable Distribution vs. Fixed Rules: Marital Property Reform and the*

Uniform Marital Property Act, 23 B.C. L. Rev. 761, 762 (1982). The three distribution theories or "systems" are the now-outdated separate property system; the community property system, which is used today in about eight jurisdictions; and the equitable distribution system, which is used today by a majority of jurisdictions.

13.3. Title Was Controlling

The outdated separate property system was based on the theory that each party was entitled to retain an asset to which that party had title. Should a couple divorce, although a rare occurrence when this theory was in vogue, the property was returned to the title-holding spouse.

The separate property system was criticized as unjust, especially in a traditional family setting where most of the property was titled in the husband's name. If a divorce occurred, a traditional homemaker was often left with nothing but a claim for alimony, which often proved difficult to enforce. The separate property system was reluctant to recognize a homemaker's nonfinancial contributions to the marriage. In some instances where both spouses worked outside the home and the husband's income was placed into investments while the wife's earnings were devoted to family expenses, upon divorce, the husband received the investments— an obvious unfair result.

EXAMPLES

Example 13-1

Assume that P and D were divorced after 20 years of marriage in a jurisdiction that applied the separate property theory of division of assets. During the marriage, D worked inside the home and was the primary caretaker for the couple's five children, and P worked outside the home. The home— purchased just after the couple married with a down payment of $10,000— some stock accumulated during the marriage, and the family automobile were all titled in P's name. When D sought an equitable share of the home, stock, and car, how would a court in this jurisdiction most likely rule?

EXPLANATIONS

Explanation

The answer is self-evident, and the problem is used to illustrate the harsh realities of the literal application of the separate property theory to a divorce. In this case, a court would most likely have awarded P the home, stock, and the automobile reasoning that title was only in his name, and therefore, it was his separate property. Most likely, D would receive only alimony.

COMMUNITY PROPERTY THEORY

13.4. Overview

It is generally understood that the community property concept is an outgrowth of the civil law influence of France, Spain, and Mexico. Arizona, California, Idaho, Louisiana, New Mexico, Nevada, Texas, and Washington are recognized as community property states. Wisconsin closely aligned itself with community property theory when it adopted the Uniform Marital Property Act.

13.5. Marriage Is a Partnership

Jurisdictions that adhere to a community property system of distribution of assets upon divorce accept the theory that a marriage is a partnership and that the partnership concept applies during the marriage, upon dissolution of the marriage, or upon the death of one of the partners. In general, both spouses are vested in all the property acquired during the marriage, other than property that by statute is specifically excluded from the community, such as a gift to one partner but not the other, or an inheritance to one partner but not the other. Some jurisdictions may also allow earnings on nonmarital property to remain separate property, but others may not. The increase in the value of a party's separate property resulting from that party's effort during marriage is usually considered community property. *See Cockrill v. Cockrill*, 601 P.2d 1334, 1336 (Ariz. 1979).

13.6. Death of Partner

In a community property state, the spouse acquires a "present vested undivided one-half interest in all property acquired during the existence of the marital relationship," regardless of the state of title. *Rodgers v. Rodgers*, 98 A.D.2d 386, 391 (N.Y. App. Div. 1983); *Hursey v. Hursey*, 326 S.E.2d 178, 181 (S.C. Ct. App. 1985).

When a spouse dies intestate, the survivor is viewed as owning one-half of the community property. The only issue that can be litigated involves the deceased's remaining one-half interest in the community property — the survivor already owns the other half. In a noncommunity property state, when a partner dies intestate, intestacy laws may provide the survivor with a portion of or all of the estate.

EQUITABLE DISTRIBUTION JURISDICTION THEORY

13.7. Marriage Is a Joint Enterprise

The separate property theory, discussed earlier in this chapter, has been rejected in all jurisdictions and replaced in 43 states with the equitable distribution theory. The remaining jurisdictions have adopted some form of the community property distribution theory.

The concept of equitable distribution is a corollary of the principle that marriage is a joint enterprise whose vitality, success, and endurance is dependent on the conjunction of multiple components, only one of which is financial. The nonremunerated efforts of raising children, making a home, performing a myriad of personal services, and providing physical and emotional support are among other noneconomic ingredients of the marital relationship. They are viewed as essential to its nature and maintenance as are the economic factors, and courts and legislatures believe that their worth is entitled to substantial recognition. The extent to which each party contributes to the marriage is measurable not only by the amount of money contributed to it, but also by a whole complex of financial and nonfinancial components. Equitable distribution recognizes that when a marriage ends, each of the spouses, based on the totality of the contributions made to the marriage, has a stake in and right to a share of the marital assets accumulated because they represent the capital product of what was essentially a partnership entity.

13.8. Defining Marital Property

In an equitable distribution jurisdiction, marital property is usually defined as not including property (1) acquired before the marriage; (2) acquired by inheritance or gift from a third party; (3) excluded by valid agreement; or (4) directly traceable to any of these sources. Marital property is generally viewed broadly and in most jurisdictions includes pensions and retirement investments acquired or earned during the marriage, as well as equity in property built up during the marriage. The controlling legal principle determining the court's division of marital property in most of these jurisdictions is the rather broad standard of what is "just and equitable."

EXAMPLES

Example 13-2

Assume P and D were married in an equitable distribution jurisdiction. Before the marriage, D owned a home valued at $100,000, which did not have a mortgage on it. During the marriage, the couple lived in the home, and when they divorced, it was valued at $200,000. P argues that because this is an equitable distribution jurisdiction, he should receive an equitable interest in the home. How will a court most likely rule?

EXPLANATIONS

Explanation

Assuming that D can meet the burden of proving her claim, a court will most likely award the entire home to D. She owned it free and clear before the marriage and is entitled to the benefit of her investment. All the increase in the value of the home is a result of market forces and is viewed as nonmarital.

13.9. Presumption of Ownership — Title Not Controlling

In a no-fault equitable distribution jurisdiction, in the absence of a valid agreement between the parties, a trial court will presume that all marital property is to be divided equally between the parties. *See Matter of Marriage of Stice*, 779 P.2d 1020 (Or. 1989). The presumption is applied regardless of how title is held — that is, regardless of whose name is on the legal document showing ownership. In jurisdictions adopting the equitable distribution theory, equality is the cardinal precept, and it is assumed that all wealth acquired by the joint efforts of the husband and wife is common property. *See In re Marriage of Wanstreet*, 364 Ill. App.3d 729 (Ill. 2006).

Obviously, if a person can show that an asset was acquired in exchange for nonmarital property, this presumption is overcome. *Kottke v. Kottke*, 353 N.W.2d 633, 636 (Minn. Ct. App. 1984), *pet. for rev. denied* (Minn. Dec. 20, 1984). In several jurisdictions, the presumption of equal contribution to the acquisition of property during the marriage may also be overcome by a finding that the property was acquired by one spouse not influenced directly or indirectly by the other spouse (i.e., the other spouse has contributed neither economically nor otherwise to the acquisition of the property in issue). *In re Marriage of Kunze*, 92 P.3d 100 (Or. 2004) (although the inquiry into the "just and proper" division necessarily includes consideration of the statutory factors, including the court's determination under the presumption of equal contribution, that inquiry also takes into account the social and financial objectives of the dissolution, as well as any other considerations that bear upon the question of what division of the marital property is equitable).

Some courts may also consider other factors, including monetary contributions to marital property such as employment income, other earnings, and funds that were separate property. The court may also consider nonmonetary contributions to marital property, such as homemaker services, child care services, labor performed without compensation, labor performed in the actual maintenance or improvement of tangible marital property, or labor performed in the management or investment of assets that are marital property. The court may consider the effect of the marriage on the income-earning abilities of the parties, such as contributions by either party to the education or training of the other party or forgoing by either party of employment and education.

Finally, a court may consider conduct by either party that may have reduced the value of marital property. *See Arneault v. Arneault*, 605 S.E.2d 590 (W. Va. 2004); *Somerville v. Somerville*, 369 S.E.2d 459, 460 (W. Va. 1988) (in the absence of a valid agreement, the trial court in a divorce case shall presume that all marital property is to be divided equally between the parties, but may alter this distribution, without regard to fault, based on consideration of certain statutorily enumerated factors); *Gantner v. Gantner*, 640 N.W.2d 565 (Wis. App. 2002) (court presumes that marital property is divided equally, and it is only in considering whether to deviate from this presumption that it looks to various statutory factors).

13.10. Tracing — Overcoming the Marital Presumption

When a party claims that an asset is nonmarital, the burden is normally placed on that party to trace the asset to its nonmarital source. *Scott v. Scott*, 161 S.W.3d 307 (Ark. 2004); *Kreilick v. Kreilick*, 831 N.E.2d 1046 (Ohio App. 2005); *Hall v. Hall*, 462 A.2d 1179, 1181-1182 (Me. 1983); *Hoffmann v. Hoffmann*, 676 S.W.2d 817, 824 (Mo. 1984); *Brandenburg v. Brandenburg*, 617 S.W.2d 871, 872 (Ky. Ct. App. 1981). In general, this means that when the original property claimed to be nonmarital is no longer owned, the nonmarital claimant must trace the previously owned property into a presently owned specific asset. If the claimant does so, then the trial court assigns the specific property, or an interest in specific property, to the claimant as his or her nonmarital property. *See Terwilliger v. Terwilliger*, 64 S.W.3d 816 (Ky. 2002).

EXAMPLES

Example 13-3

Assume that P, an experienced businessperson, was injured in an accident prior to marriage to D and received a $50,000 cash settlement. About a year after the parties married, P purchased a parcel of land only in his name, allegedly for $50,000 and allegedly using only the premarital accident injury settlement funds. The parties' marriage broke down after 20 years, and they were unable to agree on the division of property. The parcel of land purchased 19 years earlier was now valued at $500,000, and P asserted that it was his nonmarital property, and he was entitled to it. D disagreed, saying that she recalled that some of the down payment on the land came from their joint bank account, maybe as much as $15,000, and some from a $10,000 inheritance she had received when her father died. She also recalled that P purchased a new car for about $25,000, paying cash for it, the first year of their marriage. At trial, P produced a paid note issued by the previous land owner, showing that P had paid $50,000 and including a date showing it was issued two years after P and D married and backdated one year. P also submitted a copy of the release of his injury claim, which indicated that the claim was settled for $50,000 prior to the marriage. During cross-examination, P conceded that he was an experienced businessperson, juggling the assets and liabilities of a number of corporations and orchestrating complex business deals. D produced a copy of the $10,000 check given to her as a part of her father's estate, and it was dated one year after the couple married. No other evidence was introduced. Has P produced sufficient evidence to persuade a judge that the land is his nonmarital property?

EXPLANATIONS

Explanation

Although a close question, most courts will most likely conclude that P has failed in his burden to trace the asset to its nonmarital source. As a skilled businessperson, with an apparent extensive recordkeeping experience, P is not the sort of person that the court would protect from the stringent tracing requirements. A court would most likely reason that he would be expected or required to keep detailed and accurate records, and it is certainly reasonable to require him to maintain and to produce records to establish his claims of nonmarital property. Note that there is some suggestion in the case law that although tracing to a mathematical certainty is not always possible, a precise requirement might be more appropriate for skilled businesspersons who maintain comprehensive records of their financial affairs than it would be for persons with lesser business skills or persons who are imprecise in their recordkeeping abilities. *See Terwilliger v. Terwilliger*, 64 S.W.3d 816 (Ky. 2002).

13.11. Formula for Calculating Value of Nonmarital Assets

In an equitable distribution jurisdiction, a court determines the present value of a nonmarital asset used in the acquisition of marital property by calculating the proportion the net equity or contribution at the time of acquisition bore to the value of the property at the time of purchase, multiplied by the value of the property at the time of separation. The remainder of the equity increase is characterized as marital property and is equitably distributed. *Woosnam v. Woosnam*, 587 S.W.2d 262 (Ky. Ct. App. 1979). *See Keeling v. Keeling*, 624 S.E.2d 687 (Va. App. 2006) (trial court erred in failing to apply the *Brandenburg* formula, which would have apportioned the marital and nonmarital contributions of hybrid property in the same percentages as their respective contributions to the total equity in the property, to ascertain the current value of husband's separate contributions toward the purchase of the marital residence).

EXAMPLES

Example 13-4

Assume that P and D were married in an equitable distribution jurisdiction. Before the marriage, D owned a home, which on the day of her marriage was valued at $100,000 and had a $50,000 mortgage on it. During the marriage, the couple lived in the home, and D made all of the house payments. When they divorced, the home was valued at $200,000. P argues that because this is an equitable distribution jurisdiction, he should receive an interest in the home. D argues that because she made all the payments during the marriage, she should receive 100 percent of the home. How will a court most likely rule — how will a court apportion the homestead?

EXPLANATIONS

Explanation

On the day the couple married, D had a 50 percent interest in the home ($50,000 is 50 percent of $100,000). During the marriage, the value of the home increased as a result of market forces, and D's 50 percent initial investment in the home should be recognized. Therefore, on divorce, she should receive $100,000 as her nonmarital interest in the homestead (50 percent of $200,000 is $100,000). The remaining $100,000 will be divided equitably between P and D, with each probably receiving about $50,000. D will most likely receive a total of $150,000.

Example 13-5

Assume P and D were married in an equitable distribution jurisdiction. Also assume that on the date of their marriage, P owned real estate then valued at \$30,000, but subject to a \$20,000 mortgage. Shortly after they married, the couple, using marital funds and doing a lot of the work themselves, built an addition to the home and increased its value by \$10,000—from \$30,000 to \$40,000. During the course of the marriage, the parties used marital funds to pay the mortgage balance down to \$4,000. At the time of the divorce, the market value of the home was \$100,000. P and D seek a determination of their marital and nonmarital interests in the home.

Explanation

Inasmuch as the real property included both marital and nonmarital interests, the court must recognize that there are three kinds of "increase" involved in the example: (1) the increase in value attributable to the physical improvement of the property through application of marital funds and marital effort; (2) the increase in value attributable to the increase in equity by application of marital funds to reduce the mortgage indebtedness; and (3) the increase in value attributable to inflation and market forces. The hypothetical assumes an investment of cash and of property and services having a cash value in the total amount of \$40,000. Whatever amount P may have invested in the property prior to the marriage, on the date of the marriage, his nonmarital equity in the property was \$10,000 (33 ⅓ percent). During the marriage, the parties contributed marital funds and labor in the construction of an addition, which increased the value of the property by \$10,000, and they undertook to pay off the \$20,000 mortgage with marital funds, reducing the unpaid balance to \$4,000.

The present value of P's nonmarital interest is the proportion his net equity at the time of marriage (\$10,000) bore to the aggregate of the value of the property on the date of the marriage (\$30,000) plus the value of the addition on its completion (\$10,000). The interests will then be apportioned as follows:

1. \$10,000/\$40,000 = 25 percent
2. \$100,000 × .25 = \$25,000 (P's nonmarital interest)
3. \$100,000 – \$25,000 = \$75,000 (marital interest)

The net value of the property, however, is \$96,000 (\$100,000 – \$4,000 mortgage balance). Because the parties undertook payment of the mortgage debt with marital funds, reduction of the marital interests by the amount of the mortgage balance (\$75,000 – \$4,000 = \$71,000) is appropriate. Thus, \$71,000 is marital property, and \$25,000 is P's nonmarital property. *See Nardini v. Nardini*, 414 N.W.2d 184, 193 (Minn. 1987).

13.12. Active and Passive Appreciation — Stock

In an equitable distribution jurisdiction, the increase in value attributable to the efforts of the spouses is generally considered "active appreciation." The couple then share in the increase or decrease in value of the stock. However, the increase in value of property attributable to inflation, general economics, and market conditions is considered "passive appreciation." If the property increases in value because of these forces, the entire increase in value is attributed to the partner holding the stock.

Example 13-6

Assume that on the day of her marriage to P, D owned 300 shares of XYZ Company. On the date of marriage, the market value of the publicly traded, unencumbered shares was $25 per share, or $7,500. At the time of the divorce, D owned 800 shares of XYZ Company, which then had a market value of $40 per share or $32,000. The increase in the number of shares was the result of a 2-for-1 split during the marriage, which increased D's holdings from 300 to 600 shares. The additional 200 shares were acquired through the reinvestment of cash dividends paid during the marriage. D claims all 800 shares of XYZ Company as her nonmarital property. P argues that the increase in value of the shares during the marriage and the additional shares received during the marriage are marital property. How will a court most likely resolve P's claim?

Explanation

If the court applies the intent of the drafters of the Uniform Marriage and Divorce Act, section 307, comment at 204 (1970), a stock split is nonmarital property. The theory is that when stock splits, the value is determined by market forces and does not increase the shareholder's proportionate ownership interest in the corporation. Therefore, it is not considered income.

Note that if the total value of D's 800 shares of XYZ Company were worth only $10 per share at the time of the dissolution, D's 600 nonmarital shares would then be worth only $6,000, which is less than the value of the 300 shares D owned when she married P. The 200 shares purchased with marital funds would then have a present value of $2,000.

13.13. Source of Funds Theory

In the absence of a specific statute, some jurisdictions have adopted a "source of funds" or tracing theory of equitable distribution when there has been no joint titling after the marriage. *Hoffmann v. Hoffmann*, 676 S.W.2d

817, 825 (Mo. 1984). Under the source of funds theory, when property is acquired by an expenditure of both nonmarital and marital property, the property is characterized as part nonmarital and part marital. Therefore, a spouse who contributes nonmarital property to the marriage is entitled to maintain a proportionate nonmarital share in an otherwise marital asset. *See Thomas v. Thomas*, 377 S.E.2d 666, 669 (Ga. 1989) (quoting *Harper v. Harper*, 448 A.2d 916, 929 (Md. 1982); *Wade v. Wade*, 325 S.E.2d 260, 269 (N.C. Ct. App. 1985) (citing *Harper*, 448 A.2d at 929).

13.14. No Source of Funds Theory

If a jurisdiction has not adopted the source of funds theory, a spouse who commingles separate property with marital property may be viewed as causing the separate property to lose its nonmarital character, and courts in these jurisdictions may classify the commingled property as marital property subject to equitable distribution. *See, e.g., Srinivasan v. Srinivasan*, 396 S.E.2d 675, 677 (Va. Ct. App. 1990).

EXAMPLES

Example 13-7

Assume that P and D divorce after 25 years of marriage in a jurisdiction that *does not* apply the source of funds theory. During the marriage, P received $200,000 as a gift from his mother. P placed the funds in P and D's joint bank account, which they used for household expenditures. When they divorce ten years later, P asserts that the $200,000 is his nonmarital property. How will a court in this jurisdiction most likely rule?

EXPLANATIONS

Explanation

A court will most likely rule that when P failed to segregate and instead commingled separate property with marital property, the commingled property became marital property subject to equitable distribution. *See Smoot v. Smoot*, 357 S.E.2d 728, 731 (Va. 1987). The evidence in this hypothetical fails to establish that P considered his interest to be composed of discrete, segregated shares but suggests that all of P's funds were commingled and considered to be an integral part of the marital estate. *See In re Marriage of Smith*, 427 N.E.2d 1239, 1245-1246 (Ill. 1981) (holding that separate property valued at $45,000 was transmuted to marital property when improved by $3,800 of marital property).

13.15. More on Transmutation of Property

Transmutation is a judicially created doctrine generally applied to prevent unfairness in the distribution of assets. When applied, property that was once classified as separate or nonmarital can be transmuted into marital property when the spouse with title represents to the other spouse that the property will be shared. *See Kenney v. Kenney*, 30 P.2d 398, 399 (Cal. 1934); *In re Marriage of Smith*, 427 N.E.2d 1239, 1244 (Ill. 1981). Transmutation allows a spouse to transmute an item of nonmarital property into marital property by agreement, either express or implied, or by gift. For example, nonmarital property may be changed into marital property if a gift of nonmarital property into co-tenancy with the other party is made or if nonmarital property is commingled with marital property. However, technical application of the transmutation rule restricting the characterization of property precisely to title ownership may result in unfair results between the parties; therefore, equitable considerations may take precedence over mechanical application of the transmutation rule.

Nonmarital property does not become marital property solely because it may have become commingled with marital property. *D.K.H. v. L.R.G.*, 102 S.W.3d 93, 100 (Mo. App. 2003). Rather, the owner's intent to convert the property to marital property is the determining factor. *Kinsey-Geujen v. Geujen*, 984 S.W.2d 577, 579 (Mo. App.1999); *see also Ker v. Ker*, 776 S.W.2d 873, 877 (Mo. App. 1989) (holding that "[n]onmarital property may lose its character as such if there is evidence of an intention to contribute the property to the community"); *Pirri v. Pirri*, 631 S.E.2d 279 (S.C. App. 2006); *Hanson v. Hanson*, 125 P.3d 299 (Alaska 2005). Nonmarital property cannot be transmuted to marital property based on evidence—oral, behavioral, or documentary—that is easily manipulated and unreliable. *In re Marriage of Benson*, 32 Cal. Rptr.3d 471 (Cal. 2005); *Estate of MacDonald*, 272 Cal. Rptr. 153 (Cal. 1990).

Example 13-8

Assume that stocks acquired by P before and during his marriage to D were shown to be either a gift from his parents or purchased with nonmarital assets. The bank account through which P bought and sold stock and deposited dividends was occasionally used for marital purposes. When the couple divorced in a jurisdiction *that applies the source of funds theory*, P argued that the stock purchased with these funds was his nonmarital property. D contended that once P used an account that on occasion was used for marital purposes, the stock was transmuted into marital property. How will a court most likely rule?

Explanation

A court most likely will rule in favor of P. A court would observe that transmutation is a matter of intent to be gleaned from the facts of each case, and the mere use of separate properties to support the marriage without some additional evidence of intent to treat it as marital property is not sufficient to establish transmutation. In general, the spouse claiming transmutation must produce objective evidence showing that during the marriage, the parties themselves regarded the property as the common property of the marriage. Nonmarital property is transmuted into marital property when it becomes so commingled as to be untraceable. However, the mere commingling of funds does not automatically make them marital funds. Here, the sparse facts tend to support P. *See Wannamaker v. Wannamaker*, 406 S.E.2d 180 (S.C. Ct. App. 1991).

Example 13-9

Assume that P and D married in a source of funds jurisdiction and that P brought $7,000 into the marriage. These funds and approximately $3,000 that D brought into the marriage were commingled in a joint account and used throughout the ten-year marriage for various expenses. When they divorce, P argues that she is entitled to the $7,000 as her nonmarital property. How will a court in a source of funds jurisdiction most likely rule?

Explanation

Although this is a source of funds jurisdiction, a court most likely will rule that the funds have lost their nonmarital character. The mere fact that the funds were placed in a joint account does not necessarily require that they be considered marital property. In many jurisdictions, a presumption arises that when deposits are made into a joint bank account between spouses, the parties share a joint ownership in the funds on deposit. The presumption, however, is rebuttable by either spouse wishing to show that the account consists of his or her separate property only. These limiting principles probably won't save P, however. Because the premarital funds were contributed to a joint account, there has been a long passage of time, and the account was used by both parties during the marriage, a court will most likely rule that they were transmuted into marital property.

13.16. "Egregious Fault"

Most, if not all, jurisdictions have no-fault grounds for a divorce. A majority also have rejected application of fault when dividing marital property. However, if there is "egregious fault," some courts may consider the conduct when dividing property. *See Alford v. Alford*, 478 N.Y.S.2d 717, 718 (N.Y. App. Div. 1984) ("In the absence of egregious circumstances marital fault is not a proper factor to be considered under equitable distribution"). Most courts, however, limit the use of fault to an award of alimony—not a division of property. *See, e.g., Fisher v. Fisher*, 648 S.W.2d 244 (Tenn. 1983); *Compare Wilbur v. Wilbur*, 498 N.Y.S.2d 525 (N.Y. App. Div. 1986) ("[M]arital fault is, generally, a proper consideration in awarding maintenance") *with Dusenberry v. Dusenberry*, 326 S.E.2d 65 (N.C. Ct. App. 1985) (finding an adulterous affair on the part of a wife was an irrelevant and inappropriate matter in determining equitable distribution of marital property). In *Charlton v. Charlton*, 413 S.E.2d 911, 915 (W. Va. 1991), the court stated that in enacting our equitable distribution statute, the Legislature did not intend fault to be considered as a factor in determining the division of marital property. However, the Legislature did designate marital fault as a factor to be considered in awarding alimony under the provisions of W. Va. Code 48-2-15(i).

UNIFORM ACTS AND RECOMMENDATIONS

13.17. Uniform Marriage and Divorce Act (UMDA)

The Uniform Marriage and Divorce Act (UMDA) addresses the disposition of property upon divorce. As originally drafted, section 307(a) of the UMDA provided that the court "shall assign each spouse's property to him" and then divide the marital property in just proportions. The act provided that marital property did not include property acquired by gift, property acquired in exchange for property acquired by gift, or increase in value of property acquired before marriage. UMDA §307(b)(1), (2), (5). According to the Commissioners' Note to section 307 and judicial interpretation of section 307, appreciation in value of nonmarital property is not marital property, but income from nonmarital property is marital property. *See Wierman v. Wierman*, 387 N.W.2d 744, 748 (Wis. 1986).

In 1973, section 307 was amended to provide two alternatives to dividing property upon divorce. Alternative A proceeds upon the principle that all property of the spouses, however acquired, should be regarded as assets of the married couple, to be apportioned equitably between the spouses.

Alternative B is designed for community property states and permits courts to divide community property after considering certain criteria. Both of these alternatives recognize that the spouses have been partners in the marriage and require courts to look beyond title in deciding how much each spouse should share in the assets to be distributed. *See* Elizabeth A. Cheadle, Comment, *The Development of Sharing Principles in Common Law Marital Property States*, 28 UCLA L. Rev. 1269, 1287 (1981).

It should be noted that courts in jurisdictions that have adopted property distribution statutes based upon the UMDA have held that income derived from nonmarital property during the marriage is marital property. *In re Marriage of Reed*, 427 N.E.2d 282, 285 (Ill. App. Ct. 1981); *Sousley v. Sousley*, 614 S.W.2d 942, 944 (Ky. 1981); *In re Marriage of Williams*, 639 S.W.2d 236 (Mo. Ct. App. 1982); *See Brodak v. Brodak*, 447 A.2d 847, 855 (Md. 1982).

13.18. Uniform Marital Property Act (UMPA)

The Uniform Marital Property Act (UMPA) also provides that income received during the marriage is marital property, regardless of the source of income. *See* UMPA §4 cmt., 9A U.L.A. 110 (1987). In Wisconsin, where the UMPA has been adopted, property acquired with income generated by an excluded asset is also considered marital property. *Arneson v. Arneson*, 355 N.W.2d 16, 19 (Wis. Ct. App. 1984).

13.19. American Law Institute (ALI) Recommendations

The American Law Institute Principles of the Law of Family Dissolution: Analysis and Recommendations is the result of 11 years of work. The following is a summary of several sections of the ALI Principles that are associated with property division.

Section 4.03 contains the definition of marital and separate property, which follows standards held in community property and most common law jurisdictions. *See* David Westfall, *Unprincipled Family Dissolution: The American Law Institute's Recommendations for Spousal Support and Division of Property*, 27 Harv. J.L. & Pub. Pol'y 917 (2004). The section defines nonmarital property as property acquired either before marriage or as gifts (or inheritances) from third parties during marriage as the separate property of the acquiring spouse and hence not subject to division on divorce. Section 4.04 defines income and appreciation in the value of separate property as nonmarital property unless its value has been enhanced by spousal labor or it is impacted by section 4.12, which provides for gradual recharacterization of nonmarital property in marriages that last a minimum of five years. *Id.* at 947. Section

4.05(1) provides that a portion of any increase in the value of separate property is marital property whenever either spouse has devoted substantial time during marriage to the property's management or preservation.

Section 4.07 declares that occupational licenses and educational degrees should not be subject to division on divorce, and section 4.07 so provides. Section 4.09(1) mandates an equal division of marital property and marital debts, but section 4.09(2)(b) and section 4.09(2)(c) allow a court under certain circumstances to order an unequal division of debts. Section 4.09(1) exceptions provide that a court may deviate from equal division if it determines that a spouse is entitled to alimony and chooses to provide for the alimony by means of a larger property settlement. It may also deviate if a party is guilty of misappropriating marital property by making substantial gifts to third parties within a specified time period; by losing, expending, or destroying marital property by intentional misconduct within a specified time period; or by negligently losing or destroying marital property after service of the dissolution petition. A court may deviate from equal division if marital debts exceed marital assets, and it is just and equitable to unequally allocate the excess debt because of financial capacity, participation in the decision to incur the debt, or the purpose of the debt. Finally, a court may deviate from equal division if an existing debt was incurred to finance a spouse's education.

Section 4.10 allows an unequal division of property when one of the spouses has committed some sort of financial misconduct. The misconduct may involve (1) certain gifts made without the other party's consent; (2) property lost, expended, or destroyed through intentional misconduct; and (3) property lost or destroyed through negligence after the service of the dissolution petition. The suggested time period during which the conduct described is relevant is either six months — in the case of (1) or (2) — or a year prior to the service of the dissolution petition.

PROFESSIONAL LICENSES AND DEGREES

13.20. Advanced Degrees

New York treats a professional license as a marital asset and subject to equitable distribution. In *O'Brien v. O'Brien*, 489 N.E.2d 712 (N.Y. 1985), the court held this view was justified because the New York Legislature "deliberately went beyond traditional property concepts when it formulated the Equitable Distribution Law." *Id.* at 715. A court therefore must determine the present value of projected future earnings of the spouse holding the degree at the time of divorce. In *O'Brien*, the court observed that although there may be problems fixing the present value of enhanced earning capacity, the problems are not insurmountable and no more difficult than computing tort damages for wrongful death or diminished earning capacity resulting from injury. The court reasoned that fixing a value on a professional license differs only in degree from the problems presented when valuing a professional practice for purposes of a distributive award, something the courts have not hesitated to do.

A majority of jurisdictions refuse to treat professional licenses and degrees that represent one spouse's enhanced earning capacity as marital property. They take the view that a professional license is not property at all but represents a personal attainment in acquiring knowledge. They also note that a professional license is not physically or metaphysically property. An advanced degree does not have an exchange value or any objective transferable value on an open market, and any attempt to place a value on it is too speculative. It is personal to the holder, terminates on death of the holder, is not inheritable, and cannot be assigned, sold, transferred, conveyed, or pledged. An advanced degree is a cumulative product of many years of previous education, combined with diligence and hard work. It may not be acquired by the mere expenditure of money. It has none of the attributes of property in the usual sense of that term. *See Simmons v. Simmons*, 708 A.2d 949 (Conn. 1998); *Graham v. Graham*, 574 P.2d 75 (Colo. 1978). Advanced degrees are best considered when awarding alimony rather than when distributing property. *But see In re Marriage of Horstmann*, 263 N.W.2d 885 (Iowa 1978) (increased earning capacity is a distributable asset); *Inman v. Inman*, 578 S.W.2d 266 (Ky. App. 1979) (there are certain instances in which treating a professional license as marital property is the only way in which a court can achieve an equitable result). The *Inman* holding, however, is limited. *See Leveck v. Leveck*, 614 S.W.2d 710 (Ky. App. 1981) (where there was some marital property, there is no need to treat a medical degree as a marital asset).

Although a majority of jurisdictions reject treating a professional degree obtained during a marriage as marital property, they do not ignore the degree. For example, some jurisdictions suggest that the future value of a degree acquired by one of the parties during the marriage, though not subject to division or transfer upon divorce, should be considered an element in reaching an equitable award of alimony. *See, e.g., Stevens v. Stevens*, 492 N.E.2d 131, 136-137 (Ohio 1986); *Downs v. Downs*, 574 A.2d 156 (Vt. 1990). A court may consider using a cost-value approach, whereby it calculates the value of the supporting spouse's contributions, not only in terms of money for education and living expenses, but also in terms of services rendered during the marriage. *See, e.g., De La Rosa v. De La Rosa*, 309 N.W.2d 755 (Minn. 1981).

Some courts may examine a spouse's lost opportunity costs because of the marriage. When this theory is applied, a court considers the income the family sacrificed because the student spouse attended school rather than accepting employment. If, for example, the student spouse could have earned $50,000 a year at a job rather than attend school, this loss of income to the family unit is considered.

Another approach is to consider compensating the supporting spouse according to the present value of the student spouse's enhanced earning capacity. This approach recognizes the spouse's lost expectation of sharing in the enhanced earning capacity; it gives the supporting spouse a return on his or her "investment" in the student spouse, measured by the student spouse's enhanced earning capacity. For example, assume the estimated enhanced earning capacity of the husband was $266,000. The figure is "the product of multiplying the husband's after-tax annual enhanced earnings of $13,000 (the difference between the husband's annual salary as a physician and the mean salary for white college-educated males in his age group) by 32.3 (estimated years remaining in the husband's expected working life) discounted to its present value." *Haugan v. Haugan*, 343 N.W.2d 796, 803 (Wis. 1984).

EXAMPLES

Example 13-10

Assume that P and D were married in 2000. That year, D embarked on an accelerated medical school program to obtain a medical degree. P testified that while D attended medical school, she worked as a waitress five or six nights a week, earning between $30 and $40 a night. In the summers, P also was employed as Recreational Assistant. Previous to the marriage, she had worked as a nurse's aide. The monies P earned were used to support the family and possibly to some extent to pay certain medical school tuition and expenses of D. D received his medical degree in 2003 and notified P that he wanted a separation. They separated for two years, and then P began divorce proceedings. P testified that during the separation, she had obtained a nursing certificate, and at the time of the divorce, she was earning about $50,000 a year. It was estimated that D was earning about $150,000 a year. The parties had not accumulated marital property of any significant value at the time of separation, and P could not, therefore, be reimbursed for her contributions to her husband's education through a distribution of property. P also waived a request for alimony. An expert placed a value on D's medical degree at $1 million, and P sought a one-third share of it. In a majority jurisdiction, how will a court most likely treat P's argument?

Explanation

The court will not in a majority jurisdiction place a value on the medical degree and distribute it to P. It will recognize that shortly after the degree was received, the marriage failed, and P was unable to see any benefit for her sacrifice while D was able to pursue a career as a physician. A court will generally conclude that P should be compensated for the financial support she gave D while he was a student. The award will not be viewed as alimony but most likely will be considered compensation for P's contribution to attainment of the degree while they were married. *See Lehmicke v. Lehmicke*, 559, 489 A.2d 782 (Pa. Super. 1985); *Mahoney v. Mahoney*, 453 A.2d 527 (N.J. 1982). Usually, a court would award alimony in such a case, and P's contribution would be recognized in that award. However, the court is faced with a very challenging problem. A favored view is the cost-value approach, described earlier. *See, e.g., De La Rosa v. De La Rosa*, 309 N.W.2d 755 (Minn. 1981).

OTHER MARITAL PROPERTY

13.21. Workers' Compensation and Personal Injury Awards

Courts have not been uniform in their treatment of workers' compensation awards. Some courts appear to categorize them as benefits, whereas others view them as a personal injury recovery. *See Weisfeld v. Weisfeld*, 545 So. 2d 1341, 1344-1345 (Fla. 1989). The various perspectives are summarized in the following paragraphs.

Some courts take the mechanistic approach. In these jurisdictions, if a personal injury or workers' compensation award was acquired during the marriage, then it is considered marital or community property and is divided as such, unless it falls within specific but limited statutory exceptions. The courts are guided by the statutory definition of what is separate and what is marital property. Arkansas, Colorado, Illinois, Michigan, Missouri, Nebraska, Pennsylvania, and Vermont appear to have followed this view. *See Liles v. Liles*, 711 S.W.2d 447 (Ark. 1986); *In re Marriage of Fieldheim*, 676 P.2d 1234 (Colo. App. 1983); *In re Marriage of Dettore*, 408 N.E.2d 429 (Ill. App. Ct. 1980); workers' compensation proceeds are considered marital property subject to division. *Hagen v. Hagen*, 508 N.W.2d 196 (Mich. 1993) (division of payments on workers' compensation claim for injury that occurred during the marriage found proper); *Jobe v. Jobe*, 708 S.W.2d 322 (Mo. Ct. App. 1986); *Maricle v. Maricle*, 378 N.W.2d 855 (Neb. 1985); *Platek v. Platek*, 454 A.2d 1059 (Super. Ct. 1982); *Condosta v. Condosta*, 395 A.2d 345 (Vt. 1978).

The second approach is analytical and examines the nature of a workers' compensation or personal injury damage award to determine whether the property is separate and belongs to the injured spouse or is marital property subject to distribution. Under this approach, the damage award is allocated along the following lines. First, the separate property of the injured spouse includes the noneconomic compensatory damages for pain, suffering, disability, and loss of ability to lead a normal life and the economic damages that occur subsequent to the termination of the marriage of the parties, including the amount of the award for loss of future wages and future medical expenses. Second, the separate property of the noninjured spouse includes loss of consortium. Third, the marital property subject to distribution includes the amount of the award for lost wages or lost earning capacity during the marriage of the parties and medical expenses paid out of marital funds during the marriage. *Id.*

Community property states may take a third approach. In *Graham v. Franco*, 488 S.W.2d 390 (Tex. 1972), for example, the court observed that

> [t]he body of the wife brought into the marriage was peculiarly her own; and that if any "property" was involved in a personal injury to the wife, it was peculiarly hers. If her house, her separate property, were set afire and destroyed by a third person, the recovery should be her separate property. If an automobile were owned by the wife before marriage and was injured or destroyed, the recovery should go to repay the loss or damage to her separate property. So, the reasoning continues, if the arm of the wife is cut off, the recovery for the loss because of disfigurement and for the attendant pain and suffering should go to the wife. The reasoning is that the recovery is a replacement, in so far as practicable, and not the "acquisition" of an asset by the community estate.

Another view is that when a personal injury or workers' compensation claim is pending at the time of divorce, some courts have said that because of the uncertainty surrounding whether a plaintiff spouse may win or lose the claim, it does not constitute marital property. However, most now view a pending claim as constituting marital property subject to later distribution.

EXAMPLES

Example 13-11

Assume that P is injured in an industrial accident, loses his right arm, and is out of work for six months. P and D divorce in a jurisdiction that applies the analytical approach to workers' compensation awards. Six months after the divorce settlement, P receives a lump-sum payment of $100,000. P argues that compensation for an injury resulting in the loss of his right arm is a benefit and not property acquired during the marriage to be considered for distribution as marital property. P also argues that as an individual, he brought his body into the marriage, and on dissolution of the marriage, he is entitled to take it with him. He contends that his body is his separate property, and compensation received for damage or loss to it is his separate property. P also argues that a spouse's health, life, limb, personal security, and so on can be viewed as property acquired prior to marriage and later exchanged for compensation. Finally, he argues that because the final award was speculative at the time of divorce, it cannot be considered as marital property now. How will a court most likely treat these arguments and distribute the property?

Explanation

A court is likely to view the award as encompassing earnings lost both before and after the divorce and as involving individual pain and suffering. If a portion of the award is for income lost before divorce, a court would hold that the pre-divorce portion is marital property subject to division. The post-divorce portion related to loss of income will likely be viewed as nonmarital and belonging exclusively to P. *See Miller v. Miller*, 739 P.2d 163, 165 (Alaska 1987); *Queen v. Queen*, 521 A.2d 320, 324 (Md. 1987). The court would also determine that the noneconomic compensatory damages for pain, suffering, disability, and P's loss of ability to lead a normal life are P's nonmarital property.

13.22. Social Security

Social Security benefits are apparently not subject to equitable distribution. *Powell v. Powell*, 577 A.2d 576, 580 (Pa. 1990). *See Flemming v. Nestor*, 363 U.S. 603, 609-610 (1960) ("To engraft upon the Social Security system a concept of 'accrued property rights' would deprive it of the flexibility and boldness in adjustment to ever changing conditions which it demands").

OTHER PROPERTY ISSUES

13.23. Premarital Agreements

Premarital contracts or settlements validly executed and in conformity with the statutes and common law of a particular jurisdiction may determine what rights each party has in the nonmarital property upon dissolution of marriage, upon legal separation, or after the marriage's termination because of death and may bar each party of all rights in the respective estates not secured to them by their agreement. *See Gentry v. Gentry*, 798 S.W.2d 928 (Ky. 1990).

13.24. Bankruptcy

Congress changed the bankruptcy law in 1994 and again in 2005 so that divorce-related property obligations are not always dischargeable. However, to prevent discharge, the creditor spouse must meet several difficult procedural and substantive requirements.

13.25. Tax Treatment

As a result of the Tax Reform Act of 1984, the recipient of property in a divorce takes the transferor's adjusted basis for the property. Prior to the 1984 reform, when property was transferred from one spouse to another as a result of a divorce settlement, and the fair market value exceeded the asset basis, the Internal Revenue Service considered this a taxable event, and taxes were due. If property that was transferred had lost value, this was also considered a taxable event. *United States v. Davis*, 370 U.S. 65 (1962).

13.26. Qualified Domestic Relations Order (QDRO)

When a couple divorces, determining the value of and distributing their pensions has considerable significance. Most courts will place a value on vested and unvested property rights, making little distinction between them. *See Bender v. Bender*, 785 A.2d 197 (2001).

To avoid tax penalties and to enhance the means of distributing the pensions, Congress passed the Retirement Equity Act of 1984, which exempted from the spendthrift and preemption provisions "qualified domestic relations orders" or "QDROs." 29 U.S.C. §1056(d)(3)(A). *See Eller v. Bolton*, 895 A.2d 382 (Md. App. 2006). By using a QDRO, a state court can order a pension-plan administrator to distribute a portion of a pension to the other spouse. A recipient may now "roll over" a pension received as a result of a QDRO to a qualified pension account without tax consequences.

A qualified domestic relations order (QDRO) is a "special order after final judgment," and it must be denominated a "judgment" to be appealable. *Brooks v. Brooks*, 98 S.W.3d 530, 532 (Mo. En Banc, 2003).

Premarital (Antenuptial or Prenuptial) Contracts — History, Requirements, and Restrictions

14.1. Introduction

This chapter surveys the legal issues confronting a court faced with the question of whether to enforce a premarital contract. A premarital contract is referred to in various jurisdictions as a "premarital," "antenuptial," or "prenuptial" contract. If validly created, a premarital contract permits the parties to agree before they marry to waive or limit certain "rights" or "benefits" that generally flow from the marital relationship. The contract is used to control property distribution upon the occurrence of two events: the death of a spouse or a divorce.

There are three basic differences between a premarital contract and an ordinary civil contract. Judith T. Younger, *Perspectives on Antenuptial Contracts*, 40 Rutgers L. Rev., 1059, 1061 (1988). First, the state has a greater interest in a premarital contract than in a commercial contract. Because of its interest, the state assumes the role of *parens patriae* with respect to protecting the children of the relationship and, in some cases, protecting the distribution of marital and nonmarital property. Second, the relationship between the parties is different from that found in an ordinary contract situation because at the time the contract was made, courts viewed the relationship between the parties as confidential, not as an arm's-length one. Furthermore, unlike most business contracts, the parties to a premarital contract may be unevenly matched in bargaining power. Finally, a premarital contract is to be performed in the future, in the context of a personal relationship that the parties have yet to experience.

When assessing a premarital contract's validity, courts will consider the motive, extent of knowledge, and consideration involved in it. Furthermore, a court will insist that the contract meet certain minimal standards of good faith and fair dealing.

Some assert that the legal system's willingness to enforce these contracts reflects an evolving transformation of marriage from a public institution to a private contractual relationship. *See Marriage as Contract and Marriage as Partnership: The Future of Antenuptial Contract Law*, 116 Harv. L. Rev. 2075 (2003). The contracts' widespread use may also reflect a trend in favor of enforcement, more limited judicial review, and greater respect for parties' freedom of contract. *Id.*

HISTORY

14.2. Sixteenth-Century England — Limited to Use upon Death

Premarital contracts first appeared during the sixteenth century in England. Younger, *supra*, citing at nn.2, 5, W. Holdsworth, *A History of English Law* 310-312 (3d ed. 1945). Both chancery and law courts passed on their validity, and by the mid-seventeenth century, they were of sufficient importance to be included in the original Statute of Frauds. *Id.* at nn.3, 4.

Historically, a premarital contract settled property rights at the time of the death of one of the parties to the relationship. A contract was often executed when the parties were contemplating a second marriage, and one or both had substantial property and children from a first marriage to whom they wanted their property to go upon their death. Without a premarital contract, in most jurisdictions, a surviving spouse had the option of taking property provided under a will or taking a statutory share of the marital estate and ignoring the will.

14.3. Twentieth-Century Use of Contracts — Upon Death or Divorce

Until the late twentieth century, a premarital contract could not be used in the event of divorce. The common law courts reasoned that the public's interest in the enforcement of the spousal duty of support should not be thwarted by a premarital provision that they believed bore little or no reasonable relationship to the subsequent circumstance of the parties.

The common law began to change its view of the use of a premarital contract upon divorce when *Posner v. Posner*, 233 So. 2d 381 (Fla. 1970), was decided. In that decision, the Florida court took judicial notice of the fact that the ratio of marriages to divorces has

> reached a disturbing rate in many states. . . . With divorce such a commonplace fact of life, it is fair to assume that many prospective marriage partners whose property and familial situation is such as to generate a valid premarital contract settling their property rights upon the death of either, might want to consider and discuss also — and agree upon, if possible — the disposition of their property and the alimony rights of the wife in the event their marriage, despite their best efforts, should fail.

Id. at 384. Following this decision, most jurisdictions have steadily retreated from the common law view that a premarital contract could not be used upon divorce.

EXAMPLES

Example 14-1

Assume that P and D execute a premarital contract that is valid except for a provision that limits the amount of alimony D would pay should the couple divorce. In a typical common law jurisdiction, how would such a provision be treated? In a jurisdiction that applies the *Posner* perspective, how would this provision be treated?

EXPLANATIONS

Explanation

In a common law jurisdiction, the contract would not be enforced. Common law courts viewed a contract to distribute property upon divorce as contrary to public policy on the theory that it encouraged a breakdown of the marriage relationship. However, in most jurisdictions today, assuming all other matters were appropriate, the contract to limit alimony would be upheld. *See*, e.g., *Snedaker v. Snedaker*, 660 So. 2d 1070 (Fla. App. 1995) (provisions in premarital contract that neither spouse acquired any interest in property of other as a result of marriage, provisions that set the amount of the wife's support payments on escalating scale based on the length of marriage, and provisions that specifically waived a spouse's right to receive any further alimony, support, or maintenance payments were fair and reasonable to wife, given the circumstances of the spouses).

COMMON LAW STANDARDS AND PROCEDURES

14.4. Common Law Limitations and Principles

As already noted, the common law recognized and upheld a premarital contract that disposed of property upon the death of a party if the contract was validly procured and ostensibly fair in result. However, the common law firmly rejected any notion that a contract could distribute property upon divorce. *Cohn v. Cohn*, 121 A.2d 704 (Md. 1956); *In re Estate of Appleby*, 111 N.W. 305 (Minn. 1907). Again, it was believed that a divorce provision in a premarital contract might encourage a breakdown of the marriage relationship.

For a contract to be valid in most common law jurisdictions, it had to be fair, equitable, and reasonable in view of all of the surrounding facts and circumstances. There must be proof that it was entered into voluntarily by both parties, with each understanding his or her rights and the extent of the waiver of such rights. *Hockenberry v. Donovan*, 136 N.W. 389 (Mich. 1912). However, the contracts were often upheld in situations where most would agree that the division of property was unfair. *See, e.g., Estate of Serbus v. Serbus*, 324 N.W.2d 381 (Minn. 1982) (premarital contract upheld where widow received $4,000, funeral, and life estate in homestead and its furnishings, rather than about $300,000 to which she would have been entitled if permitted to take against the will or if no will were in existence).

14.5. Common Law Presumptions

Common law jurisdictions that recognized the validity of premarital contracts did not agree on the use of presumptions. For example, in some jurisdictions, a presumption of fraud immediately arose if the premarital contract provided a disproportionately small allowance for the non-monied partner. *See* Annot., 27 A.L.R.2d 873 and cases cited therein. These courts often wrote that the "consideration" for the contract was not adequate, and therefore, fraud was presumed. Other jurisdictions, however, approached the application of a presumption differently. For example, Michigan created a kind of checklist that it used to determine whether a presumption of fraud existed. *See, e.g., Matter of Benker's Estate*, 331 N.W.2d 193 (Mich. 1982) (setting forth a seven-point checklist).

In jurisdictions where fraud was automatically presumed because of a disproportionate division of property, the burden of proving the absence of fraud shifted to the proponent of the contract to show that it was voluntarily entered with full and fair disclosure of the nature, extent, and value of the other spouse's property and knowledge of the rights that were being waived. *See, e.g., Hill v. Hill*, 356 N.W.2d 49 (Minn. App. 1984).

EXAMPLES

Example 14-2

Assume that this common law jurisdiction will apply a presumption of fraud theory upon a finding that there has been a disproportionate division of property in the premarital contract. Assume that three weeks before the couple married, a premarital contract was executed at a time when P was 65 and D 68. P agreed that D could make a will after their marriage, providing that, should D die before P, P's survivor's estate in D's marital property would be limited to $4,000 in cash, a life estate in the homestead and its furnishings, and a funeral similar in nature and quality to his. P waived her right to an intestate share of the marital property. Following their marriage, a will incorporating the terms of the premarital contract was executed, signed by P, and witnessed by an attorney and a secretary in the law office where it was drafted. P selected the attorney; however, it appears that the attorney was likely representing D, but giving some advice to P regarding the contract.

Ten years later, D died, leaving an estate valued at more than $1 million. P challenged the premarital contract. The trial court ruled that the consideration of $4,000, a life estate in the home and furnishings, and a funeral like D's was inadequate and that because a confidential relationship existed at the time the contract was entered, the contract was presumptively fraudulent. Under the law in this jurisdiction, the burden to overcome the presumption then shifted to D's estate. The estate argued that P was represented by independent counsel at the time the contract was signed and that P had knowledge of the property owned by D, as evidenced by the detailed list of the property owned by D attached to the contract. Despite this evidence, the judge ruled that because of the unfair division of assets at the time of D's death, the estate had failed to overcome the presumption of fraud caused by the unequal property division. The trial court refused to uphold the contract. On appeal, how will a common law appellate court most likely rule?

EXPLANATIONS

Explanation

The appellate court will most likely reverse the trial judge's ruling. Here, because the consideration was inadequate, fraud was presumed. To overcome the presumption, the proponent of the contract (D's estate) has the burden of proving that P knew the extent, character, and value of the property involved and the nature and extent of the rights being waived. In this hypothetical, the evidence tends to suggest the absence of fraud. Here, there is no indication that P was placed under undue duress at the time the premarital contract was signed, and it appears that P was represented.

Furthermore, there was full disclosure of all assets (the attached list). The question of representation is problematic but most likely not dispositive of the case. Despite the apparent unfairness of the division of property on D's death, given the disclosure and absence of duress, a common law appellate court will most likely uphold the contract. *See Estate of Serbus v. Serbus*, 324 N.W.2d 381 (Minn. 1982).

UNIFORM ACTS

14.6. Uniform Premarital Contract Act

In 1983, the National Conference of Commissioners on Uniform State Laws promulgated the Uniform Premarital Contract Act (UPA). Uniform Premarital Contract Act, 9B U.L.A. 369 (1987 & Supp. 1994). The UPA was written to provide state legislatures with a model statute governing premarital contracts. The UPA addresses the formalities for execution, effectiveness if the marriage is valid or void, permissible content, amendment and revocation, and timeliness of actions to enforce contracts. A majority of jurisdictions have legislation dealing with premarital contracts and have been influenced by the UPA.

The UPA creates a presumption that premarital contracts are valid and enforceable and places on the party seeking to void the contract the burden of proving the contrary, which is a significant change from the common law. A comment to the UPA states that the marriage itself acts as consideration for a premarital contract. To invalidate a premarital contract, the party challenging it must prove that the contract was unconscionable, a somewhat amorphous concept.

A few states do not allow premarital contracts to modify or eliminate the right of a spouse to receive court-ordered alimony at divorce. The UPA would allow premarital contracts to do this.

The UPA in some form has been adopted in at least 29 states and the District of Columbia. Among the states are Arizona, Arkansas, California, Connecticut, Delaware, Hawaii, Idaho, Illinois, Indiana, Iowa, Kansas, Maine, Minnesota, Mississippi, Montana, Nebraska, Nevada, New Jersey, New Mexico, North Carolina, North Dakota, Oregon, Rhode Island, South Dakota, Texas, Utah, Virginia, West Virginia, and Wisconsin. More states are expected to adopt the Act.

14.7. American Law Institute Premarital Principles

The American Law Institute included provisions for drafting and evaluating premarital contracts in its Principles of Family Dissolution. *See Principles of the*

Law of Family Dissolution: Analysis and Recommendations (Tentative Draft No. 4 2000). The Principles set out procedural requirements that are already required by most states. These requirements include that a contract be signed and in writing, that there be full financial disclosure, and that consent not be obtained under duress. There is a presumption of informed consent and the absence of duress if the contract was executed at least 30 days before the parties' marriage and if the parties were advised to obtain legal counsel and had an opportunity to do so. The burden of proving the lack of duress and the presence of consent is placed on the party who is trying to enforce the contract, which is intended to "caution" the stronger party against overreaching. Judith T. Younger, *Antenuptial Contracts*, 28 Wm. Mitchell L. Rev. 697, 700, 718 (2000). Should one party fail to retain independent counsel, the informed-consent presumption will not go into effect unless the contract contains understandable language explaining the significance of its terms and the fact that the parties' interests may be adverse with respect to them. *Id.*

The American Law Institute omits any requirement of substantive fairness at the time of execution. However, at the time the contract is to be enforced, the Principles provide for "a wider substantive review of these contracts" than allowed under the Uniform Premarital Contract Act. *Id.*

SCOPE OF PREMARITAL CONTRACTS

14.8. Provisions that Trouble Courts

There are provisions found in a few premarital contracts that courts will not enforce. Courts view marriage in theory as not merely a private contract between the parties, but as creating a status in which the state is vitally interested and under which certain rights and duties incident to the relationship come into being, irrespective of the wishes of the parties. *Graham v. Graham*, 33 F. Supp. 936 (D. Mich. 1940). A private contract between persons about to be married that attempts to change the essential obligations of the marriage contract is contrary to public policy and unenforceable. *Michigan Trust Co. v. Chapin*, 64 N.W. 334 (Mich. 1895). *See* The Restatement of the Law of Contracts, §587 (a bargain between married persons or persons contemplating marriage to change the essential incidents of marriage such as to forego sexual intercourse is not enforceable). For example, a premarital contract that contains a provision stating that the parties will not live together after marriage is not enforceable (although practically it seems useless). *Mirizio v. Mirizio*, 140 N.E. 605 (Mich. 1926); *Franklin v. Franklin*, 28 N.E. 681 (Mass. 1891). Courts will also not enforce provisions that control the sharing of expenses between spouses during the marriage because this would negate one spouse's statutory duty to support the other.

Contracts regarding custody or child support are unenforceable because of public policy concerns over the welfare of minor children. Other matters such as who does the cleaning and cooking or how often to have sex will likewise not be enforced.

Example 14-3

Assume that P and D agree in a premarital contract that during their marriage, P will pay D $2,500 a month in return for D accompanying P on her business travels. D gives up his job in reliance on this written contract, which in part reads, "P hereby agrees to pay to D the sum of Two Thousand Five Hundred ($2,500.00) Dollars per month each and every month hereafter until the parties hereto no longer desire this arrangement to continue." After five years, the couple separates, and P stops making the monthly payment. D brings an action to enforce the contract, and P responds that the contract is without consideration. Alternatively, P contends that under its express provisions, the contract was to continue only until the parties no longer desired the arrangement to continue, and thus, it was terminated when they separated. How will a court most likely treat this contract?

Explanation

A court will most likely refuse to uphold this premarital contract because it will be viewed as altering by private contract the personal relationships and obligations assumed upon marriage. The court will reason that, if P and D were permitted to regulate by private contract where the parties are to live and whether the husband is to work or be supported by his wife, there would seem to be no reason why they could not contract as to the allowance the husband or wife may receive, the number of dresses she may have, the places where they will spend their evenings and vacations, and innumerable other aspects of their personal relationships. Recognizing the existence of such a right would open an endless field for controversy and bickering and would destroy the element of flexibility needed in making adjustments to new conditions arising in marital life. A wife can voluntarily pay her husband a monthly sum, and the husband by mutual understanding can quit his job and travel with his wife. The objection is to putting such conduct into a binding contract, tying the parties' hands in the future and inviting controversy and litigation between them. *Graham v. Graham*, 33 F. Supp. 936 (D. Mich. 1940).

14.9. State Statutes Control Future Uncertainty

Most jurisdictions have attempted to reduce the uncertainty surrounding the use of premarital contracts by promulgating statutes that replace the common law and contain specific procedures to follow when drafting them. The statutes and case law in a jurisdiction must be thoroughly scrutinized before drafting a contract as they vary from state to state.

REQUIREMENTS FOR PREMARITAL CONTRACTS

14.10. Consideration

Most courts have viewed premarital contracts when written as executory and consider the marriage, when it occurs, as sufficient consideration for a premarital contract. However, courts are not always clear when discussing this aspect of these contracts, and in some jurisdictions, courts consider not only the marriage as consideration for the contract, but also the ultimate division of property. These courts may find that there was "inadequate consideration" for the contract, even though the parties married, where there is a disproportionate division of property.

14.11. Duty to Disclose — Waiver

Premarital contracts are viewed as giving rise to a special duty of disclosure not required in ordinary contract relationships. It is common, for example, to find courts declaring that each person signing a premarital contract has an affirmative duty to disclose to the other the nature of his property interests so that the effect of the contract can be understandingly assessed and waived. Disclosure is important because it underscores that each party is exercising a meaningful choice when he or she agrees to give up certain rights found in statutes to protect married persons in anticipation of marriage. In the absence of a full and frank disclosure, courts will generally refuse to give effect to a contract. *See Ortel v. Gettig*, 116 A.2d 145 (Md. 1955).

The necessity of a knowing waiver has added significance in the context of premarital contracts because a majority of jurisdictions view the relationship as confidential, that is, not an arm's-length transaction. Without full and truthful disclosure of the worth of the real and personal property, the party who waives various statutory protections cannot know what is being waived. *See Newman v. Newman*, 653 P.2d 728, 732 (Colo. 1982); *Burtoff v. Burtoff*, 418 A.2d 1085, 1089 (D.C. App. 1980); *Del Vecchio v. Del Vecchio*, 143 So. 2d 17, 21 (Fla. 1962); *Frey v. Frey*, 471 A.2d 705, 711 (Md. 1984); *Fletcher v. Fletcher*, 628 N.E.2d 1343, 1346 (Ohio 1994); *Kosik v. George*, 452 P.2d 560, 563 (Or. 1969); *Button v. Button*, 388 N.W.2d 546, 550 (Wis. 1986). It is felt that the full disclosure rule also levels the bargaining field for the party in the weaker bargaining position. *Gant v. Gant*, 329 S.E.2d 106, 114 (W.Va. 1985).

The extent of what constitutes "full and fair" disclosure varies from case to case, depending on a number of factors, which may include the parties' respective sophistication and experience in business affairs; their respective worth, ages, intelligence, and literacy; their prior family ties or commitments; the duration of their relationship prior to the execution of the contract; the time of the signing of the contract in relation to the time of the wedding; and their representation by, or opportunity to consult with, independent counsel. *Randolph v. Randolph*, 937 S.W.2d 815 (Tenn. 1996). Although disclosure need not reveal precisely every asset owned by an individual spouse, at a minimum, full and fair disclosure requires that each contracting party be given a clear idea of the nature, extent, and value of the other party's property and resources. An effective method of proving disclosure is to attach a net worth schedule of assets, liabilities, and income to the contract itself. *See, e.g., Pajak v. Pajak*, 385 S.E.2d 384, 388 (Va. 1989); *Hartz v. Hartz*, 234 A.2d 865, 871, n.3 (Md. 1967). If parties wish to insulate a contract from subsequent challenge on the basis of overreaching, full, frank, and truthful disclosure is essential. *See Harbom v. Harbom*, 760 A.2d 272 (Md. App. 2000); Annot., *Failure to Disclose Extent or Value of Property Owned as Ground for Avoiding Premarital Contract*, 3 A.L.R.5th 394 (1993).

Example 14-4

Assume that this action is brought in a jurisdiction that recognizes the use of premarital contracts upon divorce. Also assume that only one day before their marriage, the parties entered into a contract prepared by P's lawyer. The contract provided, in part, that in the event of divorce or death, each party released all marital rights in the separate property of the other. Also, in the event of divorce, the division of marital property was to be based on the amount each party had invested in the property. Also assume that at the time the contract was signed, D owned no assets, except personal belongings, while P had substantial real estate holdings that were valued at approximately $800,000. In addition, assume P had liquid assets of $500,000.

The marriage broke down after ten years, and P filed for divorce, asking that the premarital contract be enforced. D testified that she did not see the contract until one day before the parties were married. D admitted that she reviewed the contract on the drive to the attorney's office, but claimed that no one explained it to her. She said that because she was responsible for a minor child and suffering from breast cancer at the time, her only choices were to sign the contract or be kicked out of the residence she and her son had shared with P for the year prior to their marriage. D also admitted that she knew at that time about some of P's property holdings, but she insisted that she was not aware of, nor did anyone disclose to her, the full extent and value of his assets and holdings.

D was not represented by counsel when she signed the contract. However, P's attorney, who drafted the contract, was present at the hearing on the contract and testified that it is his normal practice to explain such contracts to both parties to ensure a mutual understanding of the terms. He could not specifically recall following that practice with D and acknowledged that he did not provide D with a copy of P's financial statement prior to execution of the contract. Nor did he discuss the specific dollar value of P's holdings with her, but instead only discussed P's assets in general terms.

P conceded that he never specifically advised D of his net worth prior to the signing of the contract, but asserted that she was generally aware of the nature of his holdings because they had lived together for more than one year before the contract was signed, and she had accompanied him to many of his properties to collect rent. P testified that D had also reviewed the contract before signing it and had made suggestions for changes, including a provision relating to a watch. Although D conceded that she read that provision before signing the contract, she denied that the provision was included on her suggestion. Will a court most likely uphold the contract on these facts?

Explanation

This is a close question; however, a court most likely will not uphold the contract for the following reasons. Although all agree that D resided with P for about a year before their marriage, P conceded that he did not reveal the extent or value of his holdings and that D's knowledge of P's property was only general in nature. D's testimony regarding her general knowledge of P's holdings was corroborated by P and his attorney. Although specific appraisal values are not required to sustain the validity of a premarital contract, greater knowledge of the proponent spouse's overall net worth is usually necessary. In terms of the comparative sophistication and business experience of the parties, P was apparently a learned businessman, whereas D, in contrast, possessed no prior business experience or knowledge. Moreover, the contract was executed only one day before the parties were married, and D was presented with it on the way to the attorney's office, at a time when, according to her testimony, she was in ill health. She can most likely argue that she had no opportunity to personally study the contract or to seek advice from her own attorney or others close to her because of the short period of time between the presentation of the contract and the marriage. *See Randolph v. Randolph*, 937 S.W.2d 815 (Tenn. 1996).

14.12. Lack of Notice

Courts have held that the lack of negotiations or insufficient notice, standing alone, is seldom enough to invalidate an antenuptial agreement. *See, e.g.,*

Liebelt v. Liebelt, 801 P.2d 52 (Idaho Ct. App. 1990); *Howell v. Landry*, 386 S.E.2d 610 (N.C. 1989). Courts generally have treated such a claim as one of duress and have found such a defense inapplicable when the party contesting the agreement had notice of the agreement. *See, e.g., Rose v. Rose*, 526 N.E.2d 231, 235-236 (Ind. Ct. App. 1988) (parties discussed necessity of agreement several times before wedding, and husband told wife he would not marry her if she did not sign agreement); *Matter of the Marriage of Adams*, 729 P.2d 1151 (Kan. 1986) (husband approached wife morning of wedding and asked her to sign agreement; agreement was identical to one wife reviewed with her attorney); *Taylor v. Taylor*, 832 P.2d 429, 431 (Okla. Ct. App. 1991) (wife in possession of the agreement for three months prior to its execution); *Shepherd v. Shepherd*, 876 P.2d 429, 432 (Utah Ct. App. 1994) (parties discussed agreement for months prior to marriage, and each had opportunity to review and make changes to it).

14.13. Right to Counsel

Most jurisdictions view the presence of independent counsel as one factor among many in determining the enforceability of premarital contracts but have not made a lack of representation alone sufficient to void them. *See, e.g., In re Marriage of Bonds*, 5 P.3d 815, 816 (Cal. 2000). However, some jurisdictions such as California have enacted statutory provisions to strengthen the independent counsel requirement and will require that if at the time the contract was signed, an attorney did not represent the challenger, it must appear that the party was advised to seek independent legal counsel and the party expressly waived the right to counsel in a separate writing.

The American Law Institute, *Principles of the Law of Family Dissolution*, also place an emphasis on representation by independent counsel and require a clear waiver of such assistance.

14.14. Substantive and Procedural Fairness when Signed

Several jurisdictions now require that premarital contracts be examined for fairness at the time they are signed and be given a second look at the time they are to be enforced. Courts examining the procedural fairness at the time the contracts were signed will consider disclosure, duress, detailed knowledge of the property, and whether the challenger was represented by counsel.

These courts will also examine a premarital contract for substantive fairness at the time the contract was signed. Often courts will use the term "unconscionable" when looking for substantive fairness. However, they have struggled to define what is meant by the use of the term "unconscionable." Examples of the difficulty are apparent in decisions such as *Holler v. Holler*, 612 S.E.2d 469 (S.C. App. 2005), where the court stated that under South Carolina law, unconscionability is the "absence of meaningful choice on the part of one party due to one-sided contract provisions, together with terms which are so oppressive that no reasonable person would make them and no fair and honest person would accept them." A New York court in *Clermont v. Clermont*, 603 N.Y.S.2d 923 (1933), defined unconscionability as involving a bargain "such as no [person] in his [or her] senses and not under delusion would make on the one hand, and as no honest and fair [person] would accept on the other." The North Dakota Supreme Court held a contract unconscionable where the evidence indicated that the husband provided the wife with the contract only three days before their wedding, the wife did not have independent legal advice before signing the contract, the husband did not provide wife fair and reasonable disclosure of his property and financial obligations, the husband's representation of his income was not credible, and the wife did not waive her right to a fair and reasonable disclosure of husband's property or financial obligations. *Peters-Riemers v. Riemers*, 644 N.W.2d 197 (N.D. 2002).

The standard of unconscionability measured at the time of a contract's making is contained in the Uniform Premarital Agreement Act, 9C U.L.A. 35 (Master ed. 2001). Several states have also adopted this standard. *See, e.g., Scherer v. Scherer*, 292 S.E.2d 662 (Ga. 1982); *Gentry v. Gentry*, 798 S.W.2d 928, 936 (Ky. 1990); *Ferry v. Ferry*, 586 S.W.2d 782, 786 (Mo. Ct. App. 1979); *MacFarlane v. Rich*, 567 A.2d 585 (1989).

Some jurisdictions discuss the validity of a contract at the time it was signed using a fair and reasonable test, which is not perceived as identical to unconscionability. *Upham v. Upham*, 630 N.E.2d 307 (Mass. App. 1994). Although there may be substantial overlap between the standards, a standard of unconscionability is generally thought to require a greater showing of inappropriateness. Several states appear to have adopted the fair and reasonable test. *See, e.g., Ex parte Walters*, 580 So. 2d 1352, 1354 (Ala. 1991); *Harbom v. Harbom*, 760 A.2d 272 (Md. 2000), quoting *Hartz v. Hartz*, 234 A.2d 865 (Md. 1967) (premarital contract upheld if contract was "fair and equitable under the circumstances"); *Matter of the Estate of Crawford*, 730 P.2d 675 (Wash. 1986) ("if the contract makes a fair and reasonable provision for the party not seeking its enforcement, the contract may be upheld").

It is unlikely that a contract will be considered unfair and unreasonable merely because at the time of execution it failed to approximate an alimony award and property division ruling that a judge would be required to make upon divorce. The relinquishment of claims to the existing assets of a future spouse, even if those assets are substantial, also does not necessarily render a premarital contract invalid. Many valid contracts may be one-sided, and a contesting party may have considerably fewer assets and enjoy a far different lifestyle after divorce than he or she may enjoy during the marriage. It is only when the contesting party is essentially stripped of substantially all marital interests that a judge may determine that a premarital contract is not fair and reasonable and therefore not valid.

14.15. Waiving Spousal Support (Alimony or Maintenance)

Courts have considered the question of the use of premarital contracts to protect a party's property as separate from the question of whether premarital contracts containing spousal-support waivers are unenforceable. Property settlement agreements are distinct from premarital agreements, and the two are not necessarily treated identically under the law. Historically, the common law courts assumed provisions regarding waiver of spousal support were unenforceable per se and based this view on assumptions that dissolution of marriage is contrary to public policy and that premarital waivers of spousal support may promote dissolution. Today, it is argued by some that such a view is anachronistic. For example, California decided in *In re Marriage of Pendleton & Fireman*, 5 P.3d 839 (Cal. 2000), that such contracts were not per se unenforceable. Furthermore, Section 3 of the Uniform Premarital Contract Act (UPA) expressly permits the parties to a premarital agreement to contract with respect to modification or elimination of spousal support.

In *Osborne v. Osborne*, 428 N.E.2d 810 (Mass. 1981), the court held that it is permissible for parties contemplating marriage to enter into an antenuptial contract settling their alimony or property rights in the event their marriage should prove unsuccessful. The court noted, however, that the freedom to limit or waive those rights in the event of divorce is not unrestricted, and it set forth "some guidelines to be used in determining the extent to which such agreements should be enforced." In deciding enforcement, a judge must determine whether an antenuptial agreement is valid. Second, the agreement must be fair and reasonable at the time of entry of the judgment.

14.16. Substantive Fairness at the Time of Enforcement — The Second Look Doctrine

Unlike commercial contracts, family courts in a few jurisdictions are taking a second look at premarital contracts at the time they are to be enforced. These courts generally ask whether the contract is at present fair and reasonable or unconscionable. This second look examination is unique to family law and remains a principle in a minority of jurisdictions.

Whether the courts that employ the second look doctrine claim they are searching for "unconscionability," "unfairness and unreasonableness," "inequity," or something else, the judicial analysis appears remarkably similar in substance. *See* 1 H.H. Clark, Jr., *Domestic Relations in the United States* §1.9, at 52 n.51 (2d ed. 1987) ("Unconscionability seems to be defined as occurring when enforcement of the contract would leave the spouse without sufficient property, maintenance, or appropriate employment to support himself"); *MacFarlane v. Rich, supra* (defining *unconscionable* as occurring when "provisions in a premarital contract may lose their vitality by reason of changed circumstances so far beyond the contemplation of the parties at the time they entered the contract that its enforcement would work an unconscionable hardship"); *Miles v. Werle*, 977 S.W.2d 297, 303 (Mo. Ct. App. 1998) (a contract is unenforceable that attempts to "totally take from one of the spouses his or her presumed right to marital property. By contrast, where a premarital contract permits each spouse to retain a share of the marital property, albeit a disproportionately small one, courts are more likely to uphold and enforce the contract"); *Cladis v. Cladis*, 512 So. 2d 271, 273 (Fla. Dist. Ct. App. 1987) ("a trial court may determine that the contract . . . does not adequately provide for the challenging spouse and, consequently, is unreasonable"); *Button v. Button*, 388 N.W.2d 546 (Wis. 1986) ("If there are significantly changed circumstances after the execution of a contract and the contract as applied at divorce no longer comports with the reasonable expectations of the parties, a contract which is fair at execution may be unfair to the parties at divorce"); *see McKee-Johnson v. Johnson*, 444 N.W.2d 259, 267-268 (Minn. 1989) (contract must be substantively fair at the time of enforcement).

A valid premarital contract is not unenforceable at the time of divorce merely because its enforcement results in property division or an award of support that a judge might not order or because it is one-sided. A majority of courts will not relieve the parties from the provisions of a valid contract unless, because of circumstances occurring during the course of the marriage, enforcement of the contract would leave the contesting spouse "without sufficient property, maintenance, or appropriate employment to support" herself. *See* 1 Clark, Jr., *Domestic Relations in the United States, supra*, at §1.9; Younger, *Premarital Contracts, supra*, at 700 ("The review for substantive fairness is more difficult to describe. As it applies to the terms of the contract, it is not a substitution of the court's notions of what is right for the parties' bargain. It is 'amorphous,' made on a case by case basis and the standard is variously described as 'reasonable,' 'fair,' 'not unconscionable,' and 'equitable,' for example."). Such circumstances might include, for example, the unanticipated mental or physical deterioration of the contesting party as to nullify the obvious intention of the parties at the time of the contract's execution. The "second look" at a contract is to ensure that the contract has the same vitality at the time of the divorce that the parties intended at the time of its execution. *See also MacFarlane v. Rich, supra*.

EXAMPLES

Example 14-5

Assume that P and D entered into a premarital contract that in part read as follows: "In the event that the Parties terminate their present cohabitation arrangement or initiate dissolution of marriage proceedings, neither Party shall be liable to the other for living expenses, food, shelter, medical, dental or pharmaceutical expenses, or other necessities of life except as provided in this Agreement, and each Party waives and releases all rights and claims to receive money, property, or support from the other Party." Also assume that ten years into their marriage, P was in a life-shattering automobile accident. At one point, P was pronounced dead; however, P survived the accident. P suffered brain damage, internal injuries, and numerous broken bones. She underwent a dozen reconstructive surgeries and is slated to have many more. A year after the accident, D filed a petition to dissolve the marriage. Assume that a statute in this jurisdiction declares that "a premarital waiver of spousal support will not be enforced if enforcement would be unconscionable at the time sought." P asks the court to enforce their premarital contract. How will a court most likely rule?

EXPLANATIONS

Explanation

Most likely the court will not enforce the premarital contract. As a general rule, courts applying the unconscionability test at the time the contract is to be enforced will examine what the parties could have anticipated when they married. This accident was not anticipated and could not reasonably have been foreseen. As a public policy matter, requiring D to support P is consistent with public policy as expressed in most state family code provisions. *See Borelli v. Brusseau*, 16 Cal. Rptr. 2d 16 (Cal. App. 1 Dist. 1993).

14.17. Jurisdictions Applying Strict Contract Principles

A minority of jurisdictions do not follow the common law principle discussed so far in this chapter. Rather, prenuptial contracts are interpreted using traditional principles of contract law. *See, e.g., Simeone v. Simeone*, 581 A.2d 162 (Pa. 1990); *In re O'Brien*, 898 A.2d 1075 (Pa. Super. 2006). In *Simeone v. Simeone*, the court abandoned its earlier position that it would review premarital contracts for substantive fairness. It stated that such a review at the time of execution severely undermines the functioning and reliability of a contract and is therefore not a proper subject for judicial inquiry. 581 A.2d at 166. It also rejected any inquiry into substantive fairness at the time of enforcement because it believes that all such events are foreseeable.

A minority of jurisdictions also have not adopted the general requirement that a party be made aware of his or her statutory rights. They endorse the parties' right to freely contract and decline to impose the additional inquiry as to whether the parties were sufficiently advised of their statutory rights. However, because of the unique relationship of the parties, these courts do require full disclosure of the parties' financial resources. These courts believe that the parties are protected by the requirement of disclosure of financial assets and the traditional contract remedies available to them for fraud, misrepresentation, or duress. *See, e.g., Sabad v. Fessenden*, 825 A.2d 682 (Pa. Super. 2003).

14.18. Burden of Proof

Jurisdictions are not in agreement over which party carries the burden of proof in premarital disputes. Does the spouse who allegedly waived rights have the burden of proving the invalidity of the contract, or do those who rely on the contract have the burden of proving its validity? As noted earlier, the Uniform Premarital Contract Act and the newly announced ALI Principles of Family Law differ on which of the parties should bear the burden. In the following decisions, the court placed the burden of proof on the attacking spouse to prove the invalidity of the contract: *Linker v. Linker*, 470 P.2d 921 (Colo. Ct. App. 1970); *Del Vecchio v. Del Vecchio*, 143 So. 2d 17 (Fla. 1962); *Christians v. Christians*, 44 N.W.2d 431 (Iowa 1950); *In re Estate of Strickland*, 149 N.W.2d 344 (Neb. 1967).

In the following cases, the court placed the burden on those relying on the contract to prove its validity: *In re Estate of Harbers*, 449 P.2d 7 (Ariz. 1969); *Davis v. Davis*, 116 S.W.2d 607 (Ark. 1938); *Seuss v. Schukat*, 192 N.E. 668 (Ill. 1934); *In re Neis' Estate*, 225 P.2d 110 (Kan. 1950); *Truitt v. Truitt*, 162 S.W.2d 31 (Ky. Ct. App. 1942); *Hartz v. Hartz*, 234 A.2d 865 (Md. 1967); *Kosik v. George*, 452 P.2d 560 (Or. 1969); *In re Estate of Vallish*, 244 A.2d 745 (Pa. 1968); *Friedlander v. Friedlander*, 494 P.2d 208 (Wash. 1972).

The following courts initially presumed that these contracts were valid and placed the burden of proof on the party challenging them: *In re Estate of Peterson*, 381 N.W.2d 109, 112 (Neb. 1986); *Evered v. Edsell*, 464 So. 2d 1197, 1199 (Fla. 1985); *Gant v. Gant*, 329 S.E.2d 106, 116 (W. Va. 1985); *Newman v. Newman*, 653 P.2d 728, 736 (Colo. 1982): *In re Estate of Burgess*, 646 P.2d 623, 626 (Okla. App. 1982); *Counts v. Benker*, 331 N.W.2d 193, 196 (Mich. 1982); *Sunshine v. Sunshine*, 51 A.D.2d 326, 327 (1976), *affirmed sub nom. In re Sunshine*, 357 N.E.2d 999 (N.Y. App. Div. 1976).

OTHER ISSUES REGARDING PREMARITAL CONTRACTS

14.19. Ambiguous Provisions

A premarital contract must be clear regarding its applicability. For example, in *Roth v. Roth*, 565 N.W.2d 782 (S.D. 1997), the couple signed a contract to protect the interests of their respective children from previous marriages. Although the contract did not contain a provision regarding divorce, when they dissolved their relationship, the husband argued the contract should be applied to that proceeding. The court disagreed, holding that the contract was not ambiguous on its face and that it applied only at death and not on divorce. *See Parkhurst v. Gibson*, 573 A.2d 454, 458 (N.H. 1990) (contract not specifically mentioning divorce, alimony, or property settlement inapplicable to divorce); *Levy v. Levy*, 388 N.W.2d 170, 176 (Wis. 1986) (premarital contract that failed to mention divorce was not to be considered when making a property division pursuant to divorce proceedings); *see also Foster v. Foster*, 609 A.2d 1171, 1172 (Me. 1992) (holding broad "whereas" clauses do not expand the settlement provision to include divorce when it is not otherwise mentioned); *Devault v. Devault*, 609 N.E.2d 214, 216 (Ohio Ct. App. 1992) (premarital contract without reference to divorce may not be applied in divorce proceedings, noting that a court refuses to make a contract for a party).

14.20. Abandoning a Premarital Contract

In some jurisdictions, a premarital contract may be abandoned by mutual consent without consideration. *McMullen v. McMullen*, 185 So. 2d 191 (Fla. Ct. App. 1966). The abandonment of a contract may be effected when the acts of one party are inconsistent with the existence of the contract and are acquiesced in by the other party. This is tantamount to a rescission of the contract by mutual assent.

14.21. Tax Planning

Premarital contracts are sometimes related to the estate-planning wishes of one or both of the prospective spouses. Depending on the consideration being exchanged by the contract, there may be gift-tax or income-tax consequences involved.

CHAPTER 15

Cohabitation Without Formal Marriage

15.1. Introduction

This chapter covers the legal issues that may arise when unmarried cohabiting partners, who live together much like married partners, decide to end their relationship. Courts use a variety of legal theories to resolve disputes between cohabitants, and the relief afforded them varies substantially among the states.

CHANGING LIFESTYLES

15.2. Four Decades of Change

During the last four decades of the twentieth century, a revolution occurred in the United States regarding the formation of families and the roles of family members. As the number of people living together without marrying increased, most of the social stigma associated with bearing children out of wedlock was removed, as was the shame previously associated with cohabitation.

There are several reasons that couples may choose to cohabit without marrying. First, some view a period of cohabitation as a time to "test" a relationship before making it legally permanent. To the extent that an unwise marriage is prevented, cohabitation may help couples avoid the financial and emotional consequences associated with divorce. Second, some couples may realize tax savings by remaining single. Third, cohabitation offers some couples freedom from what they view as a marriage system dominated by traditional societal values. Finally, a cohabiting party may continue to receive income that would terminate if the person married, such as benefits from a public program or maintenance from a prior marriage.

Those critical of cohabitation contend that there is little evidence to suggest that a "trial run" results in a greater chance of success with marriage. They also argue that when a relationship ends, partners may be surprised to learn that courts are reluctant to assist them with issues such as property division and ongoing maintenance or alimony. Finally, they assert that the legal problems associated with a cohabitation arrangement may be as costly and as difficult to resolve as those associated with divorce. *See* Lynne Marie Kohm & Karen M. Groen, *Cohabitation and the Future of Marriage*, 17 Regent U. L. Rev. 261 (2005).

15.3. Cohabitation Data

Although the overall percentage is not high, the number of unmarried-partner households has increased significantly since the 1970s. By 1990, cohabitants constituted 3.5 percent of all households, and in 2000, unmarried-partner households accounted for 5.2 percent of all households. Of the 5.5 million cohabiting couples, 4.9 million were opposite-sex partners. According to the 2000 Census, Vermont and Alaska had the highest percentage of unmarried-partner households (7.5%), and Alabama and Utah had the fewest (3.4%). Census 2000 Briefs, Households and Families: 2000, http://www.census.gov/population/www/cen2000/briefs.html (last visited 10-24-06).

THE COMMON LAW

15.4. Criminal Conduct

Most states have laws that make it a criminal offense for unmarried persons to live together and that are designed to punish cohabitants for sodomy, fornication, and cohabitation. The decision by the United States Supreme Court in *Lawrence v. Texas*, 123 S. Ct. 2472 (2003), raises questions about the continued validity of many of these prohibitions. In that case, the Court held that a Texas statute making it a crime for two persons of the same sex to engage in certain intimate sexual conduct was unconstitutional, as applied to adult males who had engaged in consensual acts of sodomy in the privacy of their home. One may extrapolate from this opinion that other intimate acts between consenting adults are likewise now protected from criminal prosecution.

15.5. Meretricious Relationships

The common law took a dim view of contracts made between unmarried persons who were living together out of wedlock much like a husband and wife. Under the common law, oral or written agreements between unmarried cohabitants were not enforced if any part of the consideration for them involved the illicit relationship itself. Common law courts objected to the parties' disregard of traditional moral values and were concerned that enforcement of any oral or written agreements might make meretricious relationships more attractive than marriage. The common law, it was said, should not allow a man to trade sexual services as consideration for contractual promises or make a woman's virtue an article of merchandise.

15.6. States Reject Common Law Marriage

States began to eliminate common law marriages in the 1930s and 1940s, in part because the pioneering conditions that fostered them had disappeared and also because of the fear of fraudulent claims. For example, when New York abolished common law marriage in 1933, one of the expressed concerns was the absence of public marriage records that would assist in verifying the property rights of common law spouses. Another concern was that they allowed spouses to completely avoid some of the state's objectives in enacting marriage statutes, such as obtaining medical examinations to prevent the spread of disease, collecting fee payments to finance recordkeeping, and requiring waiting periods to prevent impulsive unions. There were concerns with the difficulty of proving such marriages, and some believed that recognition sanctioned immorality and debased formal marriage. Others contended that the doctrine would encourage perjury and fraud by unwed cohabitants hoping to gain the financial benefits of marriage.

With abolition of common law marriage in a majority of jurisdictions, the nuclear family was thought to be more secure. However, societal changes beginning in the 1960s brought new challenges to the concept of "family" and the legal system when large numbers of individuals began to openly live together much as husband and wife. When their relationships ended, they turned to the legal system for assistance with property and contract disputes.

Example 15-1

Assume that P and D were married to each other, and then they divorced. Subsequent to the divorce, they began living together once again, but they did not remarry. After the divorce, but a few months before P and D resumed living together, D purchased a home, and the couple resided in it for ten years until their final separation. P claimed that P and D were common law spouses and that P was entitled to part of the house under the marital dissolution statute. However, the court held that they were not common law spouses because P and D did not consistently hold themselves out as being married — they filled out legal forms designating themselves as single people, they maintained separate bank accounts, and they filed individual income tax returns. Assume that the court correctly held that P and D were not common law spouses, and also assume that P has not plead any other claims for relief. Could P still be awarded part of the value of the house under the marital dissolution statute?

Explanation

A similar situation was presented in *In re Marriage of Martin*, 681 N.W.2d 612 (Iowa 2004), where the court held that P could not be awarded any portion of the house under the marital dissolution statute because P and D were no longer married, and they were not common law spouses. P was unable to claim putative spouse status because P did not have a good-faith belief that the parties were married. Because P raised no other claims for relief, P could not recover. Note how different the outcome would have been if P and D had remained married: the house would have been marital property, and P would have had a statutory basis for a possible maintenance claim.

LEGAL RECOGNITION OF COHABITATION RELATIONSHIPS

15.7. *Marvin v. Marvin*

Legal recognition that partners in a cohabitating relationship may have enforceable rights is a by-product of a phenomenon that began in the 1960s when increasingly large numbers of adults began openly living together without a traditional marriage ceremony or state license. The legal movement was sparked by the publicity following a decision by the California Supreme Court in *Marvin v. Marvin*, 557 P.2d 106 (Cal. 1976).

Marvin v. Marvin was the first major decision handed down by a state court to clearly hold that unmarried adults who live together are free under general principles of contract law to make agreements concerning their property and earnings. The opinion received special notice because of the scope of the contract principles it said could be employed when considering live-in claims.

Under *Marvin v. Marvin*, nonmarital partners may order their economic affairs as they choose and may agree to pool their earnings and to hold all property acquired during the relationship in accordance with the law governing community property. They may also agree that each partner's earnings and the property acquired from those earnings remain the separate property of the earning partner.

15.8. *Marvin* Applied

Since *Marvin v. Marvin* was announced, various jurisdictions have responded to cohabitation claims differently. For example, in California, New Jersey, and Minnesota, the *Marvin* principles are applied quite liberally. However, even in these jurisdictions, relief is generally granted when the cohabitants have lived together in a stable, long-term relationship. In other jurisdictions, there is a more cautious application of the principles enunciated in *Marvin*. Finally, a small number of jurisdictions may adhere to the principle that cohabitation agreements under any circumstances involve immoral consideration; therefore, they are unenforceable as against public policy. To some critics, enforcement of live-in agreements will return society to acceptance of common law marriage, with a consequential increase in the law's instability.

A majority of jurisdictions distinguish between contracts that are explicitly and inseparably founded on sexual services and those that are not. They have concluded that an agreement between cohabitants is not illegal merely because there is an illicit relationship between the parties, so long as the agreement is independent of the illicit relationship, and the illicit relationship is not part of the consideration bargained for and is not a condition of the agreement. They have also recognized that by failing to enforce contract and property rights between unmarried cohabitants, one party keeps all or most of the assets accumulated during the relationship, while the other party, no more or less "guilty," is deprived of property that he or she has helped to accumulate. A decision that leaves one party in the relationship enriched at the expense of the other party who had contributed to the acquisition of the property has been criticized as unduly harsh.

Example 15-2

Assume that P and D met as teenagers and had a romantic relationship that spanned 70 years. However, the parties never married, and they never formally shared a residence together. They did stay overnight together "periodically" at various locations. In consideration for the emotional and social support that P provided to D over the years, D promised to support P for life. However, as D's health declined, his children took over his day-to-day financial affairs, and P no longer received monthly support payments. When P filed suit, the trial court dismissed her case, finding that P and D had never cohabited in a marital-style relationship. Did the trial court err in requiring that parties reside together as a condition for granting relief?

Explanation

In *Levine v. Konvitz*, 890 A.2d 354 (N.J. Super. A.D. 2006), the decision dismissing P's case was affirmed. The appellate court stated as follows: "In order to establish a *prima facie* case for palimony, a plaintiff must present competent evidence showing (1) that the parties cohabitated; (2) in a marriage-type relationship; (3) that during this period of cohabitation, defendant promised plaintiff that he/she would support him/her for life; and (4) that this promise was made in exchange for valid consideration." *Id.* at 354. The court held that P and D failed to meet the first element, cohabitation, because they never formally shared a residence. Note that some states define cohabitation more broadly.

15.9. American Law Institute

The American Law Institute approach to cohabitation issues contrasts sharply with the *Marvin* doctrine. Rather than relying on contract and equitable remedies, it creates presumptive categories of "domestic partners" who are entitled to property and support in the same manner as legal spouses. Domestic partners are defined as two unmarried people (same- or opposite-sex) who "share a primary residence and a life together as a couple" for a significant period of time. ALI, Principles of the Law of Family Dissolution: Analysis and Recommendations §§6.01-6.06 (2002).

15.10. Washington Meretricious Relationship Doctrine

Rather than creating common law marriages, the state of Washington recognizes stable, cohabiting relationships referred to as "meretricious relationships." (Note that use of the term "meretricious" in this context denotes a committed intimate relationship rather than the common use of the term to connote an illicit relationship.) Cohabiting couples may fall under the meretricious relationship doctrine based on the following factors: (1) continuous cohabitation; (2) duration of the relationship; (3) purpose of the relationship; (4) services for mutual benefit; and (5) intent of the parties. Property acquired during such a relationship is presumed to belong to both parties, and the court may be *guided* by the dissolution statute in making a fair and equitable distribution. *In re Marriage of Pennington*, 14 P.3d 764 (Wash. 2000); *Olver v. Fowler*, 126 P.3d 69 (Wash. App. 2006).

15.11. Same-Sex Partners

The principles espoused in *Marvin v. Marvin* have been applied with equal force in some jurisdictions to agreements between same-sex partners. For example, in *Whorton v. Dillingham*, 202 Cal. App. 3d 447 (1988), the court extended this principle to same-sex partners. *See also Seward v. Mentrup*, 622 N.E.2d 756, 757 (Ohio 1993); *Crossen v. Feldman*, 673 So. 2d 903 (Fla. 1996).

EXAMPLES

Example 15-3

P and D are a same-sex couple living in Washington, and they had a domestic relationship for ten years. During that time, they pooled their resources, acquired property, and accumulated some debt. The real estate was held in D's name only, but they used joint funds to make the payments. When they separated, D had significantly more income and legal title to more assets than P. The state where P and D reside has precedent for dividing property between opposite-sex cohabitants in quasi-marital relationships (known as meretricious relationships). P alleges that P and D have a quasi-marital relationship falling within the meretricious relationship doctrine, and P seeks recovery from D on this basis. D argues that the doctrine does not apply to partners who are unable to marry, such as same-sex couples, and that P cannot recover on this theory. What is the likely result?

EXPLANATIONS

Explanation

In *Gormely v. Robertson*, 83 P.3d 1042 (Wash. App. 2004) the court concluded that the state law with respect to unmarried opposite-sex cohabitants (termed quasi-marital meretricious relationships) should also apply to same-sex cohabitants. Consequently, P could seek relief in the same manner as an opposite-sex cohabitant.

LEGAL THEORIES ASSERTED BY COHABITANTS

15.12. Legal Theory and Factual Support

A cohabitant must allege a legal theory as a basis for recovery. Most commonly, cohabitation actions are based on some form of contract. However, recovery may also be sought based on imposition of a trust or finding of a gift. Some jurisdictions grant relief based on some theories but not others. Of course, plaintiffs must also be able to prove the facts necessary to sustain the claims alleged. *See Ball v. Smith*, 150 S.W.3d 889 (Tex. App. 2004) (plaintiff failed to produce more than "a scintilla of evidence" in support of claims for breach of contract and resulting trust).

15.13. Express Written Contracts

If a written agreement can be shown, and the terms are clear, it will be upheld in most jurisdictions unless some portion of the consideration for the agreement involves sexual services. The trend, as noted earlier, is to sever any part of the agreement that may arguably be based on payment for sexual services from the remainder of the contract.

In some states, *only* written agreements will be enforced. For example in Texas, all cohabitation agreements must be in writing and in accord with the state statute of frauds. In *Zaremba v. Cliburn*, 949 S.W.2d 822 (Tex. App. 1997), the court held that a palimony action was subject to a statute of frauds provision requiring that an agreement made on consideration of marriage or on consideration of nonmarital conjugal cohabitation be in writing to be enforceable. The statute was ruled to bar claims for recovery under "all causes of action" that alleged that the live-in plaintiff partner was entitled to recover for services rendered in consideration of nonmarital, conjugal cohabitation, including claims for equitable relief. *But see In re Palmen*, 588 N.W.2d 493 (Minn. 1999) (statute of frauds requiring cohabitation agreements to be in writing applies only when the "sole consideration for a contract between cohabiting parties is their contemplation of sexual relations . . . out of wedlock."

EXAMPLES

Example 15-4

Assume that D was a doctor and P was a nurse working at the same facility when D decided to move her practice to another city. To induce P to give up her job and sell her home, and to reside with D "for the remainder of P's life to maintain and care for the home," D agreed that she would provide essentially all the support for the two, would make a will leaving her entire estate to P, and would "maintain bank accounts and other investments which constitute nonprobatable assets in P's name to the extent of 100 percent of her entire nonprobatable assets." Also, as part of the agreement, P agreed to loan D $20,000, which was evidenced by a note. The agreement provided that P could cease residing with D if D failed to provide adequate support, if D requested in writing that P leave for any reason, if D brought a third person into the home for a period greater than four weeks without P's consent, or if D's abuse, harassment, or abnormal behavior made P's continued residence intolerable. D agreed to pay as liquidated damages the sum of $2,500 per month for the remainder of P's life.

P required this agreement as a condition of accompanying D to the new city. The agreement was drawn by a lawyer and properly witnessed. P feared that D might become interested in a younger companion, and four years after the parties moved to the new city, D announced, without P's consent, that she wished to move another woman into the house. When P expressed strong displeasure with this idea, D moved out and took up residence with the other woman. P now seeks to enforce the agreement that D will pay her $2,500 per month for the remainder of P's life. How will a court most likely rule?

EXPLANATIONS

Explanation

Even though no legal rights or obligations flow as a matter of law from a nonmarital relationship, there is no impediment to parties agreeing between themselves to provide certain rights and obligations. In *Marvin v. Marvin*, 557 P.2d 106 (Cal. 1976), the California Supreme Court held that adults who voluntarily live together and engage in sexual relations are nonetheless as competent as any other persons to contract respecting their earnings and property rights, so long as the agreement does not rest upon illicit meretricious consideration. Here, the parties, represented by counsel, took pains to assure that sexual services were not even mentioned in the agreement — a factor not decisive if it could be determined from the contract or from the conduct of the parties that the primary reason for the agreement was to deliver and pay for sexual services. *See Bergen v. Wood*, 14 Cal. App. 854 (1993). This contract and the parties' testimony show that such was not the case here.

The obligations imposed on P by the agreement include the obligation "to immediately commence residing with D at her said residence for the remainder of P's life." This is similar to a "until death do us part" commitment. And although the parties undoubtedly expected a sexual relationship, they contemplated much more. They contracted for a permanent sharing of, and participating in, one another's lives; therefore, the contract is enforceable. *Posik v. Layton*, 695 So. 2d 759 (Fla. App. 1997).

15.14. Express Oral Agreements

Few disputes between cohabitants involve express written agreements; consequently, courts are left to construe the meaning of claimed oral agreements, a difficult task at best. The reason for the difficulty lies in the potential barrier erected by the statute of frauds. The party attempting to establish an agreement must produce a substantial amount of evidence to support a reasonable inference of its existence. As noted previously, even if an express oral contract is proven, it may be unenforceable because of the statute of frauds. (Partial performance of an oral contract, however, normally takes the contract out of the statute of frauds.) Most courts will uphold express oral contracts.

For example, in a Florida ruling, the court held that an oral contract under which a putative father agreed to support the mother of their child during pregnancy and for a reasonable time thereafter in return for the mother quitting her job during pregnancy was enforceable. *Crossen v. Feldman*, 673 So. 2d 903 (Fla. App. 1996). The court observed, "Without attempting to define what may or may not be palimony, this case simply involves whether these parties entered into a contract for support, which is something that they are legally capable of doing." *Id.*

Example 15-5

Assume that P, who was single, met D, who was single, at a party in California. P indicated that being a bachelor, he wanted someone to take care of him, be his hostess, and make some home-cooked meals. D offered to take on those duties. For the next two years, P paid D for D's services as a housekeeper to care for P's California home. She moved into the California home, and over the next five years, their relationship grew closer, and they began having sexual relations on a regular basis. P made no attempt to hide the relationship but stated many times that he would never marry. P became ill and died. D was not included in P's will, and D brought an action against P's estate based on an oral agreement to pay the reasonable value of D's services and on an alleged indebtedness arising out of work, labor, and services rendered by D at P's request in the amount of the reasonable value of $100,000. At trial, D testified that on numerous occasions, P expressly said that he would take care of her after his death and that if D ever left him, the agreement would be terminated, but otherwise, he was going to pay her well for the services that she was performing. D testified that P said D "was taking good care of him." The deceased's sister, X, also testified that P told her that he would include D in his will. She also testified that D did the cooking and household duties at the apartment, drove the car, did the shopping, and took care of P while P was ill. The estate pleaded that the alleged agreement was illegal because it was in furtherance of a meretricious relationship. How will a court most likely rule?

Explanation

D must prove (1) an express contract to pay for services, which contract must be completely free of any agreement of meretricious relationship, (2) the rendering of the services, and (3) their reasonable value. Here there is evidence of an oral agreement, and P rendered valuable services independent of the meretricious relationship, so D will probably be able to recover. For example, D may testify that D cleaned P's apartment, did the marketing and buying of food, cooked the dinners, took care of D's personal laundry, and acted as his hostess in entertaining at the apartment. D may also have dusted, cleaned, and driven an automobile for him on his trips to and from his place of business. On these facts, in a jurisdiction that recognizes express oral contracts, the agreement most likely will be enforced.

15.15. Implied-in-Fact Contracts

Some live-in disputes involve claims resting on the implied-in-fact contract theory. An implied-in-fact contract is viewed as one that essentially meets the requirements of a written contract; therefore, the plaintiff must prove the existence of an agreement, and it must be supported by consideration. The agreement is found in the conduct of the parties rather than in express statements made by them.

For example, the decision in *In re Estate of Roccamonte*, 808 A.2d 838 (N.J. 2002), was rendered in a jurisdiction that recognizes that palimony contracts may be express or implied. The court observed that the existence of a contract and its terms are ordinarily not determinable by what was said, but primarily by the parties' acts and conduct in light of subject matter and surrounding circumstances.

The court held that the female cohabitant's marital-type relationship with her male cohabitant and the evidence of her conduct during the relationship was sufficient consideration for the now-deceased male cohabitant's promise to support her for life. Moreover, the support duty was not discharged by his death, but was enforceable against his estate. The court said that unmarried adult partners, "even those who may be married to others," have the right to choose to cohabit together in a marital-like relationship and that if one of those partners is induced to do so by a promise of support given her by the other, that promise will be enforced by the court. *Id.* at 842.

The court also observed that "the right to support in that situation does not derive from the relationship itself but rather is a right created by contract. Because, however, the subject of that contract is intensely personal rather than transactional in the customary business sense, special considerations must be taken into account by a court obliged to determine whether such a contract has been entered into and what its terms are." *Id.* at 843-844.

Some jurisdictions, such as New York, recognize express contracts but reject recognition of implied contracts when cohabitation claims are made. For example, in *Soderholm v. Kosty*, 676 N.Y.S.2d 850, 851 (N.Y. Just. Ct. 1998), the court said that recognition of implied contracts was "against New York's public policy (as evidenced by the 1933 abolition of common-law marriages) but runs in to too great a risk of error for a court, in hindsight . . . to sort out the intentions of the parties and to fix jural significance to conduct carried out within an essentially private and generally noncontractual relationship," quoting *Morone v. Morone*, 413 N.E.2d 1154 (1980). The court indicated it would enforce express oral contracts between the couple if there was evidence supporting the claim.

The nonrecognition jurisdictions contend that the complex and varied relationships between men and women, once ended, may embitter one of the parties and encourage claims based on real or imaginary facts. They also contend that the concept of an implied contract to compensate for services is conceptually amorphous. It is argued that personal service is frequently rendered by two people because they value each other's company or because they find it a convenient or rewarding thing to do. For courts to attempt through hindsight to sort out the intentions of the parties and affix jural significance to conduct carried out within an essentially private and generally noncontractual relationship runs too great a risk of error. The courts espousing this view believe that without an express agreement, there is a substantially greater risk of emotion-laden afterthought, not to mention fraud, in attempting to ascertain by implication what services, if any, were rendered gratuitously and what compensation, if any, the parties intended. *See Elkins v. Ehrens*, 251 N.Y.S.2d 560 (1964); *Trimmer v. Van Bomel*, 434 N.Y.S.2d 82 (N.Y. Sup. 1980).

These courts believe that there is very little difference in personal services between unmarried persons living together and unmarried persons whose actions flow out of mutual friendship and reciprocal regard. Consequently, an implied contract to compensate for those things that are ordinarily done by one person for another as a matter of regard and affection should not be recognized. The major difficulty with implying a contract from the rendition of services in such situations is that it is not reasonable to infer an agreement to pay for the services rendered when the relationship of the parties suggests that the services were rendered gratuitously.

EXAMPLES

Example 15-6

Assume that P and D do not marry, but they have an ongoing romantic relationship for the ten years preceding D's death. D supported P financially, and she moved into D's home early in their relationship. P worked for D, who was a radio personality and author. She edited his books, arranged for appearances, and helped with all aspects of his career. D asked P not to work outside the home, and he assured her, "This is our house, and most of what I have is going to be yours anyway." Even though he orally promised to do so, D died without executing a will in P's favor, and she seeks relief from the court. What might she claim, and what is the likely result?

EXPLANATIONS

Explanation

In *Northrup v. Brigham*, 826 N.E.2d 239 (Mass. App. Ct. 2005), P claimed that she had an oral contract with D under which he agreed to execute a will leaving property to her and to provide for her based on her years of service. Although the oral promise to execute a will was unenforceable under the statute of frauds, P's suit for recovery in *quantum meruit* was allowed to proceed past summary judgment. The court stated, "At this stage, the plaintiff has presented sufficient evidence in support of her theory that in return for the substantial services she provided to the decedent over the years, he had promised her the bulk of his estate. In making this determination, we do not consider actions and statements as strands in isolation, but as threads which, when viewed together, form the tapestry, often multi-textured, of interpersonal dynamics. In sum, the record supports that the elements of a contract — namely offer, acceptance, and an exchange of consideration or meeting of minds — have been established sufficiently to withstand summary judgment. Accordingly, the plaintiff's claim in quantum meruit may proceed." *Id.* at 243.

15.16. Equitable Contracts

Some courts may impose an equitable contract when there is no evidence of a contract, if granting no remedy would result in the unjust enrichment of one party. Quasi-contracts are not contracts based on the apparent intention of the parties to undertake the performance in question, but are contracts created by law for reasons of justice. An action for recovery based on unjust enrichment is grounded on the moral principle that one who has received a benefit has a duty to make restitution when retaining such a benefit would be unjust. The remedy is based on the reasonable value of the benefit conferred by one party that enriched the other. The value of the benefit has two components: money expended and services or forbearance rendered. Several courts have held that unmarried cohabitants may raise claims based on unjust enrichment following the termination of their relationships when one of the parties attempts to retain an unreasonable amount of the property acquired through the efforts of both.

Unlike express and implied contracts, the conduct of the parties is not critical to granting relief because no contract exists. Instead, a contract is imposed as a matter of law, not as a matter of fact. A party seeking to establish a quasi-contract must present evidence of the benefits conferred on the other party and services performed. In addition, the moving party must establish evidence of the reasonable value of those benefits and services.

15.17. Resulting Trusts

Resulting trusts are judicial fictions. They are created to carry out the presumed intent of the parties as understood by the court. The presumption in a resulting trust is that the party who purchased property and caused title to be put in another's name intended to retain a beneficial interest in the property.

15.18. Constructive Trusts

A constructive trust arises by operation of law against one who, through any form of unconscionable conduct, holds legal title to property when equity and good conscience demands that he should not hold such title. *Henkle v. Henkle*, 600 N.E.2d 791, 795-796 (Ohio App. 1991). When it is inequitable that a person retain title to property, a constructive trust may be imposed even in the absence of fraud when there exists a legal principle that can serve as a basis for equitable relief. A constructive trust closely parallels the equitable remedy of *quantum meruit* under quasi-contract, with the primary difference being that the trust transfers title, whereas the *quantum meruit* remedy is based on value, not title. The facts in a particular case may permit a plaintiff to choose which remedy is most appropriate. In many jurisdictions, a constructive trust usually requires some kind of wrongdoing, such as fraud or undue influence.

LIMITATIONS ON RECOVERY BY COHABITANTS

15.19. General Limits

Because cohabitants are not married, they cannot avail themselves of relief, such as alimony, awarded under dissolution of marriage statutes. They also have difficulty receiving various other benefits that commonly accrue to married people, including wrongful death awards and insurance recoveries.

15.20. Statutory Barriers

Courts have generally been unwilling to award benefits that flow from various statutes to cohabiting partners absent language that specifically encompasses the relationship. *See, e.g.*, *Powell v. Rogers*, 496 F.2d 1248, 1250 (9th Cir.), *cert. denied*, 419 U.S. 1032 (1974); *Ford v. American Original Corp.*, 475 F. Supp. 10 (E.D. Va. 1979) (female "friend" of the decedent was not a beneficiary because she had never become decedent's "legal wife" under the laws of Virginia, which did not recognize the common law spouse doctrine); *Lawson v. United States*, 192 F.2d 479 (2d Cir.), *cert. denied*, 343 U.S. 904 (1951) (holding that a putative wife was not a "legal" wife and therefore could not recover for wrongful death of her putative husband under DOHSA); *Tetterton v. Arctic Tankers, Inc.*, 116 F. Supp. 429 (E.D. Pa. 1953) (declaring that even if a valid common law marriage had been perfected under the law of Florida, which recognized common law marriages, the claimant still did not become a legal wife and was at most a common law wife, and the congressional intent of DOHSA was to permit the recovery of wrongful death damages only by "legal" spouses); *McPherson v. S.S. South African Pioneer*, 321 F. Supp. 42 (E.D. Va. 1971) (following the doctrine of *Lawson*).

The limited view of cohabitant relationships is in sharp contrast to that of the putative spouse — one who believes in good faith that he or she is a party to a valid marriage. For example, California recognizes that a putative spouse is entitled to take by intestacy on the death of a spouse in the same manner as a validly married spouse and is entitled to workers' compensation death benefits.

EXAMPLES

Example 15-7

P and the decedent, D, lived together for 14 years until his death but did not undergo a formal or ceremonial marriage. Three children were born of this union, and the entire household was supported by the decedent. During most of this period, the decedent was lawfully married to X, a marriage of which P was aware. D's marriage was dissolved by divorce about four years before X died, but P and D did not formally marry. In the words of P, her "marriage" was legal "in the sight of God, yes; but in the sight of man, no." P and D lived together in two states that did not recognize common law marriages. When D died in an accident, P sought death benefits as a surviving wife or widow under the applicable federal law. P argues that the court should consider her a putative spouse or recognize federal common law marriages so that application of the benefits statute would be uniform throughout the country. How will a court most likely treat P's claim?

EXPLANATIONS

Explanation

The court will ask whether the two states that P and D lived in would recognize P as a "surviving widow" on these facts. Here, the two states that P lived in did not recognize common law marriages; therefore, P cannot argue she was D's lawful wife at the time of his death.

P also cannot be treated as a putative spouse because one must believe in good faith that she is a party to a valid marriage. P had no such belief and knew that she was not a party to a state common law marriage.

Although creating a federal common law marriage doctrine might result in more uniform application of federal statutes and eliminate the element of whether the law of a particular state recognized common law marriage, the courts have taken the position that these views are more properly directed to Congress. Giving additional weight to the court's view is the fact that courts have relied on state law to supply the meaning of "surviving wife" and "widow" and Congress has not chosen to intervene. P will not be able to recover benefits.

15.21. Tort and Insurance Claim Barriers

Unmarried partners have difficulty bringing wrongful death actions after the loss of a partner. For example, in *Holguin v. Flores*, 18 Cal. Rptr.3d 749 (Cal. App. 2004), a cohabiting opposite-sex partner could not sue for the wrongful death of the other partner, even though a similarly situated same-sex registered domestic partner could bring such an action.

Courts are not in agreement over what type of relationship is needed between an injured party and a bystander before the bystander may recover for emotional damages when witnessing the injury. Whether a plaintiff can recover for negligent infliction of emotional distress after witnessing injury to another is a contentious issue. One state, New Jersey, has held that "familial relationship" with the injured person, of the kind required to permit a bystander to recover for his or her emotional distress upon witnessing injury, is not necessarily limited to relationships of marriage or blood. *Dunphy v. Gregor*, 642 A.2d 372 (N.J. 1994). Under New Jersey law, for a bystander-claimant to prevail, the claimant must demonstrate (1) that the death or serious physical injury of another was caused by defendant's negligence, (2) that a marital or intimate, familial relationship existed between the plaintiff and the injured person, (3) that the claimant observed the death or injury at the scene of the accident, and (4) that the claimant suffered resulting severe emotional distress.

In *Ortiz v. New York City Transit Authority*, 699 N.Y.S.2d 370 (N.Y. App. Div. 1 Dept. 1999), the court ruled that the named insured's same-sex, live-in partner was not entitled to underinsured motorist coverage under the supplementary uninsured motorist clause in the named insured's automobile policy. The court held that the partner was neither a "spouse" nor a "relative" of the named insured and was not covered by the policy. The supplementary uninsured motorist clause in dispute covered the named insured and "while residents of the same household, the named insured's spouse and . . . relatives."

In *390 West End Associates v. Wildfoerster*, 661 N.Y.S.2d 202 (N.Y. App. Div. 1 Dept., 1997), the court awarded possession of a rent-controlled apartment to the landlord, finding that there was an insufficient familial relationship between tenant and companion to allow for transfer of the apartment to the companion under rent-control regulations. The companion and the deceased tenant had a 20-year relationship, during which they lived together from 1976 to 1978 and again for more than two years prior to the tenant's death from AIDS in 1993. The court found that the relationship lacked the normal indicia of a familial relationship. Although the tenant's close friends testified, and the trial court found, that the tenant and respondent had a very close, loving relationship, the trial evidence failed to sufficiently establish the respondent as a family member within the meaning of the applicable rent regulations.

15.22. Housing Discrimination Based on Marital Status

The Supreme Court of California has held that California's Fair Employment and Housing Act's (FEHA) prohibition against discrimination because of "marital status" prohibits landlords from refusing to rent to prospective tenants because they are not married. The court also stated that FEHA's prohibition against discrimination based on marital status does not "substantially burden" a landlord's religious exercise under the state constitution's free exercise and enjoyment of religion clause. *Smith v. Fair Employment & Hous. Commn.*, 913 P.2d 909 (Cal. 1996).

Courts in Minnesota and Washington have not followed California's lead. *See, e.g., State by Cooper v. French*, 460 N.W.2d 2, 5-6 (Minn. 1990); *McFadden v. Elma Country Club*, 613 P.2d 146, 150 (Wash. Ct. App. 1980). The Wisconsin Supreme Court declared a county ordinance similar to California's FEHA "invalid to the extent that it [sought] to protect 'cohabitants,'" *County of Dane v. Norman*, 497 N.W.2d 714, 716 (Wis. 1993). The court reasoned that the county had no power to enact statutes that were "inconsistent with the public policy of Wisconsin, which seeks to promote the stability of marriage and family." *Id.* at 720.

15.23. Statute of Limitations

As a general principle, a *Marvin*-type agreement is breached when one of the partners ends the relationship. However, the limitations period must be construed in light of the facts of a particular case. When no time for performance is specified, a person who has promised to do an act in the future and who has the ability to perform does not violate his or her agreement unless and until performance is demanded and refused. For example, if the parties have separated, but the obligor performs as required by the *Marvin* agreement, there has been no breach, no cause of action has accrued, and the statute of limitations has not begun to run. The statute of limitation only begins to run when the breach occurs. *See Cochran v. Cochran*, 66 Cal. Rptr. 2d 337 (Cal. Ct. App. 1997).

Example 15-8

Assume that P and D had been living together for several years without getting married when D left the relationship to marry another. At one point in the relationship, D had promised P that should their relationship ever end, D would pay P $400 a month for life because she had given up her job and moved to the country to live with D. When D marries, he pays P $400 a month for the next three years. He then stops payment, and when P immediately brings an action to enforce their agreement, D asserts that the two-year statute of limitations has run. How will a court most likely rule in this case?

Explanation

A court most likely will rule that a person who has promised to do an act in the future and who has the ability to perform, and who does not violate the agreement, does not receive the benefit of the statute of limitations unless and until performance is demanded and refused. Here, the statute of limitations began to run when defendant stopped making the monthly $400 payments. *See Byrne v. Laura*, 60 Cal. Rptr. 2d 908 (Cal. Ct. App. 1997). Alternatively, it can be argued that there was no damage until the support payments stopped, and the statute of limitations does not run until a cause of action accrues.

CHAPTER 16

Determining Paternity

16.1. Introduction

This chapter examines significant legal principles involved in paternity proceedings. Paternity was important under the common law because it fixed the line of succession. In England, primogeniture, which passed property to the first-born male, made the determination of an heir very important. Consequently, much of the early English law on this topic was inherited by America and was initially concerned with making a "legitimacy" determination. Courts today are more concerned with determining paternity than with legitimacy.

There are many reasons for establishing paternity, some of which include the following: obtaining child support from the biological father; establishing the biological father's visitation and custodial rights; creating peace of mind; determining grandparentage; establishing inheritance rights; establishing insurance claims; obtaining Social Security benefits; establishing Native American tribal rights; determining the likelihood of being the biological sibling of a long-lost sister or brother; and helping a person seeking entry into the United States on the grounds that he or she is a biological relative of a citizen.

THE COMMON LAW

16.2. Disparate Treatment

The common law treated a child born during marriage and one born outside of marriage differently. If a child was born during a marriage, the common law was averse to declaring the child illegitimate — a result that could deprive the child of inheritance and succession and possibly make the child a ward of the state. It aided a child born during a marriage by applying a presumption that the child was the legitimate issue of the wife's husband. The presumption could be overcome only by evidence that the husband was incapable of procreation or had no access to his wife during the relevant period of conception.

Proof of illegitimacy was further complicated by the adoption in many jurisdictions of an evidentiary rule known as "Lord Mansfield's rule." The rule, developed in England and imported into this country, provided that neither the husband nor the wife were permitted to bastardize the issue of the wife after marriage by testifying to the nonaccess of the husband. *See Egbert v. Greenwalt*, 6 N.W. 654 (1880). The rule was apparently applied in some jurisdictions until the mid-twentieth century, when legislatures and courts abandoned its use. *See People v. C.*, 85 N.Y.S.2d 751 (N.Y. Child. Ct. 1949).

For children born out of wedlock, the common law was harsh. It labeled these children bastards and considered them *filius nullius* — the children of no one and the kin to nobody. In some jurisdictions, a child born out of wedlock remained illegitimate despite the marriage of the biological parents. Should a marriage be annulled, a child born during the relationship was considered illegitimate. Support for children born out of wedlock was almost nonexistent.

EXAMPLES

Example 16-1

Assume that 200 years ago, P and D were married, and a child was born to them in a common law jurisdiction. D suspects that the child was conceived during an affair his wife had with a neighbor, X, while P and D were separated for one year. D brings a legal action with the goal of proving that the child is the issue of X, or at least, not D's child. D is unable to produce any witnesses other than P and D. How would a common law court most likely rule on D's request that he be allowed to testify?

EXPLANATIONS

Explanation

The common law court most likely would reject the request, and the action would fail. In the common law jurisdiction that applied Lord Mansfield's rule, D would be barred from testifying to nonaccess.

SUPREME COURT MANDATES EQUAL TREATMENT

16.3. Overview

Discrimination against children born out of wedlock was practiced in most jurisdictions in the United States until well into the 1960s. The United States Supreme Court, Congress, and the National Conference of Commissioners on Uniform State Laws all played a role in causing the states to abandon their unfair treatment of these children. One of the most important factors in changing society's views of these children was the Supreme Court, which invalidated a host of state statutes that treated children born outside of marriage differently from those born during marriage.

16.4. Child's Action for Wrongful Death of the Mother

The case of *Levy v. Louisiana*, 391 U.S. 68 (1968), helped close the gap between children born to unmarried parents and children born during marriage. The dispute involved five children born outside of marriage who sued for damages as the result of the wrongful death of their mother. Under a Louisiana statute, the children did not have a legally recognizable interest in her death if they were born out of wedlock. Although not finding that illegitimacy was a suspect classification, the Court struck down the statute on equal protection grounds, holding that it was invidious to discriminate against the children "when no action, conduct, or demeanor of theirs was relevant to the harm that was done in the matter." *See also* Annot., *Discrimination on Basis of Illegitimacy as Denial of Constitutional Rights*, 38 A.L.R.3d 613 (1971).

16.5. Child Claims Inheritance Rights

The Supreme Court has also aided children born out of wedlock in their efforts to inherit from their parents. For example, *Trimble v. Gordon*, 430 U.S. 762 (1977), involved Delta Mona Trimble, the nonmarital daughter of Jessie Trimble and the deceased biological father, Sherman Gordon. Gordon had provided support and had acknowledged the parent–child relationship; however, when he died without a will, Illinois probate law prohibited Delta Mona Trimble from collecting any portion of his estate. The statute declared that as an illegitimate child, she could only inherit if she had been legitimized by the subsequent marriage of her biological mother and father.

The Court held that a classification based on illegitimacy is not suspect so as to require strict scrutiny. However, using a mid-level or mid-tier analysis, the Court held that at a minimum, a statutory classification must bear some rational relationship to a legitimate state purpose. The Court explained that "in this context, the standard just stated is a minimum; the Court sometimes requires more. 'Though the latitude given state economic and social regulation is necessarily broad, when the state statutory classifications approach sensitive and fundamental personal rights, this Court exercises a stricter scrutiny.' " *Id.* at 767. The Court concluded that the statute bore only the most attenuated relationship to the asserted goal of family relationships and was unconstitutional.

In a subsequent decision, *Lalli v. Lalli*, 439 U.S. 259 (1978), the Court rejected a constitutional challenge to a New York intestacy statute that required illegitimate children seeking to inherit from their fathers to produce an order of affiliation made by a court of competent jurisdiction during the alleged father's lifetime. The Court observed that the statute was intended to soften the rigors of previous law, which permitted illegitimate children to inherit only from their mothers. It also believed that the statute provided for the just and orderly disposition of property at death and protected innocent adults, and those rightfully interested in their estates, from fraudulent claims of heirship and harassing litigation.

The Court distinguished *Trimble v. Gordon* on the grounds that the Illinois statute in *Trimble* was constitutionally unacceptable because it effected a total statutory disinheritance of children born out of wedlock who were not legitimated by the subsequent marriage of their parents. However, inheritance under the New York statute is barred only where there has been a failure to secure evidence of paternity during the father's lifetime. "This is not a requirement that inevitably disqualifies an unnecessarily large number of children born out of wedlock." *Id.* at 273. The Court concluded "that the requirement imposed by Section 4-1.2 on illegitimate children who would inherit from their fathers is substantially related to the important state interests the statute is intended to promote." *Id.* at 275.

EXAMPLES

Example 16-2

Assume that P and D have a daughter, X, but they do not marry. D is not listed on X's birth certificate, but D was found to be X's father in a paternity action and was ordered to pay monthly child support. D paid the child support as ordered but had little contact with X. X was not included in family gatherings, many of D's friends did not know of her existence, and D described her as an "$18,000 mistake." Prior to X's birth, D executed a will disposing of his estate. He did not change the will after X's birth, and she was not included in it. D dies, and X seeks a share of the estate as an omitted child. The state where the parties live has a statute providing that an illegitimate child born after the date that a will is executed can take an intestate share of the decedent's estate if the testator "recognized" the child during his lifetime. What is the likely result?

EXPLANATIONS

Explanation

The other heirs will argue that D did not recognize X as his child because he did not treat her as his child or have a relationship with her. X will argue that if D had died intestate, she would have inherited from him based on the paternity judgment issued during D's lifetime. This example is based on the case of *In re Estate of Brewer*, 168 S.W.3d 135 (Mo. App. 2005), where the trial court found that X was not entitled to an intestate share of D's estate, but that decision was overturned on appeal. The appellate court reasoned that the paternity judgment constituted "recognition" within the meaning of the statute.

16.6. Child Claims Social Security Benefits

In *Mathews v Lucas*, 427 U.S. 495 (1976), nonmarital children sought to obtain Social Security benefits after their biological father died. There was no dispute over the issue of the deceased being the biological father. The Social Security Act provided that a child of an individual who died fully insured under the act is entitled to surviving child's benefits if the child is under 18, or a student under 22, and was dependent at the time of the parent's death. A child is considered dependent if the insured parent was living with the child or the parent was contributing to the child's support at the time of death.

The Court upheld the statute, holding that it did not violate the Equal Protection Clause of the Constitution, even though the statute treated children differently based at least in part on their parents' marital status. The Court said that the challenged statutory classifications are permissible because they are reasonably related to the likelihood of dependency at death. The Court concluded that although the act did not extend any presumption of dependency to illegitimate children as a group, it did not impermissibly discriminate against them when compared with legitimate children or those illegitimate children who are statutorily deemed dependent.

16.7. Child's Father Makes Wrongful Death Claim

In *Parham v. Hughes*, 441 U.S. 347 (1979), the Supreme Court rejected a claim by a father who had not legitimated his child and who sought to recover for the child's wrongful death. The relevant Georgia statute allowed a mother to bring a wrongful death action for the death of a child born out of wedlock and allowed the father, if he had legitimated the child, to bring an action if there was no mother. The Court found that "unlike the illegitimate child for whom the status of illegitimacy is involuntary and immutable, the [father] here was responsible for fostering an illegitimate child and for failing to change its status." *Id.* at 441. The Court indicated concern about proving the paternity of illegitimate children and the related danger of spurious claims against intestate estates. It also evinced additional concern that if paternity has not been established before the commencement of a wrongful death action, a defendant might face multiple lawsuits by individuals all claiming to be the father of the deceased child. Such uncertainty would make it difficult if not impossible for a defendant to settle a wrongful-death action because there would always exist the risk of a subsequent suit by another person claiming to be the father.

16.8. Tests to Determine Rights if Child Is Born Outside of Marriage

Since *Levy v. Louisiana*, the Supreme Court has used two tests to determine the rights of illegitimate children who are treated differently by a state statute than children born during marriage: (1) the "insurmountable barrier" test, *Gomez v. Perez*, 409 U.S. 535, 538 (1973); *Labine v. Vincent*, 401 U.S. 532, 539 (1971); and (2) the less stringent "substantial relationship" test, *Lalli v. Lalli*, 439 U.S. 259 (1978); *Trimble v. Gordon*, 430 U.S. 762, 772-774 (1977).

EXAMPLES

Example 16-3

Assume that M and D are the biological parents of child P, who was born out of wedlock in state X. A month prior to P's birth, the biological father, D, was involved in an automobile accident. He remained in a coma for five months and died intestate. Under the law in state X, there are three means by which an illegitimate child may inherit from an intestate father: (1) the father may marry the mother and recognize the child as his own; (2) the father may legitimate the child by following the statutory procedure for legitimation by written declaration; or (3) a court may make a judicial determination of paternity during the father's lifetime. P argues that she was unable to qualify under any of these provisions because her biological father was fatally injured in an automobile accident that occurred before her birth and remained in a coma until his death some four months after her birth. P attacks the law in state X as unconstitutional. How will a court most likely rule?

Explanation

Obviously, after the accident, P's father could not have married her mother or acknowledged the child by written declaration. Nor did P have a meaningful opportunity to be legitimated through a paternity proceeding, which, under X's law, must be maintained during the father's lifetime. As a practical matter, X's intestacy scheme effectively denied P any means through which to become legitimated or qualify herself to inherit from her father's estate. On these facts, a court will most likely rule that the statute creates an insurmountable barrier and, as applied, is unconstitutional.

PROCEDURAL RIGHTS

16.9. Burden of Proof

In *Rivera v. Minnich*, 483 U.S. 574 (1987), the Supreme Court held that a paternity statute that provided proof by a preponderance of evidence did not violate the Due Process Clause of the Fourteenth Amendment to the United States Constitution. It concluded that the clear and convincing standard of proof for terminating a parent-child relationship established in *Santosky v. Kramer*, 455 U.S. 745 (1982), was not applicable.

16.10. Indigent's Right to Blood Tests

In *Little v. Streater*, 452 U.S. 1 (1981), the Court held that due process requires that an indigent defendant involved in paternity matters be entitled to blood testing at state expense to establish (or disprove) paternity. The importance of blood tests magnifies the necessity for the timely assistance of counsel, who can ensure that the defendant is apprised of his right to request blood tests and who can inform him of their significance.

16.11. Indigent's Right to Counsel in Paternity Proceeding

The Supreme Court has not mandated that counsel be afforded indigents who are accused of fathering a child out of wedlock. However, some state courts have required counsel either under the exercise of their supervisory power to ensure fairness or as a requirement of the state constitution. *Hepfel v. Bashaw*, 279 N.W.2d 342 (Minn. 1979) (supervisory power). In noncriminal cases in which a right to counsel has specifically been recognized (such as contempt or paternity cases), the court should exercise the same care in assuring the understanding of the right and voluntariness of the waiver, as in criminal cases.

Those jurisdictions that have determined that counsel should be provided reason that an adjudication of paternity can mean up to 18 years of child support payments and that paternity affects the distribution of defendant's estate upon death, Worker's Compensation benefits, Social Security benefits (42 U.S.C. §402(d)(1)), and insurance proceeds. A paternity adjudication can also seriously damage the reputation of the defendant and have a deleterious effect on an already established family of the defendant. The child's rights of support, inheritance, and custody are directly affected by a paternity proceeding, and a child's health interests are involved. An accurate family medical history can be critical in the diagnosis and treatment of a child's injuries and illnesses. *See Reynolds v. Kimmons*, 569 P.2d 799, 803 (Alaska 1977) (under state constitution); *Artibee v. Cheboygan Circuit Judge*, 243 N.W.2d 248, 250 (Mich. 1976); *Salas v. Cortez*, 593 P.2d 226, 234 *cert. denied*, 444 U.S. 900 (1979) (state constitution); *Wake Cty. ex rel. Carrington v. Townes*, 281 S.E.2d 765, 769 (N.C. App. 1981).

There is contrary state authority regarding the right to counsel. *State ex rel. Hamilton v. Snodgrass*, 325 N.W.2d 740 (Iowa 1982); *Sheppard v. Mack*, 427 N.E.2d 522, 528 (Ohio App. 1980) (no due process or equal protection right to appointed counsel); *State ex rel. Adult and Family Serv. Div. v. Stoutt*, 644 P.2d 1232, 1137 (Or. App. 1982) (no due process right to appointed counsel under federal or state constitutions); *State v. Walker*, 553 P.2d 1093, 1095 (Wis. 1976) (no due process or equal protection right to appointed counsel).

16.12. Putative Father's Standing to Bring Action — Michael H

The best-known standing decision is *Michael H. v. Gerald D*, 491 U.S. 110 (1988) (STEVENS, J., concurring in the judgment; BRENNAN, J., with MARSHALL and BLACKMUN, J., dissenting; WHITE, J., with BRENNAN, J., dissenting). Justice Stevens concurred in the judgment denying the putative father an opportunity to establish his paternity, only after concluding that under the California statute at issue, the putative father "was given a fair opportunity to show that he is [the child's] natural father, that he developed a relationship with her, and that her interests would be served by granting him visitation rights." *Id.* at 135-136. The dispute involved a child fathered by the wife's lover during the marriage and born while she was cohabiting with her husband. The child was conclusively presumed by statute to be a child of the marriage unless the husband was impotent or sterile. The husband's name was placed on the birth certificate, and he claimed the child as his daughter. Blood tests indicated, however, that the wife's lover, Michael H., was actually the child's biological father.

During the child's first three years, she and her mother intermittently lived with Michael, who consistently held himself out as her father. About 18 months after the child's birth, Michael filed a filiation action to establish his paternity and visitation rights, and during the course of this lawsuit, the constitutionality of the conclusive presumption was challenged.

The Court held that the biological father had no protected liberty interest in the parental relationship and that the state's interest in preserving the marital union was sufficient to support termination of his relationship with the child. The Court balanced the nonmarital father's rights against the rights of the married father. The plurality determined that the marital family and the marital father's rights are paramount and rested its holding on history and tradition. Five justices, however, refused to foreclose the possibility that the natural father might ever have a constitutionally protected interest in his relationship with a child, whose mother was married to and cohabiting with another man at the time of the child's conception and birth.

In addition to *Michael H. v. Gerald D.*, several state courts have considered a putative father's standing to bring a paternity action. *Barnes v. Jeudevine*, 2006 WL 2075648 (Mich. 2006) (biological father lacked standing to sue under Paternity Act); *Numerick v. Krull*, 694 N.W.2d 552 (Mich. App. 2005) (paternity action barred by marriage of mother to another man); *Lisa I. v. Superior Court*, 34 Cal. Rptr.3d 927 (Cal. App. 2005) (biological with no existing relationship with child lacks standing); *J.K. v. R.S.*, 706 So. 2d 1262 (Ala. Civ. App. 1997) (alleged biological father did not count as a parent for purposes of standing to bring custody action involving child born to a married couple); *S.B. v. D.H.*, 736 So. 2d 766 (Fla. Dist. Ct. App. 1999) (putative biological father could not maintain a paternity action concerning a child conceived by a married woman over the objections of the woman and her husband); *In re Paternity of S.R.I.*, 602 N.E.2d 1014 (Ind. 1992) (interpreting the relevant statute to allow a putative father to establish paternity without regard to the mother's marital status): *Pearson v. Pearson*, 134 P.3d 173 (Utah App. 2006) (putative father lacked standing to intervene in divorce proceedings).

16.13. Accused Father's Right to Jury Trial

A paternity action today is civil in nature, and most jurisdictions allow normal discovery such as interrogatories, depositions, requests for admissions, and requests for an adverse physical or psychological examination. The Personal Responsibility and Work Opportunity Reconciliation Act of 1996 (PRWORA) required states, as a condition of receiving federal funds, to preclude jury trials in contested paternity matters.

FEDERAL LEGISLATION

16.14. Overview

With an increasingly large number of children being born outside of marriage and the federal government providing support for many of them, more than three decades ago, Congress responded with legislation that reduced the government's financial burden by shifting it to the biological parents of the child—in particular, their fathers. To accomplish this objective, the federal government created a child support enforcement program that imposed requirements on states as a condition of receiving IV-D funding. The program, titled after IV-D of the Social Security Act, requires that the states comply with various requirements, including establishment of paternity, or risk losing up to two-thirds of support payments provided by the government.

Beginning in 1975, state and local IV-D agencies were required to establish the paternity of all children who were born to unmarried parents and who either received public assistance benefits or have applied for IV-D services. In 1984, Congress required that each state permit a paternity action to be brought at any time before a child's eighteenth birthday, rather than allowing shorter statutes of limitations, which had been the practice in some states.

16.15. The Omnibus Budget Reconciliation Act of 1993

The Omnibus Budget Reconciliation Act of 1993, Pub. L. No. 103-66 (1993), required that all states adopt an in-hospital, voluntary acknowledgment process as a condition of receiving federal IV-D funds. The Personal Responsibility and Work Opportunity Reconciliation Act of 1996 (PRWORA), Pub. L. No. 103-66 (1993), modified and expanded the required paternity acknowledgment procedures earlier established by Congress.

16.16. Personal Responsibility and Work Opportunity Reconciliation Act of 1996 (PRWORA)

The Personal Responsibility and Work Opportunity Reconciliation Act of 1996 (PRWORA) mandates that states have laws requiring that genetic testing be ordered in any contested case. The party requesting the testing must execute a sworn statement that either alleges paternity, with a showing of a reasonable possibility of sexual contact between the parties, or denies paternity. The tribunal can then compel genetic testing of the child and all parties. *See State ex rel. Dept. of Justice and Division of Child Support*, 120 P.3d 1 (Ore. App. 2005) (requiring parentage testing was a reasonable "search" under state and federal constitutions).

UNIFORM PARENTAGE ACT (UPA)

16.17. Overview

The National Conference of Commissioners on Uniform State Laws (NCCUSL) first addressed parentage in 1922 with the Uniform Illegitimacy Act and continued to promulgate related acts such as the Uniform Blood Tests to Determine Paternity Act, the Uniform Paternity Act, the Uniform Probate Code, and the Blood Tests to Determine Paternity Act. One can see from the titles of the acts how societal and legal views of parentage have evolved over the last century.

The most influential current uniform law is the Uniform Parentage Act, which was originally approved in 1973 and most recently revised in 2002. The text of the Act can be found at http://www.law.upenn.edu/bll/ulc/upa/final2002.htm (last visited 10-24-06). By December of 2000, the UPA had been adopted in 19 states and had influenced development of the law in a significant number of the remaining states.

The UPA declared that the law should treat children equally, regardless of the marital status of their parents. UPA §202 (2002). Consequently, the title "illegitimate" was replace with the term "child with no presumed father."

16.18. Genetic Testing

The UPA sets forth procedures and guidelines to expedite and regulate the use of genetic testing in paternity cases. A man may be rebuttably identified as the father of a child based on certain genetic testing results described in the Act. UPA §§501 *et. seq.*; UPA §§621 *et. seq.*

In the past, proving paternity scientifically was unreliable, and verdicts were unpredictable. Often, the evidence consisted of testimony about the mother's relationships with other men, the physical resemblance of the child to the alleged father, and the relationship of the mother and alleged father. When blood-type testing came into common use, it could not reliably identify the father of a child, but could exclude possible fathers.

Recent scientific advances have led to genetic testing that is able to identify a man as the father of a child to a reasonably high degree of accuracy. By testing blood and tissue, certain genes can be identified. If a test of a child reveals a gene that did not come from the mother, the gene was contributed by the child's biological father. If the DNA test shows the alleged father could not have contributed the gene, he is excluded. However, the fact that the alleged father could have contributed the gene does not automatically prove he is the father. Ronald J. Richards, *DNA Fingerprinting and Paternity Testing*, 22 U.C. Davis L. Rev. 609, 614 (1989).

Certain genes are more or less common in given human populations. If the test reveals that the child's father possesses uncommon genes also found in the child, but not found in the mother, it is probable that he is the biological father. The probability is expressed as a high paternity index or "probability of paternity." *DNA Fingerprinting and Paternity Testing*, *supra*, at 616-617. This probability exists because it is assumed that the man had access to the mother. *See, e.g.*, *In re Paternity of M.J.B.*, 425 N.W.2d 404, 409 (1988). Regardless of the test results, if the alleged father is infertile or did not have access to the mother, he cannot be adjudicated as the father.

EXAMPLES

Example 16-4

Assume that P claims that D is the father of a child born out of wedlock. A genetic test reveals that D is the child's father to a probability of 97 percent or greater. In this jurisdiction, an individual is presumed to be the father of a child when genetic testing indicates a 96 percent or greater probability. D insists he is not the father. What evidence, if any, might D be able to introduce that will overcome the presumption?

EXPLANATIONS

Explanation

Most likely, the only way to rebut the genetic test presumption is to discredit the test results (chain of custody, evidence) or to obtain a sample from another man who had access to the mother with a 97 percent or greater probability of paternity. Evidence that there was no sexual access for the 230 to 300 days preceding the birth is admissible; however, it must be clear and convincing. One-on-one testimony more than likely will not carry this burden. Evidence of promiscuity outside the period when conception might have occurred is usually not admissible.

16.19. Voluntary Acknowledgment

Under the Personal Responsibility and Work Opportunity Reconciliation Act of 1996 (PRWORA), states became required to facilitate a man's ability to voluntarily acknowledge paternity. To this end, a valid acknowledgment of paternity is sufficient to establish the father–child relationship. UPA §201(b)(2). The UPA sets forth detailed procedures for acknowledgment and denial. UPA §300 et. seq.

Example 16-5

Assume that M gave birth to child, and D executed a voluntary acknowledgement of paternity two days later. The acknowledgment form informed D of his right to genetic testing and the legal consequences of signature. When sued for child support, D claimed that he is not the father of the child. He provided DNA testing showing that there was a 0 percent chance that he was the child's father. The state where M and D live has a statute providing that a voluntary acknowledgement becomes conclusive if it not timely rescinded, which X's was not. In contrast, D argues that if the marital presumption of paternity applied in this case, it could be rebutted by clear and convincing evidence. Will a court allow D to rescind the acknowledgement?

Explanation

This example is based on the case of *People ex rel. Dept. of Public Aid v. Smith*, 289 Ill. Dec. 1 (Ill. 2004), where the court found that the disparate treatment of the two groups of presumed fathers was logical and appropriate. The court reasoned that a man who signs an acknowledgement informing him of his rights and waiving them is in a very different position than a man assumed to be a father merely by virtue of his marital status. The court held that D could not rescind the voluntary acknowledgment of paternity.

Example 16-6

Assume that D had a sexual relationship with P, but they did not marry. A child, A, was born in 1999, and D signed a voluntary acknowledgement of paternity on the day that A was born. He did so based on assurances from P that he was the father of A. In 2000, D agreed to entry of a child support order, but several months later, he began to question whether he was actually A's father. After genetic tests were performed, it was determined that D was not A's biological father. In the state where P and D live, the statute dealing with voluntary acknowledgement provides that an acknowledgment can be overturned if based on a material mistake of fact. D claims that his belief that he was the father of A, based on P's assertions, was a material mistake of fact and that he should be allowed to rescind the acknowledgment. P claims that the acknowledgment should be enforced, and she alleges that D's error was caused by his "neglect of legal duty" because he signed the acknowledgment without insisting on genetic testing. What is the likely result?

Explanation

This example is based on *Department of Human Services v. Chisum*, 85 P.3d 860 (Okla. App. 2004), where the appellate court held that D had established a "material mistake of fact" as required under the statute. He was consequently allowed to rescind his prior acknowledgement of paternity. Note that the outcome likely would have been quite different were it not for the state statutory provision specifically providing for rescission of a voluntary acknowledgment based on a material mistake of fact.

16.20. Presumptions of Paternity

The UPA establishes five categories of presumed fathers, including the following: (1) the man is married to the mother, and the child is born during the marriage; (2) the man is married to the mother, and the child is born within 300 days of termination of the marriage; (3) the man and the mother attempted to marry, and the child is born within 300 days of the termination of the relationship; (4) after the child is born, the man and the mother marry or attempt to marry, and the man voluntarily asserts paternity through methods set forth in the Act; and (5) the man resides with the child for the first two years of the child's life and holds himself out as the father. UPA §204. An unrebutted presumption of paternity establishes a father-child relationship. UPA §201(b)(1).

The time limits and procedures for rebutting the presumptions are set forth in Article 6, Proceeding to Adjudicate Parentage. UPA §601 et seq. However, when the child has a presumed father, an action must generally be brought by the presumed father, the mother, or another individual within two years of the child's birth (unless the presumed father did not have sexual intercourse with the mother near the time of conception, and he never held the child out as his own). UPA §607. In the year 2000, 33 states had statutes or case law allowing rebuttal of the marital presumption. *But see Michael H. v. Gerald D.* 491 U.S. 110 (1989) (bar on man suing to establish paternity in face of marital presumption).

Challenging issues arise when more than one man is the presumed father of a child. The UPA previously provided that the presumption founded on "the weightier considerations of policy and logic" should control. Although this provision is no longer contained in the UPA, it does appear in some state statutes.

Example 16-7

Assume that P and D were married but had some relationship problems. They separated but did not divorce. During the separation, P had a sexual relationship with X, which resulted in the birth of a child. X's name appeared on the birth certificate as the father, and he provided some financial support for the child. X brings a paternity action. D objects to the proceeding, claiming that he is the legal father of the child because he is the husband of the child's mother, and the child was conceived and born while P and D were married. X contends that under state law, the presumption of legitimacy can be rebutted if its application is "outrageous to common sense and reason." What is the likely result?

Explanation

This situation can be viewed in several different lights. Historically, the presumption that a child born during a marriage was the child of the husband was a strong and often impossible presumption to overcome. Particularly when the married couple opposed the paternity action, a man in X's position would have lacked standing to file suit. With the advent of genetic testing and changing views of the family, some states provide that the traditional marital presumption can be rebutted under some circumstances. This example is based in part on the case of *Lander v. Smith*, 906 So. 2d 1130 (Fla. App. 2005), where the court found for X, holding that the presumption of legitimacy could be rebutted in a circumstance where "common sense and reason are outraged" by its rigid application. The court was swayed by the fact that X was eager to embrace the responsibilities of parenthood.

Example 16-8

Assume that M was married to F1 but that during the marriage, she had an affair with F2. When a child was conceived, all of the parties believed that F1 was the father. However, routine hospital testing disclosed that F2 was the biological father of the child. F2 signed a support agreement, and F2's wife regularly cared for the child. F2 told family and friends that he was the father of the child. F2 brought an action to be declared the legal father of the child. F1 claimed to be the legal father of the child because he was M's husband at the time of conception and birth and was therefore the presumed father under state law. F1 claims that he is also a presumed father based on a state statute presuming paternity for a man who "receives the child into his home and openly holds out the child as his natural child." The state statute provides that "If two or more presumptions conflict with each other, the presumption which on the facts is founded on the weightier considerations of policy and logic controls." What is the likely result?

EXPLANATIONS

Explanation

This example is based on the case of *Craig L. v. Sandy S.*, 125 Cal. App.4th 36 (Cal. App. 2004), where the trial court's initial decision quashing F2's petition was reversed. The appellate court remanded the case for further consideration, giving the greatest weight to the well-being of the child. The court stated, "As we have indicated, in weighing the conflicting interests under [the statute] the trial court must in the end make a determination which gives the greatest weight to [the child's] well-being." *Id.* at 53. On remand, the court was instructed to consider the nature of F2's relationship with the child and the impact on the child of recognizing F2's paternity.

16.21. Statutes of Limitation

In order to retain federal subsidies for child support enforcement, states have extended their statutes of limitations for establishing paternity at least until the child reaches the age of 18. State statutes of limitation generally range from age 18 to age 23. However, nine states have no age limitation.

The UPA allows a child with no presumed, acknowledged, or adjudicated father to sue for determination of parentage until the alleged parent's estate has been closed. UPA §606. When the child has a presumed father, an action must generally be brought by the presumed father, the mother, or another individual within two years of the child's birth. However, an action to disprove the relationship with a presumed father may be brought at any time if the presumed father and mother did not cohabitate or have sexual intercourse with each other near the time of conception and if the presumed father never openly held the child out as his own. UPA §607.

States historically had statutes requiring that paternity actions be brought within a year or two of the birth of the child. For example, in *Mills v. Habluetzel*, 456 U.S. 91 (1982), the mother of an illegitimate child brought suit to establish paternity. The trial court had dismissed the suit because the child was one year and seven months old when the suit was filed, and Texas law required a paternity action to be brought within one year of a child's birth. The Supreme Court held that the Texas statute effectively blocked legitimation by imposing a time limit on the initiation of paternity proceedings, which for all practical purposes was impossible to comply with. The provision was unconstitutional under both the insurmountable barrier and the substantial relationship tests. The Court said that the statute denied equal protection to illegitimate children because a state that grants opportunity for legitimate children to obtain parental support must also grant that opportunity to illegitimate children, and this opportunity must be more than illusory.

In *Clark v. Jeter*, 486 U.S. 456 (1988), the mother of a child born out of wedlock waited ten years to seek support from the putative father. He claimed that Pennsylvania's six-year statute of limitations for bringing paternity actions barred the action to establish paternity. After reviewing *Mills v. Habluetzel*, 456 U.S. 91 (1982) (invalidating one-year statute of limitations) and *Pickett v. Brown*, 462 U.S. 1 (1983) (invalidating a two-year statute of limitations), the Court struck down the Pennsylvania limitation. The Court held that for a paternity limitation to pass intermediate scrutiny, the period must be sufficiently long to present a reasonable opportunity to be heard, and any limitation placed on that opportunity must be substantially related to the state's interest in avoiding litigation of stale or fraudulent claims.

There are, however, some state limits on bringing paternity actions. For example, in *In re Estate of Smith*, 685 So. 2d 1206 (Fla. 1996), the claim of a 60-year-old alleged daughter to the estate of her deceased father was denied on the basis that the Florida statute of limitations regarding adjudication of paternity had expired. *But see R.A.C. v. P.J. S.*, 880 A.2d 1179 (N.J. Super. 2005) (man declared father of 30-year-old child after 23-year statute of limitations equitably tolled).

16.22. Registration to Receive Notice of Termination of Parental Rights

The UPA provides for the use of parentage registries in order to expeditiously free children for adoption. Any man who wants to receive notification of termination of parental rights and adoption proceedings concerning a child he may have fathered must enter his name on the registry. Failure to do so can result in termination of parental rights without notice. As of May 2000, 28 states had statutes creating paternity registries. UPA §401 et. seq.

OTHER ISSUES IN DETERMINING PATERNITY

16.23. Equitable Parent Doctrine

The equitable parent doctrine allows a court to find that a husband who is not the biological father of a child born or conceived during the marriage may be considered the natural father of that child when: (1) the husband and the child mutually acknowledge a relationship as father and child, or the mother of the child has cooperated in the development of such a relationship over a period of time prior to the filing of a complaint for divorce; (2) the husband desires to have the rights afforded to a parent; and (3) the husband is willing to take on the responsibility of paying child support.

Courts have refused to apply the doctrine to situations in which a child was not born or conceived during the marriage. *See Van v. Zahorik*, 597 N.W.2d 15 (Mich. 1999) (court refuses to apply doctrine to putative unmarried father); *People ex rel. J.A.U. v. R.L.C.*, 47 P.3d 327 (Colo. 2002) (man who waited 11 years before attacking a paternity judgment he stipulated to without demanding genetic testing waited too long); *W. v. W.*, 779 A.2d 716 (Conn. 2001) (court estopped the husband from denying his paternity when he had treated the child as his for 12 years); *In re Paternity of Cheryl*, 746 N.E.2d 488 (Mass. 2001) (man waited five years after acknowledging paternity to have genetic tests that showed his nonpaternity was not relieved of support obligation); *Huisman v. Miedema*, 644 N.W.2d 321 (Iowa 2002) (putative father's paternity action dismissed when it was brought seven years after child's birth, and mother and her husband raised child); *Killingbeck v. Killingbeck*, 711 N.W.2d 759 (Mich. App. 2005) (child not conceived or born within marital relationship).

EXAMPLES

Example 16-9

Assume P and D cohabited for five years but were never married. D claims that D and P continued their relationship for several years after they stopped living together, and P had two children in the course of this relationship. D alleges that P informed him that he was the father of the children, and he believes that he was named as the father on the birth certificates of both children. He also claims that he cared for and financially supported the children both during and after his relationship with P.

When D started a relationship with another woman, P refused to allow him to see the children. D filed a petition to establish paternity, and he alleged that he believed and continues to believe he is the father of the two children. P argued that D was not the biological father of either child and could not be an "equitable parent" to them because D and P were never married. D conceded that blood testing showed that he was not the biological father but argued that he was an "equitable parent" and that P was equitably estopped from denying that he is the father. The trial court decided for P and indicated that its ruling turned on two factors: (1) D apparently was not the biological father of the children, and (2) D and P were never married. The court noted that the state's public policy favored marriage and concluded that the doctrines of equitable estoppel, equitable parenthood, and equitable adoption require marriage. On appeal, how will the court rule most likely?

EXPLANATIONS

Explanation

The appellate court most likely will reject D's claim. As noted in the readings, there has been a general reluctance to apply the equitable parent doctrine to situations similar to this hypothetical.

CHAPTER 17

Adoption

17.1. Introduction

This chapter reviews the history, development, and application of the law involving adoptions. In general, most agree that the basic purpose of an adoption is the "welfare, protection and betterment of the child." *Reeves v. Bailey*, 126 Cal. Rptr. 51 (Cal. App. 3d 1975). Adoption acts to "maximize a child's opportunity to develop into a stable, well-adjusted adult." *Adoption of Michelle T.*, 117 Cal. Rptr. 856 (Cal. Ct. App. 1975). It is probably one of the happiest of all legal proceedings.

OVERVIEW

17.2. History

The law of adoption had its beginning early in civilization. It apparently existed in Greece and Rome and in portions of continental Europe that received Roman law. It also existed in the Middle East, Asia, and in the tribal societies of Africa and Oceania.

Adoption was unknown to the common law. The first instance in which a state legislature authorized adoption can be traced to 1847, when the Massachusetts House of Representatives ordered that the Committee on the Judiciary consider a law for adoption of children. An adoption bill was passed in 1851, and within 25 years most states followed Massachusetts' lead and passed adoption legislation.

When states first established adoption laws, adoptive children were commonly not accorded the same legal rights as children born during wedlock. For example, some states expressly provided that the relationship of parent and adopted child was to be without the right of inheritance.

During the early part of the twentieth century, states established laws requiring a pre-hearing investigation and a report by a local child welfare agency. They also required that adoption records be kept private and sealed. Secrecy was believed important because it assured anonymity, which protected the child from the stigma of illegitimacy and encouraged full integration of the child into the adoptive family.

It was not uncommon for states to allow the return of children under certain circumstances. In 1951, for example, Minnesota passed a bill that gave parents of an adopted child five years from the time the child was adopted to annul the adoption if the child developed feeblemindedness, epilepsy, insanity, or venereal infection as a result of conditions existing prior to the adoption of which the adopting parent had no knowledge. The law was repealed in 1975.

During the 1970s, discussion in the adoption area focused on two issues: first, improving the policies and adoption practices so that special needs children could be placed in permanent homes; and second, determining the considerations under which certain persons would have access to adoption records. There emerged a movement during this period in which a small number of persons organized to provide support for others interested in searching for and meeting their biological parents. Two such organizations were the Adoptees Liberty Movement Association (ALMA) and the Concerned United Birth parents (CUB) group. The American Adoption Congress (AAC) was formed in 1980 to coordinate the efforts of those persons interested in legislative changes that would provide access to information that would lead to the discovery of biological parents. These organizations have been fairly successful in obtaining new legislation that permits adopted children, under limited circumstances, to locate their biological parents.

When conducting research, one will discover that adoption laws vary considerably among the states. Although efforts have been made to achieve uniformity among the states, only about a half dozen have enacted a version of the Uniform Adoption Act. As a result, one finds differences from state to state in terminology, organization, and procedure.

17.3. Legal Effect of Adoption

Today, an adoption is viewed as completely severing the ties of a child with the child's biological parents. The child's new adoptive parents are substituted for the biological parents and may exercise the same rights toward the child as a natural parent. The child has the same right to support as a natural child born to the adoptive parents and may inherit as would such a child. The adoptive parents may bar visitation or any other contact between the child and his or her biological parents.

Example 17-1

Assume that M and D are a married couple who have three biological children. They farm land located in state X that has been in D's family for more than 100 years. They enjoy being parents, and they adopt another child, P. Unfortunately, P does not adjust well to the family and never adapts to rural living. P runs away from home repeatedly and does not develop close relationships with M, D, or the other children. M and D die suddenly in a plane crash without leaving a will. The biological children claim that, under the circumstances, P should not be allowed to inherit an interest in the family farm. Will P most likely inherit under the intestacy provisions of state X?

Explanation

P will most likely be allowed to inherit under the provisions of state X, because an adopted child is treated as a natural child of his adopted parent or parents. Just as with biological children, the quality of the adoptive parent-child relationship has no bearing on the right to inherit under intestacy provisions.

Example 17-2

Assume that P is adopted by M and D. Three years after the adoption, P learns that her natural parents, X and Y, were killed in an automobile accident and have left a sizeable estate. There is no will, and P seeks to inherit from her natural parents. What will be the likely outcome of P's effort to inherit from her natural parents?

Explanation

P will most likely be unsuccessful. The right to receive property by devise or descent is not a natural right but a privilege granted by the state, and absent a statutory provision allowing P to inherit from her natural parents, her claim will be unsuccessful. *See Hall v. Vallandingham*, 540 A.2d 1162 (Md. App. 1988). Because the states will treat P as a natural issue of M and D for intestacy purposes, it will not allow her to inherit from both her adoptive and biological parents.

17.4. Abrogation of Adoption

In the past, many states allowed an adoption to be abrogated or annulled because the child was suffering from an undisclosed illness or disability. Some allowed the child to be returned to an orphanage because of the child's poor behavior. *See, e.g., In the Matter of the Abrogation of Anonymous*, 167 N.Y.S.2d 472 (N.Y. 1951) (adoptive parents abrogate adoption of 17-year-old emancipated boy whom they adopted when he was four years old). Today, while some jurisdictions allow abrogation of an adoption on a limited basis (fraud), an annulment will not be granted unless it is in the best interest of the child. *See, e.g., M.L.B. v. Department of Health and Rehabilitative Services*, 559 So. 2d 87 (Fla. App. 1990).

FORMS OF ADOPTION

17.5. Agency Adoptions

Agency adoptions involve the placement of a child with adoptive parents by a public agency, or by a private nonprofit agency licensed or regulated by the state. The agency acts as an intermediary between potential adoptive parents and the child's natural parent or parents. Public adoption agencies generally place children who have become wards of the state as a result of abuse or because they have been abandoned. Private agencies are usually nonprofit organizations, and children placed by them are often obtained when a single mother is expecting a child and wants to give the child up for adoption.

17.6. Independent Adoption

An independent or direct adoption usually involves newborn infants. These are infants often born to young parents from 12 to 17 years of age. While the arrangements vary, sometimes there is a direct arrangement made between the birth parents and the adoptive parents. On other occasions, the arrangements are made through the use of an intermediary such as an attorney. At least three states apparently do not allow independent adoptions (Connecticut, Delaware, and Massachusetts), and this form of adoption is carefully regulated in others.

Independent adoptions are used because the adoption can be accomplished faster than working with an adoption agency. They are also viewed as advantageous to the natural parents of the child because they may participate in choosing the adoptive parents.

17.7. Stepparent Adoption

Stepparent adoption requires the consent of the spouse of the adopting stepparent and consent of the divorced parent. A divorced parent is often reluctant to relinquish his or her parental rights, and without grounds for terminating those rights, the consent cannot be overcome. A stepparent adoption is viewed as less complicated than agency or independent adoption procedures when the child's other birth parent consents to the adoption.

17.8. Near Relative Adoption

In most jurisdictions, the absence, inability, or incapacity of the natural parents to provide and care for their children has prompted other relatives to step forward to assume the benefits and responsibilities of that role. For example, grandparents may seek to adopt their grandchildren if the children's parents die while the children are minors. These adoptions are among the easiest to process.

While at one time judicial intervention was unnecessary, a body of common law developed according a custodial preference for near relatives. In most states, adoptive placement with a family member is presumptively in the best interests of a child, absent a showing of good cause to the contrary or detriment to the child. States may by statute create a preference for near relatives. *See, e.g.*, Minn. Stat. §259.57, subd. 2 (2006) ("authorized childplacing agency shall consider placement, consistent with the child's best interests and in the following order, with (1) a relative or relatives of the child, or (2) an important friend with whom the child has resided or had significant contact").

17.9. Open Adoption

The concept of open adoption is a variation on the principle that upon the entry of an order of adoption, a child is the legal child of the persons adopting him, and they become his legal parents with all the rights and duties of natural parents. Once an adoption decree is entered, the natural parents of an adopted child are relieved of all parental responsibilities for the child, and may neither exercise nor retain any rights over the adopted child or his property. As a general rule, the adoptive parents may bar any contact between the minor child and the biological parents.

Several states have statutes that expressly address the issue of post-adoption contact between the adoptive and biological parents. *See, e.g.*, Cal. Fam. Code §8616.5 (West 2006) ("Post adoption contact agreements"); Mass. Gen. Laws Ann. ch. 210, §6C (West 2006) ("Agreement for Post-Adoption Contact or Communication"); Minn. Stat. Ann. §259.58 (West 2006) ("Communication or contact agreements"); Mont. Code Ann. §42-5-301 (2005) ("Visitation and communication agreements"); Neb. Rev. Stat. §43-162 (2005) ("Communication or contact agreement; authorized; approval"); Or. Rev. Stat. Ann. §109.305 (West 2006) ("Interpretation of adoption laws; agreement for continuing contact with birth relatives"). When there are no statutory provisions, the adoptive parents to an open adoption can most likely prevent future contacts at will between the child and the natural parents.

EXAMPLES

Example 17-3

Assume that a child was born out of wedlock to P. P meets with X and Y, who agree to adopt C, and the legal adoption becomes final when C is two months old. Prior to the adoption, the parties agree that on occasion P may visit with the child, but nothing is put in writing. P visits C several times each year. When C is five years old, X and Y overhear P using inappropriate language with C, and they hear P encouraging C to disobey household rules established by X and Y. X and Y conclude that P is upsetting the child, and they terminate the visits. P is shocked that X and Y would treat her this way after five years of contact with C, and P believes that X and Y are overreacting to innocent events. P consequently brings an action to enforce the oral visitation agreement. Will P be likely to succeed?

EXPLANATIONS

Explanation

X and Y will argue that as the legal parents of C, they have the obligation and prerogative to act in C's best interest, and a court would determine that X and Y are in the best position to know and understand C's needs. Especially absent a statute authorizing ongoing contact or a written agreement to that effect, P will not be able to enforce the oral agreement.

17.10. Subsidized Adoption

Children with special needs waiting for adoptive families are difficult to place because of the costs associated with caring for them. However, most states provide financial help to parents who adopt these children. The two sources of funds used to support such programs come from the federal Title IV-E program under the Social Security Act and each state's individual program, which will vary from jurisdiction to jurisdiction.

17.11. International Adoption

The Hague Convention on International Adoption was adopted and opened for signature at the conclusion of the Seventeenth Session of the Hague Conference on Private International Law on May 29, 1993. Thirty-two countries, including the United States, have signed the Convention, 17 countries have ratified it, and one country has acceded to it. The Convention sets out norms and procedures to safeguard children involved in inter-country adoptions and to protect the interests of their birth and adoptive parents. These safeguards are designed to discourage trafficking in children and to ensure that inter-country adoptions are made in the best interest of the children involved. Cooperation between Contracting States will be facilitated by the establishment in each Contracting State of a central authority with programmatic and case-specific functions. The Convention also provides for the recognition of adoptions that fall within its scope in all other Contracting States. It leaves the details of its implementation up to each Contracting State.

In an international adoption, the new parents must satisfy the adoption requirements of both the foreign country and the parents' home state in the United States. They must obtain an immigrant visa for the child from the Bureau of Citizenship and Immigration Services (BCIS, formerly called the INS), which has its own rules for international adoptions. For example, one requirement is that the adoptive parents must be either married or, if single, at least 25 years old. The adoptive parents must apply for U.S. citizenship for the child because it is not automatically granted.

PROCEDURES

17.12. Filing a Petition

In general, a petition for adoption is filed once consent is obtained from the child's natural parent or parents, or the adoption agency handling the matter. Once a petition is filed, in most jurisdictions the child is placed with the adoptive parents on a probationary basis. If the background checks, home study, and probationary period are satisfactory, a hearing is held in which the judge reviews the potential adoptive parents' qualifications. Once the adoption is approved, a permanent decree of adoption is filed.

17.13. Investigating Prospective Parents

In most cases, a home study is conducted to determine the suitability of the potential adoptive parents' home. The adoptive parents' background is investigated, including a criminal background check. The purpose of the criminal records check is to safeguard the well-being of foster and adoptive children by ensuring that persons seeking to care for or adopt a foster child have not been arrested for or convicted of criminal charges that would place the child at risk. *See In re Adoption of Paul Y.*, 696 N.Y.S.2d 796 (N.Y. Fam. Ct. 1999).

17.14. Sealing Adoption Records

For decades, states have sealed adoption records from the public due to the stigma historically associated with bearing a child out of wedlock and concern that the biological parents would interfere with the adoptive parents if their names became known. To ensure privacy, after the adoption, statutes typically provided for the issuance of a new birth certificate which changed the adoptee's surname to that of the adoptive parents. The original birth certificate was then sealed.

Today, most state statutes provide adoptees with the opportunity to obtain the names of their biological parents from official records when certain conditions are met. For example, some states will allow the adopted children to gain access to this information when the biological family and the adoptive parents agree to allow access. In Oregon and Tennessee, adult adoptees apparently have access to their birth records without restrictions (despite challenges from birth mothers who argued they relinquished their children in reliance on promises of confidentiality).

In *In re Adoption of S.J.D.*, 641 N.W.2d 794 (Iowa 2002), the adoptee's reasons for wanting adoption records unsealed, which included satisfaction of curiosity, thanking biological parents for what they did, and obtaining medical information, did not constitute sufficient good cause to entitle records to be unsealed, even though adoptee had been treated for manic depression. The adoptee presented no medical evidence that linked his manic depression to his status as an adopted child and the adoptee was viewed as expressing more of a curiosity over whether manic depression was hereditary than any particular medical reason for wanting to know.

In *In re Long*, 745 A.2d 673 (Pa. Super. 2000), the adoptee sought disclosure of the identity of her biological parents and their medical histories. In support of her petition, she submitted a letter from her physician who stressed the importance of obtaining a complete family medical history to diagnose and treat her recent complicated medical issues. She also asserted that she suffered from depression, panic attacks, and similar psychological afflictions because of her lack of identity.

The court said that an adoptee had the burden of showing by clear and convincing evidence that there is good cause for unsealing, given the overriding privacy concerns of the adoption process and this statute. It warned that unsealing adoption records is not to be lightly undertaken, and a court must consider the ramifications to those specifically affected by that unsealing, including the adoptive and biological parents and their families, as well as the impact on the integrity of the adoption process in general. Only if the adoptee's need for the information clearly outweighs the considerations behind the statute may the records be unsealed.

QUALIFICATIONS OF POTENTIAL ADOPTIVE PARENT

17.15. Race

Race may be considered legitimately as one factor in making an ultimate adoption placement decision. *See, e.g.*, *J.H.H. v. O'Hara*, 878 F.2d 240, 244 (8th Cir. 1989). Race may not, of course, be used in an automatic fashion to prescribe the appropriate adoptive placement. *See Palmore v. Sidoti*, 466 U.S. 429, 434 (1984). Race also may not be used as the sole basis for making long-term foster care placements or in determining who may adopt a child. *See In re Moorehead*, 600 N.E.2d 778, 786 (Ohio App. 1991) ("The difficulties inherent in interracial adoption justify consideration of race as a relevant factor in adoption, but do not justify race as being the determinative factor.").

17.16. Sexual Orientation

The issue of whether gay and lesbian partners can jointly adopt a child is a matter of current controversy. In most states, involvement in a gay or lesbian relationship does not preclude adoption where adoption would otherwise be in the best interests of the child. *See In re Infant Girl W.*, 845 N.E.2d 229 (Ind. App. 2006); *Sharon S. v. Superior Court*, 2 Cal. Rptr. 3d 699 (Cal. 2003); However, in 1977 Florida adopted a statute expressly prohibiting homosexual adoption and it survived recent constitutional challenge on equal protection grounds. *Lofton v. Sec'y of Dept. of Children and Family Services*, 358 F.3d 804 (11th Cir. 2004); Florida Stat. §63.042(3) (West 2003). *See also* Sonja Larsen, *Adoption of Child By Same-Sex Partners*, 27 A.L.R.5th 54 (1995); Miss. Code Ann. §93-17-3 (West 2004) (prohibiting adoption by couples of the same gender); Utah Code Ann. §78-30-1 (West 2004) (unmarried cohabiting couples prohibited from adopting); Conn. Gen. Stat. Ann. §45a-726A (West 2006) (child-placing agency may consider sexual orientation of adoptive or foster parent).

17.17. Age

The age of a potential adoptive parent may play a role in some adoption matters. For example, California requires that a prospective adoptive parent be at least ten years older than the child, unless the adoption is by a stepparent, sister, brother, aunt, uncle, or first cousin and the court is satisfied that adoption by the parent and, if married, by the parent's spouse is in the best interests of the parties and is in the public interest regardless of the ages of the child and the prospective adoptive parent. *See* Cal. Fam. Code §8601 (West 2006). Being elderly does not absolutely bar adoption. For example, in *Adoption of Michelle T.*, 117 Cal. Rptr. 856 (Cal. App. 1975), the court granted a petition to proposed parents, who were 71 and 55 years of age, who had a stable marriage, were financially secure, in good health, and had cared for the child for nine months prior to filing the petition. *See also In re T.S.*, 7 Cal. Rptr. 3d 173 (Cal. App. 2003) (grandparents aged 58 and 61 allowed to adopt despite objections that they were too old and had not passed physical examinations).

WHO MUST CONSENT TO AN ADOPTION?

17.18. Pre-birth Consent

All states mandate that consent to adoption be obtained from the natural mother after the birth of the child unless her rights are terminated. Most states mandate a waiting period following the birth of a child during which the natural mother may revoke her consent to the adoption. *See Sims v. Adoption Alliance*, 922 S.W.2d 213 (Tex. App. 1996) (legislation that required that a biological mother must wait 48 hours after the birth of the child before signing an affidavit of relinquishment is constitutional). This is to ensure that the consent is a fully deliberative act on the part of the biological parent and to provide a legal framework within which a future adoption can be undertaken with reasonable guarantees of permanence and with humane regard for the rights of the child, the natural mother, and the adoptive parents.

Occasionally, consent is obtained prior to the birth of the child, the child is born and adopted, and the birth mother seeks to void the adoption on the grounds that the pre-birth consent is void *ab initio*. Courts that have examined this issue have concluded that in the case of a pre-birth consent, such consent is ratified by a post-birth act that sufficiently manifests a present intention to give the child up for adoption. *See, e.g., Matter of Pima City Juvenile Action*, 806 P.2d 892, 895 (Ariz. 1990). These courts have said that the statutory notice prerequisites and the mandate that a consent must be executed after the birth of the child are aimed at safeguarding the rights and interests of the biological parents in adoption proceedings, rather than affording some kind of protection for the public at large. Under these statutes, the rights of a parent may be surrendered by a formally executed paper. However, the purpose of the statute is to protect the abandonment of the parent's right, and if this is done before birth and is after birth observed, recognized, and honored by all parties, the purpose of the law is fulfilled by the parent's ratification. *See In re Adoption of Krueger*, 448 P.2d 82 (Ariz. 1968); *Anonymous v. Anonymous*, 530 N.Y.S.2d 613, 617 (N.Y. App. Div. 3 Dept. 1988); *In re Adoption of Long*, 56 So. 2d 450 (Fla. 1952).

Example 17-4

P arranged with an adoption agency to place her child for adoption as soon as the child was born. The state statute requires that a birth mother's consent be obtained not sooner than 48 hours after the birth of a child. However, P signed adoption consent forms two weeks before the child was born and once again on the day after the child was born. When the child is one month old, P changes her mind about the adoption and brings an action to void her consent. The adoptive parents argue that P waived the 48-hour requirement by giving consent both before and after the birth of the child. How will a court most likely rule?

Explanation

Because of the intimate nature of the proceeding, and the unambiguous language in the statute, it is likely that a court will consider the consent invalid. This is particularly likely if a statute provides for a waiting period. In some jurisdictions, a mother may recover a child legally placed for adoption if there has not been an adoption decree entered, if she is fit, and if returning the child to the mother is in the child's best interests.

17.19. Minor Child's Consent

In most jurisdictions the consent of a child over the age of 12 to the adoption is necessary.

17.20. Putative Father's Consent

As the climate for children born out of wedlock has changed over the past 50 years, so has the view of unmarried biological fathers. New recognition meant that they had the opportunity for a voice in adoption proceedings. In the leading case, *Stanley v. Illinois*, 405 U.S. 645 (1973), Stanley, an unwed father, lived with his children and their mother intermittently for 18 years prior to her death. When she died, under state law the children automatically became wards of the state and Stanley was presumed unfit to care for them. The statutory presumption applied even though there had not been a hearing regarding his fitness or proof of neglect on his part. Stanley sought custody of the children, arguing that he should be afforded a hearing on his fitness. When the Illinois Supreme Court refused to provide him with a hearing, the United States Supreme Court granted review.

The Court held that a putative father's interest in the companionship, care, custody, and management of his children was greater than the state's interest in the children as long as the putative father was a fit parent. It ordered that a hearing be held to determine whether Stanley was in fact fit to have custody of the children. The Court did not, however, articulate the scope of the protection afforded an unwed father, especially when the state interests were more substantial. (On remand, the trial court found that Stanley was not a fit parent.)

Five years after *Stanley*, the Supreme Court clarified the principles articulated in *Stanley v. Illinois* in *Quilloin v. Walcott*, 434 U.S. 246 (1977), *reh', denied*, 435 U.S. 918 (1978). The Court held that a putative father who had little or no contact with his child did not have a constitutional right to veto the child's adoption. A unanimous Court rested its decision on the putative father's failure to seek actual or legal custody of the child and the fact he had played no part in the child's daily supervision, education, protection, or care. *Quilloin v. Walcott* established the principle that when there is no significant commitment on the part of the biological father to a child born out of wedlock, the state is not required to find anything more than that the adoption, and denial of legitimization, are in the best interests of the child.

In a third ruling, *Caban v. Mohammed*, 441 U.S. 380 (1979), both the mother and the putative father had emotionally and financially supported children born to them out of wedlock. When their relationship broke down, the mother married another man and then initiated proceedings asking the court to allow her new husband to adopt the children. The putative father filed a cross-petition in which he asked to adopt the children. Under New York law, a putative father could not adopt his children without the mother's consent. However, the mother could legally adopt the children without first obtaining the putative father's consent. The trial court permitted the mother and her new husband to adopt the children over their putative father's objection and the Supreme Court granted review.

The Court reversed, holding that the New York statute had inappropriately created a gender-based distinction between unwed mothers and unwed fathers, which bore no substantial relation to any legitimate state interest. Because the putative father had demonstrated a substantial interest in his children, the Court said he had certain constitutionally protected rights that the state could not take from him.

In another significant decision, *Lehr v. Robertson*, 463 U.S. 248 (1983), the Court considered whether the Due Process and Equal Protection Clauses of the Fourteenth Amendment provided a putative father with the right to notice and an opportunity to be heard before a child is adopted, although he had not established a substantial relationship with his biological child born out of wedlock. Lehr had never lived with his child or its mother, had never registered with the state putative-father registry as the child's father, and had failed to provide any financial support for the child following birth. When the child was eight months old, the mother married, and her husband adopted the child.

The Court rejected Lehr's claim that he had a constitutional right to notice and a hearing before adoption. The Court reasoned that his rights had not been violated because he had failed to establish a substantial relationship with the child. The "mere existence of a biological link," wrote the court "does not merit equivalent constitutional protection."

EXAMPLES

Example 17-5

Assume that P is unmarried when she gives birth to C. The biological father, D, is aware of C's birth. However, he and P have a hostile relationship, and D avoids all contact with her. Consequently, D does not attempt to visit C and does not provide any financial support. P meets X and she and X marry. After a year of marriage, when C is two years old, X moves to adopt C. When D learns of the adoption action, he appears in opposition to it, insisting that the court cannot terminate his rights to the child. How should a court rule?

EXPLANATIONS

Explanation

D has failed to manifest any "indicia of parenthood," which would provide him with constitutional protection of his parental rights. It is doubtful that his rights could be resurrected even with testimony that D is now ready to assume parental responsibilities for the child. D knew of the child's birth and could have played a role in the child's life well before the adoption action was begun. *See Caban, supra.*

17.21. Putative Father Consents by Failing to Use Adoption Registry

Some states have created a statutory adoption registry for the purpose of determining the identity and location of a putative father of a minor child who is, or who is expected to be, the subject of an adoption. The purpose of the registry is to provide notice to a putative father that a petition for adoption has been filed. States have adopted strict provisions regarding the registry. Some require that the putative fathers register within 30 days after the child's birth or the date the adoption petition is filed, whichever occurs later. If a father fails to do so, he is not entitled to notice of the child's adoption.

A putative father's failure to register not only waives his right to notice of the adoption but also irrevocably implies his consent. *See, e.g., In re J.D.C.*, 751 N.E.2d 747 (Ind. App. 2001). Courts have held that a putative father was not entitled to notice of an adoption petition and that his consent was irrevocably implied when the biological mother did not disclose his identity or address and he failed to register with the putative father's registry until six months after the adoption petition was filed. *In re Paternity of Baby Doe*, 734 N.E.2d 281 (Ind. Ct. App. 2000). *See Robert O. v. Russell K.*, 604 N.E.2d 99 (N.Y. Ct. App. 1992) (putative father's notice or consent was not needed for the adoption when he failed to avail himself of the methods to qualify for notice until some ten months after the adoption became final); *Heidbreder v. Carton*, 645 N.W.2d 355 (Minn. 2002) (requirement that putative father not otherwise entitled to notice of an adoption petition must register with the Minnesota Fathers' Adoption Registry no later than 30 days after birth of child to assert a claim to a child who is the subject of an adoption petition is not a statute of limitations that can be tolled by fraudulent concealment); *Petition of K.J.R.*, 687 N.E.2d 113 (Ill. App. 1 Dist. 1997) (birth mother's misrepresentation that another man was child's father did not excuse putative father's failure to register, and provision of Adoption Act that operated to deprive putative father of right to proceed with parentage petition did not deprive him of equal protection of the laws or due process); *M.V.S. v. V.M.D.* 776 So. 2d 142 (Ala. Civ. App. 1999) (requirements and procedures of Putative Father Registry Act to establish parental rights did not violate due process or equal protection).

These statutes and court decisions reflect a strong interest in providing stable homes for children early in their lives and a belief that permanent placement of children with adoptive families is of the utmost importance. If a father fails to register within the specified amount of time allowed under the statute, the state's obligation to provide the child with a permanent, capable, and loving family becomes paramount.

EXAMPLES

Example 17-6

Assume that P and D have a casual sexual relationship and P becomes pregnant and gives birth. D, the biological father, does not know of P's pregnancy or the birth of the child until the child is six months old and is in the process of being adopted. D resides in a jurisdiction with an adoption registry requiring that registration take place within 30 days of the birth of the child, but D has no idea what an adoption registry is or how to go about registering. He consequently fails to do so. How will a court most likely treat D's effort to block the adoption?

EXPLANATIONS

Explanation

D most likely will not succeed. The adoption registry statute protects those putative fathers who have taken certain specified actions to preserve their rights. If the putative father has not so acted within the time limits provided by statute, the child's right to a stable environment and finality becomes paramount, and the putative father loses all right to intervene in adoption proceedings or to vacate a finalized adoption order. *See Lehr v. Robertson*, 463 U.S. 248 (1983). D's failure to register may well bar him from preventing the adoption.

UNIFORM ACTS

17.22. Uniform Adoption Act of 1994

The Uniform Adoption Act of 1994 was promulgated by the National Conference of Commissioners on Uniform State Laws (NCCUSL) as an attempt to codify and make uniform the current legal practice regarding adoption. However, only a half dozen states have adopted some provisions of the proposed uniform act. *See* Uniform Adoption Act: http://www.law.upenn.edu/bll/ulc/fnact99/1990s/uaa94.htm (last visited 10-23-06).

FEDERAL GOVERNMENT'S ROLE

17.23. Indian Child Welfare Act (ICWA)

The Indian Child Welfare Act (ICWA), 25 U.S.C. §§1901 *et seq.*, governs the placement of Native American children for adoption. The ICWA contains procedural and substantive provisions that apply to Native American children. The ICWA protects the best interests of Indian children by promoting the survival and stability of Indian families and tribes. It is aimed at preventing wholesale separation of Indian children from their families through state court proceedings. The ICWA applies to any child who is either a member of an Indian tribe, or eligible to be a member, and the biological child of a member of a tribe.

State courts must follow the jurisdictional requirements of the ICWA and an adoption decree entered in violation of the Act can be invalidated by the tribe or custodian. *See* 25 U.S.C. §1914 (West 2006); *Mississippi Band of Choctaw Indians v. Holyfield*, 490 U.S. 30 (1989). (Note that there is additional discussion regarding this Act in Chapter 27, Jurisdiction.)

EXAMPLES

Example 17-7

Assume that P and D are members of an Indian tribe living on a reservation and they conceive a child. They do not want the child born on the reservation, and they prefer that the child be adopted and raised by non-Indians. The child is born off reservation and within two weeks the child is adopted by non-Indian parents. The child is healthy and thriving in the adoptive home. When the tribe learns of the adoption four months later, it moves to vacate the adoption decree, claiming it had exclusive subject matter jurisdiction under the ICWA. How will a court most likely rule on the tribe's motion?

EXPLANATIONS

Explanation

Because the child's domicile is that of its mother, who apparently lives on the reservation, and there is no evidence the child was abandoned, a court most likely will vacate the judgment. One of the purposes of ICWA is to prevent Indian children from being adopted by non-Indians without the oversight of the tribe.

17.24. Multiethnic Placement Act (MEPA)

The Multiethnic Placement Act (MEPA), passed into law in 1994, allowed states to consider race as a factor when making adoptive placements. It also prohibited states from refusing to place children solely on the basis of the adoptive parents' race. The Act was amended in 1996 and made it illegal for a state to delay or deny an adoptive placement solely on the basis of race. Indian children were exempted from the MEPA; therefore, adoptions involving these children continue to be controlled by the ICWA. 42 U.S.C. §1996b(3) (West 2006). By statute, Congress has declared that no state or other entity receiving federal funds can deny to any individual the opportunity to become an adoptive or a foster parent on the basis of race, color, or national origin. 42 U.S.C. §1996b (West 2006).

17.25. Adoption and Safe Families Act (ASFA)

The Adoption and Safe Families Act of 1997 (ASFA) (Pub. L. No. 105-89, 111 Stat. 2115), enacted in November 1997, amended the foster care provisions of the Social Security Act. The increase in children in foster care during the past two decades, with the number nearly doubling since the mid-1980s to an estimated 520,000 children in 1998, was the catalyst for the Act. There was also concern that more children were entering foster care facilities each year than were leaving and that their stay in foster settings was getting much longer.

The Act was also passed to change a perception held by child welfare practitioners regarding the relationship between child safety and the requirement that a state make "reasonable efforts" to prevent removal of a child from a home or to return a child home. Long stays in foster care were often believed to be the result of well-intentioned efforts to preserve the family through prolonged and extensive services, without giving adequate consideration to the child's need for a permanent home. In these situations, adoption or an alternate permanent home was rarely considered until the child had been in out-of-home care for 18 months.

Under the provisions of the Act, states no longer needed to pursue efforts to prevent removal from home or to return a child home if a parent had already lost parental rights to that child's sibling, committed certain felonies, including murder or voluntary manslaughter of the child's sibling, or had subjected the child to aggravated circumstances such as abandonment, torture, chronic abuse, and sexual abuse. In these egregious situations, the Act gave a court authority to determine that services to preserve or reunite the family — that is, the "reasonable efforts" requirement established in earlier law — are not required. Once the court makes such a determination, the state must begin within 30 days to find the child an alternate permanent home.

The Act also mandates that States begin termination proceedings if an infant has been abandoned, the parent has committed certain felonies, or the child has been in foster care 15 of the last 22 months. States may exempt a child from this requirement if the child is placed with a relative, the state has not provided services needed to make the home safe for the child's return, or there is a compelling reason why filing a petition to terminate parental rights is not in the child's best interests. As states begin the process of terminating parental rights, they must also find the child a qualified adoptive family. The Act authorized $20 million for bonuses to states for adoption of foster-care children, $5 million for health care for adopted children with special needs, and $11 million for subsidies for special-needs children if their adoptions are disrupted or their adoptive parents die.

CLAIMS

17.26. Fraud

Most states recognize a cause of action for fraud in the adoption setting. For example, in *In re Lisa Diane G.*, 537 A.2d 131 (R.I. 1988), the court held that it possessed the authority to decide whether to vacate an adoption order based upon a claim of fraud or misrepresentation. In *Allen v. Allen*, 330 P.2d 151 (Or. 1958), Oregon recognized fraud as a cause of action in adoption matters while holding that the evidence was insufficient to support a determination that a decree of adoption was void by reason of fraud. Minnesota has ruled that if a party can demonstrate that an adoption decree was fraudulently obtained, the party is entitled to relief. *In re Welfare of Alle*, 230 N.W.2d 574, 577 (Or. 1975). The Supreme Judicial Court of Massachusetts held that one may annul an adoption decree based on fraud, even after death. *Tucker v. Fisk*, 28 N.E. 1051 (Mass. 1891). The same court later held that if a person dominates his wife to such an extent that it amounts to "undue influence" and he thereby forces her to bring a petition for adoption of his son, he commits a "gross fraud" upon both her and the court. In such a case, the decree of adoption should be set aside. *Phillips v. Chase*, 89 N.E. 1049, 1051-1052 (Mass. 1909).

The elements of a cause of action for fraudulent misrepresentation require that one must show (1) a false statement of material fact, (2) known or believed to be false by the party making it, (3) intent to induce the other party to act, (4) action by the other party in reliance on the truth of the statement, and (5) damage to the other party resulting from such reliance. The party must be justified in his reliance; he must have a right to rely. *See, e.g., Roe v. Catholic Charities of the Diocese of Springfield*, 588 N.E.2d 354 (Ill. 1992).

17.27. Claims Against Agencies

Some states recognize claims against adoption agencies for negligent misrepresentation. The tort is based on the theory that an adoption placement agency owes prospective adoptive parents a duty of reasonable care to disclose information pertinent to the adoption. Courts find such a duty partly in a state's adoption statutes and partly in the existence of a "special relationship" between the agency and the prospective parents. Even if a state statute does not provide for such an action, the special relationship between adoption placement agencies and adopting parents argues strongly for recognition of a cause of action in tort. The purposes are not only to enable adoptive parents to obtain timely and appropriate medical care for the child, but also to enable them to make an intelligent and informed adoption decision. *See, e.g., Price v. State*, 57 P.3d 639 (Wash. App. Div. 2, 2002). The duty that emanates from the relationship of the potential adoptive parents and the agency is to exercise reasonable care in disclosing information pertinent to the adoption, thus enabling the adoptive parents to obtain timely and appropriate medical care for the child and make an intelligent and informed adoption decision. *See Young v. Van Duyne*, 92 P.3d 1269 (N.M. App. 2004) (Adoptive father whose wife was beaten to death by adoptive son could maintain wrongful death claim against agency regarding pre-adoption knowledge and conduct).

EXAMPLES

Example 17-8

Assume that P adopted a Russian baby girl who was discovered to be carrying the hepatitis C virus when the girl was examined by a pediatrician in the United States. P sued Adoption Center D for breach of contract, wrongful adoption/malpractice, and related counts. P adopted the child X in 1993. The contract between P and D reads as follows: "P understands that D cannot guarantee the health of the child, but will make best efforts to ensure that the child's health is known to the parent(s) prior to placement. However, P understand[s] that it is very difficult to know all of the health issues involved."

In addition to this contract language, P was made aware that even though D knew her highest priority was adoption of a healthy baby, no baby available for adoption would have a clean medical record because Russian law at that time prohibited foreign adoption of healthy Russian babies. Further, Russian orphanages rarely supplied prospective foreign parents with complete medical histories of children available for adoption. A photograph and a medical excerpt (three pages long when translated into English) were the only documentation made available to P or D, as was the standard practice in Russian adoptions at the time. The medical excerpt referenced one hospitalization for a respiratory infection, negative results on blood tests for HIV and hepatitis B, and some developmental delays, and a diagnosis that loosely translated as "encephalopathy."

When X was examined following the adoption in the United States, it was discovered that she contracted hepatitis C from blood transfusions when hospitalized in Russia, and also was suffering from fetal alcohol syndrome/fetal alcohol effect (FAS/FAE). Given these facts, which are not in dispute, D moved for summary judgment. How will a court most likely rule?

EXPLANATIONS

Explanation

Because Adoption Center D was not aware of X's hepatitis C status or of her transfusions prior to her diagnosis in the United States, the motion for summary judgment will most likely be granted. It is undisputed that none of the defendants withheld any medical information made available to them. P also adopted X knowingly in the face of incomplete information.

OTHER ISSUES REGARDING ADOPTION

17.28. Adults Adopting Adults

Cases involving adult adoptions are not necessarily consistent among jurisdictions. Many of them involve inheritance issues. The trend, however, is to allow them under limited circumstances. For example, in *Berston v. Minnesota Dept. of Public Welfare*, 206 N.W.2d 28 (Minn. 1973), the trial court's denial of the adoption of an adult woman by her natural son was reversed on public policy grounds. The court said that the broad language of Minnesota's adult adoption statute unequivocally foreclosed any limiting construction. In *Harper v. Martin*, 552 S.W.2d 690 (Ky. App. 1977), the court approved the adoption of a 47-year-old male by a terminally ill petitioner for the express purpose of making him the heir at law of a third person. In *Matter of Fortney's Estate*, 611 P.2d 599, 604-605 (Kan. App. 1980), the court upheld a trial court ruling allowing an adult adoption effectuated for purposes of inheritance. However, in *Matter of Griswold's Estate*, 354 A.2d 717 (N.J. Co. 1976), the court ruled that an adoption to make an adoptee a beneficiary of a trust was found to be an abuse of the adoption process. In *333 East 53rd Street Associates v. Mann*, 503 N.Y.S.2d 752 (N.Y. 1986), the petitioner adopted an adult woman to ensure that she would succeed to the tenancy of a rent-controlled apartment. The appellate court found nothing inherently wrong with an adoption intended to confer an economic benefit on the adopted person.

The states are not in agreement on whether to allow gay and lesbian adults to adopt each other. The Delaware Supreme Court allowed such an adoption in *In re Adoption of Swanson*, 623 A.2d 1095 (Del. 1993). On the other hand, in *Matter of Adoption of Robert Paul P.*, 471 N.E.2d 424 (1984), the New York Court of Appeals ruled that a 57-year-old man could not adopt a

50-year-old man with whom he shared a homosexual relationship. The court reasoned that adoption is not a quasi-matrimonial device to provide unmarried partners with a legal imprimatur for their sexual relationship.

17.29. Adoption for an Illegal or Frivolous Purpose

Courts will not countenance an adoption to effect a fraudulent, illegal, or patently frivolous purpose. For example, the court in *In re Jones*, 411 A.2d 910 (R.I. 1980), rejected the adoption petition of an older married man who sought to adopt his 20-year-old paramour to the economic detriment of his wife and family.

CHAPTER 18

Alternative Reproduction — History, Restrictions, and Requirements

18.1. Introduction — History

The first so-called hi-tech test tube baby was Louise Brown. She was conceived in 1978 from an embryo created in a British laboratory and implanted in a female who carried her to birth. Since that event, scientific advancements have provided a number of alternative reproduction methods.

According to the Centers for Disease Control and Prevention (CDC), of the approximately 60 million women of reproductive age in 1995, about 1.2 million, or 2 percent, had an infertility-related medical appointment within the previous year and an additional 13 percent had received infertility services at some time in their lives. (Infertility services include medical tests to diagnose infertility, medical advice and treatments to help a woman become pregnant, and services other than routine prenatal care to prevent miscarriage.) Additionally, 7 percent of married couples in which the woman was of reproductive age (2.1 million couples) reported they had not used contraception for 12 months and the woman had not become pregnant.

The Centers for Disease Control and Prevention also reported in the year 2000 that doctors in the United States performed about 100,000 in vitro "cycles," which are attempts at impregnation. Approximately 10,000 of the impregnation attempts involved egg donors, and approximately 1,000 of the attempts involved surrogate carriers.

There are several medical alternatives that may be used to achieve parenthood. For example, a wife could bear a child conceived of a donor's egg and her husband's sperm. Or a surrogate could carry a child to birth that was conceived using the wife's egg and her husband's sperm. A child could also be conceived using her husband's sperm and the surrogate's egg. It is also possible that a surrogate or the wife could carry a child to term who was conceived using a donated third-party egg and the husband's sperm.

Although most states have provisions regarding sperm donors, there is a paucity of legislation dealing with the many other procedures now available to men and women to achieve parenthood. The absence of clarifying legislation in many jurisdictions has left a cloud of uncertainty over the legality of the process and has erected legal barriers that are difficult, if not impossible, to overcome. For example, a couple contracting with a surrogate mother in order to achieve parenthood faces a series of complex legal issues. Absent legislation, there is a presumption that the woman giving birth to the child is the child's mother — not that of the contracting couple. In a jurisdiction where surrogacy is allowed, after a child is born to the surrogate, the surrogate parents will normally petition the court to have their parental rights terminated following the child's birth. If the intended father donated the sperm, he will normally have to prove his right to the child via a paternity hearing and then his wife may file for stepparent adoption. Where neither the husband nor the wife donated the egg and sperm, both must file for adoption following the termination of the parental rights of the surrogate and her husband.

UNIFORM ACTS AND PROPOSALS

18.2. Uniform Parentage Act

The Uniform Parentage Act (UPA), as approved by the National Conference of Commissioners on Uniform State Laws in 1973, deals only superficially with parental rights of a child born as a result of artificial insemination. *See* Rodgers, *Equal Protection for the Illegitimate Child: Uniform Parentage Act of 1977*, 6 Colo. Law 1299, 1307 (1977). The UPA declares that a husband of a woman who is artificially inseminated is treated as if he were the natural father of the child that is conceived. UPA §5a, 9B U.L.A. 301 (1987).

Whether the UPA intended to extinguish parental rights of semen donors who are known to the recipient woman is the subject of some debate. *See* George P. Smith II, *The Razor's Edge of Human Bonding: Artificial Fathers and Surrogate Mothers*, 5 W. New Eng. L. Rev. 639, 652 (1983) ("obvious" purpose of section 5 is "to protect anonymous [semen] donors from all legal responsibility for those children fathered as a consequence of their donation of semen"); and Note, *Contracts to Bear a Child*, 66 Calf. L. Rev. 611, 614 (1978) (purpose of section 5 "is clearly to protect anonymous donors from legal responsibility for any children fathered by the use of their semen"). *See also* Kern & Ridolfi, *The Fourteenth Amendment's Protection of a Woman's Right to Be a Single Parent Through Artificial Insemination by Donor*, 7 Women's Rts. L. Rep. 251, 256 (1982).

18.3. Uniform Putative and Unknown Fathers Act; Uniform Status of Children of Assisted Conception Act

The Uniform Putative and Unknown Fathers Act §2(a), 9B U.L.A. 80 (1996) (approved 1988), excludes the semen donor in cases of artificial insemination from being a putative father. Likewise, the Uniform Status of Children of Assisted Conception Act (USCACA) §4(a), 9B U.L.A. 191 (1966) (approved 1988), provides that a semen donor of a child conceived through assisted conception does not have parental status. The USCACA offers two alternative approaches to surrogacy. Alterative "A" allows surrogacy contracts if they have received court approval. This alternative also establishes the procedures for obtaining that approval. Alternative "B" states that surrogacy contracts are invalid and makes the surrogate parent the mother and her husband the father.

18.4. ABA Pre-embryo Proposal

The American Bar Association Family Law Section endorsed in principle a proposal for dealing with pre-embryos when the parents divorce. In the absence of an agreement of the parties specifying what is to happen, the person who wished to implant the pre-embryos would have rights superior to the person who wished to destroy them. The proposal would terminate financial responsibility of the one wishing to discard them. *See* Linda D. Elrod & Robert G. Spector, *A Review of the Year in Family Law: A Search for Definitions . . . and Policy*, 31 Fam. L.Q. 613, 625 (1998) (citing Minutes, ABA Family Law Section Fall Meeting 1996).

INSURANCE

18.5. Who is Covered?

Dealing with infertility is often traumatic and can be costly and time consuming. The average cost of one in vitro fertilization (IVF) cycle in the United States, and it frequently takes multiple cycles in order to succeed, has been estimated at $12,400, which usually is not covered by health insurance. *See Morrison v. Sadler*, 821 N.E.2d 15 (Ind. App. 2005). In *Knight v. Hayward Unified School Dist.*, 33 Cal. Rptr. 3d 287 (Cal. App. 1 Dist. 2005), the provisions of a school district's health insurance did not include coverage of IVF treatment. The court held that it did not constitute disability discrimination under Fair Employment and Housing Act (FEHA) against the teacher and his wife, who were obliged to obtain IVF treatment at their own expense.

However, some jurisdictions have statutorily required insurance carriers to provide coverage for diagnosing and treating infertility. *Goodridge v. Department of Public*, 798 N.E.2d 941 (Mass. 2003) n.31. In *Ralston v. Connecticut General Life Ins. Co.*, 617 So. 2d 1379 (La. Ct. App. 1993) the court held that in vitro fertilization procedures to induce pregnancy was treatment for a "sickness" and covered by a health insurance policy.

ARTIFICIAL INSEMINATION — STATUTORY PROVISIONS

18.6. Typical Statutory Provisions

Most jurisdictions have enacted legislation covering artificial insemination, a process that allows the sperm of a male to be used to artificially impregnate a female. Statutes eliminate claims of adultery, illegitimacy, and child support. Typically, sperm donor statutes provide that the husband of a woman who bears a child with donated sperm is automatically the legal father and the donor is relieved of any responsibility for supporting the child born of this procedure. *See Gursky v. Gursky*, 242 N.Y.S.2d 406, 409 (N.Y. Sup. Ct. 1963) (child conceived by artificial insemination is illegitimate).

Artificial insemination legislation serves several purposes: First, it allows married couples to have children, even though the husband is infertile, impotent, or ill. Second, it allows an unmarried woman to conceive and bear a child without sexual intercourse. Third, it resolves potential disputes about parental rights and responsibilities; that is, the mother's husband, if he consents, is father of the child and an unmarried mother is freed of any claims by the donor of parental rights. Fourth, it encourages men to donate semen by protecting them against any claims by the mother or the child. Finally, it legitimizes the child that is born and gives it rights against the mother's husband, if he consents to the insemination. *See, e.g., McIntyre v. Crouch*, 780 P.2d 239, 243 (Or. Ct. App. 1989).

Legislation typically requires that the artificial insemination occur under the supervision of a licensed physician and with the consent of the wife's husband. When a wife is inseminated artificially with semen donated by a man who is not her husband, the legislation treats the husband as if he were the natural father of the child. Statutes normally require that a husband's consent be in writing and the physicians involved are required to certify their signatures, the date of the insemination, and file the husband's consent with the appropriate governmental authorities, where it remains confidential in a sealed file. All papers and records pertaining to the insemination, whether part of the permanent record of a court or of a file held by the supervising physician or elsewhere, are subject to inspection only upon an order of the court for good cause shown.

Example 18-1

Assume that pursuant to a typical state artificial insemination statute, wife P, with husband D's express written permission, is impregnated under the supervision of a physician using the sperm of Y. When the child is born to P, the local prosecutor decides to put a "sperm donor clinic" out of business by charging the donors with adultery and demanding that they pay child support. The prosecutor learns that Y was the sperm donor in the above matter and charges Y with adultery in criminal court and asks for a child support order in civil court. A motion to dismiss the charge is brought in both courts by Y, the sperm donor. How will the criminal and civil courts most likely treat the motions?

Explanation

Although such a claim has a possibility of success in a jurisdiction without a typical artificial insemination statute, it should have no possibility of success in a jurisdiction that has adopted one. The criminal charge will most likely be dismissed, and Y will not have to pay child support. *See J.F. v. D.B.*, 848 N.E.2d 873 (Ohio App. 2006) (If a woman is the subject of a non-spousal artificial insemination, the donor shall not be treated in law or regarded as the natural father of a child conceived as a result of the artificial insemination, and a child so conceived shall not be treated in law or regarded as the natural child of the donor); *Levin v. Levin*, 645 N.E.2d 601, 604 (Ind. 1994) (holding father of child conceived through artificial insemination using donor's semen was equitably estopped from denying his child support obligation).

Example 18-2

Assume that D is a sperm donor in a jurisdiction that does not have an artificial insemination statute. The sperm is used to artificially inseminate X, a single woman, and a child is born. X discovers the identity of the sperm donor (D) and brings an action seeking support from him. How will a court most likely rule on the child support request?

Explanation

The court will most likely grant the request. Because the jurisdiction does not have a statute to guide the court in making a decision, it may not distinguish between artificial and natural conception. The child is clearly the genetic issue of D; therefore, D will most likely be required to pay X child support.

Example 18-3

Assume that P sues D, her former boyfriend, seeking to establish paternity and to impose support obligations for twin boys conceived through artificial insemination by an anonymous donor. They live in a jurisdiction that has a typical artificial insemination statute. At the trial, evidence was admitted showing that during their ten-year relationship, the parties discussed marriage but D told P that he did not believe in marriage. They also discussed P's desire to have children with D but it became apparent that D could not father children. P testified that D suggested that she be artificially inseminated by an anonymous donor as a means to have their child. P claims that D promised her that he would provide financial support for any child born by means of artificial insemination. According to P, with D's continuing consent and active encouragement, she attempted to become pregnant through artificial insemination and twin children were born. Evidence showed that D provided financial assistance for the insemination procedure, accompanied P to the doctor's office for examinations, injected P with medication designed to enhance her fertility, and participated in selecting the donor so that the offspring would appear to be a product of their relationship. D also participated in selecting names for the children, although he did not allow his name to be placed on their birth certificates. He provided them with monthly payments of cash and the purchase of food, clothing, furniture, toys, and play equipment. When the children were three years old,

P discovered that D was married. The relationship broke down and P now wants to establish paternity and child support. D states that he has no responsibility toward the children because they are not his genetic issue and he is not married to their mother. How will a court most likely rule?

Explanation

This is a relatively close case; however, most courts will likely find that D is the legal father of the twins. D will be held liable on either an estoppel or waiver theory. The court will most likely rule that the failure to execute a written consent did not bar further inquiry into the circumstances surrounding the decision to use artificial insemination. D's alleged conduct evinces a powerful case of actual consent. The allegations demonstrate a deliberate course of conduct with the precise goal of causing the birth of the children. Thus, if an unmarried man who biologically causes conception through sexual relations without the premeditated intent of birth is legally obligated to support a child, the equivalent resulting birth of a child caused by the deliberate conduct of artificial insemination should receive the same treatment in the eyes of the law. Regardless of the method of conception, a child is born and needs support. Under the alleged facts of this case, to hold otherwise would deprive the children of financial support merely because of deception and a technical oversight. *See generally In re Parentage of M.J.*, 787 N.E.2d 144 (Ill. 2003).

18.7. Husband's Consent

As noted earlier, most artificial insemination statutes normally require the written consent of the wife's husband before he will be found the father of a child born of this procedure and ordered to pay child support should the relationship break down. However, most courts agree that the best interests of children and society are served by recognizing that parental responsibility may be imposed based upon conduct evincing actual consent to the artificial insemination procedure. *See Gursky v. Gursky*, 242 N.Y.S.2d 406, 409 (N.Y. Sup. Ct. 1963). A New Jersey court in *K.S. v. G.S.*, 440 A.2d 64, 68-69 (N.J. Super. Ch. 1981), found that oral consent of the husband was effective at the time pregnancy occurs unless he can establish by clear and convincing evidence that consent was revoked or rescinded. The court in *In re Marriage of L.M.S.*, 312 N.W.2d 853, 855 (Wis. Ct. App. 1981), held that a man who was sterile must support a child born from this procedure. He had suggested to his wife that she become pregnant by another man and promised that he would acknowledge the child as his own and the legal obligation "to support the child for whose existence he is responsible." *See generally, In re Baby Doe*, 353

S.E.2d 877 (S.C. 1987) (husband's consent to artificial insemination may be express or implied from conduct).

EXAMPLES

Example 18-4

Assume that wife P and husband D orally agree to have a child by artificial insemination because husband D is infertile. They live in a jurisdiction that will recognize a child born of this procedure as the child of P and D. The artificial insemination of P is successful. Two months before the child is born, husband D and wife P separate. Following the child's birth, husband D is listed as the father on the birth certificate. During divorce proceedings, D brings an action seeking a declaration that he is not the father. Wife counterclaims for child support. D argues that his consent must have been in writing (it was not) and that he was not living with P when the child was born. How will a court most likely rule on P and D's claims?

EXPLANATIONS

Explanation

A court most likely will find the husband D to be the father of the child and order the payment of child support. D's knowledge of and assistance with his wife's efforts to conceive through artificial insemination will be viewed as constituting implied consent on his part, rendering him the legal father. *See In re Baby Doe*, 353 S.E.2d 877, 878 (S.C. 1987). The fact that D was not living with P at the time of the child's birth will most likely be considered irrelevant to the decision.

18.8. Do Artificial Insemination Statutes Apply to Wives?

The question of whether an artificial insemination statute applies to both wives and husbands has been answered in the affirmative in California. In *In re Karen C.*, 124 Cal. Rptr. 2d 677 (2002), the court considered the scope of subdivision (d) of section 7611 of the California Code, which states that a man is presumed to be the natural father of a child if "[h]e receives the child into his home and openly holds out the child as his natural child." The court held that the subdivision applies equally to women. This conclusion was echoed in *In re Salvador M.*, 4 Cal. Rptr. 3d 705 (2003), where the court stated, "Though most of the decisional law has focused on the definition of the presumed father, the legal principles concerning the presumed father apply equally to a woman seeking presumed mother status." *See Elisa B. v. Superior Court*, 33 Cal. Rptr. 3d 46 (Cal. 2005).

18.9. Known Donors and Unmarried Recipients

A state statute that extinguishes the parental rights of donors of semen to any child conceived by artificial insemination does not necessarily apply to known semen donors and unmarried recipients who agree that the donor will be treated as the father of the child. *In Interest of R.C.*, 775 P.2d 27 (Colo. 1989).

In *C.M. v. C.C.*, 377 A.2d 821 (N.J. Sup. Ct. 1977), the known donor gave semen to an unmarried woman, who artificially inseminated herself without the aid of a licensed physician. The court held the donor was entitled to visitation rights with the resulting child. The court reasoned that the best interests of the child are served by recognizing the donor as its father, rather than by leaving the child with no father at all. The court found it significant that the woman and the donor had a long-standing dating relationship prior to her artificial insemination, that the child had "no one else who was in a position to assume the responsibilities of fatherhood when the child was conceived" because the woman was unmarried, and that the donor "fully intended to assume the responsibilities of parenthood" at the time of the insemination. *Id.* at 824. The New Jersey legislature subsequently enacted a statutory provision that provided that a donor of semen to someone other than his wife has no parental rights to a child conceived through artificial insemination unless the donor and the woman have entered into a written contract to the contrary. *See* N.J. Rev. Stat. §9:17-44(b) (2003).

In *Jhordan C. v. Mary K.*, 224 Cal. Rptr. 530 (Cal. Dist. Ct. App. 1986), the court construed California's statute precluding recognition of a sperm donor to apply only when a physician performs the procedure or otherwise provides the semen. In *Jhordan*, the mother had self-inseminated, and the court declared that the sperm donor was the legal father of the child. The court also extended the protection it provided to married women (fear of a paternity lawsuit from sperm donor) to unmarried women. *Id.* at 392.

The Oregon Court of Appeals in *McIntyre v. Crouch*, 780 P.2d 239 (Or. Ct. App. 1989), held that Oregon's legislature had excluded a semen donor from the rights or obligations of fatherhood with respect to the resulting child, even though the insemination process was not conducted by a doctor and the recipient knew the donor. The court indicated, however, that should the parties agree that the man would be actively involved in the child's life, applying the artificial insemination statute to treat him solely as a donor, and not a father, would violate his constitutional rights. *Id.* at 244.

18.10. Using Husband's Sperm to Achieve Posthumous Reproduction

The law regarding the rights of posthumously conceived children is unsettled. Posthumous reproduction may occur if a married man and woman arrange for sperm to be withdrawn from the husband for the purpose of artificially impregnating the wife, and the woman is impregnated with that sperm after the man, her husband, has died.

In *Hecht v. Superior Court*, 20 Cal. Rptr. 2d 275 (Cal. Dist. Ct. App. 1993), the California Court of Appeal considered whether a decedent's sperm was "property" that could be bequeathed to his girlfriend. It answered in the affirmative and noted, in dicta, that under the provisions of California's Probate Code, "it is unlikely that the estate would be subject to claims with respect to any such children" resulting from insemination of the girlfriend with the decedent's sperm. *Id.* at 290.

In *Matter of Estate of Kolacy*, 753 A.2d 1257 (N.J. Super. Ct. Ch. Div. 2000), the plaintiff brought a declaratory judgment action to have her children, who were conceived after the death of her husband, declared the intestate heirs of her deceased husband in order to pursue the children's claims for survivor benefits with the Social Security Administration. A Superior Court judge held that, in circumstances in which the decedent left no estate and an adjudication of parentage did not unfairly intrude on the rights of others or cause "serious problems" with the orderly administration of estates, the children would be entitled to inherit under the state's intestacy law. *Id.* at 1257.

Woodward v. Commissioner of Social Sec., 760 N.E.2d 257 (Mass. 2002), involved a dispute where the husband was informed that he had leukemia when the couple was childless. Because the husband's leukemia treatment might leave him sterile, the couple arranged for a quantity of the husband's semen to be medically withdrawn and preserved, in a process commonly known as "sperm banking." The husband subsequently died from cancer, and the wife was appointed administratrix of his estate.

The wife gave birth to twin girls who were conceived through artificial insemination using the husband's preserved semen. She then applied for Social Security survivor benefits for the children. In rejecting her claim, the court said the question of recognition depends as a threshold matter upon a showing that the surviving parent or the child's other legal representative has a genetic relationship between the child and the decedent. Then, the survivor or representative must establish both that the decedent affirmatively consented to posthumous conception and to the support of any resulting child. Even then, circumstances such as time limitations may preclude commencing a claim for succession rights on behalf of a posthumously conceived child.

The court also observed that because death ends a marriage, posthumously conceived children are always nonmarital children. And because the parentage of such children can be neither acknowledged nor adjudicated prior to the decedent's death, it follows that, under the intestacy statute, posthumously conceived children must obtain a judgment of paternity as a necessary prerequisite to enjoying inheritance rights in the estate of the deceased genetic father.

Example 18-5

Assume that P and D are married and that D learns he has a serious heart problem and must undergo an operation. Because they have no children, P and D agree that a quantity of the husband's semen will be medically withdrawn and preserved in case D should die during the surgery. They consult you regarding the legal procedures to follow to ensure that any posthumous children will be protected. What advice might you give P and D?

Explanation

You might advise them to make the sperm donor's intent to support any posthumous children clear. This can be done by drafting a will that sets out in detail the sperm donor's intention of supporting such children. The client can also inform the sperm bank in writing of the reason for banking the sperm and special care should be exercised to keep a record so that, should D die and children be born posthumously, establishing paternity will be relatively easy. The will and the witnesses to the will should provide enough evidence to persuade a court that the children are eligible to receive Social Security benefits similar to those available to other children following the death of a parent.

SURROGACY

18.11. Surrogate Parent — History and Definition

Surrogacy has been mentioned historically as early as Biblical times: Abram's wife Sara could not bear Abram any children so she gave her maid servant, Hagar, to Abram for this purpose, saying, "the Lord has kept me from bearing children. Have intercourse, then, with my maid; perhaps I shall have sons through her." Genesis 16:3. The Bible also declares that a child, Ishmael, was born of this arrangement.

Black's Law Dictionary 1145 (8th ed. 2006) defines a surrogate parent as "a person who carries out the role of a parent by court appointment or the voluntary assumption of parental responsibilities." It defines a surrogate mother as "a woman who carries out the gestational function and gives birth to a child for another; esp. a woman who agrees to provide her uterus to carry an embryo throughout pregnancy, typically on behalf of an infertile couple, and who relinquishes any parental rights she may have upon the birth of a child." *Black's Law Dictionary* 1036 (8th ed., 2006).

Some question the accuracy of the term *surrogate* when used to describe a woman who is in fact the actual biological mother of a child. One author expressed the opinion that "[t]he term 'surrogate' mother, coined by advocates of commercial surrogacy, is a misnomer. The woman who bears the child is an actual mother; she is a surrogate 'wife.'" Kathryn D. Katz, *The Public Policy Response to Surrogate Motherhood Agreements: Why They Should Be Illegal and Unenforceable*, N.Y. St. B. J., May 1988.

18.12. Legislation Allowing and Banning Surrogacy

In contrast to artificial insemination statutes found in most states, only a handful of jurisdictions have legislation governing the subject of surrogacy. It appears that a majority of those that have promulgated legislation on the subject make such contracts void if they involve money. *See, e.g., Doe v. Attorney General*, 487 N.W.2d 484 (Mich. App. 1992).

Several states have apparently banned surrogacy contracts as contrary to public policy regardless of whether the woman carrying the baby is compensated or not. These states include New York, Utah, Michigan, and Arizona. *See, e.g.*, N.Y. Dom. Rel. Law §123 (McKinney Supp. 2003), Utah Code Ann. §76-7-204(1)(d) (2003), Mich. Comp. Laws Ann. §722.855 (2003), Ariz. Rev. Stat. Ann. §25-218(A) (2003). Washington, Louisiana, and Kentucky prohibit by statute surrogacy contracts that include a compensation element. *See* Wash. Rev. Code Ann. §26.26.230 (2003), La. Rev. Stat. Ann. §9:2713 (West 2003), Ky. Rev. Stat. Ann. §199.590 (Banks-Baldwin 2003).

18.13. Common Surrogacy Processes

There are two common surrogacy processes currently utilized. One technique involves the artificial insemination of the surrogate mother with the sperm of a male, usually when the parties contemplate that the sperm-donor male and his spouse will raise the child as the child's "parents." *See, e.g., Matter of Baby M*, 537 A.2d 1227 (N.J. 1988). The second technique, which is referred to as gestational surrogacy, involves a process by which couples who wish to have a child provide both the ovum and the sperm that undergo fertilization in a medical laboratory (in vitro fertilization). The embryo is then placed in the uterus of a woman who is not the ovum donor. This woman serves as the surrogate mother, who carries and gives birth to the child. *See, e.g., Huddleston v. Infertility Center of America*, 700 P.2d 453 (Pa. Super. 1997).

18.14. Baby M

In *In re Baby M*, 537 A.2d 1227 (N.J. 1988), William Stern and a surrogate, Mary Beth Whitehead, entered into a surrogacy contract. It recited that

Stern's wife, Elizabeth, was infertile, that they wanted a child, and that Mrs. Whitehead was willing to provide that child as the mother with Mr. Stern as the father. The contract provided that through artificial insemination using Mr. Stern's sperm, Mrs. Whitehead would become pregnant, carry the child to term, bear it, deliver it to the Sterns, and thereafter do whatever was necessary to terminate her maternal rights so that Mrs. Stern could thereafter adopt the child. Mrs. Whitehead's husband was also a party to the contract, although Mrs. Stern was not. Mr. Whitehead promised to do all acts necessary to rebut the presumption of paternity under the New Jersey Parentage Act and Mary Beth Whitehead agreed to be artificially inseminated with Mr. Stern's sperm and to relinquish her parental rights to the baby following its birth so that Mr. and Mrs. Stern could raise the baby. When Mrs. Whitehead refused to relinquish her rights to the baby according to the terms of the contract, the Sterns brought an action to enforce the contract. The claim was rejected, with the court concluding it was in direct conflict with existing statutes and conflicted with the public policy of the state, as expressed in its statutory and decisional law, and providing a series of reasons to justify the decision. *Id.* at 422.

The court held that surrogacy contracts are directly contrary to the objectives of New Jersey's laws because they guarantee the separation of a child from its mother, allow adoption regardless of parental suitability, totally ignore the child, remove a child from the mother regardless of her wishes and her maternal fitness, and accomplish their goals through the use of money. The court indicated that money should not be used in a private adoption and feared that it was actually being paid to obtain an adoption and not for the personal services of Mary Beth Whitehead. It felt that such conduct was similar to baby selling, illegal, and perhaps criminal.

The court also found that there is the coercion of contract when the natural mother's irrevocable agreement is obtained prior to birth, even prior to conception, to surrender the child to the adoptive couple. It felt that such agreements were totally unenforceable in private placement adoption. It observed that even where the adoption is through an approved agency, the formal agreement to surrender occurs only after birth.

The court also noted that surrogacy arrangements focus exclusively on the parents' desires and interests. Accordingly, the parties are apt to be insensitive to what would be in the child's best interests. That position is in direct opposition to the child custody laws, the guiding principle of which is the best interests of the child. There is also concern that a child's best interests could not be protected by an agreement in which the surrogate gave up her right to the child before she has the slightest idea of what the natural father and adoptive mother are like. Surrogacy contracts obviously do not serve the needs of the child because the child is placed without regard for whether the adoptive parents are suitable, the natural mother receives no counseling and guidance, and the adoptive parents may not be fully informed of the natural parents' medical history.

The agreement was contrary to termination statutes, which require a showing of intentional abandonment or a very substantial neglect of parental duties without a reasonable expectation of a reversal of that conduct in the future before a court will order the rights of a natural parent to be terminated. The surrogacy agreement also conflicted with state adoption laws that provide a mother with a period following the birth of the child to reflect on whether she wants the child adopted.

Another strong interest expressed in *Baby* M involves the potential exploitation of women. It is argued that surrogacy-for-profit arrangements may demean women by reducing them to the status of "breeding machines." *Doe v. Attorney General*, 487 N.W.2d 484, 487 (Mich. Ct. App. 1992). It is argued that if surrogacy contracts were recognized, every surrogate mother would soon be cast in the role of an "unfeeling, emotionless machine whose purpose is to create a life and then disappear." *See* Steven M. Recht, *"M" Is for Money: Baby M and the Surrogate Motherhood Controversy*, 37 Am. U. L. Rev. 1013, 1022 (1988).

EXAMPLES

Example 18-6

Assume that this is a jurisdiction where no surrogate statute exists. Also assume that P and X are sisters and that P, for medical reasons, cannot carry a child to term. P and X agree that X will be artificially inseminated with P's husband's sperm and that X will carry the child to term. When the child is born, X agrees to turn the child over to P. Before going through with the procedure, P consults you to determine the potential implications of the procedure. What advice should you give P?

EXPLANATIONS

Explanation

You will obviously review the various arguments that were outlined by the court in *Baby M*. However, *Baby M.* is distinguishable on two grounds. First, courts may view the close family relationship as important; i.e., the surrogate is the biological sister of the woman seeking parenthood. Second, no money is being exchanged between the parties. Therefore, the concerns about baby selling and female exploitation are lessened. While the woman seeking parenthood in this fashion may eventually achieve that goal, the legal obstacles are formidable in a state without a guiding statute.

GESTATIONAL SURROGACY

18.15. Gestational Surrogacy Defined

"Gestational surrogacy" is used to describe the situation in which one woman agrees to be impregnated with an embryo formed from another woman's fertilized egg. Among the technologies related to gestational surrogacy are in vitro fertilization, embryo and gamete freezing and storage, gamete intra-fallopian transfer, and embryo transplantation. Gestational surrogacy is the result of two of these techniques: in vitro fertilization and embryo transplantation.

In vitro fertilization (IVF) is the fertilization of a human egg outside the human body in a laboratory. Children conceived in this way are sometimes referred to as "test tube babies," because their actual conception may have occurred in a petri dish. Although a majority of states do not have gestational surrogacy statutes, there is a slow movement toward legislation in this area. States such as California and Texas have enacted such legislation. *See, e.g., Roman v. Roman*, 193 S.W.3d 40 (Tex. App. 2006).

18.16. State Theories

Johnson v. Calvert, 851 P.2d 776 (Cal. 1993), is a leading case on gestational surrogacy. In *Johnson v. Calvert*, a married couple supplied the egg and sperm and a surrogate agreed to carry and deliver the child. The surrogate was not related to the genetic providers, and was to be compensated for the surrogacy. A dispute arose over the compensation, and the surrogate claimed to be the parent.

The court recognized that either the gestational surrogate or the genetic parents could be recognized as the natural and legal parents, depending upon which party intended to procreate and raise the child. *See Robert B. v. Susan B.*, 135 Cal. Rptr. 2d 785 (Cal. Dist. Ct. App. 2003). The court explained that when Anna Johnson had agreed to bear the genetic child of the plaintiffs, both Johnson (the surrogate) and Crispina Calvert (the genetic mother) had equal claims. However, because the child would not have existed but for the surrogacy agreement, the tie was broken in favor of Calvert, the "intended" mother under the contract. Therefore, because the genetic mother intended to procreate, she was the natural parent.

In *McDonald v. McDonald*, 608 N.Y.S.2d 477 (N.Y. App. Div. 1994), the gestational surrogate received the egg from an anonymous donor and her husband provided the sperm. The sperm of the husband was mixed with the eggs of a female donor, and the fertilized eggs were then implanted in the wife's uterus. The wife gave birth to the children, twin girls. When the relationship broke down, the husband brought an action challenging the right of his wife to consider the children her natural issue. The court rejected the claim, saying that in a true egg donation situation, where a woman gestates and gives birth to a child formed from the egg of another woman with the intent to raise the child as her own, the birth mother is the natural mother. *Id.* at 480.

In *Belsito v. Clark*, 644 N.E.2d 760 (Ohio Com. Pl. 1994), two fertilized eggs created through in vitro fertilization by the use of the wife's eggs and the husband's sperm were transferred into the wife's sister's uterus by her physician. The surrogate was to receive no compensation for her role and she agreed that she planned to be no more than an aunt to the child or children.

When the wife spoke with the hospital regarding the birth certificate of the child being carried by the surrogate, she was told that the woman who gave birth to the child would be listed on the birth certificate as the child's mother. Further, she was told that because the surrogate and the wife's husband are not married to each other, the child will be considered illegitimate. The husband and wife sought a declaratory judgment challenging the hospital's position.

The court held that because the husband and wife provided the child with its genetics, they should be designated as the legal and natural parents. It stated that individuals who provide the genes of a child are the natural parents if the genetic providers have not waived their rights and have decided to raise the child.

18.17. Lesbian Issues

In *K.M. v. E.G.*, 33 Cal. Rptr. 3d 61 (Cal. 2005), a woman who had donated her eggs so that her former lesbian partner, with whom she was registered in a domestic partnership, could bear a child through in vitro fertilization, filed a petition to establish parental relationship with her partner's twin children after the relationship ended. The partner argued that the California statute that treats a sperm donor as if he was not the natural father of a child so conceived did not apply to this situation despite the fact that the relationship had ended and the woman egg donor had executed a written waiver of her rights to the children at the time of donation.

The court reasoned that both the couple in *Johnson v. Calvert* and the couple here intended to produce a child that would be raised in their own home. In *Johnson*, it was clear that the married couple did not intend to "donate" their semen and ova to the surrogate mother, but rather permitted their semen and ova to be used to impregnate the surrogate mother in order to produce a child to be raised by them. In this case, K.M. contended that she did not intend to donate her ova, but rather provided her ova so that E.G. could give birth to a child to be raised jointly by K.M. and E.G. E.G. asserted that K.M. donated her ova to E.G., agreeing that E.G. would be the sole parent.

The court observed that the couple lived together and they intended to bring the child into their joint home. It concluded that K.M. did not intend to simply donate her ova to E.G., but rather provided her ova to her lesbian partner with whom she was living so that E.G. could give birth to a child that would be raised in their joint home. It held that both lesbian partners were parents of the children and that the California statute providing that a sperm donor is treated as if he was not the natural father of a child so conceived did not apply to this situation.

EXAMPLES

Example 18-7

Assume that in this jurisdiction there is no surrogate statute, that a birth certificate can be prepared up to five days after the birth of a child, and that the adoption law provides that in recognition of the emotional and physical changes in the mother that occur at birth, voluntary surrenders are not valid if taken within 72 hours after the birth of the child. Assume further that X is the unmarried sister of P and the sister-in-law of P2. The biological parents, P and P2, entered into a gestational surrogacy contract with X. X, without financial compensation, agreed to have embryos implanted into her uterus that were created from the sperm of her brother-in-law, P2, and the ova of her sister, P. The child is due to be born in about two weeks at the county hospital. P and P2 file a complaint to declare the maternity and paternity of unborn Baby A. They seek a pre-birth order establishing them as the legal mother and father of unborn Baby A, and placing their names on the child's birth certificate. They argue that a pre-birth order is appropriate with a gestational surrogacy. How will a court most likely treat P and P2's request in a jurisdiction that is influenced by the *Baby M* decision?

EXPLANATIONS

Explanation

The court will most likely reject the request for a pre-birth order because it is contrary to the existing 72-hour statute. The gestational mother may surrender the child 72 hours after giving birth, which is 48 hours before the birth certificate must be prepared. If X chooses to surrender the infant, and she certifies that she wishes to relinquish all rights, the original birth certificate will list the two biological parents, P and P2, as the baby's parents. If X changes her mind once the baby is born, she will have a chance to litigate for parental rights to the child. *See generally* A.H.W. v. G.H.B., 772 A.2d 948 (N.J. Super. Ch. 2000).

18.18. Constitutional "Right" to Gestational Surrogacy?

Some argue that the use of techniques such as gestational surrogacy is constitutionally protected and should be restricted only on a showing of a compelling state interest. *See, e.g.*, John A. Robertson, *Procreative Liberty and the Control of Conception, Pregnancy, and Childbirth*, 69 Va. L. Rev. 405, 427 (1983); John A. Robertson, *Embryos, Families, and Procreative Liberty: The Legal Structure of the New Reproduction* 59 S. Cal. L. Rev. 939, 960 (1986). The theory is that procreation is protected under decisions of the United States Supreme Court that affirm the basic civil right to marry and raise children, and the right to procreate should extend to persons who cannot conceive or bear children. Some contend, however, that the broad application of the right of privacy for all procreational techniques has been questioned by the Court in such decisions as *Michael H. v. Gerald D.*, 491 U.S. 110 (1989).

IN VITRO FERTILIZATION

18.19. In Vitro Procedure Explained

The in vitro fertilization (IVF) procedure requires a woman to undergo a series of hormonal injections to stimulate the production of mature oocytes (egg cells or ova). The medication causes the ovaries to release multiple egg cells during a menstrual cycle rather than the single egg normally produced. The egg cells are retrieved from the woman's body and examined by a physician who evaluates their quality for fertilization. Egg cells ready for insemination are then combined with a sperm sample and allowed to incubate for approximately 12 to 18 hours. Successful fertilization results in a zygote that develops into a four- to eight-cell pre-embryo. At that stage, the pre-embryos are either returned to the woman's uterus for implantation or cryopreserved at a temperature of −196°C and stored for possible future use.

In IVF programs, the embryo will be transferred to a uterus when it reaches the four-, six-, or eight-cell stage, some 48 to 72 hours after conception. It is also at this stage that the embryo would be cryopreserved for later use. In vitro culture until the blastocyst stage may be possible, but beyond that it has not occurred. Finally, only one in ten pre-embryos at this stage goes on to initiate a successful pregnancy. Moreover, cryopreservation poses risks to the fertilized ova, which have only a 70 percent rate of viability after having been frozen.

18.20. Pre-embryo Agreements

There is an emerging majority view that written embryo agreements between embryo donors and fertility clinics to which all parties have consented are valid and enforceable so long as the parties have the opportunity to withdraw their consent to the terms of the agreement. In the absence of agreement, courts will weigh the relative interests of the male and female providers of reproductive cells and the parties' intent. *In re C.K.G.*, 173 S.W.3d 714 (Tenn. 2005). A sampling of issues raised in pre-embryo disputes follow.

In *Davis v. Davis*, 842 S.W.2d 588 (Tenn. 1992), the issue was who was entitled to control seven of the ex-wife's ova fertilized by the ex-husband's sperm through the in vitro fertilization process. The fertilized ova were cryopreserved at the Fertility Center of East Tennessee in Knoxville. The ex-husband was vehemently opposed to fathering a child that would not live with both parents in light of his boyhood experiences and the ex-wife's only interest in the embryos was to donate them to another couple.

The Tennessee Supreme Court held that disputes involving disposition of pre-embryos produced by in vitro fertilization should be resolved first by looking to the preferences of the progenitors. If their wishes cannot be ascertained, or if there is a dispute, their prior agreement concerning disposition should be carried out. If there is no prior agreement between the progenitors as to disposition of the pre-embryos, a court is to weigh the relative interests of parties in using or not using the pre-embryos. Ordinarily, the party who wishes to avoid procreation should prevail if there is a dispute as to custody of pre-embryos, assuming that the other party has a reasonable possibility of achieving parenthood by means other than use of the pre-embryos in question. However, if no other reasonable alternative exists, arguments in favor of using the pre-embryos to achieve pregnancy should be considered. In this case, because the party seeking control of the pre-embryos intends merely to donate them to another couple, the objecting party has the greater interest and should prevail.

In *J.B. v. M.B.*, 783 A.2d 707, 719 (N.J. 2001), the husband wanted to preserve the frozen embryos for his use or that of an infertile couple. The wife wanted the frozen embryos destroyed, and she did not want her former husband to retain them for his own use or to donate them to anyone else. The trial court ruled in favor of the wife, who wanted the embryos destroyed, because the family unit was no longer intact. The supreme court held that the parties' consent agreement did not "manifest a clear intent by [the parties] regarding disposition of the pre-embryos in the event of a dissolution of their marriage." In reaching its decision, the court considered the constitutional rights of the parties and stated that, "[w]e will not force [the wife] to become a biological parent against her will." *Id.* at 717. The court held that it will "enforce agreements entered into at the time in vitro fertilization has begun, subject to the right of either party to change his or her mind about disposition up to the point of use or destruction of any stored pre-embryos." *Id.* at 719. If the parties disagree about disposition because one party has reconsidered his or her decision, the court stated, "the interests of both parties must be evaluated." The court also stated that it expressed "no opinion in respect of a case in which a party who has become infertile seeks use of stored pre-embryos against the wishes of his or her partner, noting only that the possibility of adoption also may be a consideration, among others, in the court's assessment." 783 A.2d at 720.

In *Roman v. Roman*, 193 S.W.3d 40 (Tex. App. 2006), the court held that parties may voluntarily decide the disposition of a frozen embryo in advance of cryopreservation, and the embryo agreement between former husband and wife, which provided that frozen embryos were to be discarded in the event of divorce, was valid and enforceable.

One commentator has suggested that the gamete donation process that both husband and wife experience provides the consideration for an embryo agreement. Marysol Rosado, *Sign on the Dotted Line: Enforceability of Signed Agreements, upon Divorce of the Married Couple, Concerning the Disposition of Their Frozen Preembryos*, 36 New Eng. L. Rev. 1041, 1069 (2002).

18.21. Physician's Tort Liability to Parents

Physicians may become liable to patients in tort because of their failure to act or to properly inform the husband and wife. For example, a doctor who counseled a childless couple on artificial insemination and agreed to perform the procedure on the wife using the husband's sperm was held subject to suit by the couple as well as other legal consequences when he substituted his own sperm for that of the wife's husband. *See generally James v. Jacobson*, 6 F.3d 233 (4th Cir. 1993); *United States v. Jacobson*, 785 F. Supp. 563 (E.D. Va. 1992); *see St. Paul Fire and Marine Ins. Co. v. Jacobson*, 826 F. Supp. 155, 158, n.3 (E.D. Va. 1993) (listing civil actions against physician for unauthorized use of physician's own semen).

In *Harnicher v. University of Utah Medical Center*, 962 P.2d 67 (Utah 1998), the Utah Supreme Court upheld the dismissal of a couple's claim against a medical center that used sperm from a donor other than the one the couple selected for artificial insemination, resulting in the birth of triplets. The court held that the parents failed to raise a triable issue of fact that they had suffered bodily harm, and had failed to show that the medical center's alleged negligence was of the type that was likely to cause severe and unmanageable mental distress in a reasonable person.

18.22. Clinic's Tort Liability

A California clinic was sued by a child who claimed its negligence had deprived her of her legal parent because it failed to certify the signature of the mother's husband on the consent form used for artificial insemination. In a subsequent divorce action, the divorce court ruled that the husband did not have a legal obligation to support the child born of the procedure. The child, who was now fatherless, sued the clinic. The court held that the clinic and its doctors could not be sued for negligence action for denying her a legal parent or child support. The court reasoned that failure to certify the signature was not the proximate cause of any injury to the child, because certification was not required to establish the husband's consent under the statute that treated a husband who consents to a wife being inseminated artificially by a donor as the natural father of the child conceived. *Alexandria S. v. Pacific Fertility*, 64 Cal. Rptr. 2d 23 (Cal. Dist. Ct. App. 1997).

In *Jeter v. Mayo Clinic Arizona*, 211 Ariz. 386, 121 P.3d 1256 (Ariz. App. Div. 1 2005), a couple sued a reproductive medicine clinic for alleged negligent destruction or loss of five of the couple's frozen pre-embryos that the clinic had agreed to cryopreserve and store. They brought claims for wrongful death, negligent loss of irreplaceable property, breach of fiduciary duty, and breach of bailment contract. The court held that cryopreserved, three-day-old eight-cell pre-embryo, was not a "person" for purposes of recovery under wrongful death statute; but they could use it to pursue claims of negligent loss or destruction of pre-embryos and for breach of bailment contract.

18.23. Constitutional Issues

There have been a small number of constitutional challenges made to state statutes attempting to provide guidance in this area. For example, an Oregon court, in dictum, stated that, had its state statute prevented a sperm donor from exercising paternity rights, it would most likely be held unconstitutional in certain situations (as applied) under the Due Process Clause of the Fourteenth Amendment. *See McIntyre v. Crouch*, 780 P.2d 239, 244 (Or. Ct. App. 1989). The unconstitutionality of the barrier becomes apparent in situations in which a sperm donor establishes that he and the woman inseminated with his sperm agreed that he should have the rights and responsibilities of fatherhood, and in reliance on the agreement, he provided the sperm. *See, e.g., Lehr v. Robertson*, 463 U.S. 248 (1983).

At least one court has specifically held that a woman possesses the constitutional right to become pregnant by artificial insemination because a woman has a constitutional privacy right to control her reproductive functions. *Cameron v. Board of Educ. of Hillsboro*, 795 F. Supp. 228, 237 (S.D. Ohio 1991). The court relied on the Supreme Court's decisions in *Cleveland Board of Education v. LaFleur*, 414 U.S. 632, 640 (1974) (freedom of personal choice in matters of marriage and family life is one of the liberties protected by the Due Process Clause); *Roe v. Wade*, 410 U.S. 113, 153 (1973) (woman's right to privacy includes the right to terminate a pregnancy); and *Griswold v. Connecticut*, 381 U.S. 479, 485-486 (1965) (criminalizing purchasing contraceptives violates one's right to privacy).

18.24. Clinic Liability when Child Born "Imperfect"

In *Paretta v. Medical Offices for Human Reproduction*, 760 N.Y.S.2d 639 (N.Y. Sup. 2003) a New York court held that a right of recovery for emotional distress did not exist for a child's birth with cystic fibrosis but that a right of recovery did exist for pecuniary expense for the infant's care and treatment. Evidence at trial indicated that it was the custom and practice of the program used by the clinic to screen donors for various diseases, including cystic fibrosis, and to inform the patient that a potential donor was a carrier. If a couple elected to go forward, they had the option or choice to be screened to see if there was a carrier status. No one remembered ever telling the plaintiffs that the available donor was a carrier of cystic fibrosis, and the husband was not tested to ascertain whether he was a carrier of the disease.

18.25. Clinic Liability when Mix-up Occurs During Handling of Genetic Material

In *Robert B. v. Susan B.*, 135 Cal. Rptr. 2d 785 (Cal. Dist. Ct. App. 2003), a child, Daniel, was born to Susan B., a single woman, after a fertility clinic implanted embryos belonging to Robert and Denise B. into Susan. In an action to determine paternity, the trial court ruled that Susan was Daniel's mother and Robert was his father. Denise was dismissed for lack of standing.

Robert and Denise B. had contracted with an anonymous ovum donor to obtain the donor's eggs for fertilization with Robert's sperm. The contract reflected the intent of the contracting parties that Robert and Denise would be the parents of any children produced from the resulting embryos.

Susan went to the same fertility clinic with the intent of purchasing genetic material from "two strangers who would contractually sign away their rights" so that "there would be no paternity case against her, ever." She therefore contracted with the clinic for an embryo created from anonymously donated ova and sperm.

About 13 embryos were produced for Robert and Denise and some of them were implanted in Denise's uterus. Through an apparent clinic error, Susan received three of these embryos. When she became pregnant, Susan believed that the child she was carrying was the result of the anonymous donation procedure for which she had contracted. In February, ten days apart, Susan gave birth to Daniel and Denise gave birth to Daniel's genetic sister, Madeline.

In December 2001, the fertility physician informed Robert and Denise that "a mistake had occurred," in that the clinic had "inadvertently" implanted some of Robert and Denise's embryos in Susan's uterus, resulting in Daniel's birth. Robert and Denise promptly sought contact with Daniel. Susan was initially receptive, but after the three adults and two children met, she refused to relinquish custody, and Robert and Denise brought this parentage action. Over Susan's opposition, the trial court determined that Robert had standing to bring a paternity action under section 7630, subdivision (c), and it ordered genetic testing. After receiving the test results, the court declared Robert to be the father of Daniel.

In resolving the dispute, the court noted that Susan was the gestational mother and that Denise had no genetic connection with Daniel, and it concluded that "there really is only one mother in this case at this point." *Id.* at 787. Any contractual rights Denise had were to embryos, "but now what we're talking about is a live person, not an embryo."

CHAPTER 19

Domestic Violence

19.1. Introduction

The existence of domestic violence has been traced as far back as ancient Rome. Even during the 1800s, an American husband could legally "chastise" his wife in the exercise of his property rights. Awareness of domestic violence has increased dramatically over the last half century and domestic violence is no longer explicitly approved under the law. However, society remains ambivalent about when and how to intervene in family matters.

UNDERSTANDING THE PROBLEM

19.2. Risk Factors for and Consequences of Abuse

Despite years of research, there is little consensus about how social scientists should define and measure domestic violence. Risk markers for abuse include growing up in a violent home, socioeconomic status, personality issues, substance abuse, biological factors, and situational dynamics. Rates of violence may be higher when dating, in early marriage, during pregnancy, and at the time of divorce. Glenda Kaufman Kantor & Jana L. Jasinski, *Dynamics and Risk Factors in Partner Violence*, in *Partner Violence* 1, 41, 42 (Jana L. Jasinski et al. eds., 1998).

Although men are also victims of domestic violence, women are four times as likely to suffer serious and potentially life-threatening assault. They are twice as likely to be victims of repeated assault, and women are more likely than men to be killed as a result. Women and children may be at increased risk of fatal assault at the time of separation. *See* Peter G. Jaffe, Nancy K.D. Lemon & Samantha E. Poisson, *Child Custody and Domestic Violence*, 4-8, 2003.

19.3. Types of Partner Violence

During the late 1970s, Lenore Walker theorized that violent couples become enmeshed in a repetitive cycle of violence and control. Her seminal work suggesting a three-phase "cycle of violence" was instrumental in raising societal consciousness about domestic abuse. Other researchers have expanded on Walker's work and theorized that couples experience different types of violence. *See* Janet R. Johnston & Linda Campbell, *Parent-Child Relationships in Domestic Violence Families Disputing Custody*, 31 Fam. & Conciliation Cts. Rev. 282 (1993); Janet Johnston & Vivienne Roseby, *In the Name of the Child: A Developmental Approach to Understanding and Helping Children of Conflicted and Violent Divorce* (1997); Desmond Ellis & Noreen Stuckless, *Mediating and Negotiating Marital Conflicts* (1996).

Researcher Michael P. Johnson differentiates types of domestic violence based on the motivation of the aggressor and the overall pattern of the violence. Under his typology, Intimate Terrorism (IT) involves an *escalating pattern of coercive control* perpetrated by men upon women. The Intimate Terrorist exerts control over the victim through physical and sexual abuse but also through threats, emotional abuse, isolation, economic control, and manipulation of children. As a result of the abuse, victims may suffer from Post Traumatic Stress Syndrome and other health issues. Victims of Intimate Terrorism may actively seek formal help and leave the abuser. In contrast to Intimate Terrorism, Situational Couple Violence (SCV) occurs when a disagreement spirals into a violent incident because the partners lack adequate conflict resolution skills. Situational Couple Violence does not involve a larger pattern of coercive control. Situational Couple Violence may be initiated equally by men and women; however, women suffer more injuries and other negative consequences than men. Michael P. Johnson & Kathleen Ferraro, *Research on Domestic Violence in the 1990s: Making Distinctions*, 62 *Journal of Marriage and Family* 948 (2000) and Michael P. Johnson, *Patriarchal Terrorism and Common Couple Violence, Two Forms of Violence Against Women*, 7 *Journal of Marriage and the Family* 283 (1995).

The assertion that families experience different types of domestic violence has far reaching implications for research and policymaking. To a large extent, the legal system takes a one-size-fits-all approach to domestic violence, and unfortunately, the consequent failure to differentiate among violent families heightens the danger for some and at the same time prevents others from accessing helpful services. Nancy Ver Steegh, *Differentiating Types of Domestic Violence: Implications for Child Custody*, 65 La. L. Rev. 1379 (2005). Additional research is needed in this area to substantiate the existence of different types of domestic violence and develop more finely tuned screening tools.

19.4. Impact on Children

Children who witness domestic abuse suffer a range of emotional and behavioral consequences. They are sometimes more fearful and inhibited or they may act more aggressively than other children. Some children exhibit anxiety, depression, and trauma-related symptoms. Of course, the extent of the impact varies depending on the child's overall situation. Jeffrey L. Edleson, *Should Childhood Exposure to Adult Domestic Violence Be Defined as Child Maltreatment Under the Law?*, in *Protecting Children From Domestic Violence* 8, 10 (Peter G. Jaffe et al. eds., 2004). Approximately half of the children who witness domestic violence are themselves physically abused. Lundy Bancroft & Jay G. Silverman, *The Batterer as Parent* 42 (2002) (finding 40-70% concurrent child abuse).

To the extent that it can be determined, the type of violence experienced by the family may have significance for children. For example, under the typology discussed previously, children whose fathers are Intimate Terrorists should probably only have contact with them in supervised settings, and courts should keep in mind the willingness of Intimate Terrorists to manipulate children in an effort to control and intimidate the mother. Evan Stark, *Re-Presenting Woman Battering: From Battered Women Syndrome to Coercive Control*, 58 Albany L. Rev. 973, 40 (1995) (describing batterer's extension of coercive tactics to the children as "tangential spouse abuse").

19.5. Screening for Domestic Violence

Victims of domestic violence often downplay or deny the abuse. Consequently, lawyers and professionals working with families must be alert for signs of abuse and should routinely screen for it. Some attorneys use a written questionnaire or screening instrument in addition to inquiring about whether domestic violence has taken place. Asking questions about whether a client is afraid of her partner may be more productive than directly asking whether the client has been abused. Lawyers must also listen carefully for indications of control and intimidation. *See* Margaret Drew, *Lawyer Malpractice and Domestic Violence: Are We Revictimizing Our Clients?*, 39 Fam.

L. Q. 7 (2005) (exploring malpractice and ethical mistakes likely to occur when representing clients in cases involving domestic violence).

Family law attorneys routinely assist domestic violence victims with safety planning and make appropriate referrals to community resources. This is a key aspect of providing competent representation.

DOMESTIC ABUSE ACTS

19.6. History

During the 1960s, society became increasingly aware of the frequency and consequences of domestic violence, and more victims of domestic violence sought help. The need for safe shelter became immediately apparent and volunteers cooperated to create safe homes and eventually to start shelters for battered women. Shelter staff soon learned that the existing legal framework was inadequate to protect victims of domestic violence and their children. At a minimum, victims needed a way to remove the abuser from the home, establish child custody and support, and keep the abuser from contacting them. Even if the violence resulted in criminal prosecution, prospective relief was not readily available. Domestic abuse acts were developed to meet these needs.

Between 1975 and 1980, 45 states passed some type of civil domestic abuse legislation. Currently, every state has a statute granting prospective civil relief to victims of domestic violence.

19.7. Defining Domestic Violence

Although each state's domestic abuse statute defines domestic violence somewhat differently, the definitions usually focus on physical (as opposed to emotional or psychological) abuse. Section 102 of the Model Code on Domestic and Family Violence defines domestic violence in the following way:

> Domestic or family violence means the occurrence of one or more of the following acts by a family or household member, but does not include acts of self defense:
>
> (a) Attempting to cause or causing physical harm to another family or household member;
> (b) Placing a family or household member in fear of physical harm; or
> (c) Causing a family or household member to engage involuntarily in sexual activity by force, threat of force, or duress.

Typical acts of violence falling within this definition include pushing, slapping, choking, punching, use of weapons, use of household objects as weapons, and rape. Thus, the definition of domestic violence encompasses a continuum of behavior from verbal threats to homicide.

EXAMPLES

Example 19-1

P and D decided to divorce. As they were separating, they had a heated argument about who should move out of the marital home. P heard D say that if he couldn't stay in the home, he would burn it down. P seeks an order for protection based on a statute allowing for an order of protection to be issued upon a showing of "actual or imminent domestic violence." D claims that he said that they should sell the house or burn it. The court issues an order for protection on P's behalf and D appeals. What is the likely result?

EXPLANATIONS

Explanation

In a similar case, P obtained an order for protection from the trial court; however, that decision was overturned on appeal. In *Ficklin v Ficklin*, 710 N.W.2d 387 (N.D. 2006), the court found that there was evidence that P was fearful that D would burn the house; however, the court ruled that the evidence was not sufficient to establish that she was in fear of *imminent* harm. The appellate court noted that the trial court erroneously focused on eliminating the mere possibility of harm.

EXAMPLES

Example 19-2

Assume P proves that D committed the following acts: (1) he shouted profanities at P, grabbed her hand, and pushed her against a bar; (2) he pushed a car door against P's arm; and (3) he yelled profanities at P's son. P alleges that she and her son are afraid of D. The domestic abuse act in P's state defines domestic and family violence as the occurrence of at least one of the following acts: (a) attempting to cause, threatening to cause, or causing physical harm to another family or household member; (b) placing a family or household member in fear of physical harm; (c) causing a family or household member to involuntarily engage in sexual activity by force, threat or force, or duress. D opposes entry of the order for protection, claiming that P's testimony is insufficient to establish that these events occurred. Is the evidence sufficient to issue and order for protection?

EXPLANATIONS

Explanation

In *Aiken v. Stanley*, 816 N.E.2d 427 (Ind. App. 2004), the trial court issued the order for protection and the court's decision was upheld on appeal. The appellate court found that the evidence outlined previously was sufficient to support issuance of the order for protection under the statute. The court noted that under the language of the statute, it was sufficient for P to show that she and her son were in fear of D. No particular threats or actions were specifically required as long as this showing was made.

19.8. Who Is Covered?

State domestic abuse acts provide relief to spouses and former spouses of abusers. Most statutes extend coverage to children, other family members, household members, and unmarried parents of a common child. Many statutes include same gender intimate partners and some include dating couples.

EXAMPLES

Example 19-3

P files for an order for protection after she is assaulted by her cohabiting boyfriend, D. P and D are not married. The domestic violence statute in their state extends to "a person living as a spouse." The state has amended its constitution to include a Defense of Marriage Amendment (DOMA) stating the following: "Only a union between one man and one woman may be a marriage valid in or recognized by this state and its political subdivisions. This state and its political subdivisions shall not create or recognize a legal status for relationships of unmarried individuals that intends to approximate the design, qualities, significance or effect of marriage." D asserts that applying the domestic violence statute to an unmarried couple violates the state constitution and that P is consequently not entitled to relief under the domestic violence statute. What is the likely result?

EXPLANATIONS

Explanation

In *State v. Ward*, 2006 WL 758540 (Ohio App. 2006), the court agreed with D and held that the domestic violence statute provision extending protection to "a person living as a spouse" violated the state DOMA. However, due to a split among the Ohio courts, the question is expected to be reviewed and resolved by the Ohio Supreme Court. *See State v. Logsdon*, 2006 WL 1585447 (Ohio App. 2006).

19.9. What Relief Is Granted?

The workhorse of domestic abuse legislation is an injunctive order, which may be referred to as an order for protection, civil protective order, protective order, or restraining order. The relief available varies by state but typically includes a prohibition against further abuse, a no-contact order, award of exclusive possession of the residence, child custody and visitation arrangements, and/or a support order.

19.10. Ex Parte and "Permanent" Orders

Obtaining a protective order is usually a two-step process: first obtaining an *ex parte* order and then seeking a "permanent" order after notice and possibly a hearing. In many cases, the victim needs immediate relief, and giving notice to the abuser would subject the victim to additional harm. If the victim can demonstrate a substantial likelihood of abuse or an immediate and present danger of abuse, the victim can seek an *ex parte* order. In some jurisdictions this can be done by affidavit, but in other jurisdictions testimony is required. The relief available in an *ex parte* order is likely to be limited in scope. In many jurisdictions a full hearing is scheduled and the defendant is served with the *ex parte* order and the hearing date. (If the defendant is served but fails to appear at the hearing, the defendant can be defaulted.) In other jurisdictions, after the defendant is served, the defendant can request a hearing. If the defendant does not do so, the *ex parte* order becomes a permanent order. Final or permanent orders typically remain in effect for a year, although some states issue them for shorter or longer periods of time.

EXAMPLES

Example 19-4

Assume that P lives in a jurisdiction that authorizes temporary (*ex parte*) and permanent orders for protection. In order to obtain a temporary order for protection under the statute P would be required to show "imminent danger." The statute authorizes issuance of a permanent order "If . . . the judge or magistrate is of the opinion that [a spouse] has committed acts constituting grounds for issuance of a civil protection order and that unless restrained will continue to commit such acts, the judge or magistrate shall order the temporary civil protection order to be made permanent or order a permanent civil protection order with different provisions from the temporary civil protection order." P seeks a permanent order, and after notice is given to D and a hearing is held, the court issues a permanent order without making a finding of imminent danger. D alleges that a finding of imminent danger was necessary, and D appeals on that basis. Will D succeed on appeal?

Explanation

In a similar case, the court held that although a showing of imminent danger was required to obtain a temporary order, it was not statutorily required for issuance of a permanent order. The court reasoned that temporary orders are issued under urgent circumstances and often without notice to the respondent, whereas permanent orders are designed to prevent future harm. *In re Marriage of Fiffe*, 2005 WL 3244043 (Colo. App. 2005).

Example 19-5

P and D reside in Illinois. Due to domestic violence, P leaves Illinois to stay with family members in New Jersey. She obtains an *ex parte* temporary restraining order against D from a New Jersey court. D has never been to New Jersey and D claims that the New Jersey court lacked personal jurisdiction over him. What is the likely result?

Explanation

In the similar case of *Shah v. Shah*, 875 A.2d 931 (N.J. 2005), the court held that it did not have personal jurisdiction over the defendant and that it consequently could not issue a final restraining order requiring the defendant to perform affirmative acts. However, the court determined that a temporary restraining order issued by the New Jersey court was valid to the extent that it provided prohibitory relief. In addition, the court ruled that the temporary restraining order could remain in effect indefinitely.

19.11. Due Process Constitutional Challenges

Defendants have challenged state domestic abuse acts, alleging that issuance of *ex parte* orders of protection violate their due process rights. However, these challenges have not been successful. *See State ex rel. Williams v. Marsh*, 626 S.W.2d 223 (Mo. 1982); *Baker v. Baker*, 494 N.W.2d 282 (Minn. 1992). In analyzing constitutional claims, courts have used the balancing test set forth in *Mathews v. Eldridge*, 424 U.S. 319 (1976). Although the defendant has a property interest in the home and a liberty interest in the children, the government has a strong interest in preventing future violence. Furthermore, procedural safeguards exist, including requiring affidavits, taking testimony, having a judge or referee make the decision, giving notice of rights, and holding an immediate hearing.

Example 19-6

Assume that P and D have been married for five years. D is at work one day when he is served with an *ex parte* order of protection granting P exclusive possession of the residence, prohibiting D from contacting P, and barring D from seeing their children until after a hearing scheduled ten days later. In the petition, P accuses D of several acts of violence, which D denies, and P alleges that D has threatened to "kidnap" the children if P moves out of the marital home. D is outraged that he cannot go home, cannot see his children, and that all of this can happen to him without his having a chance to tell his side of the story. He contacts an attorney for advice. Have D's due process rights been violated?

Explanation

D's due process rights have not been violated. Although state action is involved and D clearly has a liberty interest in seeing the children and a property interest in the residence, this private interest is outweighed by the state's interest in preventing further abuse and possible parental kidnapping. D is protected by the requirement that P file a verified affidavit and appear before a judge who assessed P's credibility and most likely took testimony on the record. The deprivation is temporary because D has received notice and will have a full hearing shortly.

Example 19-7

Assume that D assaults P, and P files for an order for protection. Under the state domestic abuse statute, before an order is issued, the court is required to make findings in an official record or in writing. In emergency situations, the court is required to examine the petitioner under oath and review a verified petition for relief. In this case, the court issued an order for protection but did not make findings or a record of testimony. D petitions to have the order overturned, arguing that significant provisions of the domestic abuse act were not followed. P argues that these were mere technicalities. What is the likely result?

Explanation

D is likely to have the order of protection overturned because D did not receive important procedural protections. In a similar case, *Hedrick-Koroll v. Bagley*, 816 N.E.2d 849 (Ill. App. 2004), the appellate court held that the trial court failed to comply with the Domestic Violence Act requirement of specific findings. The case was remanded for further proceedings.

19.12. Access to the Court Issues

A victim of domestic violence who is not represented by counsel may have difficulty procuring a protective order and obtaining other necessary relief. Some statutes require clerks of court to assist unrepresented victims seeking to file petitions. Women's advocates also provide information and support and in some jurisdictions their communications with the victim are privileged. *See People v. Turner*, 109 P.3d 639 (Colo. 2005). Nevertheless, legal representation for victims is a serious and ongoing problem. In an effort to make protection more readily available, a few courts provide for issuance of emergency orders outside of business hours.

19.13. Issuance of Mutual Orders

Either in settlement or at hearing, a defendant may request that an order for protection be issued against the victim as well as the defendant. This practice is known as issuing mutual or cross orders of protection. In *Deacon v. Landers*, 587 N.E.2d 395 (Ohio Ct. App. 1990), the trial court granted mutual orders over the objection of the victim and without any presentation of evidence showing that she had been violent. The appellate court overruled the trial court and held that issuance of mutual orders violated the victim's right to due process.

Unless clearly warranted by the evidence, issuance of mutual orders of protection can be dangerous. Such orders empower the abuser, put the victim and her children at additional risk, and confuse police, who are trying to enforce the orders.

EXAMPLES

Example 19-8

P and D cohabited for a period of years but did not marry. During this time, D committed several severe acts of domestic violence against P, and D was imprisoned three times for these assaults. P sought a restraining order against D, and D appeared at the hearing where P was granted a three-year restraining order. About a week later, D filed a separate action for a domestic violence temporary restraining order against P alleging that P harassed him while he was in prison by sending him letters, and that P later threatened to report him for stealing her ATM card. The court issued a temporary restraining order against P. The state where P and D reside has a statute stating that the court may not issue mutual restraining orders unless both parties personally appear in court to present evidence of abuse and the court makes detailed findings that both acted as primary aggressors and not in self-defense. P claims that mutual orders have been issued in violation of the statute. D claims that the requirements of the statute have been met because, with respect to both orders, the petitioner appeared personally and the court made detailed findings. Does this situation describe mutual orders within the meaning of the statute?

Explanation

In the similar case of *Conness v. Satram*, 18 Cal. Rptr. 3d 577 (Cal. App. 2004), the appellate court found that the term "mutual order" meant a single order imposing parallel requirements on each party. The orders issued against P and D were deemed to be separate orders that included findings of credibility by the trial court. Consequently, according to the appellate court, the orders were not "mutual" under the state statute and both orders could remain in effect.

19.14. Enforcement of Orders

Most domestic abuse statutes make violation of a protective order a criminal offense, typically a misdemeanor, although some violations may be charged as a felony in some states. Despite such provisions, the Supreme Court has held that a domestic abuse victim who has obtained a restraining order does not have a constitutionally protected property interest in police enforcement of the order, even where there is probable cause to believe that the order was violated. *Town of Castle Rock, Colo. v. Gonzales*, 125 S. Ct. 2796 (2005).

In addition to being a criminal offense, violation of a protective order may constitute criminal contempt. Although both types of proceedings are useful, some commentators favor criminal contempt proceedings because victims have more control over the process, and contempt actions may proceed more quickly than criminal prosecutions. *See* David M. Zlotnick, *Empowering the Battered Woman: The Use of Criminal Contempt Sanctions to Enforce Civil Protection Orders*, 56 Ohio St. L.J. 1153 (1995).

Special enforcement issues can arise if the parties decide to reconcile but do not petition the court to dissolve an existing protective order. For example, in *Cole v. Cole*, 556 N.Y.S.2d 217 (Fam. Ct. 1990), the couple reconciled after issuance of a protective order and then separated again. Subsequent to the separation, the husband broke into the residence, choked the wife, and threatened to kill her. The police refused to enforce the order because of the intervening reconciliation. The court ultimately found that the order remained in effect and held the husband in contempt of court. In so doing, the court noted that the husband could have returned to court to vacate the order and that reconciliation did not license the husband to commit further abuse.

Example 19-9

P and D had a history of domestic violence. After twenty years of marriage, P initiated divorce proceedings against D and obtained a no-contact order. Six months later, after another incident, D pleaded *nolo contendere* to charges of domestic disorderly conduct and violation of the no-contact order. D's probation officer met with him to explain the terms of the order, but shortly after the meeting D mailed two birthday cards to P. P claimed that D violated the no-contact order by sending the cards, but D claimed that the no-contact order did not specifically prohibit mailings. Did D violate the no-contact order?

Explanation

In the similar case of *State v. John*, 881 A.2d 920 (R.I. 2005), the court held that the order was reasonably clear and specific in restraining D from "any contact" with P. "Any contact" included sending mail to P. Consequently, D was in violation of the order. Although such a violation may sound trivial, batterers commonly test the victim's resolve to enforce the protective order once it is obtained. Additionally, if there is a history of coercive control over the victim, gestures that seem innocent to an onlooker may actually have a threatening hidden meaning.

19.15. Effectiveness of Orders

Victims frequently report that protective orders have been helpful and empowering. However, researchers are still investigating how and when protective orders are most effective in preventing further abuse. For example, one study found that 60 percent of temporary orders of protection were violated within a year. Victims who had been more seriously abused suffered more serious violations and abusers who objected to entry of the order were more likely to violate it. Adele Harrell & Barbara E. Smith, *Effects of Restraining Orders on Domestic Violence Victims*, in Do Arrests and Restraining Orders Work? (Buzawa & Buzawa eds., 1996). Protective orders *may* be less effective if the abuser has a past criminal history, the couple has minor children, and/or they have low incomes. *See* Eve S. Buzawa & Carl G. Buzawa, *Domestic Violence: The Criminal Justice Response* 242-245 (2003).

The decision about whether to obtain an order for protection must be made on a case-by-case basis. Victims should be counseled concerning the availability of relief and the costs and benefits of seeking an order in light of the victim's particular circumstances. Victims should be aware that jurisdictions vary in terms of the difficulty of obtaining an order and how seriously violations are viewed by police, prosecutors, and judges.

EXAMPLES

Example 19-10

Assume that P and D were married and that D was violent with P throughout the marriage. Most recently, D broke P's nose and threatened to kill her and take the children if she left him. P does not work outside the home and does not have relatives in the area. What factors should P be counseled about in deciding whether to obtain an order of protection?

EXPLANATIONS

Explanation

With respect to obtaining a protective order, P should be carefully counseled about the possibility that D might violate the order. P would probably have an accurate assessment of D's reaction to entry of the *ex parte* order — some respondents comply with orders and others become more violent. Also, some police departments respond more quickly and some jurisdictions prosecute violations more vigorously than others. P's safety is more important than staying in the house. Consequently, P should seriously consider making a temporary move to a shelter or having someone stay at the house with P and the children. In any event, P and the children should have a detailed safety plan.

RELATED AREAS OF LAW

19.16. Violence Against Women Act

The federal Violence Against Women Act (VAWA) was originally passed in 1994 and was reauthorized in 2000 and 2005. Among other provisions, the Act requires states to enforce protective orders from different states so long as the issuing court had jurisdiction and provided due process. In cases in which mutual orders of protection were issued, only the order issued on behalf of the petitioner is enforceable unless the respondent filed a counter-petition and the court made specific findings. 18 U.S.C. §2265 (2003). *See* Emily J. Sack, *Domestic Violence Across State Lines: The Full Faith and Credit Clause, Congressional Power, and Interstate Enforcement of Protection Orders,* 98 N.W. U. L. Rev. 827 (2004). The VAWA also includes criminal penalties for crossing state lines to injure an intimate partner or violate a protective order and the Act criminalizes possession of a firearm by respondents subject to protective orders. *See* 18 U.S.C. §§922(g)(8)(9); Lisa D. May, *The Backfiring of the Domestic Violence Firearms Bans,* 14 Colum. J. Gender & L. 1 (2005).

EXAMPLES

Example 19-11

Assume that after a full hearing, an order for protection is issued against D in the State of X. D continues to contact P in spite of a "no contact" provision in the order. P no longer feels safe at the residence, so P goes to stay with a friend who lives an hour away in State Y. D tracks P down and goes to the house where P is staying with the friend. P calls the police when D arrives. Can the police in State Y enforce the order?

EXPLANATIONS

Explanation

Prior to passage of the VAWA, only a few states recognized protective orders from other states. However, the VAWA requires states to give full faith and credit to protective orders issued by other states so long as due process was provided. Consequently, the police and the courts in State Y can enforce the order originally issued in State X.

19.17. Criminal Sanctions

Violence between intimate partners involves commission of crimes such as assault, battery, rape, attempted murder, etc. Police historically were trained not to arrest abusive partners, and domestic violence was, for the most part, not treated as a crime by prosecutors. This practice changed dramatically during the 1980s due to increased awareness of the issue, studies documenting the value of arrest as a deterrent, and lawsuits against police departments.

Arrest and criminal sanctions remain an important tool for victims of abuse—especially where police, prosecutors, and courts coordinate enforcement efforts. However, research indicates that arrest is less effective with some defendants than others. Eve S. Buzawa & Carl G. Buzawa, *Domestic Violence: The Criminal Justice Response* 104 (2003) (an excellent discussion of the history and effectiveness of arrest in cases of domestic violence). For example, arrest may not be as effective with unemployed defendants and may reduce violence only in the short run. Janell D. Schmidt & Lawrence W. Sherman, *Does Arrest Deter Domestic Violence?* in Do Arrests and Restraining Orders Work? (Buzawa & Buzawa eds., 1996). Clearly, more research is needed in this area.

19.18. Mandatory Arrest and No-Drop Policies

Some jurisdictions have adopted mandatory arrest (with probable cause) and/or no-drop policies so that the decision to press criminal charges is taken out of the hands of the victim. Such policies are designed to protect traumatized victims from pressure to drop charges by having the police and prosecutor bring the charges and subpoena the victim as a witness. Critics of these policies argue that they ignore the preferences of the victims and further disempower them.

19.19. Confrontation Clause

Particularly if a victim does not testify at trial, prosecutors may seek to introduce statements made to police and medical personnel. However, under the Sixth Amendment, perpetrators facing criminal prosecution have the right to confront witnesses, and testimonial out-of-court statements cannot be admitted into evidence unless the witness is unavailable and the defendant had a prior opportunity to cross-examine. *Crawford v. Washington*, 541 U.S. 36 (2004). Recently, the United States Supreme Court held that a domestic abuse victim's statements to a 911 operator were not subject to the Confrontation Clause because they were not testimonial in nature. In contrast, a victim's written statements in an affidavit provided to police were testimonial and thus subject to the Confrontation Clause. *Davis v. Washington*, 126 S. Ct. 2266 (2006).

19.20. Tort Actions

In recent years, creative advocates have brought various tort actions on behalf of battered spouses. Such actions can be based on torts such as assault and battery, wrongful death, false imprisonment, defamation, wiretapping, and intentional infliction of emotional distress. *See* Clare Dalton, *Domestic Violence, Domestic Torts and Divorce: Constraints and Possibilities*, 31 New Eng. L. Rev. 319 (1997).

For example, in *Feltmeier v. Feltmeier*, 777 N.E.2d 1032 (Ill. Ct. App. 2002) *aff'd*, 2003 LEXIS 1421 (Ill. 2003), the court upheld an action for intentional infliction of emotional distress based upon a finding of "extreme and outrageous" conduct. The husband unsuccessfully argued that a "reasonable wife" should have been able to endure 11 years of abuse. *See also* Curtis v. Firth, 850 P.2d 749 (Idaho 1993) (upholding damage award for intentional infliction of emotional distress); *Xiao Yang Chen v. Fischer*, 843 N.E.2d 723 (N.Y. 2005) (personal injury action for damages for physical and emotional abuse during marriage not barred by res judicata). *But see Hakkila v. Hakkila*, 812 P.2d 1320 (N.M. Ct. App. 1991) (husband's conduct did not meet "outrageousness" standard).

CHAPTER 20

Child Abuse and Termination of Parental Rights

20.1. Introduction — The Scope of the Problem

In the year 2004, 872,000 children were victims of some type of child maltreatment. Most (62.4 percent) suffered neglect, 17.5 percent were abused physically, 9.7 percent were abused sexually, 7 percent were abused psychologically, and 2.1 percent were medically neglected. Nearly 1,500 children died as a result of the abuse, and 81 percent of the children who were killed were younger than four years of age. U.S. Dept. of Health and Human Services, Administration for Children and Families, *Child Maltreatment* 2004, *http://www.acf.hhs.gov/programs/cb/pubs/cm04/index.htm* (last visited 10/17/06).

State intervention into the family unit has historically been focused on strengthening and reuniting the family unit. In cases of substantiated child abuse and neglect, the state child protection agency worked with the family, sometimes for years, with the goal of returning the child to the home. This approach was questioned in the 1990s as experts expressed concern that some children who might be made available for adoption were instead stranded in foster care without any realistic hope of reunification. Thus, in recent years, new emphasis has been placed on faster termination of parental rights in order to free children in foster care for adoption.

As of 2003, 523,000 children were in foster care, and the average age of a child in foster care was ten years old. Twenty-three percent were placed in the home of a relative, but others lived in placements including non-relative foster family homes (46%), institutions (10%), and group homes (9%). The mean length of stay in foster care was 31 months. In about half the cases (48%) reunification was the stated case goal, and of children exiting foster care in 2003, 55 percent were reunited with their parent or primary caretaker. Adoption and Foster Care Analysis Reporting System (AFCARS) U.S. Department of Health and Human Services, Administration for Children and Families, Administration on Children, Youth and Families, Children's Bureau, *www.acf.hhs.gov/programs/cb/stats_research/afcars/tar/report10.htm* (last visited 10/17/06).

STANDARDS FOR STATE INTERVENTION

20.2. Parents' Right to Privacy — Liberty Interests

The raising and disciplining of children has long been considered a private family matter, and this liberty interest has historically been given constitutional protection. *Meyer v. Nebraska*, 262 U.S. 390 (1923); *Pierce v. Socy. of Sisters*, 268 U.S. 510 (1925); *Troxel v. Granville*, 530 U.S. 57 (2000). However, parents' prerogatives are not without limit. As the Supreme Court stated in *Prince v. Massachusetts*, 321 U.S. 158, 166 (1944):

> And neither rights of religion nor rights of parenthood are beyond limitation. Acting to guard the general interest in youth's well being, the state as *parens patriae* may restrict the parent's control by requiring school attendance, regulating or prohibiting the child's labor, and in many other ways.

Consequently, if there is compelling justification, such as when a child is "at risk of harm," the state may intervene in the family. *In re Juvenile Appeal* (83-CD), 455 A.2d 1319 (Conn. 1983). However, statutes prescribing when intervention may occur may not be vague or overly broad. *Roe v. Conn*, 417 F. Supp. 769, 778 (D.C. Ala. 1976) (standard that "the child is in such condition that its welfare requires" is unconstitutionally vague and infringes on fundamental right); Scott A. Davidson, *When Is Parental Discipline Child Abuse? The Vagueness of Child Abuse Laws*, 34 U. Louisville J. Fam. L. 403, 409 (1996).

20.3. Indian Child Welfare Act (ICWA)

Special protections are provided for Native American children under the Indian Child Welfare Act (ICWA). The Act requires clear and convincing evidence of serious emotional or physical damage before a child is removed from the home. 25 U.S.C. §1912(e). In addition, absent good cause to the contrary, if an Indian child is removed from the home, the Act requires that the child be placed in foster care with extended family, in a foster home approved by the tribe or a licensing authority, or in an institution approved of or operated by an Indian organization. 25 U.S.C. §1915(b).

20.4. Defining Abuse, Neglect, and Dependency

State statutes define the circumstances under which the state will intervene in the family. States historically have separately defined abuse, neglect, and dependency. Abuse typically involves excessive corporal punishment, sexual abuse, or serious psychological abuse. Neglect is associated with failure to provide food, housing, or meet medical or educational needs. Dependency is similar to neglect except that the lack of care occurs due to circumstances beyond the parent's control and without fault on the part of the parent.

Some states do not distinguish among abuse, neglect, and dependency but instead use a definition that includes all three. For example, the relevant California statute merges neglect and abuse into the definition of dependent child.

Cal. Welf. & Inst. Code §300 (West 2006). Children Subject to Jurisdiction. . . .

Any child who comes within any of the following descriptions is within the jurisdiction of the juvenile court which may adjudge that person to be a dependent child of the court.

(a) The child has suffered, or there is a substantial risk that the child will suffer, serious physical harm inflicted nonaccidentally upon the child by the child's parent or guardian. . . .

(b) The child has suffered, or there is a substantial risk that the child will suffer, serious physical harm or illness, as a result of the failure or inability of his or her parent or guardian to adequately supervise or protect the child, or the willful or negligent failure of the child's parent or guardian to adequately supervise or protect the child from the conduct of the custodian with whom the child has been left, or by the willful or negligent failure of the parent or guardian to provide the child with adequate food, clothing, shelter, or medical treatment, or by the inability of the parent or guardian to provide regular care for the child due to the parent's or guardian's mental illness, developmental disability, or substance abuse. . . .

(c) The child is suffering serious emotional damage, or is at substantial risk of suffering serious emotional damage, evidenced by severe anxiety, depression, withdrawal, or untoward aggressive behavior toward self or others, as a result of the conduct of the parent or guardian or who has no parent or guardian capable of providing appropriate care. . . .

(d) The child has been sexually abused or there is substantial risk that the child will be sexually abused. . . .
(e) The child is under the age of five and has suffered severe physical abuse by a parent, or by any person known by the parent, if the parent knew or reasonably should have known that the person was physically abusing the child. . . .
(f) The child's parent or guardian caused the death of another child through abuse or neglect. . . .
(g) The child has been subjected to an act or acts of cruelty by the parent or guardian or a member of his or her household or the parent or guardian has failed to adequately protect the child from an act or acts of cruelty when the parent or guardian knew or reasonably should have known that the child was in danger of being subjected to an act or acts of cruelty.
(h) The child's sibling has been abused or neglected. . . .

The following sections discuss how courts have interpreted and applied similar statutory provisions.

POSSIBLE FORMS OF ABUSE AND NEGLECT

20.5. Use of Unreasonable Force to Correct a Child

Parents can legally use reasonable force to correct a child. *South Carolina Dept. of Soc. Servs. v. Father and Mother*, 366 S.E.2d 40, 42 (S.C. Ct. App. 1988) (force or violence of discipline must be "reasonable in manner and moderate in degree"); *State v. Lefevre*, 117 P.3d 980 (N.M. App. 2005).

The Restatement (Second) of Torts §147 provides that "[a] parent is privileged to apply such reasonable force or to impose such reasonable confinement upon his child as he reasonably believes to be necessary for its proper control, training, or education. . . ." Section 150 lists factors to be considered in determining whether the action was reasonable:

(a) whether the actor is a parent;
(b) the age, sex, and physical and mental condition of the child;
(c) the nature of his offense and his apparent motive;
(d) the influence of his example upon other children of the same family or group;
(e) whether the force or confinement is reasonably necessary and appropriate to compel obedience to a proper command;
(f) whether it is disproportionate to the offense, unnecessarily degrading, or likely to cause serious or permanent harm.

20.6. Spanking

Spanking children is a matter of some controversy, and judges may be called upon to distinguish reasonable use of force from that which is excessive. For example, in *Raboin v. North Dakota Dept. of Human Servs,* 552 N.W.2d 329 (N.D. 1996), the court held that bruising on the buttocks resulting from the use of a wooden spoon, plastic spoon, or belt did not constitute child abuse. However, the concurring judge frowned upon the use of corporal punishment, stating that it "can only diminish a child's sense of self-worth, and thereby unnecessarily limit the resources that child can bring to life's battles." *Id.* at 335.

Sweden, Norway, Denmark, Finland, and Austria have prohibited corporal punishment, and opponents of the practice have urged the United States to ratify the United Nations Convention on the Rights of the Child, which would prohibit its use.

Example 20-1

Assume that a 13-year-old girl, X, comes home at 2:00 A.M. from a party even though she promised to be home by 11:00 P.M. Her father, D, is angry and frightened by X's failure to return home on time or call. He strikes the girl twice with his belt, leaving two large purple bruises, one on her thigh and the other on the back of her leg. D claims that X bruises easily and that he didn't use excessive force. X reports that D also struck her in the face with his hand, causing her ears to ring for the next 24 hours. D denies hitting X in the face and argues that X had no bruises on her face and no witnesses to support her claim. Assume that the jurisdiction has a civil dependency statute identical to the statute presented in Section 21.4 above. Is it likely that a court would declare X to be dependent?

Explanation

The state child protection agency will argue that X falls under paragraph (a) of the dependency statute because X has suffered serious physical harm inflicted nonaccidentally by her parent. D will argue that the bruises on X's thigh and leg do not constitute serious physical harm because X has no broken bones and no permanent disfigurement and that there is no evidence of a substantial risk that future serious harm will occur. Given that D struck X with a belt with enough force to leave physical marks, a court would likely rule that X is dependent under the statute. However, without more, the court will probably require that D participate in a parenting class or go to counseling rather than placing X in foster care. *See South Carolina Dept. of Soc. Servs. v. Father and Mother,* 366 S.E.2d 40 (S.C. Ct. App. 1988).

20.7. Sexual Abuse

Girls are three times more likely to be sexually abused than boys, and children from families with incomes below $15,000 per year are as much as 18 times more likely to be sexually abused. However, half of sexually abused children are abused by someone other than a parent or parent-substitute. U.S. Dept. of Health & Human Services, Administration for Children and Families, *Executive Summary of the Third National Incidence Study of Child Abuse and Neglect* (1996) *http://www.healthieryou.com/cabuse.html* (last visited 10-17-06).

In *State v. J.Q.*, 617 A.2d 1196 (N.J. 1993), the court discussed behavioral indications of possible sexual abuse, known as the Child Sexual Abuse Accommodation Syndrome (CSAAS). These behaviors include overt or indirect disclosures, sexualized play, withdrawal, feelings of shame and guilt, falling grades, pseudomature personality development, sexual promiscuity, problems with peer relationships, attempted suicide, exhibiting positive relationship with the abuser, and being frightened or phobic.

Proving sexual abuse can be especially difficult because sexual abuse is rarely observed by a third party. Expert testimony is often required. *See State v. Waddell*, 504 S.E.2d 84 (N.C. Ct. App. 1998), *aff'd as modified*, 527 S.E.2d 644 (N.C. 2000) (discussion of issues related to child competency, hearsay, and use of anatomically correct dolls); *In re Jaclyn P.*, 179 A.D.2d 646 (N.Y. 1992), *aff'd*, 658 N.E.2d 1042 (N.Y. Ct. App. 1995). In cases of sexual abuse, some states specifically authorize the use of anatomically correct dolls to aid courtroom testimony. 42 Pa.C.S.A. § 5987 (2004).

20.8. Failure to Protect from Harm

In addition to not harming children, parents have a legal obligation to protect children from known or reasonably anticipated danger. Thus a parent who fails to intercede to protect a child may be the focus of scrutiny by the child protection agency even though he or she did not affirmatively harm the child. For example, in *People v. T.G.*, 578 N.W.2d 921 (S.D. 1998), a mother knew that the stepfather was sexually molesting her daughters but ignored and concealed the abuse. Sadly, the mother herself had been "sold" to adoptive parents and sexually abused as a child. Nevertheless, her parental rights were terminated because of her failure to protect her daughters.

EXAMPLES

Example 20-2

Assume the same facts as in Example 21-1except that M, X's mother, was present during the incident. M was extremely alarmed when X did not return home on time, and she began calling hospital emergency rooms, fearing that X had been in an accident. M feared that she was losing control of X, and she asked D, the father, to "lay down the law" to X. M saw D strike X multiple times with the belt and saw D hit X in the face. M told the child protection worker that D's use of force was appropriate and justified in order to "get X's attention." Assume that the statute found in Section 21.4 is in effect in this jurisdiction. Is M also likely to be the subject of the child protection investigation?

Explanation

The child protection agency could argue that M falls within paragraph (i) of the dependency statute under the theory that M witnessed X being subjected to acts of cruelty by D and that M failed to adequately protect X. M will argue that D acted reasonably to discipline X and that X was not subjected to acts of cruelty under the statute. Furthermore, no other incidents of abuse are alleged. In many cases where failure to protect is alleged, there is an ongoing pattern of abuse such as sexual abuse. However, under the terms of the statute, failure to protect can be shown based on one incident. In a case somewhat similar to this hypothetical, the court found that M was guilty of neglect because she did not intervene or report the incident. *South Carolina Dept. of Soc. Servs. v. Father and Mother*, 366 S.E.2d 40 (S.C. Ct. App. 1988). *See also In re Craig T.*, 744 A.2d 621 (N.H. 1999) (mother did not intervene to protect young child who was hit and shaken by father at shopping mall).

20.9. Failure to Protect from Harm: Domestic Violence

Removal of children for failure to protect has been especially controversial in cases of domestic violence. As noted in Chapter 20, there are many reasons why a victim of domestic violence may remain in the home, including the fact that the abuser may threaten to kill the victim or kidnap the children if the victim attempts to leave. Nevertheless, children growing up in violent homes suffer harm from witnessing abuse, and they may also be physically abused themselves. Consequently, if the victim does not leave the home, her children may be removed by the state on the basis that she failed to protect them. However, in a lawsuit regarding a New York policy, *Nicholson v. Scoppetta*, 820 N.E.2d 840 (Ct. App. N.Y. 2004), the court held that evidence that a caretaker allowed a child to witness domestic abuse was insufficient on its own to establish neglect. *See* Justine A. Dunlap, *Sometimes I Feel like a Motherless Child: The Error of Pursuing Battered Mothers for Failure to Protect*, 50 Loy. L. Rev. 565 (2004); Beth A. Mandel, *The White Fist of the Child Welfare System: Racism, Patriarchy, and the Presumptive Removal of Children from Victims of Domestic Violence in Nicholson v. Williams*, 73 U. Cin. L. Rev. 1131 (2005); and Evan Stark, *A Failure to Protect: Unraveling the "Battered Mother's Dilemma,"* 27 W. St. U. L. Rev. 29 (1999-2000).

20.10. Prenatal Drug Abuse

Drug and alcohol use are frequently linked to child abuse and neglect. Many children are exposed to drugs and alcohol prior to birth. As a result, these children are likely to have special needs and be particularly difficult to parent. Unfortunately, a mother's ability to cope is likely to be severely compromised by continued substance abuse. Because this is a dangerous combination of dynamics, child protection workers frequently try to intervene in such cases. *See* Elizabeth Bartholet, *Nobody's Children* 68-69 (1999). However, intervention may be limited by the fact that some state courts hold that a fetus is not a "child" within the meaning of child protection statutes. *State ex rel. Angela M.W. v. Kruzicki,* 561 N.W.2d 729 (Wis. 1997). Policy makers also fear that criminal prosecution of substance-abusing mothers would discourage these women from seeking prenatal care and consequently bring more harm than benefit to unborn children. *Johnson v. State,* 602 So. 2d 1288 (Fla. 1992).

In contrast, other state courts have held that the term *child* includes a viable fetus and that a mother can be criminally liable for the death of a stillborn child related to drug use. *State v. McKnight,* 576 S.E.2d 168 (S.C. 2003). In addition, some state statutes include prenatal substance abuse in the definition of neglect. For example, Minn. Stat. §626.556(2)(f)(6) (2006) defines neglect to include prenatal exposure to a controlled substance as evidenced by withdrawal symptoms, toxicological testing, medical effects, or developmental delays during the first year of life.

EXAMPLES

Example 20-3

Assume that a twelve-year-old boy resides with his mother and father. He was awake in his bedroom when law enforcement officers executed a search warrant based on the alleged drug use of his parents. The officers found one gram of marijuana in a trash can and another gram loose on a coffee table. They uncovered residual amounts of cocaine in the kitchen and other drugs in the parents' bedroom. The police called child protection, and the trial court found that the child was abused, neglected, and at imminent risk of being abused and neglected. The parents argued that there was no evidence presented that the child had come in contact with the drugs or paraphernalia and there was similarly no evidence that the child was denied food, clothing, or medical care. They appealed the decision. What is the likely outcome?

Explanation

In this case the appellate court reasoned that exposing a child to controlled substances is harmful if it occurs during the mother's pregnancy or when chronic drug use by a parent "demonstrably adversely" affects the child. The appellate court found that there was no evidence presented to support either assertion in this case. The court further reasoned that the child was not neglected because he was not deprived of food, clothing, shelter, etc. as defined under the statute. Finally the court found that the child was not in imminent danger of abuse or neglect because no nexus was shown between the parents' behavior and impending abuse or neglect of the child. *J. B., III v. Dept. of Children and Families*, 2006 WL 1027006 (April 7, 2006).

20.11. Emotional or Mental Abuse

Emotional abuse or neglect can be grounds for state intervention. Emotional abuse often accompanies physical abuse but can be more difficult to prove. Emotional abuse can also arise on its own. For example, in *In Interest of B.B.*, 500 N.W.2d 9 (Iowa 1993), a child suffered emotional harm when, because of his mother's obsession with his health, he was not allowed to attend school.

Example 20-4

Assume that X is a five-year-old child who attends kindergarten. His teacher is concerned that he is very anxious and withdrawn. X has never spoken and he cries easily. He is sometimes observed pinching himself until he has black and blue marks. The teacher contacts X's parents and asks them to attend a meeting about X. X's father comes to the meeting with X. At the meeting he calls X a "dummy" and tells the teacher that X is "nothing but trouble." The teacher urges the father to accept help for X, but the father refuses to do so. After the meeting, the teacher reports the situation to child protection. Assume that this hypothetical situation takes place in a jurisdiction with a statute identical to that found in Section 21.4. Is this the sort of case in which child protection services should intervene?

Explanation

The child protection worker could argue that X falls under paragraph (c) of the statute because X is suffering serious emotional damage evidenced by severe anxiety and withdrawal as a result of the belittling conduct of the father. The father might argue that X is merely having trouble adjusting to kindergarten and that X's behavior has nothing to do with the father's parenting style. Paragraph (c) of the statute is carefully drafted to focus on the impact of alleged emotional abuse on the child. In this case the teacher feels strongly that X is exhibiting behavior not normally seen in children adjusting to kindergarten. Although there is not a great deal of evidence linking the father's conduct to X's problems, the father's behavior at the meeting and his refusal to accept help for X would likely spur additional investigation by child protection.

20.12. Neglect

The term *neglect* refers to many situations and conditions that may occur separately or concurrently. Common themes include lack of food, lack of appropriate housing, lack of medical care, lack of supervision, failure to thrive, and irregular school attendance. Not surprisingly, findings of neglect are often linked to poverty. *See* Elizabeth Bartholet, *Nobody's Children*, 33 (1999) (noting that children from families with incomes under $15,000 annually are 44 times more likely to be neglected than children from families with annual incomes over $30,000).

Example 20-5

Assume that a father was incarcerated and left his three children in the care of his longtime girlfriend. She did not have legal custody over them, and the children were consequently taken briefly by their drug-using biological mother. Neglect proceedings were filed, and the state argued that an incarcerated parent *ipso facto* could not adequately care for children. The father argued that he had arranged for someone else (his girlfriend) to care for the children and that no nexus was shown between his unavailability and the condition of the children. What is the likely result?

Explanation

In *In re* T.T.C., 855 A.2d 1117 (D.C. 2004), the court agreed with the father that incarceration did not *ipso facto* constitute neglect. However, the court found that the father had put the children at risk by not granting his girlfriend (or someone else) legal authorization to care for the children and had consequently left them open to being taken by their unsuitable biological mother. The adjudication of neglect was affirmed.

20.13. Housing and Housekeeping

Children are sometimes removed from their parents' care because of housing problems. Critics allege that caseworkers may be overzealous in removing children from "dirty houses." However, courts commonly intervene in such cases.

Example 20-6

Assume that a child protection worker visits the home of a child while investigating a complaint of neglect. The worker finds that the apartment reeks of cat feces and urine and is filled with garbage and overflowing ash trays. Dirty dishes are stacked all over the kitchen, and the only food in the refrigerator is milk, eggs, and ketchup. Two litters of cats are living under the bed, and cats have defecated in the bathtub and on some of the child's clothing. Do these conditions constitute neglect? If so, should the child be placed in foster care?

Explanation

This fact situation is based on *In Interest of N.M.W.*, 461 N.W.2d 478, 479 (Iowa Ct. App. 1990), in which the appellate court upheld the finding of neglect. The dissenting judge agreed that the mother was "an extremely poor housekeeper," but argued that the child's interest would have been better served by having the house cleaned instead of placing the child in foster care. *Id.* at 482. She argued that a wealthier mother would have been able to hire someone to clean and that there was no evidence that "only people in clean houses were good parents." *Id.* at 483.

20.14. Medical Treatment

Difficult issues arise when parents withhold medical treatment for religious reasons. Some states have statutes providing that good-faith treatment by prayer does not constitute neglect. Del. Code Ann. tit. 10 §901(11) (2006). However, if the child dies, the parent may be subject to criminal prosecution. For example, in the case of *Walker v. Superior Court*, 763 P.2d 852 (Cal. 1988), a parent was criminally prosecuted for failure to seek medical care for a child who died of meningitis after being treated through prayer. *See also In re McCauley*, 565 N.W.2d 411 (Mass. 1991) (court authorized blood transfusion over contrary religious beliefs of parents).

DISCOVERING ABUSE AND NEGLECT

20.15. Mandated Reporting

Professionals who come into frequent contact with children are required to report abuse and neglect. Mandatory reporters typically include teachers, physicians, and therapists, although clergy and attorneys may also be required to report. With respect to physical abuse occurring in 2004, 24.1 percent of incidents were reported by educators, 21.8 percent by law enforcement, and 11 percent by medical personnel. U.S. Dept. of Health & Human Services, Administration for Children and Families, *Child Maltreatment 2004, http://www.acf.hhs.gov/programs/cb/pubs/cm04/chapterthree.htm.*

States grant immunity for good-faith mistakes in making reports that turn out to be unfounded. However, mandated reporters can be civilly or criminally liable for failing to report abuse and neglect. *See Landeros v. Flood,* 551 P.2d 389 (Cal. 1976).

20.16. Central Registry of Reports

Some states maintain a central registry of reports that can be used by some prospective employers. For example, a New York reporting statute required health care workers, social workers, education employees, law enforcement agents, and judicial officers to report child maltreatment. After investigation, if there was "some credible evidence" of maltreatment, the name of the alleged perpetrator was placed on a central register made available to child care employers. Noting a high risk of possible error, the Second Circuit found that the alleged perpetrators' due process rights were violated by the statutory scheme. *Valmonte v. Bane,* 18 F.3d 992 (2d Cir. 1994). *See also Division of Youth and Family Services v. D.F.,* 781 A.2d 699 (N.J. Super. A.D. 2005) (mother's name placed on registry even though no child protective action filed) and *DuBray v. S.D. Dept. of Social Services,* 690 N.W.2d 657 (S.D. 2004) (removed mother's name from registry after it had been placed there based on hearsay evidence).

ADJUDICATION AND DISPOSITION

20.17. Two-Stage Proceedings

Civil juvenile proceedings usually involve a two-stage procedure. First, a jurisdictional hearing is held to establish that the child falls within the relevant state statutory definition of a neglected, abused, or dependent child. *People ex rel. U.S.*, 121 P.3d 326 (Col. Ct. App. 2005) (court did not have statutory authority over a mother where there was no adjudication of dependency or neglect by her). Second, a dispositional hearing is held to determine whether the child should remain with the parent subject to conditions, should be placed in foster care, or should be sent to an institution. If the child is removed from the home, the state agency will begin to plan concurrently for the reunification of the family and the possibility of terminating parental rights.

20.18. Procedures when Child Is in Immediate Danger

In emergency situations, when a child is in immediate danger, the state may assume temporary custody of children. For example, Kentucky Revised Statutes provide as follows:

§620.060. Emergency custody orders

(1) The court for the county where the child is present may issue an ex parte emergency custody order when it appears to the court that removal is in the best interest of the child and that there are reasonable grounds to believe, as supported by affidavit or by recorded sworn testimony, that one (1) or more of the following conditions exist and that the parents or other person exercising custodial control or supervision are unable or unwilling to protect the child:

(a) The child is in danger of imminent death or serious physical injury or is being sexually abused;
(b) The parent has repeatedly inflicted or allowed to be inflicted by other than accidental means physical injury or emotional injury. This condition shall not include reasonable and ordinary discipline recognized in the community where the child lives, as long as reasonable and ordinary discipline does not result in abuse or neglect as defined in KRS 600.020(1); or
(c) The child is in immediate danger due to the parent's failure or refusal to provide for the safety or needs of the child.

In Kentucky, a petition must be filed with the court within 72 hours of taking the child into custody. *See also Doe v. Kearney*, 329 F.3d 1286 (11th Cir. 2003) (upholding Florida statute permitting removal of children without court order when caseworker had probable cause to believe that children were in imminent danger of abuse). *See also* Mark R. Brown, *Rescuing Children from Abusive Parents: The Constitutional Value of Pre-Deprivation Process*, 65 Ohio St. L.J. 913 (2004).

Example 20-7

Assume that you are a judge in a jurisdiction with a statute identical to the Kentucky statute found in Section 21.18. On a Friday afternoon you are presented with an affidavit stating that a teacher has reported a fourth-grade student who came to school that day with bruises and what appear to be cigarette burns on her arms. The child told the investigating caseworker, who was called to the school by the teacher, that the bruises resulted from an accidental fall down the stairs and that the other marks were bug bites. The experienced caseworker does not believe the child and asserts that the child will be in danger over the weekend. Will you issue an *ex parte* removal order?

Explanation

The statute allows issuance of an *ex parte* custody order if it is in the best interests of the child and there are reasonable grounds to believe that the child is in danger of serious physical injury or the child is in immediate danger because of a parent's failure to provide for the child's safety. This is the sort of case that is difficult to resolve without expert medical evidence. However, a judge is likely to give more credence to physical indications and the opinions of the teacher and caseworker than the protestations of a child who may be afraid to disclose the possible abuse. The judge probably has reasonable grounds to believe that the child is in immediate danger.

20.19. Alternative Responses

Intervention of the state into the family system is inherently coercive in nature and can be upsetting to families in and of itself. Consequently, states are exploring innovative approaches aimed at establishing more positive relationships with struggling families. States such as Kentucky, Minnesota, Missouri, New Jersey, Oklahoma, and Wyoming authorize alternative approaches that are less confrontational and more assessment-oriented (and which may not require a formal finding of abuse or neglect) where children are at lower risk. Gila R. Shusterman et al., *Alternative Responses to Child Maltreatment: Findings from NCANDS, http://aspe.hhs.gov/hsp/05/child-maltreat-resp/* (last visited 10-17-06).

20.20. Alternative Dispute Resolution

In order to promote better communication and planning, more than half the states offer mediation or some form of alternative dispute resolution in child protection cases. There is some evidence that mediation shortens the length of time spent by children in foster care as well as reducing costs. *See* Kelly Browe Olson, *Lessons Learned from a Child Protection Mediation Program: If at First You Don't Succeed and Then You Don't . . .*, 41 Fam. Ct. Rev. 480 (2003).

20.21. Foster Care: Safety and Accountability

In the well-known case of *DeShaney v. Winnebago County Dept. of Soc. Servs.*, 489 U.S. 189 (1989), a boy was beaten and permanently injured by his father after repeated involvement with the department of social services. The Court held that there was no due process violation because there was no special relationship giving rise to a duty to protect. Because the boy was in the physical care of his father, the state had no obligation to protect him from abuse. Following *DeShaney*, courts have recognized due process violations where the state has established a special relationship with the child or if the state affirmatively places an individual in danger. *Waubanascum v. Shawano County*, 416 F.3d 658, 665 (7th Cir. 2005). *See also Radke v. County of Freeborn*, 694 N.W.2d 788 (Minn. 2005) (wrongful death action against workers for negligent investigation of abuse reports).

When a child is placed in foster care, the state is viewed as having a special relationship with that child and the state may have a consequent duty to protect him or her while in foster care. *Lewis v. Anderson*, 308 F.3d 768 (7th Cir. 2002) (state must know or suspect likely abuse); *Nicini v. Morra*, 212 F.3d 798 (3d Cir. 2000) (conduct did not "shock the conscience"); *Lintz v. Skipski*, 25 F.3d 304 (6th Cir. 1994) (insufficient evidence of deliberate indifference); *Braam ex rel. Braam v. State*, 81 P.3d 851 (Wash. 2003) (whether state conduct falls substantially short of the exercise of professional judgment, standards, or practices); *Weatherford ex rel. Michael L. v. State*, 81 P.3d 320 (Ariz. 2003) (whether workers acted with deliberate indifference); *Miller v. Martin*, 838 So. 2d 761 (La. 2003) (state vicariously liable for intentional abuse by foster parents); *Mosher-Simons v. County of Allegany*, 783 N.E.2d 509 (N.Y. 2002) (court ordered home study "cloaked in judicial immunity").

Experts believe that frequent visits from caseworkers are key to keeping children safe in foster care. As a result of lawsuits, consent decrees, and collaborations with child advocacy groups, 43 states have adopted standards calling for monthly caseworker visits to children in foster care. However, 27 states have been cited as needing improvement in this area. Department of Health and Human Services, Office of Inspector General, *State Standards and Capacity to Track Frequency of Caseworker Visits with Children in Foster Care* (2005) http://oig.hhs.gov/oei/reports/oei-04-03-00350.pdf (last visited 10-17-06).

CHILD WITNESSES (TRIAL CONSIDERATIONS)

20.22. Victim as Witness

Proving abuse, particularly sexual abuse, can be especially challenging because the abuse takes place in private and a young child may be the only witness. Consequently, the state may call the child as a witness, seek to admit out-of-court statements, and/or attempt to use "syndrome" testimony.

20.23. Competency to Testify

Under the Federal Rules of Evidence Rule 601, children can testify without first establishing competence. While some states have adopted this approach, other states require inquiry about the child's understanding of the oath (truthfulness) or a full inquiry voir dire. Lucy S. McGough, *Child Witnesses: Fragile Voices in the American Legal System* 96 (1994); Nancy Walker Perry & Lawrence S. Wrightsman, *The Child Witness: Legal Issues and Dilemmas* (1991).

20.24. Right of Criminal Defendant to Confront Child

A child traumatized by abuse is likely to be traumatized again if required to testify in the presence of the abuser. On the other hand, a criminal defendant accused of abuse has a Sixth Amendment right to confront witnesses. In *Maryland v. Craig*, 497 U.S. 836 (1990), the Supreme Court accommodated both interests by approving the use of one-way closed circuit television. The court noted that at the time of the decision a majority of states allowed use of videotaped testimony under similar circumstances.

In some criminal prosecutions, the child victim may be deemed incompetent to testify. In such cases, prosecutors may attempt to introduce testimony about statements that the child made to medical personnel or investigators. In some situations this testimony may run afoul of the Supreme Court's holding in *Crawford v. Washington*, 541 U.S. 36 (2004), that testimonial out-of-court statements are not admissible in criminal cases unless the witness is unavailable and the defendant had a prior opportunity to cross-examine the witness. However, in *State v. Scacchetti*, 711 N.W.2d 508 (Minn. 2006), statements made by a 3½-year-old to a pediatric nurse were held not to be testimonial, and their admission into evidence did not violate the Sixth Amendment. In reaching its decision, the court placed particular emphasis on the identity (nongovernmental actor) and purpose (medical treatment) of the questioner. *See also* Kamala London et al., *Disclosure of Child Sexual Abuse: What Does the Research Tell Us About the Ways That Children Tell?*, 11 Psychol. Pub. Pol'y & L. 194 (2005) (exploring empirical data).

20.25. Syndrome Testimony

During the 1960s researchers labeled a cluster of symptoms as the "battered child syndrome." Battered child syndrome involves the infliction of multiple injuries over a period of time. When discovered, the injuries are in various stages of healing and the parents' explanations of the injuries are inconsistent with the medical evidence. Expert knowledge is necessary to identify battered child syndrome. *Estelle v. McGuire*, 502 U.S. 62, 66 (1991) (battered child syndrome exists when "a child has sustained repeated and/ or serious injuries by nonaccidental means"). *See also Commonwealth v. Rodgers*, 528 A.2d 610 (Pa. Super. 1987); *State v. Dumlao*, 491 A.2d 404 (Conn. App. 1985).

Significant controversy exists over the use of testimony concerning syndromes such as Child Sexual Abuse Accommodation Syndrome (CSAAS), Battering Parent Syndrome (BPS), and Battered Child Syndrome (BCS). *See* Sarah J. Ramsey & Robert F. Kelly, *Social Science Knowledge in Family Law Cases: Judicial Gate-Keeping in the Daubert Era*, 59 U. Miami L. Rev. 1 (2004); *Estelle v. McGuire*, 502 U.S. 62, 70 (1991) (testimony regarding BCS did not violate defendant's right to due process); *People v. Peterson*, 537 N.W.2d 857 (Mich. 1995) (limited use of CSAAS testimony); *State v. MacLennan*, 702 N.W.2d 219 (Minn. 2005) (admissibility of BCS determined under rules of evidence).

TERMINATION OF PARENTAL RIGHTS

20.26. Legal Consequences of Termination

Termination of parental rights severs the parent-child relationship and makes the child available for adoption. The parent loses the right to see the child, and the child has no right to financial support from the parent or to inherit property upon the parent's death. *But see In re Stephen Tyler R.*, 584 S.E.2d 581 (W. Va. 2003) (under specially drafted statutory provision, terminated father ordered to pay child support) and Richard L. Brown, *Disinheriting the "Legal Orphan": Inheritance Rights of Children after Termination of Parental Rights*, 70 Mo. L. Rev. 125 (2005) (arguing for a change in the law to allow inheritance after termination). Because termination involves constitutional rights and is such a drastic remedy, special procedural precautions are required. In 2005, 66,000 children had their parental rights terminated. *Trends in Foster Care and Adoption — FY 2000-FY 2005*, U.S. Department of Health and Human Services, Administration for Children and Families, Children's Bureau *http://www.acf.hhs.gov/programs/cb/stats_research/afcars/trends.htm* (last visited 11-02-06).

20.27. Grounds for Termination

Statutes typically provide specific grounds and requirements for termination of parental rights. Termination may be sought when there has been chronic abuse and neglect, abandonment, parental incapacity, and abuse of a sibling or termination of parental rights of a sibling. As discussed below, with some exceptions states may seek termination of parental rights pursuant to the Adoption and Safe Families Act if a child has been placed outside of the home for 15 of the preceding 22 months. *See In re Parental Rights as to D.R.H.*, 92 P.3d 1230 (Nev. 2004) (upholding termination where child placed outside the home for 14 of 20 months).

20.28. Adoption Assistance and Child Welfare Act (AACWA)

In 1980 Congress passed AACWA as a result of concern about children languishing in foster care. The Act stressed reunification of the family but encouraged adoption in cases where reunification was not realistic. In order to receive matching funds, states were required to make "reasonable efforts" to prevent removal or reunify the family. States were also required to undertake "permanency planning" and make periodic case reviews. In *Suter v. Artist M.*, 503 U.S. 347 (1992), the Supreme Court held that there was no implied right of action to enforce the reasonable efforts language in AACWA.

20.29. Adoption and Safe Families Act (ASFA)

In 1997 Congress enacted ASFA to limit the amount of time children spend in foster care (known as foster care drift) and to speed adoption. The Act requires states to pursue termination of parental rights if children have been in foster care for 15 of the preceding 22 months. (This provision does not apply if the child has been placed with a relative, if termination is not believed to be in the best interests of the child, or if reunification services have not been provided.) Permanency hearings are to occur within a year, but "reasonable efforts" to reunify are not required where there are "aggravated circumstances" (such as sexual abuse) or parental rights to a sibling have been terminated. *See* Stephanie Jill Gendell, *In Search of Permanency: A Reflection on the*

First Three Years of the Adoption and Safe Families Act, 39 Fam. & Conciliation Cts. Rev. 25 (2001) and Kurtis A. Kemper, *Construction and Application by State Courts of the Federal Adoption and Safe Families Act and Its Implementing State Statutes*, 10 A.L.R. 6th 173 (2006).

Critics of ASFA believe that inadequate resources and the Act's aggressive timelines have worked to the detriment of children and families. William Wesley Patton & Amy M. Pellman, *The Reality of Concurrent Planning: Juggling Multiple Family Plans Expeditiously without Sufficient Resources*, 9 U.C. Davis J. Juv. L. & Pol'y 171 (2005); Martin Guggenheim & Christine Gottliev, *Justice Denied: Delays in Resolving Child Protection Cases in New York*, 12 Va. J. Soc. Pol'y & L. 546 (2005); Catherine J. Ross, *The Tyranny of Time: Vulnerable Children, "Bad" Mothers, and Statutory Deadlines in Parental Termination Proceedings*, 11 Va. J. Soc. Pol'y & L. 176 (2004).

20.30. Reasonable and Active Efforts by the State

Under the Adoption Assistance and Child Welfare Act, states are required to make "reasonable efforts" to prevent removal and reunify the family prior to terminating parental rights. However, under ASFA, such efforts are not required when there are "aggravated circumstances" or parental rights to a sibling have been terminated. *See* Anne Kathleen S. Bean, *Reasonable Efforts: What State Courts Think*, 36 Tol. L. Rev. 321 (2005).

If termination proceedings involve a Native American child, the Indian Child Welfare Act requires that "active efforts" be made to provide services designed to prevent removal of the child from the family, and this requirement is not overridden by AFSA. 25 U.S.C. §1912(d); *People ex rel J.S.B., Jr.*, 691 N.W.2d 611 (S.D. 2005). However, in *J.S. v. State*, 50 P.3d 388 (Alaska 2002), the father was convicted of sexual abuse, and, citing the aggravating circumstances language in ASFA, the court held that active efforts to reunify the family were not required under ICWA.

Example 20-8

Assume that a 4½-year-old child, C, was placed in a foster home after her mother, D, developed cancer and was diagnosed with a schizoid personality disorder. At the time C was placed in foster care, she was dirty and hungry, and her mother characterized her as a defiant child. C was formally evaluated by a team of experts and was diagnosed with reactive attachment disorder, ADHD, and oppositional-defiant disorder. It was determined that she consequently needed a particularly high level of care. The child protection agency developed a case plan aimed at reunifying the family and the plan was accepted by the court. The mother attended therapy sessions individually and with C in compliance with the treatment plan, but she failed to attend parenting classes, participate in a bonding study, or maintain regular contact with C. The therapist who saw C and her mother jointly strongly recommended termination of parental rights. In contrast, the foster parents coped well with C. After C had been in foster care for two and a half years, the state moved to terminate D's parental rights. In order to terminate, the state was required to show that reasonable efforts had been made to assist D in parenting and that there was little likelihood that the situation would change in the foreseeable future. D argued that, given her health and psychological problems, she had complied with as much of the treatment plan as she could and that she needed more assistance from child protection. At trial one of the experts described the mother as "an eccentric person with a 'crusty demeanor' and a tendency to 'shut down' when she is feeling defensive," but he did note some improvement in her interpersonal skills. Is a court likely to terminate parental rights under these circumstances?

Explanation

This fact situation is based on the case of *State ex rel. Children, Youth & Families Dept.*, 47 P.3d 859 (N.M. Ct. App. 2002), in which the court upheld termination of the mother's parental rights. The court considered the requirements of ASFA with respect to the state's obligation to make reasonable efforts to reunify the family and determined that the state had made reasonable, if not perfect, efforts to assist D. Because of the child's special needs and the mother's major parenting deficits, the court did not see any likelihood of change in the foreseeable future.

Example 20-9

Assume that three minor children were placed in foster care because their mother, due to drug use, had failed to protect them and they suffered serious emotional damage. As a part of the treatment plan, the mother was required to stop using drugs. However, she continued to use methamphetamine and was in fact arrested for drug use while the children were in foster care. The mother repeatedly sought visitation with the children but was prevented from seeing them because she failed to pass a drug test as required in the treatment plan. Pursuant to a statutory provision, after six months of no contact, the state ended reunification services and scheduled a permanency planning hearing likely to lead to termination of parental rights. The mother claimed that the department had actively prevented her from visiting the children despite her requests and was now accusing her of not maintaining contact with the children. She asserted that she was entitled to a full year of reunification services before her parental rights could be terminated. What is the likely result?

Explanation

In the similar case of *Sara M. v. Superior Court*, 116 P.3d 550 (Cal. 2005), the court found that the department made reasonable efforts to reunify the family. The appellate court upheld the trial court's finding that the mother was appropriately prevented from seeing the children while under the influence of drugs. Furthermore the court held that under California law, reunification services could be terminated where clear and convincing evidence showed that a parent had not contacted the children for six months after the start of services. *But see In re O.S.*, 848 N.E.2d 130 (Ill. App. 2006) (termination reversed where department kept true identity of mother a secret from young son — she was introduced to the child as "Jenny" — but her parental rights were ultimately terminated in part because she had not established a parent-child bond with the boy).

Example 20-10

Assume that a child, X, was placed in foster care based on his mother's inability to deal effectively with his health and behavioral problems. As part of the family treatment plan, the mother was required to maintain appropriate housing, which she had some difficulty affording, and to work on her parenting skills. She did not attend a parenting class because it was some distance away and she had transportation problems, but she did meet with a family support worker who assisted her with parenting. The worker testified that the mother had made improvements that were evident when the worker made home visits. The worker also observed that the mother had a warm and playful relationship with X. The child protection agency seeks termination of parental rights under a statutory provision allowing termination of parental rights if a child is in foster care for more than 15 months of the most recent 22 months. The mother argues that she has made substantial progress with respect to her case plan and that the termination or parental rights is not in the best interests of the child. The family support worker testifies that the child would be harmed by the termination. However, the state argues that it is not in X's best interest to remain in foster care and that the mother has had sufficient time to make the required improvements. What is the likely outcome?

Explanation

In *In re Interest of Aaron D.*, 691 N.W.2d 164 (Neb. 2005), the court held that, under the facts presented, termination based solely on length of stay in foster care was not in the child's best interest. The court stated as follows: "The 15-month condition set forth in [the statute] serves the purpose of providing a reasonable timetable for parents to rehabilitate themselves . . . But termination based on the ground that a child has been in out-of-home placement for 15 of the preceding 22 months is not in a child's best interests when the record demonstrates that a parent is making efforts toward reunification and has not been given a sufficient opportunity for compliance with a reunification plan. We do not mean to suggest that termination solely on the basis of [the statutory section] cannot be appropriate. Obviously, there will be cases in which clear and convincing evidence to that effect will be presented. But that may prove difficult in cases where the record is insufficient to prove any of the other statutory grounds i.e., where the parent did not abandon the child, did not neglect to protect or provide for a child, was not unfit or unable to parent, did not fail to participate in necessary rehabilitation, and was not abusive." *Id.* at 261.

TERMINATION PROCEDURE

20.31. Standard of Proof

Because termination of parental rights is such a drastic remedy, the standard of proof is "clear and convincing evidence." In *Santosky v. Kramer*, 455 U.S. 745 (1982), the Supreme Court held that a New York statute requiring only a "fair preponderance of the evidence" violated a parent's right to due process in termination of parental rights proceedings. The Court found that parents have a fundamental liberty interest in the care and upbringing of children and that the state had an advantage over parents with respect to proof and expertise.

The Indian Child Welfare Act requires proof "beyond a reasonable doubt" when termination of parental rights is at issue. 25 U.S.C. §1912(f).

20.32. Right to Counsel?

In *Lassiter v. Department of Soc. Servs.*, 452 U.S. 18 (1981), the Supreme Court ruled that due process does not require appointment of counsel for indigent parents in all termination actions. However, states generally appoint counsel in termination cases either as required by state statute or under state constitutional provisions. *See* Bruce A. Boyer, *Justice, Access to the Courts, and the Right to Free Counsel for Indigent Parents: The Continuing Scourge of Lassiter v. Department of Social Services of Durham*, 36 Loy. U. Chi. L.J. 363 (2005).

CHAPTER 21

Abortion

HISTORY AND BACKGROUND

21.1. Nineteenth Century

Laws prohibiting abortions began to appear in the United States during the early part of the nineteenth century. At that time, feminists opposed abortion because it was an unsafe medical procedure for women. This was particularly true prior to the development of antiseptics and until their general acceptance at the turn of the twentieth century. As a consequence, abortion mortality was high, and even after 1900 they were often unsafe.

By 1840, when Texas had received the common law, only eight U.S. states had statutes dealing with abortion. *Roe v. Wade*, 410 U.S. 113, 139 (1973). After the War Between the States, legislation began generally to replace the common law, and these initial statutes dealt severely with abortion after quickening but were lenient with abortion before quickening. *Id.* Most punished attempted abortions equally with completed abortions. Many early statutes included the exception for an abortion thought by one or more physicians to be necessary to save the mother's life, but that provision soon disappeared and the typical law required that the procedure actually be necessary for that purpose. *Id.*

Gradually, in the middle and late nineteenth century the quickening distinction disappeared from the statutory law of most states, and the degree of the offense and the penalties were increased. By the end of the 1950s, a majority of jurisdictions banned abortion unless done to save or preserve the life of the mother. The exceptions—Alabama and the District of Columbia—permitted an abortion to preserve the mother's health. *Id.* Three states permitted abortions that were not unlawfully performed or that were not without lawful justification, leaving interpretation of those standards to the courts. *Id.*

The ban continued through the 1960s, although the American Law Institute's Model Code had persuaded several states to allow an abortion to save the life of the mother, in cases of rape or incest, if the fetus was deformed, and when continuation would impair a mother's mental or physical health (therapeutic abortions). As the Supreme Court developed and unfolded its privacy theory in a series of important cases, the realistic possibility that certain state statutes that completely banned abortions could be successfully challenged on constitutional grounds began to emerge.

PRIVACY

21.2. Roots of Privacy

Although privacy is not mentioned in the Constitution, most agree that the roots of the privacy theory can be found in *Meyer v. Nebraska*, 262 U.S. 390, 400 (1923) (recognizing that the liberty interest protected by due process includes the right of parents "to control the education of their own") and *Pierce v. Society of Sisters*, 268 U.S. 510, 534 (1925) (recognizing that "the liberty of parents and guardians" includes the right "to direct the upbringing and education of children under their control").

In *Griswold v. Connecticut*, 381 U.S. 479 (1965), the Court held that the Constitution does not permit a state to forbid a married couple to use contraceptives. The Court also held that although the word "liberty" is not defined in the Constitution, it includes at least the fundamental rights "retained by the people" under the Ninth Amendment. *Id.* at 484.

The right to privacy was not explicitly recognized until *Eisenstadt v. Baird*, 405 U.S. 438 (1972). In that case, the defendant was convicted under a criminal statute for exhibiting contraceptive articles in the course of delivering a lecture on contraception to a group of students at Boston University and for giving a young woman a package of vaginal foam at the close of his address. The state argued that the legislative purpose of the criminal statute was to promote marital fidelity and discourage premarital sex. The Supreme Court invalidated the law saying that under the existing statute, contraceptives may be made available to married persons without regard to whether they are living with their spouses or the uses to which the contraceptives are to be put. Therefore, the legislation has no deterrent effect on extramarital sexual relations.

The decision extended the "right of privacy" established in *Griswold v. Connecticut*, 381 U.S. 479 (1965), to all individuals, regardless of marital status and explicitly recognized a constitutional right to privacy. Under *Griswold*, a Connecticut statute that barred the distribution of contraceptives to married persons was struck down on the ground that it unconstitutionally intruded upon the right of marital privacy. *Eisenstadt* granted individuals the right "to be free from unwarranted governmental intrusion into matters so fundamentally affecting a person as the decision whether to bear or beget a child." This decision is viewed by many as providing the legal foundation for *Roe v. Wade*, 410 U.S. 113 (1973).

Note that the Court subsequently struck down a statute that barred distribution of all contraceptives except by a licensed pharmacist. *Carey v. Population Services International*, 431 U.S. 678 (1977). In *Carey*, the majority held that limitations on access to contraceptives impose burdens similar to limitations on their use; therefore, both must satisfy the compelling state interest test.

Example 21-1

Assume that D, a druggist, stocks and sells contraceptives in direct violation of a state criminal law that permits their sale only to married couples. D has provided contraceptives to unmarried adults. When the state brings criminal charges against D for selling contraceptives to unmarried couples, he contends that the criminal law is unconstitutional. The state argues that the law is constitutional and that its purpose is to deter premarital sex and prevent unwanted out-of-wedlock pregnancies. Is it likely that D would be convicted of a crime after the decisions in *Griswold* and *Eisenstadt*?

Explanation

It is unlikely that D would be convicted of a crime. Here, the statute provides dissimilar treatment for married and unmarried persons who are similarly situated. This would clearly be considered a violation of the Equal Protection Clause.

21.3. Criminal Abortion Statute Struck Down

In *Roe v. Wade*, 410 U.S. 113 (1973), the Supreme Court was asked to review a Texas criminal abortion statute that made an abortion illegal except for the purpose of saving a mother's life. The statute's challenger, Jane Roe, an unmarried pregnant woman, asserted that she was unable to obtain an abortion because her life was not threatened and she did not have the funds to travel to another state where an abortion was legally permitted. She alleged that the statute was unconstitutional. The government argued that the statute was constitutional and provided three specific reasons to support it: (1) it discouraged illicit sexual conduct outside marriage; (2) it protected a pregnant woman from the dangerous nature of an abortion; (3) it protected the state's interest in potential life.

The Court found that the protection of a pregnant woman and the protection of potential life were compelling state interests and weighed those interests against a woman's right to privacy. It struck down the statute, holding that in the first trimester, a pregnant woman possesses an unqualified right to an abortion and that right may not be infringed upon by the state. The decision is left with the woman in conjunction with her physician. After the first trimester and until viability — viability defined as the point when a fetus is capable of survival outside the womb (*Roe*, 410 U.S. at 160, 163) — the state may regulate abortions but may not place an outright ban on them. It may, however, regulate the abortion procedure to protect the mother's health and safety. During the third trimester, the state's interest in protecting potential life justifies regulating and banning abortions except when necessary for the preservation of life or health of the mother.

The Court relied primarily on the Ninth Amendment to the United States Constitution, declaring that "the Ninth Amendment's reservation of rights to the people, is broad enough to encompass a woman's decision whether or not to terminate her pregnancy." *Roe*, 410 U.S. at 153. It reasoned that from a practical perspective, modern medical techniques had significantly reduced the medical risks of an abortion, stating that prior to the end of the first trimester, although not without its risk, abortion is now relatively safe. *Id.* at 149.

21.4. Residency, Advance Approval

Doe v. Bolton, 410 U.S. 179 (1973), was a companion decision to *Roe v. Wade*. In this case, the Court invalidated a Georgia statute that required a woman seeking an abortion because of a threat to her life or health to meet certain residency and procedural requirements. The Court held that the requirement that the abortion be performed in an accredited hospital was invalid because accreditation was not legitimately related to the state's objective of protecting the woman's life. It also invalidated the requirement that a woman secure advance approval from a hospital committee for an abortion because this limits a woman's right to medical care and a physician's right to make medical decisions. Finally, it rejected a provision that required three physicians to justify the abortion.

EXAMPLES

Example 21-2

Assume that a state is concerned that abortions should not threaten the life of the mother. To protect her health, state X promulgates a statute that allows abortions only in a state-accredited hospital and after two doctors have concurred in the abortion decision. The statute is challenged.

EXPLANATIONS

Explanation

For the reasons outlined in *Doe v. Bolton* above, the statute would be held unconstitutional.

21.5. Expanding the Meaning of Privacy

In *Whalen v. Roe*, 429 U.S. 589 (1977), the Court expanded on the meaning of privacy. A high school swim team coach, suspecting that a teenage team member was pregnant, required the young woman to take a pregnancy test. She and her mother filed a Section 1983 action claiming *inter alia* that the pregnancy test unconstitutionally interfered with the daughter's right to privacy regarding personal matters. It held that the fact that the coach compelled the student to take the test, coupled with an alleged failure to take appropriate steps to keep the information confidential, infringed upon the girl's right to privacy.

DEFERENCE TO PHYSICIANS

21.6. Pennsylvania Abortion Control Act

In *Colautti v. Franklin*, 439 U.S. 379 (1979), the Court held impermissibly vague a section of the Pennsylvania Abortion Control Act that required a physician to adopt a particular standard of care whenever the physician determined that a fetus was viable or "there [was] sufficient reason to believe that the fetus may be viable." *Colautti*, 439 U.S. at 391. The Court emphasized that, while "viable" and "may be viable" presumably had different meanings, a physician could not know from the statute what they were. It said that the law provided no guidance and conditioned potential physician liability on "confusing and ambiguous criteria," and was therefore impermissibly vague. *Id.* at 394. Note that *Roe v. Wade* indicated viability was about 28 weeks; however, in *Planned Parenthood of Southeastern Pa. v. Casey*, 505 U.S. 833, 869 (1992), the Court placed viability at 23 to 24 weeks.

21.7. Physician's Duty: Second-Trimester Abortions

The approach of courts to defer to physicians probably reached its apex in *City of Akron v. Akron Center for Reproductive Health, Inc.*, 462 U.S. 416 (1983) (*Akron I*). In this case, a local city ordinance required that a physician inform a woman of the status of her pregnancy, the development of her fetus, the date of possible viability, the physical and emotional complications that may result from an abortion, and the availability of agencies to provide assistance and information. *Id.* at 442. The physician was also required to advise the woman of the risks associated with the abortion technique to be employed and other information. *Id.* The law was invalidated based on the physician's right to practice medicine in the way he or she saw fit. According to Court, "[i]t remains primarily the responsibility of the physician to ensure that appropriate information is conveyed to his patient, depending on her particular circumstances." *Id.* at 443. The ordinance was viewed by the Court as an unwarranted "intrusion upon the discretion of the pregnant woman's physician." *Id.* at 445. According to the Court, a physician under this ordinance was placed in an "undesired and uncomfortable straitjacket." *Id.*

Note that, even though the Supreme Court later overruled portions of *Akron* in *Planned Parenthood of Southeastern Pennsylvania v. Casey*, 505 U.S. 833 (1992), the Court did not readdress the unconstitutionality of requiring second-trimester abortions to be performed in hospitals. The Court in *Casey* discussed the informed consent requirement struck down in *Akron* and held that *Akron* was wrong on this point. The *Casey* court stated that the doctor-patient relation was only "entitled to the same solicitude it receives in other contexts." 505 U.S. at 884.

PERSONAL HISTORY; CONSENT; WAITING PERIOD

21.8. Personal History and Health-Related Interests

In *Thornburgh v. American Coll. of Obst. & Gyn.*, 476 U.S. 747 (1986), the Supreme Court held the requirements of a Pennsylvania statute unconstitutional because they went "well beyond the health related interests" that may justify reporting requirements in some cases. 476 U.S. at 766. Among the defects noted by the Court was the fact that the statute required information "as to the woman's personal history." 476 U.S. at 766. The Court also held that withholding a minor's name is not enough by itself to protect her anonymity where the publicly available information could identify the minor. 476 U.S. at 766-68. Because the potentially identifying information contained in the file is often so detailed that the absence of the minor's name will not protect her interests, the use of a fictitious name does not appear adequate to protect a pregnant minor's confidences.

Note that *Thornburgh* was in part overruled by *Planned Parenthood of Southeastern Pennsylvania v. Casey*, 505 U.S. 833 (1992), and in particular the portions of the decision that addressed the issue of informed consent. However, the Supreme Court left intact *Thornburgh* to the extent that it relied upon *Roe's* approach to postviability regulation of abortions, which was expressly re-affirmed in *Casey*.

21.9. Waiting Period, Informed Consent

In *Planned Parenthood of Southeastern Pennsylvania v. Casey*, 505 U.S. 833 (1992), a portion of the Pennsylvania Abortion Control Act was challenged. The Act required that women seeking abortions sign a statement 24 hours before the procedure giving an informed consent. The Act also required that, except in special cases, a parent must also give an informed consent for a minor child. Another section of the statute required a wife to sign a statement that she had notified her husband that she intended to get an abortion.

The Court upheld all of the Pennsylvania requirements except the spousal notification provision. It stated that requiring a doctor to make certain information available to the woman is permissible as long as the information is truthful and not misleading and was not an undue burden. The Court, relying on the doctrine of stare decisis, did not overrule the legality of abortions premised in *Roe v. Wade*. The Court also seemed to shift its view of abortion as a fundamental right to that of a liberty interest. It declared that only state restrictions that impose an "undue burden" on a woman are subject to strict scrutiny.

Note that in upholding the Act's consent provisions, the Court effectively overruled *Akron v. Akron Center for Reproductive Health, Inc.*, 462 U.S. 416, 103 (1984) and *Thornburgh v. American College of Obstetricians and Gynecologists*, 476 U.S. 747 (1986), which held that a state could not require a physician to provide a woman with certain information designed to dissuade her from having an abortion. The Court upheld the essential holding in *Roe v. Wade* on the legality of abortion while narrowing *Roe* to permit a state to regulate abortions as long as the regulations would not unduly burden women.

Example 21-3

Assume that a state legislature passes a statute that requires a physician to provide a woman seeking an abortion with information that suggests the fetus is a human being capable of life. P, who is seeking an abortion, challenges the notice requirement. How will a court most likely rule on the challenge?

Explanation

The court will most likely uphold the notice requirement if the information supplied to the woman is truthful and not misleading and was not an undue burden. The argument will center on the status of the fetus and whether it can truthfully be viewed as capable of life.

PICKETING

21.10. Buffer Zones

Madsen v. Women's Health Center, 512 U.S. 753 (1994), involved anti-abortion protesters who threatened to picket and demonstrate around a Florida abortion clinic. The protestors sought a declaration that a criminal statute prohibiting any person from knowingly approaching within eight feet of another person near a health care facility without that person's consent violated the First Amendment, and they sought injunction against statute's enforcement.

The Court held that the statute prohibiting persons from knowingly approaching within eight feet of an individual who was within 100 feet of health care facility entrance, for purposes of displaying a sign, engaging in oral protest, education, counseling, or passing leaflets or handbills, unless the individual consented to that approach, was content-neutral time, place, and manner regulation for First Amendment purposes, even if it might be necessary to examine content of oral statements made by the approaching speaker to determine whether the speaker violated the statute. The Court said that the statute regulated only places where some speech could occur, applied equally to all demonstrators, regardless of viewpoint, and did not make any reference to content of speech, and the state's interests in protecting access to medical facilities and privacy. It concluded that the statute provided the police with clear guidelines that were unrelated to content of demonstrators' speech. The injunction was not subject to heightened scrutiny as content or viewpoint based simply because it restricted only the speech of anti-abortion protesters.

LEGISLATION THAT MAY CREATE UNDUE BURDEN

21.11. Regulating Partial-Birth Legislation

In *Stenberg v. Carhart*, 530 U.S. 914 (2000), the Court held that a Nebraska statute regulating so-called "partial-birth abortions" imposed an undue burden. Without deciding the issue of whether a statute that outlawed only intact dilation and evacuation (D & E) would be unduly burdensome, the *Stenberg* Court held that an abortion ban that failed to differentiate in its statutory language between intact D & Es and non-intact D & Es unquestionably constituted an undue burden, for the obvious reason that it would prohibit most second-trimester abortions. *Stenberg*, 530 U.S. at 938-946. As part of its analysis, the *Stenberg* Court provided legislatures with guidance about how to draft statutes that would adequately distinguish between the two forms of D & E.

The Court explained that a legislature can make clear that a statute intended to regulate only intact D & Es applies to that form of the procedure only, by using language that "track[s] the medical differences between" intact and non-intact D & Es or by providing an express exception for the performance of non-intact D & Es and other abortion procedures. *Stenberg*, 530 U.S. at 939. In her concurring opinion, Justice O'Connor emphasized how, by employing the latter approach, a legislature could easily make clear that a statute intended to regulate intact D & E was in fact narrowly tailored to reach only that form of the D & E procedure. *Stenberg*, 530 U.S. at 950. Citing three state statutes prohibiting intact D & Es that had specifically excluded from their coverage other abortion methods, Justice O'Connor described the language each statute used, providing legislatures wishing to prohibit only intact D & Es with a clear roadmap for how to avoid the problems regarding the scope of coverage that undid the Nebraska statute. *Id.*

PARENTAL NOTIFICATION

21.12. Making Mature Decisions

In *Bellotti v. Baird*, 443 U.S. 622 (1979), the Supreme Court, in separate opinions by Mr. Justice Powell and Mr. Justice Stevens, held that a Massachusetts statute that required a pregnant minor seeking an abortion to obtain the consent of her parents or obtain judicial approval following notification to her parents unconstitutionally burdened the right of the pregnant minor to seek an abortion. The Court stated that if a state decides to require a pregnant minor to obtain one or both parents' consent to an abortion, it also must provide an alternative procedure whereby authorization for the abortion can be obtained. A pregnant minor is entitled in such a proceeding to show either that she is mature enough and well enough informed to make her abortion decision, in consultation with her physician, independently of her parents' wishes, or that even if she is not able to make this decision independently, the desired abortion would be in her best interests. Such a procedure must ensure that the provision requiring parental consent does not in fact amount to an impermissible "absolute, and possibly arbitrary, veto."

The decision is consistent with *Planned Parenthood of Central Missouri v. Danforth*, 428 U.S. 52 (1976), where a Missouri abortion statute required written consent of parent or person in loco parentis to an abortion of an unmarried woman under 18 during the first 12 weeks of pregnancy unless a licensed physician certifies that the abortion is necessary to preserve the mother's life. The Court held that such a provision was unconstitutional, at least insofar as it imposed a blanket parental consent requirement. *Id.*

21.13. Physician Notifying Parents

In *Hodgson v. Minnesota*, 497 U.S. 417 (1990), an action was brought challenging the parental notification requirement of Minnesota's Abortion Law. The Supreme Court held that the statute, which with certain exceptions, required a physician to notify both parents at least 48 hours before performing an abortion on a minor, would be unconstitutional in the absence of a judicial bypass. *Id.* at 450. The Court said that "the requirement that both parents be notified . . . does not reasonably further any legitimate state interest." *Id.* The Court rejected as justifications for the two-parent requirement (a) the parents' concern for the child's welfare and (b) the State's interest in protecting the parents' independent right to determine and strive for what they believe best for their child. *Id.* at 452. Neither of these reasons can justify the two-parent notification requirement.

The Court recognized that the second parent may well have an interest in the minor's abortion decision, making full communication among all members of a family desirable in some cases, but the Court said that such communication may not be decreed by the state. The State has no more interest in requiring all family members to talk with one another than it has in requiring certain of them to live together. *Id.* The Court stated that to the extent a parental consent or parental notification provision legitimately supports the parents' authority to act in the minor's best interest, and thus "assures that the minor's decision to terminate her pregnancy is knowing, intelligent, and deliberate," that interest is fully served by notice to one parent. *Id.* at 450.

21.14. Notifying One Parent

In *Akron v. Akron Center for Reproductive Health*, 497 U.S. 502 (1990) (*Akron II*), the Court upheld a statute requiring a minor to notify one parent before having an abortion, subject to a judicial bypass provision. It declined to decide whether a parental notification statute must include some sort of bypass provision to be constitutional. The Court allowed a judge to waive the notification requirement if it was determined by clear and convincing evidence "that notice is not in the minor's best interests" (not that an abortion is in her best interests). 497 U.S. at 508. The Court explicitly held that such a provision must meet the requirement that "the procedure must allow the minor to show that, even if she cannot make the abortion decision by herself, the desired abortion would be in her best interests." 497 U.S. at 511.

21.15. Best Interests and Notification

In *Lambert v. Wicklund*, 520 U.S. 292 (1977), physicians and other medical personnel filed suit seeking a declaration that Montana's Parental Notice of Abortion Act was unconstitutional, and an order enjoining its enforcement. The Supreme Court held that the Montana statute was constitutional.

The Court was satisfied with the provision that allowed a judge to waive a state notice requirement if (a) there is clear and convincing evidence that the minor is mature enough to make the decision independently, (b) if there is evidence that the minor is a victim of "physical, sexual, or emotional abuse" by a parent or guardian, or (c) that the notification is not in the minor's best interest. The Court ruled for the first time that a judge can consider the minor's best interests in relationship to both the abortion and to the notification of a parent.

Example 21-4

Assume that in 1972 P, age 17, underwent an abortion. D, the physician who performed the abortion, obtained an informed consent signed by P's mother but did not obtain P's consent to the abortion. Also assume that the statute of limitations does not bar a civil action against D and that P sues D, alleging the physician was negligent in failing to consult with P prior to the abortion. In support of her claim, D responds that in 1972 D was not required to obtain the minor's consent. How will a court most likely rule on D's request that the lawsuit be dismissed?

Explanation

D's motion will most likely be granted. Even if the trial court examines *Roe v. Wade*, a case decided a year after this event, *Roe* did not create a legal duty of a physician to obtain the consent of a minor patient before an abortion. Furthermore, at the time of the abortion, P was a minor who could not give effective consent. Given the purpose of requiring a physician to disclose information—that is, to help the person who will consent, or withhold consent, to make an informed decision—a physician was not required to make full disclosure to a minor, when the minor could not give legally effective consent. *See Powers v. Floyd*, 904 S.W.2d 713 (Tex. App. 1995).

21.16. Health Risks and Parental Notification

Ayotte v. Planned Parenthood of New England, 126 S. Ct. 961 (2006), involved New Hampshire's Parental Notification Prior to Abortion Act, which prohibited physicians from performing an abortion on a minor until 48 hours following the delivery of written notice to the minor's parent or guardian. Although the Act did make an exception in cases where an abortion was necessary to preserve the life of the mother, it contained no corresponding health exception. The First Circuit invalidated the law in its entirety for want of the health exception. In a unanimous opinion, the Supreme Court, Justice

O'Connor writing, held that the constitutional challenge to New Hampshire's parental notification law, which did not contain an exception allowing a minor to obtain an abortion without notice to her parent when necessary to preserve the minor's health, was, as to that particular requirement, unconstitutional.

The Court then announced a test consisting of three principles to guide its inquiry into the validity of a state statute. It said that it would "not nullify more of a legislature's work than is necessary." It also said that it was resisting "rewrit[ing] state law to conform it to constitutional requirements" even as it "strived to salvage it." Finally, it said that "the touchstone for any decision about remedy is legislative intent."

The Court concluded that complete invalidation of the statute was an unnecessarily "blunt" remedy in light of the relatively few potentially unconstitutional applications of the statute. 126 S. Ct. 969. It said that "the lower courts can issue a declaratory judgment and an injunction prohibiting the statute's unconstitutional application." The Court's sole reservation was whether this was consistent with legislative intent, as it had been alleged that the legislature intended for the statute to be nonseverable. The Court remanded the case to the lower court to assess the merit of this argument and declared that, if the court found the argument unavailing, it must then craft an injunction prohibiting unconstitutional application of the law.

POST-AYOTTE RULING

21.17. Federal Partial Birth Abortion Ban Act

Two weeks after *Ayotte* had been decided, two circuit courts issued opinions on the same day finding constitutional problems with the federal Partial-Birth Abortion Ban Act of 2003. Pub. L. No. 108-105, 117 Stat. 1201 (codified at 18 U.S.C. §1531 (Supp. III 2003)). In *Planned Parenthood Federation of America, Inc. v. Gonzales*, 435 F.3d 1163 (9th Cir. 2006), the Ninth Circuit held that the federal partial birth abortion ban statute was constitutionally deficient because it failed to offer a health exception, its potential to impose an undue burden on the abortion right, and its vagueness. On the subject of remedy, the court invalidated the law in its entirety, distinguishing *Ayotte* on the ground that the statute in that case had lacked only a health exception.

In *National Abortion Federation v. Gonzales*, 437 F.3d 278 (2d Cir. 2006), a divided Second Circuit panel agreed with the Ninth Circuit that the absence of an explicit health exception in the federal partial birth abortion ban statute created a constitutional infirmity. The court requested further briefing in light of *Ayotte* before selecting a remedy.

ABORTION FUNDING

21.18. Medicaid Coverage

In 1977 the Court decided three cases permitting states to refuse Medicaid coverage for nontherapeutic abortions. *Beal v. Doe*, 432 U.S. 438 (1977); *Mather v. Roe*, 432 U.S. 464 (1977); *Poelker v. Doe*, 432 U.S. 519 (1977). In *Beal v. Doe*, 432 U.S. 438 (1977), the Court held that Title XIX of the Social Security Act does not require a state Medicaid program to fund elective (nontherapeutic) abortions, declaring that states have broad discretion to determine the extent of medical assistance that is "reasonable" and "consistent" with the objectives of the Act. *Id.* at 444 of 432 U.S. The Court explained that it was "not unsympathetic to the plight of an indigent woman who desires an abortion, but the Constitution does not provide judicial remedies for every social and economic ill."

21.19. Subsidizing Indigent Abortions

Although the government subsidized continued pregnancy and childbirth but not abortion for an indigent, a majority in *Maher v. Roe*, 432 U.S. 464 (1977), found no "unduly burdensome interference" with a woman's abortion decision and that the exclusion of elective abortions from Medicaid did not violate the Equal Protection Clause. The court treated the refusal to fund abortion as state inaction calling for the rational basis test rather than the strict scrutiny test applied in *Roe*. Because Connecticut encouraged childbirth over abortion, this was viewed as satisfying application of the rational basis test.

21.20. Abortion Funding Barred

In *Harris v. McRae*, 448 U.S. 297 (1980), the Court held that the language in the Medicaid statute prohibiting the use of federal funds to reimburse the cost of abortions "except where the life of the mother would be endangered if the fetus were carried to term" was facially constitutional under the Equal Protection Clause.

21.21. Selective Funding

In *Rust v. Sullivan*, 500 U.S. 173 (1991), the Court held that Congress may "selectively fund a program to encourage certain activities it believes to be in the public interest, without at the same time funding an alternative program which seeks to deal with the problem in another way." 500 U.S., at 193. In doing so, "the Government has not discriminated on the basis of viewpoint; it has merely chosen to fund one activity to the exclusion of the other." *Ibid.*; *see also Maher v. Roe*, 432 U.S. 464, 475 (1977) ("There is a basic difference between direct state interference with a protected activity and state encouragement of an alternative activity consonant with legislative policy"). *Rust's* holding has been limited to situations in which the government is itself the speaker, or instances in which the government used private speakers to transmit its own message

21.22. Barring Use of Public Facilities

In *Webster v. Reproductive Health Services*, 492 U.S. 490 (1989), Missouri legislation prohibited the use of public facilities for abortion and required that a physician rigorously examine a pregnant woman seeking an abortion if the physician thought that the woman's pregnancy was past 20 weeks. The medical tests were to determine "the gestational age, weight, and lung maturity of the unborn child." *Id.* at 512. The legislation was successfully challenged in the United States District Court for the Western District of Missouri, which held the act unconstitutional. The Eighth Circuit Court of Appeals upheld the lower court decision and review was granted by the Supreme Court. Although overturning *Roe v. Wade* was urged by the Solicitor General, the Court did not do so. However, five of the nine justices agreed that restrictions such as Missouri's prohibition on the use of public facilities and funds for abortions and the state's required tests to determine viability do not burden procreational choice and are constitutional. In other words, the Court upheld a requirement that no public employees or facilities be used for nontherapeutic abortions.

CHAPTER 22

Mediation

22.1. Introduction

Mediation is an increasingly popular alternative to traditional adversarial divorce. This form of alternative dispute resolution is designed to avoid the animosity and expense associated with divorce litigation. Although the widespread use of mediation in family cases is relatively recent in the U.S. legal system, similar processes have been historically documented in ancient China, the New Testament, and Navajo Peacemaking.

THE PROCESS OF MEDIATION

22.2. Definition Under the Model Standards

The Model Standards of Practice for Family and Divorce Mediation define *mediation* as

> A process in which a mediator, an impartial third party, facilitates the resolution of family disputes by promoting the participants' voluntary agreement. The family mediator assists communication, encourages understanding and focuses the participants on their individual and common interests. The family mediator works with the participants to explore options, make decisions and reach their own agreements.

Andrew Schepard, *An Introduction to the Model Standards of Practice for Family and Divorce Mediation*, 35 Fam. L. Q. 1, 3 (2001).

The process of family mediation assists couples in communicating and determining their own post-divorce outcomes. However, it is not intended to supplant either legal advice or therapy. The process keeps the needs of children in the forefront, while reducing the emotional and financial costs of divorce.

In practice, mediation programs differ significantly from each other. Some mediation takes place under the auspices of the court, and some mediation occurs in private practice settings. Other differences include the number of sessions offered, the qualifications of the mediator, and possible limitations on the issues considered. Mediators also adhere to different models of mediation. Consequently, when people refer to mediation, they may be discussing significantly different processes.

22.3. Structured Process

Mediation is a structured problem-solving process that is likely to include the following steps: (1) identifying issues to be mediated; (2) gathering and documenting facts related to the issues; (3) reaching consensus on standards of fairness for each issue; (4) brainstorming possible solutions and considering the ramifications of each; and (5) making decisions about the issues. *See* Stephen K. Erickson & Marilyn S. McKnight, *The Practitioner's Guide to Mediation* 63 (2001). For example, if a couple is considering how to divide assets, they might first make a list of their assets and document the existence and value of each one. Next they would explore fair ways to divide the assets — for example, they might choose to divide their assets equally between themselves. With this information in mind, the couple is prepared to brainstorm about concrete plans for asset division, often with the use of a spreadsheet. After considering the pros and cons of each proposed plan, the couple would agree upon an option for dividing the assets.

22.4. Interest-Based Process

The mediation process focuses on the underlying needs and interests of the parties. Most couples have some common interests, such as the well-being of their children, and the mediation process encourages the participants to focus on ways they can work together to achieve common goals. Individual interests are also identified and spouses consider how they can meet their own needs by also meeting the needs of the other person. For example, if one spouse feels strongly about continuing to live in the marital home and the other spouse is willing to move, the spouse staying in the home might agree to a division of assets that allocates liquid assets to the moving spouse so that he or she will be in a position to make a down payment on a new residence. Couples are thus encouraged to look for ways to "enlarge the pie" rather than becoming locked into a win-lose, rights-based orientation. Couples are discouraged from taking fixed positions and instead are encouraged to look for creative ways to satisfy important interests of both parties. Although the past actions of the parties can be relevant in trouble-shooting agreements, the mediation process is primarily forward-looking in nature.

22.5. Standard of Fairness

Couples are encouraged to consider and define their own standards of fairness regarding particular issues. If both parties see their final agreement as being fair, they are more likely to comply with it and make it work. Of course, before the couple is divorced, their agreements are generally reviewed by attorneys and must be approved by the court.

22.6. Focus on Children's Needs

The focus on children's needs is a hallmark of the mediation process. Mediators continually ask parents to consider how their decisions will affect their children, and they encourage parents to build agreements around the particular needs of their children. Parents are given information about the impact of divorce on children, the developmental needs of children at various ages, and the effects of continuing parental conflict on children.

Most mediation involves the preparation of a detailed "parenting plan." Typical parenting plans contain agreements about child-rearing practices, decision-making methods and authority, scheduling of physical residence and/or parenting time, budgeting and financial support, parental communication, and dispute resolution. Parenting plans focus on anticipating the needs of the children rather than enforcing the "rights" of the parents. Thus, where state law allows it, parenting plans avoid the use of custody labels because detailed parenting-time schedules and agreements about decision making obviate the need for these often contentious labels. The American Law Institute (ALI) adopted this approach, replacing the terms *custody* and *visitation* with the concept of *custodial responsibility*. ALI, Principles of the Law of Family Dissolution: Analysis and Recommendations §2.03(3) cmt. E, at 124 (2002). See Section 5.8 *supra* for a discussion of parenting plans.

Parties commonly develop a parenting plan and then implement it informally for a period of time before incorporating it into a final agreement or court order. This allows parents to "test-drive" arrangements and make desired changes prior to finalizing agreements.

THE MEDIATOR

22.7. The Role of the Mediator

The mediator functions as a neutral third party who facilitates the mediation process but does not express a point of view on the substantive issues. Instead, the mediator helps the participants reach their own decisions. This is quite different from the role of judges and arbitrators who make final decisions for the parties.

EXAMPLES

Example 22-1

Assume that P and D, who plan to divorce, disagree about issues such as parenting time and child support. The court appoints an attorney to act as a guardian *ad litem*, which entails functioning as an independent fact finder and evaluator who reports to the court regarding the best interests of the child. In the same order, the judge appoints the same lawyer to mediate the economic aspects of the divorce. As a guardian *ad litem*, the attorney criticizes some of P's parenting practices, and P contends that the attorney is biased toward her and consequently not a suitable mediator of economic issues. Was appointing the attorney to both roles in the same case improper?

EXPLANATIONS

Explanation

In the similar case of *Isaacson v. Isaacson*, 792 A.2d 525 (N.J. Super. 2002), the court found that the two roles were indeed incompatible. In New Jersey, the guardian *ad litem* functions as an independent fact finder and evaluator who reports to the court. That role was inconsistent with that of the mediator, who operates as a neutral party in a confidential setting. The court stated that "We are not persuaded that the language limiting the role of [the attorney] as mediator to mediate economic issues and her role as guardian *ad litem* to protect the best interests of the children presents a defining distinction allowing her to serve in both capacities. Despite the seeming disparate nature of the roles, they were not so distinct as to avoid the necessary overlap generating the conflict." *Id.* at 534.

22.8. Control of Process

The mediator actively controls the mediation process by setting the agenda, deciding who will speak and in what order, creating ground rules, and framing the discussion. Through modeling and discussion, the mediator teaches the couple effective conflict-resolution and problem-solving skills. In addition, the mediator watches for power imbalance and uses techniques such as verifying facts, meeting in separate caucuses, and asking probing questions to ensure that couples make informed and voluntary decisions. Mediators carefully monitor the behavior of the participants and remain alert for lopsided agreements.

Research shows that mediation is most effective when the mediator actively structures the sessions, stays in "flexible control" of the process, "shapes" communication, and keeps the focus on problem solving and the parties' underlying interests. Joan B. Kelly, *A Decade of Divorce Mediation Research: Some Answers and Questions,* 34 Fam. & Conciliation Cts. Rev. 373, 382 (1996).

22.9. Mediator Qualifications

The skill and experience of the mediator directly affect the quality of the mediation process. The Model Standards of Practice for Family and Divorce Mediation suggest that, at a minimum, family mediators should:

1. have knowledge of family law;
2. have knowledge of and training in the impact of family conflict on parents, children, and other participants, including knowledge of child development, domestic abuse and child abuse and neglect;
3. have education and training specific to the process of mediation; and
4. be able to recognize the impact of culture and diversity.

Model Standards of Practice for Family and Divorce Mediation, Standard X (2001).

Family mediation is a multidisciplinary practice, and mediators are likely to be psychologists, social workers, and/or lawyers. Because mediators come from different professional backgrounds and mediation is a relatively new field, regulation and quality control have been controversial issues. Mediators and commentators continue to debate about how to effectively promote professional diversity and innovation while maintaining quality control. Despite disagreements over licensure, research shows that participants generally find that mediators are impartial, sensitive, and skilled. Joan B. Kelly, *A Decade of Divorce Mediation Research: Some Answers and Questions,* 34 Fam. & Conciliation Cts. Rev. 373, 378 (1996).

Example 22-2

P and D decided to divorce and were ordered by the court to attend mediation. After mediation concluded, the wife objected to the mediated agreement because during the mediation, the mediator (1) told the wife she would lose in court on an issue, (2) threw papers on the table and announced "that's it, I give up," (3) threatened to report to the court that mediation had failed because of the wife, (4) guessed about the value of assets, and (5) applied time pressure, saying that "you guys have five minutes to hurry up and get out of here" after eight hours of mediation. The mediator argued that P was represented by counsel and could have objected to the process, terminated the mediation, or simply not agreed to the terms. Will the wife be successful in having the mediated agreement overturned?

Explanation

This mediator did not behave professionally during the mediation—the mediator should have remained neutral and should not have coerced the wife into agreeing to a settlement. A court will not adopt an agreement that is not made voluntarily and would not approve this one. *See Vitakis-Valchine v. Valchine*, 793 So. 2d 1094, 1099 (Fla. Dist. Ct. App. 2001).

Example 22-3

P and D mediate their divorce. Afterward, P claims that she was under duress because she had not slept during the 24 hours prior to the mediation, she was in pain from recent surgery, and she had a migraine headache. During the mediation, she took narcotic pain medication, an antidepressant, and a migraine-related injection. D presented evidence that (1) P was herself an experienced mediator who was represented by counsel at the mediation; (2) P appeared to understand what was transpiring; and (3) P did not seem confused or mentally incapacitated. Based on this evidence, the court ruled that P was not under duress. What is the likely result on appeal?

Explanation

In the similar case of *McMahan v. McMahan*, 2005 WL 3287475 (Tenn. Ct. App. 2005), the trial court found that P's testimony was "not persuasive." The appellate court did not overturn this finding on appeal and held that, based on the trial court's credibility finding, P's testimony did not rise to the level necessary to prove duress. *See also Ford v. Ford*, 68 P.3d 1258 (Alaska 2003) (agreement enforceable despite husband's poor health and desire to "get away from the intolerable stress of the mediation").

22.10. Mediator Testimony

The confidential nature of mediation allows participants to brainstorm and speak candidly during mediation sessions. Consequently, mediators object to being called as witnesses if mediation is unsuccessful and the parties return to court. For example, in *Marchal v. Craig*, 681 N.E.2d 1160, 1161 (Ind. Ct. App. 1997), the parties failed to reach a mediated agreement but stipulated that the mediator could testify as a witness for both parties. The husband later changed his mind, but the lower court allowed the mediator to testify. *Id.* at 1162. The appellate court found that the testimony violated Indiana ADR Rule 2.12 providing that a "[m]ediator shall not be subject to process requiring the disclosure of any matter discussed during the mediation, but rather, such matter shall be considered confidential and privileged in nature." *Id.* State laws vary concerning the extent to which mediation sessions are protected. For a discussion of confidentiality and privilege under the Uniform Mediation Act, *see* Scott H. Hughes, *The Uniform Mediation Act: To the Spoiled Go the Privileges*, 85 Marq. L. Rev. 9 (2001). *See also* ALI, Principles of the Law of Family Dissolution: Analysis and Recommendations §2.07(4), (5) (2000).

EXAMPLES

Example 22-4

A and B attended divorce mediation pursuant to a court order that specifically provided that the mediation process was to be confidential and "nonevidential." After the mediation ended, the parties disagreed about whether they had actually reached a settlement. A calls the mediator to testify on that question. A asserts that an agreement was reached and argues that the mediator was present when the agreement was made and that the mediator is in an ideal position to testify objectively about what occurred. B asserts that no settlement was reached and argues that the under the court order the mediation process was confidential and nonevidential and that mediator testimony would violate that order. Should the mediator be compelled to testify?

EXPLANATIONS

Explanation

In a similar case, the court recognized that the ability to be open and honest during mediation is key to the success of the process and that parties would be less likely to speak candidly if their statements could later be used in court. The court concluded that there had been no express waiver of the confidentiality provision and that mediator testimony was consequently improper. *See Lehr v. Afflitto*, 889 A.2d 462 (N.J. Super. 2006); *In re Marriage of Kieturakis*, 41 Cal. Rptr. 3d 119 (Cal. App. 2006).

ROLE OF ATTORNEYS

22.11. Legal Advice in Mediation

Attorneys play different roles in mediation depending upon the model of mediation used. Sometimes lawyers attend mediation sessions with their clients and participate in the process. In other cases, the participants consult with their attorneys as needed between mediation sessions. Some people in mediation seek legal advice only after the mediation has concluded. A few people never consult an attorney and appear *pro se* in court. Mediators prefer that participants consult separate attorneys as needed throughout the process and also before a final divorce decree is entered in court.

ROLE OF THE COURT

22.12. Approval of Agreements

A divorce is not final until the mediated agreement is approved and a decree is entered by the court. Thus, even when private mediation is used, the court retrospectively oversees the process and may refuse to approve a mediated agreement for various reasons. For example, a court might refuse to adopt an agreement if the court believes that the parenting arrangements are not in the best interests of the children or if the mediated agreement departs substantially from state law without good reason. Under ALI section 2.06, courts are cautioned to reject parenting plans agreed to by parents if the agreement was not "knowing or voluntary" or if the plan would harm the child. *See* ALI, The Allocation of Custodial and Decisionmaking Responsibility for Children §2.06 (2000).

EXAMPLES

Example 22-5

P and D, who are divorcing, have one child. They attended mediation sessions, where they entered into an agreement under which D was to have sole physical custody of the child but P was not ordered to pay any child support. Instead, D paid P a reduced amount of alimony. D later objected to the agreement on the basis that, under state law, child support could not be waived. P argued that the arrangement did not affect the amount of money available for support of the child; it just prevented the couple from exchanging unnecessary checks. Will a court adopt the mediated agreement?

Explanation

In the similar case of *Swanson v. Swanson*, 580 S.E.2d 526 (Ga. 2003), the court found that the right to child support belonged to the child and could not be waived by the parents in a mediated agreement. The court refused to incorporate the settlement agreement into a final decree, and the case was consequently reversed and remanded. *See also Esser v. Esser*, 586 S.E.2d 627 (Ga. 2003).

22.13. Mediation as Condition Precedent to Post-Decree Actions

If a final divorce decree requires the parties to mediate before filing post-decree motions in court, the provision is likely to be enforced by the court. For example, in *Gould v. Gould*, 523 S.E.2d 106, 107 (Ga. Ct. App. 1999), at the time of the divorce, the parties agreed to mediate conflicts prior to returning to court. Consequently, the court refused to hear a petition for modification and contempt until after mediation had taken place. *Id.* at 108. *But see Maurer v. Maurer*, 872 A.2d 326 (Vt. 2005) (claim by father that mediation was condition precedent to litigation was rejected by the court because the father was the party who refused to attend mediation).

EFFECTIVENESS OF MEDIATION

22.14. Time

Research shows that mediated divorces generally take less time to complete than divorces that are not mediated. *See* Kenneth Kressel & Dean G. Pruitt, *Mediation Research: The Process and Effectiveness of Third-Party Intervention* 398 (1989); Jay Folberg, *Mediation of Child Custody Disputes*, 19 Colum. J.L. & Soc. Probs. 413, 431 (1985). In fact, some research shows that mediated divorce may be completed in half the time it would normally take the case to make its way through the court system. Joan B. Kelly, *A Decade of Divorce Mediation Research: Some Answers and Questions*, 34 Fam. & Conciliation Cts. Rev. 373, 376 (1996).

22.15. Expense

Studies show that mediated divorces are generally less expensive than traditional divorces. Kressel & Pruitt, *supra*; Kelly, *supra*. Couples save money on attorney fees and through the use of neutral experts — if expert opinions are necessary, couples hire one neutral expert to advise them rather than each hiring a "battling expert." The amount of money saved depends upon the type of mediation process used and how early the divorce is diverted from the adversarial system. *See* Connie J. A. Beck & Bruce D. Sales, *A Critical Reappraisal of Divorce Mediation Research and Policy*, 6 Psychol. Pub. Poly. & L. 989, 1041 (2000).

22.16. Settlement Rates

Mediation settlement rates vary by program. Overall settlement rates range from 40 to 80 percent with an average settlement rate of 60 percent. Desmond Ellis & Noreen Stuckless, *Mediating and Negotiating Marital Conflicts* 103 (1996); Jeanne A. Clement & Andrew I. Schwebel, *A Research Agenda for Divorce Mediation: The Creation of Second Order Knowledge to Inform Legal Policy*, 9 Ohio St. J. Disp. Resol. 95, 99 (1993) (40 to 75 percent); Jay Folberg, *Mediation of Child Custody Disputes*, 19 Colum. J.L. & Soc. Probs. 413, 422 (1985) (58 percent).

22.17. Satisfaction Levels

Research indicates that participants express satisfaction with the mediation process in 60 to 93 percent of cases. Couples who reach settlement are predictably more satisfied than couples who do not settle. However, even among those who do not reach agreement, 81 percent would recommend the process to a friend. Ellis & Stuckless, *supra* at 93, Folberg, *supra* at 413, 424.

Researchers have found that both men and women are more satisfied with mediation than with the adversarial divorce process. Ellis & Stuckless, *supra* at 95. Seventy-seven percent of mediating couples are pleased with the mediation process, but only 40 percent of litigating couples report satisfaction with the court procedure. Jessica Pearson & Nancy Thoennes, *Divorce Mediation: Reflections on a Decade of Research*, 437 in *Mediation Research* (Kenneth Kressel et al. eds., 1989). Mediation is seen as involving less pressure, protecting people's rights better, giving couples more control over decisions, and being less coercive. National Center for State Courts, Multi-State Assessment of Divorce Mediation and Traditional Court Processing 72 (1992).

22.18. Compliance with Agreements

Couples who mediate are more likely to comply with the agreements they have made. Not surprisingly, couples who participate in multiple mediation sessions have higher compliance rates than those participating in a single session. Ellis & Stuckless, *supra* at 116; Pearson & Thoennes, *supra* at 21. These higher compliance rates result from the voluntary nature of the agreements made in mediation and the thoughtful consideration given to various options before decisions are finalized.

22.19. Relitigation

While studies show that relitigation rates are lower for mediating couples, other studies limit this finding to the first few years following the divorce. *See* Ellis & Stuckless, *supra* at 115; Clement & Schwebel, *supra* at 95, 100.

22.20. Ongoing Contact with Children

Children whose parents attend mediation may have more long-term, ongoing contact with the nonresidential parent. In a study where families were randomly assigned to a divorce process (mediation or adversarial), 30 percent of nonresidential parents who mediated continued to see their children at least once per week 12 years after the divorce. In contrast, only 9 percent of nonresidential parents who participated in adversarial divorce had weekly face-to-face contact 12 years later. Similarly, 54 percent of the mediating nonresidential parents had weekly phone contact 12 years after the divorce compared with 13 percent of the adversarially divorced nonresidential parents. Robert E. Emery, David Sbarra, & Tara Grover, *Divorce Mediation: Research and Reflections*, 43 Fam. Ct. Rev. 22 (2005).

REQUIRING PARTIES TO MEDIATE

22.21. Mandatory Mediation

Because mediation is cost-effective and reduces animosity, some states require divorcing couples to participate in mediation. For a state-by-state analysis, see Carrie-Anne Tondo et al., *Mediation Trends: A Survey of the States*, 39 Fam. Ct. Rev. 431 (2001). Proponents of mandatory mediation note high levels of satisfaction with the process and believe that all nonabusive couples can benefit from exposure to mediation. Andrew Schepard, *Children, Courts and Custody: Interdisciplinary Models for the Twenty-First Century* (2004).

In contrast, the Model Standards of Practice for Family and Divorce Mediation endorse the notion of informed consent by participants in mediation. Standard IIIC provides that "[a] mediator should not agree to conduct the mediation if the mediator reasonably believes one or more of the participants is unable or unwilling to participate." Because mediation is about self-determination, many mediators strongly object to the idea of requiring participation in mediation. *See* Ann Milne & Jay Folberg, *The Theory and Practice of Divorce Mediation: An Overview, in Divorce Mediation: Theory and Practice* 19 (Jay Folberg & Ann Milne eds., 1988); René L. Rimelspach, *Mediating Family Disputes in a World with Domestic Violence: How to Devise a Safe and Effective Court-Connected Mediation Program*, 17 Ohio St. J. Disp. Resol. 95, 102 (2001); ALI, The Allocation of Custodial and Decisionmaking Responsibility for Children §2.07 (2000).

22.22. Domestic Violence

Commentators express serious reservations about the use of mediation in cases involving domestic violence. Concerns include the possibility of coercion and retribution by the abusive partner as well as subjecting the victim to additional danger. Consequently, even states with mandatory mediation programs generally make an exception or have special provisions for cases involving domestic violence. Other states are "victim choice" states in that they have followed the Model Code on Domestic and Family Violence (1994), which provides:

> Section 407. Duty of the mediator to screen for domestic violence during mediation referred or ordered by court.
>
> 1. A mediator who receives a referral or order from a court to conduct mediation shall screen for the occurrence of domestic violence between the parties.
> 2. A mediator shall not engage in mediation when it appears to the mediator or when either party asserts that domestic or family violence has occurred unless:
>   (a) Mediation is requested by the victim of the alleged domestic or family violence;
>   (b) Mediation is provided in a specialized manner that protects the safety of the victim by a certified mediator who is trained in domestic and family violence; and
>   (c) The victim is permitted to have in attendance at mediation a supporting person of his or her choice, including but not limited to an attorney or advocate.

This approach allows victims of domestic violence to mediate if they choose to do so but does not require victims to engage in face-to-face negotiations with an abusive partner. *See also* ALI, Principles of the Law of Family Dissolution: Analysis and Recommendations §2.07(2000). For a discussion of factors to be considered by victims of domestic violence in deciding whether to mediate their divorces and the special safety and procedural precautions that are needed, see Nancy Ver Steegh, *Yes, No, and Maybe: Informed Decision Making About Divorce Mediation in the Presence of Domestic Violence*, 9 Wm. & Mary J. of Women & L. 145 (2003).

Example 22-6

Assume that P and D were divorced because during the marriage P was physically abusive to D and was arrested and convicted of assault and domestic violence. P and D return to court to resolve an issue related to parenting time, and the court orders them to attend mediation before a hearing date will be set. The jurisdiction has a statute providing that "[a]ny court of record may, in its discretion, refer any case of mediation services or dispute resolution programs . . . except that the court shall not refer the case to mediation services or dispute resolution programs where one of the parties claims that it has been the victim of physical or psychological abuse by the other party and states that it is thereby unwilling to enter into mediation services or dispute resolution programs." D objects to the mediation. What is the court likely to do?

Explanation

In most states the court will not require D to mediate with P if she objects to the mediation based on the occurrence of domestic violence. The statute clearly states that the court "shall not" refer to mediation if one of the parties "claims" to be a victim of domestic violence. Here, P has been convicted of assault and domestic violence and D is opposed to mediating. *See Pearson v. District Court*, 924 P.2d 512 (Colo. 1996).

CHAPTER 23

Professional Responsibility

23.1. Introduction

This chapter focuses on issues of professional responsibility that are especially relevant to practitioners of family law. The changing role of the family attorney is also discussed.

23.2. Client Dissatisfaction with Family Law Attorneys

Unfortunately, some divorcing couples express dissatisfaction with their attorneys, and there is some evidence that more ethical complaints are filed against family attorneys than attorneys practicing in other areas. *See* Andrew Schepard, *The Evolving Judicial Role in Child Custody Disputes: From Fault Finder to Conflict Manager to Differential Case Management*, 22 U. Ark. Little Rock L. Rev. 395, 410 (2000); Susan Daicoff, *Lawyer, Know Thyself: A Review of Empirical Research on Attorney Attributes Bearing on Professionalism*, 46 Am. U. L. Rev. 1337 (1997). In one survey, divorcing parents reported that their attorneys lacked genuine interest in their cases and did not pay sufficient attention to their cases. These clients did not feel involved in important decisions and were concerned about the lack of attorney communication: "nobody hears you and nobody talks to you." Marsha Kline Pruett & Tamara D. Jackson, *The Lawyer's Role During the Divorce Process: Perceptions of Parents, Their Young Children, and Their Attorneys*, 33 Fam. L.Q. 283, 297 (1999). In partial explanation, attorneys point out that divorce clients sometimes have unrealistic expectations, are undergoing serious emotional stress, and may not have dealt with the legal system or an attorney before.

Of course, many divorce clients are pleased with the representation they receive. These clients report that their attorneys helped them keep perspective, "interpreted" the legal proceedings for them, and provided emotional support. Connie J.A. Beck & Bruce D. Sales, *A Critical Reappraisal of Divorce Mediation Research and Policy*, 6 Psychol. Pub. Pol'y. & L. 989, 1014 (2000); Pruett & Jackson, *supra* at 294-295. In addition, lawyers serve an important function in protecting the interests of their clients.

SEXUAL RELATIONSHIPS WITH CLIENTS

23.3. Rule 1.8(j)

The 2005 Model Rules of Professional Conduct provide that "[a] lawyer shall not have sexual relations with a client unless a consensual sexual relationship existed between them when the client-lawyer relationship commenced." Rule 1.8(j). The comments following the rule explain the reasons for the prohibition of sexual relationships with clients. First, the attorney occupies a position of trust and has a fiduciary obligation to the client. The lawyer may not use this trust to disadvantage or exploit the client. Second, because of the nature of the relationship, the lawyer's independent professional judgment may be impaired. Third, it may be difficult to distinguish confidences protected by the attorney-client privilege from those that are not protected. Under these circumstances, the client is not considered able to give informed consent.

23.4. Existing Relationships Exception

Rule 1.8(j) provides for an exception when the lawyer and client have a preexisting sexual relationship. Even in this circumstance, the comments direct the lawyer to consider whether the relationship would materially limit the lawyer's ability to represent the client.

23.5. Special Concerns in Family Cases

Sexual relationships with clients are especially problematic in divorce cases. If the client is involved in a custody dispute, the existence of an affair or cohabitation may adversely affect the outcome. The lawyer may, in fact, be called as a witness. At a minimum, the sexual relationship exacerbates an already emotionally charged situation, making resolution of the issues more difficult. Most people experiencing a divorce are more emotionally vulnerable than they normally would be and exploitation is more likely to occur.

Example 23-1

A lawyer engages in a consensual sexual relationship with a client he is representing in a domestic relations matter and she later files a disciplinary complaint against him. The attorney practices in a state with no specific rule prohibiting such a relationship and he claims that he would not have engaged in the relationship if it were specifically barred. The attorney further argues that the former client has not presented any evidence of impaired representation. Does the attorney nevertheless have a conflict of interest?

Explanation

In a somewhat similar case, *In re Application for Disciplinary Action Against Chinquist*, 714 N.W.2d 469 (N.D. 2006), the court was not persuaded by either the absence of a "bright-line rule" prohibiting sexual relationships or the notion that evidence of impaired representation was necessary. The court found that the lawyer's relationship placed his interests above those of his client and was a conflict of interest.

Example 23-2

A lawyer has a sexual relationship with a woman, and while the relationship is ongoing, he undertakes representation of her in her divorce. If the jurisdiction doesn't have a specific rule forbidding this behavior, what other rules might apply?

Explanation

This behavior may violate rules related to (1) competent and diligent representation, (2) attorney acting as advocate and potential witness, and (3) conduct prejudicial to the administration of justice. In the similar case of *State ex rel. Oklahoma Bar Assn. v. Downes*, 121P.3d 1058 (Okla. 2005), the court noted that such behavior was adverse to the client's interest and added "even more hostility to an already acrimonious divorce."

REPRESENTING BOTH PARTIES

23.6. Dual Representation

Sometimes attorneys are asked to represent both parties in a divorce action. This is most likely to occur when the case is "uncontested." Unfortunately, once the lawyer starts to investigate the issues and assets, he or she is likely to uncover an issue or asset that the parties failed to consider and about which they disagree. Parties may also need to be advised concerning conflicting legal rights. Consequently, dual representation is ill advised, and the attorney should represent one party or the other in a divorce case.

23.7. Representing Opposing Parties (Rule 1.7(b)(3))

Rule 1.7(b)(3) of the 2005 Model Rules of Professional Conduct disallows representation that involves "the assertion of a claim by one client against another client represented by the lawyer in the same litigation or other proceeding before a tribunal." Thus, the rule prohibits the representation of opposing parties in the same litigation. Comment [30] to Rule 1.7(b)(3) warns that the attorney-client privilege will not attach between commonly represented clients. If such representation proceeds and adverse interests surface, the attorney would have to withdraw from both representations, thus creating unnecessary hardship and expense for the clients. Comment [29] to Rule 1.7(b)(3).

Example 23-3

A lawyer met briefly with a husband about pending divorce proceedings and an action for a restraining order. The husband did not retain the lawyer to represent him and instead hired other counsel. Some time later, the lawyer was contacted by the wife, met with her, and agreed to represent the wife in the divorce proceeding. Was this a conflict of interest?

Explanation

Under similar facts, in *In re Conduct of Knappendberger*, 108 P.3d 1161 (Or. 2005), the court found that the lawyer did have a conflict of interest. The court characterized the husband as a former client in a significantly related matter.

CONTINGENT FEES

23.8. Forbidden Fee Arrangement (Rule 1.5(d)(1))

Sometimes potential clients are unable to pay hourly attorney fees and are interested in entering into a contingent fee arrangement.

Rule 1.5(d)(1) of the 2005 Model Rules of Professional Conduct forbids attorneys from charging or collecting "any fee in a domestic relations matter, the payment or amount of which is contingent upon the securing of a divorce or upon the amount of alimony or support, or property settlement in lieu thereof . . ." Use of contingent fees in divorce cases goes against public policy because (1) the attorney would have a financial stake in the divorce proceeding and might promote divorce instead of encouraging reconciliation by the parties, and (2) a percentage fee might be unduly burdensome in the context of the work done and the financial circumstances of the parties.

23.9. Exceptions

Contingent fees are allowed in domestic relations cases involving collection of post-judgment amounts due "under support, alimony or other financial orders." Comment [6] to Rule 1.5(d)(1). *See Burns v. Stewart*, 188 N.W.2d 760 (Minn. 1971).

EXAMPLES

Example 23-4

Assume that P and D are divorcing. D is unemployed and cannot afford to pay an attorney an hourly fee. However, in the divorce, D expects to be awarded a parcel of land located on a lake. D agrees that if the land is awarded to D, D will sell it and give half of the payment received to the attorney. D is very happy with this arrangement because otherwise D will not be represented in the divorce. Is this an appropriate fee arrangement?

EXPLANATIONS

Explanation

This is the type of contingent fee prohibited under Rule 1.5(d)(1) because the arrangement gives the lawyer a financial interest in having D proceed with the divorce. The arrangement also gives the lawyer a vested stake in a certain outcome. If D decides to reconcile with P, or if D and P decide that P should have the lake property, the lawyer may have difficulty giving D objective advice because of the lawyer's own financial interest in the divorce.

COMMUNICATING WITH CLIENTS

23.10. Special Needs of Family Clients

Divorce clients often experience serious emotional turmoil as the legal action proceeds. Many clients have not been party to a lawsuit or dealt with an attorney before. As a result, most divorce clients have frequent questions and desire some level of emotional support. Clients experiencing serious distress should be referred for counseling. However, all clients are entitled to a reasonable amount of communication with their attorneys.

23.11. Informing and Consulting (Rule 1.4)

2005 Model Rule of Professional Conduct 1.4 provides as follows:

(a) A lawyer shall:
  (1) promptly inform the client of any decision or circumstance with respect to which the client's informed consent, as defined in Rule 1.0(e), is required by these Rules;
  (2) reasonably consult with the client about the means by which the client's objectives are to be accomplished;
  (3) keep the client reasonably informed about the status of the matter;
  (4) promptly comply with reasonable requests for information; and
  (5) consult with the client about any relevant limitation on the lawyer's conduct when the lawyer knows that the client expects assistance not permitted by the Rules of Professional Conduct or other law.

(d) A lawyer shall explain a matter to the extent reasonably necessary to permit the client to make informed decisions regarding the representation.

EXAMPLES

Example 23-5

Lawyer L agreed to represent P in a divorce from D. P was shocked when D filed for divorce and was extremely upset by the entire proceeding. At first, P called L four or five times a week to "check on the case." Lawyer L became weary of the calls and stopped returning them. L continued to ignore P's calls and only contacted P when L had a particular need to talk to P. P didn't hear from L for a period of two months, and P became distraught when P's calls were never returned. P finally filed a disciplinary complaint against L. Did L violate Rule 1.4?

EXPLANATIONS

Explanation

L should have referred P for counseling so that P could deal with the emotional aspects of the divorce more appropriately. L should also have had a conversation with P about the number of times P was calling the office — P needed information about how P could stay informed about the case and under what circumstances P should call. L's decision not to return calls or contact P for two months was unreasonable and violates Rule 1.4.

PRO SE LITIGANTS

23.12. Increasing Lack of Representation

In recent years, the number of unrepresented litigants in family cases has dramatically increased. A 1990 American Bar Association study conducted in Arizona found that at least one party was unrepresented in 88 percent of divorce cases. In contrast, a 1980 study found that one party was unrepresented in only 24 percent of cases. Steven K. Berenson, *A Family Law Residency Program?: A Modest Proposal in Response to the Burdens Created by Self-Represented Litigants in Family Court*, 33 Rutgers L.J. 105, 109 (2001). This trend raises several issues for family practitioners.

23.13. Dealing with Unrepresented Parties (Rule 4.3)

Attorneys dealing with unrepresented parties have special obligations under Rule 4.3 of the 2005 Model Rules of Professional Conduct. First, the lawyer cannot imply that he or she is disinterested. Second, the lawyer should make reasonable efforts to correct the unrepresented person's misunderstandings of the lawyer's role. Third, the lawyer must not give legal advice to the unrepresented person but should advise the person to obtain counsel if there is a reasonable possibility that the person's interest will conflict with the client's interests. Within these guidelines, the Rule does not prohibit negotiating with an unrepresented person or explaining the lawyer's view of the meaning of documents prepared by the lawyer. *See* Comment [2] to Rule 4.3.

EXAMPLES

Example 23-6

Attorney L represents P in a divorce against D, who is unrepresented. P and D live in a jurisdiction where the sole custodian of a child can move to another state so long as the child is not endangered by the move. D is willing to agree to P having sole physical custody but does not want P to move from the state. D does not know that P could easily do so if D agrees to the sole custody arrangement. Attorney L wants to wrap up the case and allows D to continue to think that P can't permanently leave the state without D's permission. Has L violated Rule 4.3?

EXPLANATIONS

Explanation

L has likely violated Rule 4.3. Even though L had no obligation under the rule to give D legal advice, L should have strongly encouraged D to retain a lawyer. Furthermore, L's client, P, is not well served by making an agreement based on a misunderstanding.

23.14. Need for Pro Bono Representation (Rule 6.1)

All family law attorneys should provide pro bono representation to people who are unable to afford representation. Rule 6.1 of the 2005 Model Rules of Professional Conduct suggests that lawyers render at least 50 hours of pro bono representation each year.

EXAMPLES

Example 23-7

Assume that as part of an organized clinic, lawyers provide limited advice to people who can't afford to retain an attorney. These lawyers occasionally assist in preparing documents for filing, but they do not appear in court or establish an ongoing professional relationship. Clients are informed of the limited nature of the representation and that the attorneys will not make court appearances. Does this arrangement violate the rules of professional conduct?

EXPLANATIONS

Explanation

In Formal Opinion 2005-F-151 (2005), the Tennessee Supreme Court's ethics board concluded that such limited assistance was appropriate. Rule 1.2(c) allows lawyers to limit the scope of representation if reasonable under the circumstances. The board suggested that written client consent be sought and that documents drafted by the lawyers be labeled "Prepared with Assistance of Counsel." The board also cautioned lawyers to be mindful of potential conflicts of interest.

NEW AND CHANGING ROLES FOR LAWYERS

23.15. Dissatisfaction with Adversarial Divorce

Couples have increasingly expressed dissatisfaction with the adversarial approach to dissolution. Research shows that from 50 to 70 percent of litigants describe the adversarial process as "impersonal, intimidating, and intrusive." Mary R. Cathcart & Robert E. Robles, *Parenting Our Children: In the Best Interest of the Nation* 39 (1996). In another study, 71 percent of parents reported that the process escalated the level of conflict and distrust "to a further extreme." Marsha Kline Pruett & Tamara D. Jackson, *The Lawyer's Role During the Divorce Process: Perceptions of Parents, Their Young Children, and Their Attorneys*, 33 Fam. L.Q. 283, 298 (1999). This escalation of conflict makes it more difficult for parents to interact in the future and has long-term ramifications for children.

23.16. Attorney as Counselor

Attorneys practicing family law have begun to reexamine their traditional role as zealous advocates. Some have encouraged assumption of a more moderate role of attorney as counselor. *See* Nancy Ver Steegh, *Using Externships to Introduce Family Law Students to New Professional Roles*, 43 Fam. Ct. Rev. 138 (2005).

A group of commentators suggests that family attorneys have an ethical obligation to actively promote conflict resolution in the following ways:

1. counseling clients about the negative consequences of custody disputes and the availability of resources to reduce conflict;
2. discussing alternatives to litigation such as mediation;
3. encouraging cooperation with custody and mental health evaluations;
4. realistically evaluating cases and avoiding false expectations;
5. seeking early intervention in high-conflict cases and making referrals;
6. cooperating in narrowing the issues, procedures, and evidence needed to consider the best interests of the child;
7. maintaining a civil demeanor and encouraging clients to do so;
8. avoiding use of the media or protective services to exacerbate conflict;
9. seeking training in child development, abuse and neglect, domestic violence, family dynamics, and alternative conflict resolution and becoming knowledgeable about community resources; and
10. developing continuing legal education programs improving lawyers' ability to reduce conflict.

The Wingspread Report and Action Plan, *High Conflict Custody Cases: Reforming the System for Children*, 39 Fam. Ct. Rev. 146, 150 (2001). *See also* Andrew Schepard, *Children, Courts and Custody: Interdisciplinary Models for the Twenty-First Century* (2004).

23.17. Mediation

As discussed in Chapter 25, mediation is commonly used to resolve family disputes without undue escalation of conflict. Lawyers are increasingly involved in various aspects of mediation. For example, some lawyers have become mediators, while others represent clients in mediation.

23.18. Collaborative Law

Collaborative law is a model of practice in which each party is represented by a separate attorney who agrees to use cooperative problem-solving strategies to resolve the issues. If settlement does not occur, both attorneys withdraw and are replaced by litigation counsel. The parties voluntarily disclose information to each other and neutral experts are jointly retained. *See* Pauline H. Tesler, *Collaborative Family Law*, 4 Pepp. Disp. Resol. L.J. 317 (2004); William H. Schwab, *Collaborative Lawyering: A Closer Look at an Emerging Practice*, 4 Pepp. Disp. Resol. L.J. 351 (2004); New Jersey Supreme Court Advisory Comm. on Professional Ethics, Op. 699 (2005).

CHAPTER 24

Jurisdiction

24.1. Introduction

There are two initial jurisdictional considerations one must make when handling a marital dispute. The first is to determine whether the court assigned to hear the dispute has subject matter jurisdiction. The second assumes that subject matter jurisdiction exists but asks whether the court has personal jurisdiction over the parties. Absent subject matter jurisdiction, the court does not possess the power to hear any portion of the dispute. Without personal jurisdiction over both parties, a court with subject matter jurisdiction may dissolve the relationship but may not impose personal obligations such as alimony, child support, or attorney fees. This chapter examines a variety of family law legal problems that involve these two jurisdictional concepts.

SUBJECT MATTER JURISDICTION IN FEDERAL COURT

24.2. Domestic Relations and Probate Exceptions

Federal courts are courts of limited subject matter jurisdiction. *See, e.g.*, 28 U.S.C. §1331 (federal question); 28 U.S.C. §1332(a)(1) (diversity actions between citizens of different states involving matters in controversy exceeding $75,000 exclusive of costs and interest). Given their limited jurisdictional reach, the question in family law is what is the nature and extent of their power in domestic matters?

Among longstanding limitations on federal court jurisdiction otherwise properly exercised are the so-called "domestic relations" and "probate" exceptions. Neither is compelled by the text of the Constitution or federal statute. Both are judicially created doctrines stemming in large measure from "misty understandings" of English legal history. In view of lower federal court decisions expansively interpreting the two exceptions, the Court "reined in" the domestic relations exception in *Ankenbrandt v. Richards*, 504 U.S. 689 (1992), and endeavored similarly to curtail the probate exception in *Markham v. Allen*, 326 U.S. 490 (1946). However, in *Marshall v. Marshall*, 126 S. Ct. 1735 (2006), the Court held that the probate exception was not applicable to deprive a bankruptcy court of jurisdiction over a widow's claim that her stepson tortiously interfered with her expectancy of inheritance or gift from her deceased husband. The Court said that a ruling by a state probate court that it had exclusive jurisdiction over all of the widow's claims against her stepson did not deprive a federal district court of jurisdiction over the widow's tort claim against her stepson asserted in her bankruptcy proceeding.

The Supreme Court birthed the federal courts' domestic relations exception in diversity matters in 1859, declaring that federal courts were without power to hear disputes involving "the subject of divorce, or for the allowance of alimony." *Barber v. Barber*, 62 U.S. 582, 584 (1858). Though the exception was not clearly explained, it has been refined since the *Barber* decision and remains in use to the present day.

The domestic relations exception is based on the history underlying the congressional grant of power to the federal courts and on policy considerations that the states have traditionally adjudicated marital and child custody disputes, and have developed competence and expertise in adjudicating such matters, which federal courts lack. *See Mansell v. Mansell*, 490 U.S. 581, 587 (1989) ("[D]omestic relations are preeminently matters of state law"); *Moore v. Sims*, 442 U.S. 415, 435, (1979) ("Family relations are a traditional area of state concern"); *Ankenbrandt v. Richards*, 504 U.S. 689 (1992). It is also thought that state courts are peculiarly suited to enforce state regulations and domestic relations decrees involving alimony and child custody — particularly in light of the fact that such decrees often demand substantial continuing judicial oversight. *See Firestone v. Cleveland Trust Co.*, 654 F.2d 1212, 1215 (6th Cir. 1981). State courts also have close connections to local agencies, which resolve conflicts resulting from domestic decrees. Such conflicts are probably better handled in this venue because the state courts are accustomed to handling these cases.

The domestic relations exception was delineated in *Ankenbrandt v. Richards*, where the Court stated that federal courts are divested of the power to issue divorce decrees, alimony, and child custody orders. *Ankenbrandt*, 504 U.S. at 703. Because the limitation is one of subject matter jurisdiction, it is not waivable by the parties.

Ankenbrandt v. Richards made clear that the exception is narrowly limited and that lawsuits affecting domestic relations, however substantial, are not within the exception unless the claim at issue is one to obtain a divorce or establish alimony or child custody. This narrow construction led the Court to hold that the exception did not apply to the tort claims at issue in *Ankenbrandt v. Richards* despite their intimate connection to family affairs. *Id.* at 704.

Example 24-1

Assume that P, acting on behalf of himself and his severely disabled son, brought suit against P's former wife and the son's mother, D, alleging various tort claims arising from the former wife's care of the son while the couple were separated but during the marriage. The parties were of diverse citizenship and the amount of damages sought exceeded the minimum requirements of 28 U.S.C. §1332. D moved to dismiss the action on the ground that this was a domestic matter and outside the jurisdiction of the federal court. How will a federal court most likely rule on D's motion?

Explanation

The federal court will most likely find that it has subject matter jurisdiction to hear this case and reject D's motion. While the action arises from the husband-wife relationship, it does not involve issuing a divorce decree, alimony, child support or custody. *See Dunn v. Cometa*, 238 F.3d 38 (1st Cir. 2001).

Example 24-2

Assume that P, who was not married at the time, began a relationship with D, who was married. P was employed as an elementary school teacher, a position she had held for some years. She resigned her teaching position allegedly in response to D's urging. She claimed that she quit so that she could be free to spend more time with him and travel around the world with D. She also claimed that she quit her job in reliance on D's promises to provide for her and eventually marry her. D provided P with an extravagant lifestyle as a result of her relationship with D. She traveled around the world with him, and he provided her with sundry material benefits and comforts.

He paid the rent on homes they shared in two different states, purchased and maintained her automobiles, allowed her the use of his luxury yachts, and presented her with lavish gifts. P states that she trusted D and believed that he would get a divorce. Occasionally, she and D discussed plans for their wedding. However, after ten years, D ended the relationship. P filed an action in federal district court relying on the court's diversity subject matter jurisdiction (citizens of different states and claims exceeding $75,000) and asserted claims involving the following: (1) promissory estoppel, (2) intentional infliction of emotional distress, (3) the tort of outrage, (4) fraud, and (5) breach of promise to marry. D brought a motion to dismiss on the ground the court lacked subject matter jurisdiction. How will the court most likely rule?

EXPLANATIONS

Explanation

The court will most likely reject the claim that it lacks subject matter jurisdiction. Despite the breadth of the phrase "domestic relations exception" and the potential reach of the exception's aim, *Ankenbrandt* made clear that the exception is narrowly limited. In general, lawsuits affecting domestic relations are not within the exception unless the claim at issue is one to obtain, alter or end a divorce, or to seek alimony, child custody, or child support. *Dunn v. Cometa*, 238 F.3d 38, 41 (1st Cir. 2001). Notwithstanding the fact that this hypothetical grows out of the dissolution of an intimate relationship, P's claims do not sound in family law, let alone the specific areas of divorce, alimony, child support, or child custody. Instead, P brought tort and contract claims. *See Norton v. McOsker*, 407 F.3d 501 (1st Cir. 2005).

24.3. Federal Question Jurisdiction — Liberty Interest

Under the federal Constitution, there is a protected liberty interest in familial relations. *Stanley v. Illinois*, 05 U.S. 645 (1972); *Hurlman v. Rice*, 927 F.2d 74 (2d Cir. 1991). For example, questions of visitation between a parent and a child placed in foster care may implicate this liberty interest. *Winston v. Children and Youth Servs. of Del. County*, 948 F.2d 1380 (3d Cir. 1991); *Blair v. Supreme Court of Wyo.*, 671 F.2d 389, 390 (10th Cir. 1982). Thus, the adjudication of whether the state's procedure used to separate a parent from a child complies with constitutional due process requirements is within a federal court's question jurisdiction, and does not necessarily entail any investigation by the federal court into the fitness of the parent to care for the child.

Example 24-3

Assume that P filed an action in federal district court claiming under 42 U.S.C.A. §1983 that he was unconstitutionally deprived of his right to a relationship with his son when the trial judge in state X terminated his parental rights. The state judge held a full hearing at which P testified and was represented by counsel. The judge found that P willfully failed to contribute to the support of his child for one year and that it would be in the child's best interests to be adopted by his stepfather, with whom he had been living since his mother and stepfather's marriage. In the lawsuit filed in federal court, P does not attack state X's statute on termination of parental rights as unconstitutional, or claim that his rights were terminated without a due process hearing. Rather, P contends the court in state X did not have subject matter jurisdiction to terminate his parental rights because the custody of his child had previously been determined by a court in state Y, an argument P also made before the court in state X. P brings a motion to dismiss the federal action. How will a court most likely rule?

Explanation

The federal court will most likely dismiss the lawsuit. It is true that the relationship between parent and child is constitutionally protected. As such, the state's power to legislate, adjudicate, and administer all aspects of family law, including determinations of custodial and visitation rights, is subject to scrutiny by the federal judiciary within the reach of the Due Process and/or Equal Protection Clauses of the Fourteenth Amendment.

It is clear, however, that the state has a compelling interest in the welfare of minor children and has authority to terminate parental rights under certain limited circumstances, so long as it makes that determination in the best interest of the child and after a hearing. *See Lassiter v. Dept. of Soc. Serv.*, 452 U.S. 18 (1981). Here, P appears to be relitigating issues identical to those raised in the state court. Under such circumstances, the federal court most likely will apply collateral estoppel to bar P's claim. *See Blair v. Supreme Court of State of Wyo.*, 671 F.2d 389 (10th Cir. 1982).

24.4. Abstention Doctrine

Where timely and adequate state court review is available, a federal court, despite the fact that it has subject matter jurisdiction, may abstain from hearing a case. The United States Supreme Court has suggested that abstention might be relevant in a case involving elements of the domestic relationship even when the parties do not seek divorce, alimony, or child custody. This would be so when a case presents "'difficult questions of state law bearing on policy problems of substantial public import whose importance transcends the result in the case then at bar.'" *Ankenbrandt*, 504 U.S. at 705 (quoting *Colorado River Water Conservation Dist. v. United States*, 424 U.S. 800, 814 (1976)).

In *Younger v. Harris*, the Supreme Court required that a federal court abstain from enjoining a pending state criminal proceeding. 401 U.S. 37 (1971). In *Middlesex County Ethics Comm. v. Garden State Bar Assn.*, 457 U.S. 423, 432 (1982), the Court applied *Younger* to noncriminal judicial proceedings when important state interests are involved. Later, the Court extended the *Younger* principles to state civil proceedings. *Pennzoil Co. v. Texaco, Inc.*, 481 U.S. 1 (1987). In *Pennzoil*, the Court held that "federal courts must abstain from hearing challenges to pending state proceedings where the state's interest is so important that exercising federal jurisdiction would disrupt the comity between federal and state courts." *Id.* at 17.

Younger requires federal courts to abstain when (1) state proceedings are pending, (2) the state proceedings involve an important state interest, and (3) the state proceedings will afford the plaintiff an adequate opportunity to raise his constitutional claims.

Example 24-4

Assume that P filed a lawsuit challenging the constitutionality of state X's domestic violence statute, which enabled domestic violence victims to receive ex parte civil protection orders (CPOs) in a divorce proceeding and to obtain a restraining order without a hearing. The statute in state X, which is similar to that found in most jurisdictions, states that a victim of domestic violence may "receive an ex parte civil protection order (CPO) by filing a petition detailing (1) the nature and extent of the domestic violence, (2) the relationship between the respondent, the petitioner, and the victim, and (3) the relief requested." The statute also requires that the petition allege the "immediate and present danger of domestic violence," which constitutes good cause.

D obtained such an order during the course of the divorce proceedings between P and D, and the order granted D exclusive possession of their residence and household furniture. While the divorce matter was being litigated in state court, P filed an action in federal district court and sought injunctive relief pursuant to 42 U.S.C. §1983, a federal civil rights statute. P alleged that service and execution of the CPO denied him due process. The federal court applied the abstention doctrine, finding that the pending divorce proceedings implicated important state issues regarding the resolution of domestic disputes and that the state court provided P with an adequate opportunity to present his constitutional challenges. P has appealed. How will the federal appeals court most likely treat the lower court's decision to abstain from hearing the civil rights claim?

EXPLANATIONS

Explanation

The appellate court will most likely affirm the decision to abstain. Here it is undisputed that the underlying divorce case was pending at the time P filed his federal action. Thus, the first element of *Younger* is satisfied.

State X also has a strong state interest in regulating domestic violence and in protecting property from both parties to a pending divorce. In addition, in *Ankenbrandt*, the Court narrowed the scope of the traditional domestic relations exception, but did not overrule its prior decisions holding that domestic relations is a traditional area of state concern. Here, the challenged statutes affect the underlying divorce and involve important state interests, thus satisfying the second *Younger* criterion.

P has failed to prove the inadequacy of the courts in state X. There is no reason to question their ability or willingness to address P's constitutional issue. Because state X courts provide an adequate forum for P's constitutional claim, the third criterion of *Younger* is satisfied. Thus, most courts would rule that the trial judge did not abuse her discretion when she applied the abstention principles to this dispute. *Kelm v. Hyatt*, 44 F.3d 415 (6th Cir. 1995).

SUBJECT MATTER JURISDICTION IN STATE COURT

24.5. Residency Requirements

In *Sosna v. Iowa*, 419 U.S. 393 (1975), a wife, whose petition for divorce had been dismissed by an Iowa court because she failed to meet the state statutory requirement that a petitioner in a divorce action be a resident of the state for one year preceding the filing of the petition, brought a class action seeking to have the residency requirement declared unconstitutional. The Court held that the durational requirement is not unconstitutional on the ground that it establishes two classes of persons and discriminates against those who have recently exercised their right to travel to Iowa. The petitioner was not irretrievably foreclosed from obtaining a divorce, and the requirement is reasonably justified on grounds of the state's interest in requiring those seeking a divorce from its courts to be genuinely attached to the state, as well as of the state's desire to insulate its divorce decrees from the likelihood of successful collateral attack. The durational residency requirement does not violate the Due Process Clause of the Fourteenth Amendment on the ground that it denies a litigant the opportunity to make an individualized showing of bona fide residence and thus bars access to the divorce courts. The Court states that there is no total deprivation of access to divorce courts but only a delay in access to them.

24.6. Are Residency Requirements Subject Matter Requirements?

Most states have statutes governing divorce proceedings that require the plaintiff to show a minimum period of residency. The period may be from six weeks to two years. A person seeking a divorce must offer proof that he or she has resided and become a domiciliary within the state for the required length of time. If one spouse meets the residency requirement of a state and of the country, a divorce obtained in the state is valid in other jurisdictions, even if the other spouse resides elsewhere. However, the residency requirements may not necessarily be viewed as subject matter jurisdictional prerequisites unless they contain specific language stating that this is the case. *See Lacks v. Lacks*, 359 N.E.2d 384 (N.Y. 1976). If the jurisdiction accepts the *Lacks* analysis, the residency requirements are elements of a cause of action.

EXAMPLES

Example 24-5

Assume that the marriage of P and D breaks down. P serves D with a petition to dissolve the marriage. D does not appear and the matter goes by default. Assume that the residency requirement for a divorce in this jurisdiction is one year. Furthermore, assume that two years following the divorce, D moves to vacate the judgment, claiming that the court lacked subject matter jurisdiction when it was entered because D had been a resident for only six months. Will a court most likely vacate the judgment?

EXPLANATIONS

Explanation

A court will most likely reject the argument for vacating the judgment. A court will probably rule that the statutory residence requirements for maintaining an action for divorce go only to the substance of the cause of action, not to the competence of the court to adjudicate the cause, and accordingly, even if the court that granted the final judgment of divorce erred in determining the issue of residence, the error did not deprive it of jurisdiction to render the judgment, and the judgment was not subject to vacature on post-judgment motion made after the time for appeal had been exhausted.

24.7. State Jurisdiction to Grant Ex Parte Divorce — The Divisible Divorce Theory

The Supreme Court has stated that personal jurisdiction over a nonresident spouse is not necessary to dissolve a marriage because dissolution is a status determination. *Pennoyer v. Neff*, 95 U.S. 714, 735 (1877). The theory is that a state possesses in rem jurisdiction over the res, or "thing," which is the marriage itself. This theory, when coupled with in personam jurisdiction over the plaintiff, provides a court with power to grant a valid ex parte divorce on whatever basis it sees fit. A state is entitled, moreover, to give to the divorce decree absolute and binding finality within the confines of its borders. This principle rests on the theory that every state possesses jurisdiction to determine the civil status and capacities of all its inhabitants and the authority to prescribe the conditions on which proceedings affecting them may be commenced and carried on within its territory. Consequently, a state is viewed as having an absolute right to prescribe the conditions upon which the marriage relation between its own citizens shall be created, and the causes for which it may be dissolved.

Under the theory of "divisible divorce," issues other than the dissolution of the marriage are severed from the divorce action when the court does not have personal jurisdiction over one spouse. *Conlon by Conlon v. Heckler*, 719 F.2d 788, 795-796 (5th Cir. 1983); *see also Vanderbilt v. Vanderbilt*, 354 U.S. 416, 418-419 (1957) (where wife not subject to Nevada jurisdiction, Nevada court could not extinguish right to support in another state even though not reduced to judgment in the other state); *Estin v. Estin*, 334 U.S. 541, 549 (1948) (Nevada court lacking personal jurisdiction over wife could not terminate husband's preexisting obligation for support ordered in another state).

The divisible divorce theory was developed by the United States Supreme Court in *Estin v. Estin*, *supra*. In *Estin* the husband and wife were married and lived in New York until they separated. The wife brought an action in New York for separation, and the husband entered a general appearance. The New York court granted the separation and awarded the wife alimony. The husband then went to Nevada and instituted an action for divorce. The wife was notified of the action by constructive service, but entered no appearance. The Nevada court granted the husband a divorce, but made no provision for alimony. The Supreme Court found that the Nevada court did not have personal jurisdiction over the wife because she was not a resident of Nevada, nor had she submitted to the jurisdiction of the Nevada court. The Court held that the absence of personal jurisdiction over the wife made the divorce "divisible"—accommodating the interest of both states but restricting each state to the matters of "dominant concern." *Id.* at 549. Based on this "divisible divorce," the Court held that the Nevada decree was effective only in changing the parties' marital status, but that the order had no effect on alimony.

EXAMPLES

Example 24-6

Assume that P and D were married for ten years when their relationship began to sour. They entered into a separation agreement in state X that provided that D was to pay P $750 per month for child support until their child reached age 18, plus $1,000 per month in alimony. The court in state X had subject matter and personal jurisdiction when it entered the order. Eight months later, D filed an action for divorce in state Y, and P was served by constructive service. P was not a resident of state Y, was not served in state Y, and did not submit to the jurisdiction of state Y. The court in state Y granted a divorce and awarded D custody of their child, even though the child was in state X with P at the time and had never lived in state Y with D. The court did not award alimony or child support. P challenges enforcement of the judgment from state Y in state X. How will a court most likely treat the challenge?

EXPLANATIONS

Explanation

Based on *Estin v. Estin*, a separation agreement that is entered by a court in state X that had in personam jurisdiction over both parties, and that provided for alimony or child support, is not superseded by a subsequent divorce decree obtained in a foreign state where the foreign state did not have in personam jurisdiction over both parties. *See Burnett v. Burnett*, 542 S.E.2d 911 (W. Va. 2000). Here, the parties are now divorced but the absence of jurisdiction over P means that the child support and alimony awards made in state X remain in effect.

24.8. In Rem Divorce

In some divorces, one of the parties cannot be located when a divorce is sought. All jurisdictions have promulgated statutes that must be complied with if one is seeking such a divorce. The legal action is usually labeled "in rem" and requires compliance with the local rules relating to service of process and proper notice with publication acting as a surrogate for service. As noted earlier, in personam jurisdiction is not necessary to the dissolution of a marriage because such a proceeding affects only the status of the marriage itself. The action is in rem and a valid judgment requires only that the res be before the court on proper notice. *In re Marriage of Breen*, 560 S.W.2d 358, 361 (Mo. App. 1977). In addition to dissolving the marriage, a proper in rem action is usually viewed as providing the state with the power to adjudicate interests in land located within that state, even though the person who claims an interest in it is not personally before the court. *Id.* 560 S.W.2d at 361; Restatement (Second) of Conflict of Laws §59, p. 197 (1971).

EXAMPLES

Example 24-7

Assume that P wanted to dissolve her marriage to D, but D could not be found. P's lawyer prepared a publication notice asking the state court to exercise in rem jurisdiction in the matter. The local statute states that service by publication notice for in rem civil actions shall include "a description of any property to be affected. When service is sought by means of constructive notice, strict compliance with the statute and rule allowing service by publication is required." Assume that a description of the property was not included in the service by publication notice. The court grants P a divorce. When P dies, D's daughter X seeks her intestate share of P's estate. P's executor contends that the divorce action provided P with the real estate once owned by P and D. How will a court most likely rule?

EXPLANATIONS

Explanation

Because the description of the property was not included in the service by publication notice, the defect constitutes a violation of the service by publication requirements set out by the statute. The theory is that the service by publication requirements was not met; therefore, the court was without jurisdiction to enter a judgment. Thus, the judgment of the court relating to the property within the state was wholly void.

FULL FAITH AND CREDIT

24.9. State Recognition of Ex Parte Divorce — Full Faith and Credit

If a state's ex parte divorce decrees are to be accorded full faith and credit in the courts of her sister states, it is essential that the state issuing the decree have proper jurisdiction over the divorce proceedings. This means that a state must have jurisdiction over at least one of the parties to the ex parte proceeding. *See Vanderbilt*, 354 U.S. at 420, 422 (1957). An ex parte decree not based on domicile may not be entitled to full faith and credit. *See Williams v. North Carolina*, 325 U.S. 226 (1945).

24.10. State Recognition of Same-Sex Marriages (Defense of Marriage Act)

State and federal statutes currently exist that permit both state and federal governments to deny recognition of same-sex marriages originating in other states. The Federal Defense of Marriage Act (DOMA) was enacted after the Supreme Court of Hawaii determined the state statute banning same-sex marriage fell under strict scrutiny, leading some to believe that constitutionalization of same-sex marriage was imminent. The federal DOMA declares that "No State . . . shall be required to give effect to any public act, record, or judicial proceeding of any other State . . . respecting a relationship between persons of the same sex that is treated as a marriage under the laws of such other State." 28 U.S.C. §1738C (Supp. 2000). The statute provides each state with the power to determine the validity of same-sex marriage within its own borders. The statute is, in effect, an exception to the Full Faith and Credit Clause of the United States Constitution.

24.11. Full Faith and Credit for Child Support Orders Act

In 1996, Congress enacted the Full Faith and Credit for Child Support Orders Act, 28 U.S.C.A. §1738(B) (1996). The Act ensures that only one child support order at a time is in effect, and it incorporates many of the concepts contained in the Uniform Interstate Family Support Act. For example, it requires that a state enforce a child support order made in another state at a time when that state had jurisdiction over both parties.

EXAMPLES

Example 24-8

Assume that P and D were divorced in state X. At that time, state X ordered that P pay D $1,000 a month permanent maintenance and $600 a month child support. Shortly after the divorce, P moved to state Y, while D remained in state X. P had the original divorce judgment registered in state Y. A few months after registering the judgment, P lost his job and brought an action in state Y to modify the maintenance and child support. Neither party objected to the court hearing the matter and the judge drastically reduced the support payments. D has appealed the reduction in support. How will the appellate court most likely view the action?

Explanation

The court in state Y does not have subject matter jurisdiction, and the lower court's judgment should be vacated and the entire matter dismissed *sua sponte*. When the Full Faith and Credit for Child Support Orders Act became effective, the federal statute deprived courts in state Y of jurisdiction to modify an amount of child support of an order entered by another state and registered under URESA (now UIFSA). *See, e.g., Paton v. Brill*, 663 N.E.2d 421 (Ohio Ct. 1995). The Full Faith and Credit for Child Support Orders Act requires each state to enforce a child support order made by a court of another state. Pursuant to the federal statute, courts should refrain from modifying a foreign order unless the court of the other state no longer has continuing and exclusive jurisdiction of the child support order either because the child or any contestant is no longer a resident of the state, or each party has filed written consent in the original state, agreeing to permit the new state to modify the order. Here, D continues to reside in state X with the child.

LONG-ARM STATUTES

24.12. Requirements

For a court to exercise personal jurisdiction over a nonresident, there must be a statute authorizing it to do so and sufficient contacts between the defendant and the forum state to satisfy "traditional notions of fair play and substantial justice." *Milliken v. Meyer*, 311 U.S. 457, 463 (1940). State legislatures have generated a variety of long-arm statutes and when one is used, the legislative language must be carefully scrutinized to ensure that it applies to the facts of thc particular dispute. Some states have passed long-arm provisions that allow a state court to exercise jurisdiction on any basis not inconsistent with the constitution of the state or of the U.S. Constitution, and others contain more restrictive language.

The advent and growth of long-arm statutes represent attempts by one state to provide a litigation forum for the convenience of its own citizens at the expense of citizens of other states. Most agree that the use of such statutes is natural in a mobile, industrialized society that has effectively reduced the time and rigors of travel between states. *See* Annot., *Long-Arm Statutes: Obtaining Jurisdiction Over Nonresident Parent in Filiation or Support Proceeding*, 76 A.L.R.3d 708, 714-715 (1977).

Often Courts have applied the phrases *transacting business* or *tortious conduct* to divorce matters, even though such terms are usually found in traditional long-arm statutes and generally used in commercial activities. For example, in *Prybolsky v. Prybolsky*, 430 A.2d 804 (Del. Fam. Ct. 1981), the court held that it had acquired jurisdiction over a nonresident husband by means of the "doing business" provision of the Delaware long-arm statute. *Id.* at 807. (This decision was later overruled by statute. *T.L. v. W.L.*, 820 A.2d 506 (Del. Fam. Ct. 2003).) It emphasized that marriage, from its perspective, is a contract, and the support and other rights springing from that contract have financial and business implications.

Some courts have construed the phrase "a tortuous act" as consisting of a failure on the part of the alleged defendant to support a child following birth. Tortuous act has been defined to include any act committed in a state that involved a breach of duty to another and has resulted in ascertainable damages. *See Poindexter v. Willis*, 231 N.E.2d 1 (Ill. Ct. App. 1967); *accord In re Marriage of Highsmith*, 488 N.E.2d 1000, 1003 (1986); *Black v. Rasile*, 318 N.W.2d 475, 476 (Mich. App. 1982); *State ex rel. Nelson v. Nelson*, 216 N.W.2d 140, 143 (Minn. 1974); *In re Custody of Miller*, 548 P.2d 542, 546 (Wash. 1976). Failure to pay child support fits within this general rationale.

Example 24-9

Assume that P, a citizen of state X, and D, a citizen of state Y, allegedly had a series of sexual encounters in state X that led to a pregnancy and birth of a child. P, the child's mother, now seeks to establish paternity and obtain child support from D, who lives in state Y. Assume that the only long-arm statute available permits the exercise of jurisdiction over a nonresident who transacts business in state X, causes tortious injury in it, or has an interest in real property there. When D is served in state Y, he challenges the application of the long-arm statute to a domestic proceeding. How will a court in state X most likely rule on D's challenge?

Explanation

A court will most likely rule that the language of the long-arm statute applies to these facts. Note, of course, that the constitutional issue remains to be answered: that is, whether application of the long-arm statute to these facts is constitutional. Also note that the Uniform Interstate Family Support Act, which has been adopted in some form in all states, provides that a person who has sexual intercourse within a state submits to the jurisdiction of that state's courts with respect to a child who may have been conceived. *See Garvey v. Mendenhall*, 404 S.E.2d 613 (Ga. Ct. App. 1991) (alleged father's social visits to state did not constitute transacting business so as to subject him to personal jurisdiction under Georgia's long-arm statute).

24.13. Due Process Barriers to Application of Long-Arm Statutes

It is axiomatic that even though a state's long-arm statute applies to a domestic dispute, the Constitution may bar its application because the Due Process Clause of the Fourteenth Amendment operates as a limitation on the jurisdiction of state courts to enter judgments affecting the rights or interests of nonresident defendants. *Kulko v. Superior Court of California*, 436 U.S. 84 (1978). Under *Kulko*, the existence of personal jurisdiction depends upon the presence of reasonable notice to the defendant that an action has been brought and a sufficient connection between the defendant and the forum state to make it fair to require defense of the action in the forum.

In *Kulko*, after separating, the husband remained in New York, the state of marital domicile, and the wife moved to California. The couple executed a separation agreement in New York that provided that the parties' two children were to reside with Mr. Kulko in New York during the school year and with their mother during their Christmas, Easter, and summer vacations. Mr. Kulko also agreed to pay $3,000 a year in child support. The terms of this agreement were later incorporated into a Haitian divorce decree obtained by Mrs. Kulko.

Subsequently, the parties' daughter expressed a desire to live full-time with her mother. Mr. Kulko acquiesced and paid the child's airfare to California. A few years later, the couple's son expressed to his mother a desire to live with her. Without Mr. Kulko's knowledge, Mrs. Kulko sent the boy a plane ticket, which he used to join his mother and sister in California.

Shortly afterward, Mrs. Kulko filed suit in California to obtain an increase in child support. Mr. Kulko resisted on the ground that he had insufficient contacts to warrant the California court's assertion of personal jurisdiction over him. The California Supreme Court rejected this argument, reasoning that by sending his daughter to reside permanently in California, Mr. Kulko had "purposely availed himself of the benefits and protections of the laws of California." *Id.* at 89.

The U.S. Supreme Court rejected the California court's analysis, pointing out that the mere fact that Mr. Kulko "acquiesced" in the desire of his daughter to live with her mother was not a sufficient contact with the State of California to warrant imposition of the unreasonable burden of having to litigate a child support action there. The Court observed that there was no other activity that would bring Mr. Kulko in contact with the State of California. The Court also made the point that the former wife was not without remedy, as she could initiate a proceeding under the Uniform Reciprocal Enforcement of Support Act "and have its merits adjudicated in the State of the alleged obligor's residence, without either party's having to leave his or her own State." *Id.* at 86.

EXAMPLES

Example 24-10

Assume that P and D were married and lived in Wisconsin for five years. When P lost his part-time job at a local fast-food restaurant, he decided he needed more education. He applied and was accepted to graduate school at the University of North Carolina. While D remained in Wisconsin because of her good job that helped pay for P's room, board, and tuition, P moved to North Carolina to attend the University. After seven months, D was served with a divorce petition begun by P in North Carolina. In it, P asked for alimony of $150 a month, an equal division of the couple's personal and real property, and sole possession of a 1987 Porsche. D did not answer, and a decree of divorce was granted to P in North Carolina. The court granted P's alimony request, divided the personal and real property equally, and awarded P sole possession of the Porsche. After graduation, P moved back to Wisconsin and sought to enforce the North Carolina judgment. D countered by asking the Wisconsin court to declare P's North Carolina divorce decree void. How should a Wisconsin court rule?

EXPLANATIONS

Explanation

Recall *Pennoyer v. Neff*, where the Court said

> The jurisdiction which every State possesses to determine the *civil status* and capacities of all its inhabitants involves authority to prescribe the conditions on which proceedings affecting them may be commenced and carried on within its territory. The State, for example, has absolute right to prescribe the conditions upon which the marriage relation between its own citizens shall be created, and the causes for which it may be dissolved. One of the parties guilty of acts for which, by the law of the State, a dissolution may be granted, may have removed to a State where no dissolution is permitted. The complaining party would, therefore, fail if a divorce were sought in the state of the defendant; and if application could not be made to the tribunals of the complainant's domicile in such case the injured citizen would be without redress.

95 U.S. 714, 734-735 (1877). Therefore, so long as P has met the conditions North Carolina established for a divorce, P is divorced. D's action to have the divorce voided would have no effect despite the fact that the divorcing court did not have personal jurisdiction over D.

However, that part of the North Carolina decree dealing with the $150 monthly alimony payment, dividing the couple's personal and real property, and granting P sole possession of a 1987 Porsche will not be recognized in Wisconsin. At the time the North Carolina court issued its decree, it did not have personal jurisdiction over D. There is no suggestion that she consented or waived the personal jurisdiction defense. Those issues may be litigated between the couple in Wisconsin.

Example 24-11

Assume a statute in state X reads as follows: "In a proceeding to establish, enforce, or modify a support order or to determine parentage, a tribunal of this state may exercise personal jurisdiction over a nonresident individual or the individual's guardian or conservator if the child resides in this state as a result of the acts or directives of the individual." Assume that P, a citizen of state Y, was awarded custody in a divorce five years ago. However, last month, P became angry with the child, purchased a bus ticket, and sent the child to live with D, the child's mother, who lives in state X. Assume that D brought an action in state X asking for child support. P, who has never been to state X, challenges the court's exercise of personal jurisdiction over him on a constitutional basis. How will a judge most likely rule on the challenge?

Explanation

This question is based on *Kulko v. Superior Court*. The facts, of course, are somewhat different than in *Kulko*, but probably not so different as to change the jurisdictional outcome. Here, regardless of the statutory language, the Due Process Clause of the Fourteenth Amendment will bar the application of the long-arm statute. D must seek to obtain child support under state X's Uniform Interstate Family Support Act, which will allow an eventual establishment of support.

THE POWER OF PERSONAL JURISDICTION

24.14. Traditional View

Personal jurisdiction may be exercised over an individual by virtue of being served with legal process while he or she is present within the forum state.

This rule applies even if the person served is an out-of-state resident who comes into the forum state only briefly. *Burnham v. Superior Court*, 495 U.S. 604 (1990). In *Burnham*, the wife brought a divorce action in California and served her husband with divorce papers when he visited children in that state. The Court ruled that his physical presence within the state conferred personal jurisdiction over him — no additional "minimum contacts" were required. *Id.* at 619.

Justice Scalia, writing for a plurality of four in *Burnham*, determined that "jurisdiction based on physical presence alone constitutes due process because it is one of the continuing traditions of our legal system that define the due process standard of 'traditional notions of fair play and substantial justice.' " *Id.* Three other justices joined in a concurring opinion filed by Justice Brennan. In their view, tradition alone was not dispositive; they would judge the constitutionality of in-state service on a nonresident by examining contemporary notions of due process. *See id.* at 629-32 (BRENNAN, J., concurring). The justices ultimately concluded that "as a rule the exercise of personal jurisdiction over a defendant based on his voluntary presence in the forum will satisfy the requirements of due process." *Id.* at 639. They reasoned that by visiting the forum state, a defendant avails himself of significant benefits, such as the protection of his health and safety. *See id.* at 637-38. Justice Stevens joined neither Justice Scalia's nor Justice Brennan's opinion, but concurred in the judgment based on considerations of history, fairness, and common sense.

EXAMPLES

Example 24-12

Assume that P asserts that D is the father of a child born out of wedlock. P is a citizen of Texas and D a citizen of New Mexico. P initiates a paternity action in Texas. D is served with a summons and complaint when D's private airplane touched down at a Texas airport. The plane was traveling from Colorado to New Mexico when it made the 30-minute stop to refuel. D argues that Texas does not have personal jurisdiction over D. How will a court most likely rule on the challenge?

EXPLANATIONS

Explanation

The Texas court has personal jurisdiction over D because D was served within the boundaries of Texas. There is no basis for D's argument. *See In re Gonzalez*, 993 S.W.2d 147 (Tex. Ct. App. 1999).

Example 24-13

Assume that P and D divorced in Pennsylvania and that, at the time, Pennsylvania had personal jurisdiction over both parties. Neither was awarded alimony, and alimony was not reserved. Two years following entry of the divorce decree, D moves to Texas and remarries. P goes to Texas and brings an action seeking alimony. D contends the Texas court may not hear the action. How will a court most likely rule?

Explanation

D will most likely be successful in preventing the court from hearing the action. D will contend that the action in Pennsylvania is *res judicata* and must be enforced under the Full Faith and Credit Clause of the federal Constitution, which reads as follows: "Full Faith and Credit shall be given in each state to the public acts, Records, and Judicial Proceedings of every other state." U.S. Const. Art. 4, §1. When there is nothing in the decree reserving maintenance, all jurisdictions will take the view that it has been waived.

24.15. Continuing Jurisdiction

Most states take the view that they possess continuing jurisdiction over the parties to a dissolution if a court possessed personal jurisdiction over the parties at the time the divorce judgment was entered. Consequently, obligors who move from a jurisdiction where a judgment was properly entered, and remain away for several years, cannot block modification or enforcement efforts on the ground the forum court lost personal jurisdiction once they moved out of state. *See Bjordahl v. Bjordahl*, 308 N.W.2d 817 (Minn. 1981); *but see Zent v. Zent*, 281 N.W.2d 41 (N.D. 1979) (enforcement of a divorce judgment is a new and independent action, requiring independent jurisdictional contacts).

Example 24-14

Assume that P and D divorced at a time when the court in state X had subject matter and personal jurisdiction over both parties. D left the jurisdiction and had remained away for ten years when P brought an action against D in state X to enforce provisions in the original divorce decree. P alleges that D has ignored provisions in the original decree relating to a car that was to be delivered in new condition but was delivered in used condition and five years late, that insurance policies D was required by the divorce decree to keep in effect have lapsed, and that alimony and child support totaling $17,175 remain unpaid. D argues that state X cannot obtain personal jurisdiction over him for these claims because of his long absence from that jurisdiction. How would a court most likely rule on these hypothetical facts?

EXPLANATIONS

Explanation

Courts are not necessarily in agreement, but it is quite likely a court will agree with P and reject D's claim. Here state X was the original marital domicile. A due process argument can be made to support P as follows: The parties chose to resolve their marital dispute in state X and thus defendant purposefully availed himself of the privilege of conducting activities within state X. At the time, it was entirely foreseeable that breach of the agreement could lead to D being called into a court in state X in the future if D failed to comply with the judgment.

Furthermore, a court may reason that a finding that state X continues to have jurisdiction protects D from arbitrarily being sued in any other state. D is subject to suit only in state X, the state of original marital domicile and the state with the sole divorce judgment against D. While it is true that D has not been a resident or transacted business in state X for ten years since the divorce decree, the obligations of that judgment have attached, and the obligations may constitute continuing contacts sufficient to satisfy due process.

24.16. Waiving Personal Jurisdiction

Personal jurisdiction may be conferred upon a party by a failure to properly raise the issue at the first opportunity to do so. For example, if a defendant appears generally in a divorce action and fails to challenge the court's exercise of personal jurisdiction, she may not subsequently attack the divorce decree for lack of personal jurisdiction. *Sherrer v. Sherrer*, 334 U.S. 343 (1948).

EXAMPLES

Example 24-15

Assume that P and D's marriage broke down and that P brought a divorce action in state X. D, who lives in state Y, appeared in state X through her lawyers. Following entry of the divorce decree, D discovered to a certainty that the court in state X did not have personal jurisdiction over her. D now attacks enforcement of the divorce action in state Y, claiming that the court in state X lacked personal jurisdiction over her. How will a court in state Y most likely rule?

Explanation

A court in state Y will most likely dismiss D's challenge. Once parties participate in a proceeding, even if it is later discovered that the court lacked personal jurisdiction, the issue cannot be successfully raised collaterally. The reason for this is that the party has made an appearance and the party has been afforded an opportunity to be heard. *Id.* at 350-351.

STATUS AS A JURISDICTIONAL THEORY

24.17. Overview of Status Theory

Some jurisdictions have begun to more actively use "status" as a theory upon which to adjudicate family law issues without obtaining personal jurisdiction over an out-of-state member of the family. The theory originally sprang from actions where one party sought a divorce and the other could not be found. The "status" theory allowed courts to grant an in rem divorce to the party before the court even though the other party was absent or could not be found. Status is also being used as a theory in some child custody disputes, which some argue is in contravention of the Supreme Court's view of the matter. One view of jurisdiction in custody disputes is found in *May v. Anderson*, 345 U.S. 528 (1953). In this case, the Court held that a child custody decree of one state was not entitled to full faith and credit in another state when the decree was entered by a court that had no personal jurisdiction over the nonresident parent. However, application of the holding has been challenged by a number of courts. For example, the Tennessee courts rejected *May* on the ground that subsequent Supreme Court decisions had "abolished the distinctions between in rem and in personam" jurisdiction, and "recognized that exceptions can be made to the 'minimum contacts' standard" in "status" cases, such as child custody decisions. *Fernandez v. Fernandez*, 1986 WL 7935 (Tenn. Ct. App. 1986); *see also Brown v. Brown*, 847 S.W.2d 496, 499 n.2 (Tenn. 1993). The court followed the rule that courts of a state "having the most significant connections with the child and his family have jurisdiction to make a custody adjudication even in the absence of personal jurisdiction over a parent who does not reside in the forum state." *Fernandez*, 1986 WL 7935, at 2. *See also Roderick v. Roderick*, 776 S.W.2d 533 (Tenn. Ct. App. 1989).

A Texas court explained that "unlike adjudications of child support and visitation expense, custody determinations are status adjudications not dependent upon personal jurisdiction over the parents. Generally, a family relationship is among those matters in which the forum state has such a strong interest that its courts may reasonably make an adjudication affecting that relationship even though one of the parties to the relationship may have had no personal contacts with the forum state." *In re S.A.V.*, 837 S.W.2d 80, 84 (Tex. 1992); *see also In re Marriage of Los*, 593 N.E.2d 126 (Ill. App. 1992).

The status exception has been extended to parental termination proceedings. *See In re Appeal in Maricopa County, Juvenile Action No. JS-734*, 543 P.2d 454, 459-460 (Ariz. Ct. App. 1975); *In re Interest of M.L.K.*, 768 P.2d at 316, 319-320 (Kan. Ct. App. 1989); *In re Adoption of Copeland*, 43 S.W.3d 483, 487 (Tenn. Ct. App. 2000) (relying on status exception in parental rights termination proceeding against a father in prison); *Wenz v. Schwartze*, 598 P.2d 1086, 1091-1092 (Mont. 1979) (concluding personal jurisdiction over a parent is not necessary in order to terminate parental rights, without specifically discussing status exception), *cert. denied*, 444 U.S. 1071 (1980); *In re A.E.H.*, 468 N.W.2d 190, 198-200 (Wis. 1991) (focusing on child's contacts with the state in order to terminate parental rights), *cert. denied*, 502 U.S. 925 (1991).

The Oklahoma Supreme Court applied the status rationale in *In re Adoption of J.L.H.*, 737 P.2d 915 (Okla. 1987). In that case, the children's natural father and stepmother petitioned Oklahoma for the nonconsensual adoption of the father's children by the stepmother on the ground that their mother, a nonresident of Oklahoma, had willfully failed to pay child support. *See also Bartsch v. Bartsch*, 636 N.W.2d 3 (Iowa 2001) (protective order may issue without personal jurisdiction over the defendants).

24.18. Restatement of Conflict of Laws — Status

The Restatement of Conflict of Laws recognizes that an adjudication of status does not require personal jurisdiction. It provides the following illustration: Assume that "A leaves his home in state X and goes to state Y, where he becomes domiciled and there obtains an ex parte divorce from B, his wife. Assuming that the requirements of proper notice and opportunity to be heard have been met, this divorce is valid and must be recognized in state X under full faith and credit even though B was not personally subject to the jurisdiction of the state Y court and at all times retained her domicile in state X." Restatement (Second) of Conflict of Laws §71 cmt. *a*, illus. 1 (1971).

INDIAN CHILD WELFARE ACT

24.19. Overview of Act

The Indian Child Welfare Act (ICWA), §§1901 and 1911, gives tribal courts exclusive jurisdiction over proceedings concerning an Indian child who resides or is domiciled on an Indian reservation. 25 U.S.C. §§1901, 1911 (1978). In *Mississippi Band of Choctaw Indians v. Holyfield*, 490 U.S. 30 (1989), the Court held that custody and adoption decisions involving Indian children born off an Indian reservation to parents who were domiciled on the reservation at the time of birth gave the tribe to which the parents belonged exclusive jurisdiction to decide those issues. Domicile was defined as physical presence with the intent to remain on the reservation. Minors will take the domicile of their parents because they are legally incapable of forming the requisite state of mind (intent) to create a domicile. The Court made it clear that parents could not defeat the intent of the ICWA absent changing their domicile.

Section 1911(a) of the ICWA states that the tribe has "jurisdiction exclusive as to any State over any child custody proceeding involving an Indian child who resides or is domiciled within the reservation of such tribe, except where such jurisdiction is otherwise vested in the State by existing Federal law."

A "child custody proceeding," as defined by the ICWA, refers to any proceeding involving foster care placement, termination of parental rights, preadoptive placement, or adoptive placement. 25 U.S.C. §1903(1) (1978). The only two exceptions to that definition are awards of custody to one of the parents in divorce proceedings and delinquency proceeding placements. 25 U.S.C. §1903(1) (1978). The ICWA defines an "Indian child" as "any unmarried person who is under age eighteen and is either (a) a member of an Indian tribe or (b) is eligible for membership in an Indian tribe and is the biological child of a member of an Indian tribe." 25 U.S.C. §1903(4) (1978).

Under section 1911(a), the tribal court possesses exclusive jurisdiction "over any child custody proceeding involving an Indian child who resides or is domiciled within the reservation of such tribe." 25 U.S.C. §1911(a) (1978). In the case of Indian children not domiciled or residing within the reservation of the child's tribe, section 1911(b) creates concurrent but presumptively tribal jurisdiction, and requires state courts to transfer jurisdiction over the proceedings to the tribal court except in cases of "good cause," objection by either parent, or declination of jurisdiction by the tribal court. 25 U.S.C. §1911(b) (1978).

EXAMPLES

Example 24-16

Assume that P, an Indian, and D, a non-Indian, lived together for a time and a child, B, was born of the relationship. D has never lived on an Indian reservation. A paternity action was held in state X's court and D was awarded custody of the child for ten months of the year and P was given custody for two months. Assume that P exercised her custodial rights sparingly over the next three years. P is an enrolled member of an Indian tribe and lives on the reservation. At a custody modification hearing in a state X court, held a few months before D died, D was granted sole physical custody of the minor child. When D died, D's sister brought an action to terminate P's rights to B and to adopt B, whom she had cared for during D's illness, which lasted several months. In the termination action, the aunt asserts that P had essentially abandoned B during the two years before the adoption action. The tribe has intervened on behalf of P and asserts that jurisdiction in this matter is exclusive with the tribal courts. How will a court most likely rule?

EXPLANATIONS

Explanation

Traditionally, in the case of children born out of wedlock, the child takes the domicile of the mother. Although P was domiciled on the reservation, D was not, had never been, and did not want to be. His domicile was in state X. Because he had sole custody of the child, state X was the child's domicile as well. Upon D's death, the domicile of the child would normally have reverted to P. An exception to this general rule has been recognized in situations in which the surviving parent has abandoned the child. Restatement (Second) of Conflict of Laws §22, Cmts. *e*-i (1971). If a child is left parentless as a result of death and/or abandonment, and no legal guardian of the child's person has been appointed, the child takes the domicile of the person who stands in *loco parentis* to him and with whom he lives. Restatement (Second) of Conflict of Laws §22, Cmt. i (1971). Accordingly, if P were found to have abandoned her child, the child's domicile would remain in state X even after D's death.

For the purposes of establishing domicile, abandonment occurs when the parent deserts the child or when the parent gives custody of the child to another with the intention of relinquishing his parental rights and obligations. To determine whether an abandonment has taken place, the rules of the forum are normally applied. A hearing must be held to determine whether the child has been abandoned by P. If the hearing discloses that there has not been abandonment, the child is domiciled on the reservation and the tribe would have exclusive jurisdiction under section 1911(a) of the ICWA (25 U.S.C. §1911(a) (1978)). If P were proven to have abandoned the child, the tribe would not have exclusive jurisdiction under section 1911(a) because the child would then neither reside nor be domiciled on the reservation. Instead, the operative provision would be section 1911(b) of the ICWA, which confers concurrent jurisdiction on the state courts along with the tribal court when the child is not domiciled and does not reside on the reservation. Under section 1911(b), there is still a presumption that the tribal court should hear the case, but transfer to the tribal court is not required when there is objection by either parent or when the trial court finds good cause to deny such a transfer. *In re Adoption of S.S.*, 657 N.E.2d 935 (Ill. 1995).

EXAMPLES

Example 24-17

Assume P and D are married and domiciled on the White Earth Indian Reservation in Minnesota. For a variety of reasons, they decide that a child to be born to them in about two months should be put up for adoption. They move from the reservation to a town in North Dakota, where the infant is born. Six weeks later, non-Indians through a North Dakota state court adopt the infant. Two months later, the tribe to which P and D belong move in North Dakota state court to vacate the adoption decree on the ground that under the ICWA, exclusive jurisdiction was vested in the tribal court. The parents of the newly adopted infant respond that P and D waived the jurisdiction of the ICWA by word and act. They present a written waiver signed by P and D in which P and D state that their intention is to "waive any provisions of law under the ICWA that might prevent the adoption under state law." How should a court rule?

EXPLANATIONS

Explanation

Despite the efforts of P and D, the court will most likely rule that the adoption is void and that subject matter jurisdiction rests with the Indian tribe. *Mississippi Band of Choctaw Indians v. Holyfield*, 490 U.S. 30 (1989) (removing Indian children from cultural setting seriously impacts long-term tribal survival and has damaging social and psychological impact on many individual Indian children — a rule of domicile that permits individual Indian parents to defeat the ICWA's jurisdictional scheme is inconsistent with what Congress intended).

SOLDIERS AND SAILORS CIVIL RELIEF ACT

24.20. Overview of the Act

The Soldiers and Sailors Civil Relief Act (SSCRA) of 1940 is essentially a reenactment of the 1918 statute, with a number of amendments. 50 U.S.C.

app. §521. It was first amended in 1942, and again in 1991 as a result of the First Gulf War. In November 2002, Congress passed a law (the Veterans Benefits Act of 2002, Pub. L. No. 107-330 §305), which provides SSCRA protection to National Guard members called to state active duty under Title 32 if the duty is because of a federal emergency, the request for active duty is made by the President or Secretary of Defense, and the member is activated for longer than 30 days. An example of this would be the National Guard members who were activated by the states, at the request of the President, to provide security for airports after the attacks of September 11.

The Soldiers and Sailors Civil Relief Act states that a service member who is either the plaintiff or the defendant in a civil lawsuit may request a stay, or postponement, of a court proceeding in which he or she is a party. A service member may request a stay at any point in the proceedings. However, courts are reluctant to grant stays at the pretrial phase of a lawsuit, such as discovery or depositions. If a judgment is entered against a service member who is unavailable because of military orders, the service member may be able to have that judgment voided.

In general, courts take the view that the provisions of the Act are to be liberally construed toward protecting the rights of men and women in the service. *See Omega Industry, Inc. v. Raffaele*, 894 F. Supp. 1425 (Nev. Dist. Ct. 1995) (Civil Relief Act was intended to be liberally construed, and applied in a broad spirit of gratitude toward service personnel).

The provisions of the Soldiers and Sailors Civil Relief Act may be applied by federal and state courts. 50 U.S.C. app. §512(1). However, the Act does not empower a court to collaterally review, vacate, or impede the decisions of a state court. *See Scheidegg v. Dept. of Air Force*, 715 F. Supp. 11, 13-14 (D.N.H. 1989); *Sarfaty v. Sarfaty*, 534 F. Supp. 701, 704 n.4 (Pa. D. & C. 1982). Judgments made in violation of the Act are subject to attack only in the courts that rendered the judgments. *See* 50 U.S.C. app. §520(4).

EXAMPLES

Example 24-18

Assume that P and D divorce and P is awarded custody of their two minor children by a judge in state X. D, who is upset with the ruling and who is in the military, files a petition in federal district court asking that it issue an order staying the enforcement of the child custody order pending the end of D's military service in Saudi Arabia. A motion to dismiss the action has been brought by P, who contends the matter should be heard in state court. How will a court most likely rule?

EXPLANATIONS

Explanation

On these sparse facts, the federal court will most likely dismiss the request for injunctive relief. Note that under the Anti-Injunction Act, 28 U.S.C. §2283 (1948), a federal court may not stay a state court proceeding "except as expressly authorized by Act of Congress, or where necessary in aid of its jurisdiction, or to protect or effectuate its judgments." It is not likely that the Soldiers and Sailors Civil Relief Act "expressly" authorizes this court to issue a stay against a state court proceeding. The federal court does not have the authority to impede the decisions of a state court.

Table of Cases

Index